Gods, Heroes, and Ancestors

AMERICAN ACADEMY
of RELIGION

RELIGION IN TRANSLATION

Series Editor
John Nemec, University of Virginia
A Publication Series of The American Academy of Religion and Oxford University Press

The Study of Stolen Love
Translated by David C. Buck
and K. Paramasivam

The Daoist Monastic Manual
A Translation of the Fengdao Kejie
Livia Kohn

Sacred and Profane Beauty
The Holy in Art
Gararadus van der Leeuw
Preface by Mircea Eliade
Translated by David E. Green
With a new introduction and bibliography
by Diane Apostolos-Cappadona

The History of the Buddha's Relic Shrine
A Translation of the Sinhala Thūpavamsa
Stephen C. Berkwitz

Damascius' Problems & Solutions Concerning First Principles
Translated with Introduction and Notes
by Sara Ahbel-Rappe

The Secret Garland
Āṇṭāḷ's Tiruppāvai *and* Nācciyār Tirumoḻi
Translated with Introduction and Commentary
by Archana Venkatesan

Prelude to the Modernist Crisis
The "Firmin" Articles of Alfred Loisy
Edited, with an Introduction by C. J. T. Talar
Translated by Christine Thirlway

Debating the Dasam Granth
Robin Rinehart

The Fading Light of Advaita Ācārya
Three Hagiographies
Rebecca J. Manring

The Ubiquitous Śiva
Somānanda's Śivadṛṣṭi and His Tantric
Interlocutors
John Nemec

Place and Dialectic
Two Essays by Nishida Kitarō
Translated by John W. M. Krummel and
Shigenori Nagatomo

The Prison Narratives of Jeanne Guyon
Ronney Mourad and Dianne Guenin-Lelle

Disorienting Dharma
Ethics and the Aesthetics of Suffering in
the Mahābhārata
Emily T. Hudson

The Transmission of Sin
Augustine and the Pre-Augustinian Sources
Pier Franco Beatrice
Translated by Adam Kamesar

From Mother to Son
The Selected Letters of Marie de l'Incarnation to
Claude Martin
Translated and with Introduction and Notes
by Mary Dunn

Drinking From Love's Cup
Surrender and Sacrifice in the Vārs
of Bhai Gurdas
Selections and Translations with Introduction and
Commentary by Rahuldeep Singh Gill

Gods, Heroes, and Ancestors
An Interreligious Encounter in Eighteenth-Century
Vietnam
Anh Q. Tran

Gods, Heroes, and Ancestors

An Interreligious Encounter in Eighteenth-Century Vietnam

Errors of the Three Religions

Edited, translated and introduced by

ANH Q. TRAN

OXFORD
UNIVERSITY PRESS

OXFORD
UNIVERSITY PRESS

Oxford University Press is a department of the University of Oxford. It furthers
the University's objective of excellence in research, scholarship, and education
by publishing worldwide. Oxford is a registered trade mark of Oxford University
Press in the UK and certain other countries.

Published in the United States of America by Oxford University Press
198 Madison Avenue, New York, NY 10016, United States of America.

© Oxford University Press 2018

All rights reserved. No part of this publication may be reproduced, stored in
a retrieval system, or transmitted, in any form or by any means, without the
prior permission in writing of Oxford University Press, or as expressly permitted
by law, by license, or under terms agreed with the appropriate reproduction
rights organization. Inquiries concerning reproduction outside the scope of the
above should be sent to the Rights Department, Oxford University Press, at the
address above.

You must not circulate this work in any other form
and you must impose this same condition on any acquirer.

Library of Congress Cataloging-in-Publication Data
Names: Tran, Anh Q., 1965– author, translator.
Title: Gods, heroes, and ancestors : an interreligious encounter in
eighteenth-century Vietnam / Anh Q. Tran.
Other titles: Container of (expression): Tam giáo chư vọng. English.
Description: New York : Oxford University Press, [2018] |
Series: AAR religion in translation series |
Includes bibliographical references and index.
Identifiers: LCCN 2017007445 (print) | LCCN 2017012745 (ebook) |
ISBN 9780190677619 (updf) | ISBN 9780190677626 (epub) |
ISBN 9780190677633 (oso) | ISBN 9780190677602 (cloth)
Subjects: LCSH: Tam giáo chư vọng. | Vietnam—Religion. |
Vietnam—Church history—18th century. | Christianity and other religions—Vietnam. |
Christianity and culture—Vietnam. |
Christian converts—Vietnam—History—18th century.
Classification: LCC BL2055 (ebook) |
LCC BL2055 .T69 2018 (print) |
DDC 270.09597/09033—dc23
LC record available at https://lccn.loc.gov/2017007445

1 3 5 7 9 8 6 4 2
Printed by Sheridan Books, Inc., United States of America

Ân Cha như núi cao vời vợi
Nghĩa Mẹ tựa biển cả mênh mông
High as a mountain is your merit, Dad
Vast as an ocean is your love, Mom

For my parents
To whom I am forever indebted for my Vietnamese heritage
Ad Majorem Dei Gloriam

Contents

Acknowledgments ix

Preface xi

Abbreviations xvii

Introduction 1

PART ONE: *Errors of the Three Religions in Context*

1. When the Cross Met the Lotus: Catholic Mission in Tonkin During the Seventeenth and Eighteenth Centuries 21

    Tonkin of the Seventeenth and Eighteenth Century 21
    The Development of Catholicism in Tonkin 25
    Reception of Christianity in Tonkin 30
    The Rites Controversy and Its Impact in Vietnam 36

2. Text and Context: *Errors of the Three Religions* 47

    Defending the True Faith 48
    The Text: History, Content, and Method 62

3. Of Gods and Heroes: Worship in Traditional Vietnam 76

    An Overview of Traditional Vietnamese Worship 77
    A Christian Evaluation of Traditional Worship 106

4. In the Realm of the Dead: Filial Piety and Ancestral Worship   108

    Vietnamese Anthropology and Ancestral Worship   108
    The Ancestral Rites in Practice   113
    A Christian Interpretation of the Cult of the Ancestors   126

5. Refutation and Dialogue: Christianity vis-à-vis the Three Religions   133

    The Theological Message of *Errors*   136
    The Legacy of *Errors of the Three Religions*   140
    Meeting the Religious Others   145

Conclusion   156

PART TWO: *An Annotated Translation of TAM GIÁO CHƯ VỌNG*

Preface   161

Book 1: The Errors of Confucianism   164

Book 2: The Errors of Daoism   233

Book 3: The Errors of Buddhism   270

Appendix A: Adriano di Santa Thecla's Opusculum   323
Appendix B: Glossary of Sino-Vietnamese Terms Used in the Translation   331
Bibliography   337
Index   355

Acknowledgments

THIS BOOK IS based on my doctoral research and studies of Vietnamese traditional religions under the guidance of Peter C. Phan of Georgetown University. I am extremely grateful to him for being my teacher and mentor over the years. From the earliest days of this project, I have been benefited by the assistance and advice of many individuals. For their direction and support, I owe a debt of gratitude to John Witek (1933–2010) and Leo D. Lefebure of Georgetown University, and Cuong Tu Nguyen of George Mason University. In my initial research, Antoine Tran Van Toan (1932–2013) of the Catholic University of Lille in France introduced me to the text of *Tam Giáo Chư Vọng*. The curator of the archives of the Missions Étrangères de Paris (AMEP) Gérard Moussay (d. 2012) and his assistant Brigitte Appavou helped me access the manuscript of the text and related materials. Father Pietro Scalia of the Discalced Augustinians in Rome generously gave me some private publications of the order. In Vietnam, I owe thanks to Ms. Lã Thị Minh Hằng of the Institute of Hán-Nôm Studies in Hanoi who helped locate some Sino-Vietnamese materials; and Br. Trần Kim Vinh and Mr. Nguyễn Trọng Hóa of the Catholic Hán-Nôm Translation Project (*Nhóm Dịch thuật Hán Nôm Công giáo*) in Hochiminh City for their help in deciphering difficult Sino-Vietnamese passages. Special thanks to Leon Hooper, the director of the Woodstock Library, and his associates, who provided me a haven for initial research and writing.

At different stages of writing and revising, various scholars and educated readers have read parts or all of the present work in various iterations. I am grateful for the insights, comments, suggestions, and corrections by, in alphabetical order, Katherine Barush, George Dutton, Sophie LeVan, Marcia McMahon, Ron Murphy, Lan Ngo, Phuong-Lan Nguyen, Charles Phipps, Hung T. Pham, John Siberski, Duc Vu, and the late James Walsh. Thanks also to Lisa Maglio-Brown and Melody Noll for their tremendous help in preparing the final manuscript. I also want to acknowledge the invaluable assistance of Su-chi Lin for the cover illustration, the Chinese texts and the index.

I would like to express my gratitude to all who have accompanied me on my academic pursuit. Your generosity, encouragement, support, and prayer have made this project possible. They include my colleagues at Santa Clara University's Jesuit School of Theology whose constant presence has lifted me up on occasional blue days of writing and revising. Thanks to the generosity of the former dean of the school, Tom Massaro, I had a semester off to work on this project while juggling other academic duties, and thanks to the Santa Clara Jesuit Community for offering material support during my revision of this project.

I am also honored to work with my editors at Oxford University Press, in particular, Cynthia Reed and John Nemec, as well as the anonymous reviewers of this book, who provided critical comments and feedback to sharpen the arguments and clarify the ideas. Thanks too, to Drew Anderla, Rajakumari Ganessin, Henry Southgate, and their team for their patience and care as production and copy editors.

Finally, many thanks for my family, friends, and my Jesuit brothers for their moral support and practical help.

Preface

IN OCTOBER 1773, two Catholic prisoners—one Spaniard, one Vietnamese, both of the Dominican order—appeared at the court of Trịnh Sâm, the viceroy of Tonkin (North Vietnam), each carrying a yoke stamped with four words: *Hoa Lang Đạo Sư* (Teacher of the Portuguese Religion). They were accused of spreading the "Portuguese religion," a foreign and heterodox sect by the court's standards. Fathers Jacinto Castaneda and Vicente Liêm de la Paz were allowed to defend themselves in an interreligious panel conducted by the presiding judge of their case, Prince Six, who was a relative of the viceroy. During the debate, the Catholic priests used Christian apologetic arguments and examples from the Chinese classics to explain the merits of Catholic doctrines and practices against those of their Confucian, Daoist, and Buddhist opponents. Their eloquence was well received by the audience and even earned the admiration of the judge. Nevertheless, the sympathetic official could not save the two Dominicans from execution. On November 7, 1773, the two priests were beheaded for violation of the imperial prohibition of Catholicism.[1] Their famous debate and martyrdom were etched upon the memory of generations of Vietnamese Catholics. The content of their legendary defense of the Christian faith[2] was later written down as the *Conference of the Four Religions* (Hội Đồng Tứ Giáo), a multiedition Catholic apologetic text that was printed during the last half of the nineteenth and the mid-twentieth centuries.[3]

---

1. Both were canonized on June 19, 1988 by Pope John Paul II as two of the 117 holy martyrs of Vietnam.

2. In this study, the word "Christian" will be used to refer to the whole Christian tradition, whereas "Catholic" is restricted to the Catholic Church, its doctrines, and practices. Before the twentieth century, Christianity in Vietnam was identified with Catholicism.

3. The text, also known as *Hội Đồng Tứ Giáo Danh Sư* (Conferences of the Representatives of the Four Religions) appeared in at least twenty-three editions between 1864 and 1959, both in demotic script (*nôm*) and romanized characters (*quốc ngữ*). For an introduction to this text, see Anh Q. Tran, "Inculturation, Mission, and Dialogue in Vietnam: The 'Conference of

Catholicism has been a minor but significant religion in Vietnam since its arrival during the sixteenth century. During its first three centuries of existence, however, the Catholic community was largely shaped by the experience of being marginalized and persecuted. More than the result of a concern for national security, the suppression of Catholicism by various Vietnamese rulers between the seventeenth and nineteenth centuries represented a clash of culture and ideology between the converts and their fellow citizens, especially on religious worship. A study of Vietnamese religions of this period is thus essential to understand the nature of such conflict. Yet, the scholarly study of the Christian mission in Vietnam has generally neglected the religious and cultural context from which Vietnamese Christianity emerged. Compared to the scholarly attention given to the Christian encounters with the religious cultures of China and Japan, little has been written on similar encounters and interactions in Vietnam.

Scholars who want to study the Vietnamese traditions have to rely on the description about the social, cultural, and religious life of Tonkin found in missionary reports and merchant's travelogues of earlier centuries. Jesuit missionaries to Tonkin in the seventeenth century were pioneers in giving Europeans information about the little-known kingdom south of China. Besides the annual reports given to their superiors in Macau and Rome and in addition to their occasional letters, a few missionaries published their traveling accounts—often called "relations" in later collections. Travelogues by the Jesuit missionaries Giuliano Baldinotti, Alexandre de Rhodes, Giovanni Filippo de Marini, and Joseph Tissanier were influential eye-witness accounts that provide a general picture of the situation in Tonkin.[4] Missionary accounts of Tonkin were translated into many European languages, and the information therein was often summarized in later dictionaries and encyclopedias.

Traders and merchants who visited or settled in Tonkin also composed their own accounts of what was going on. Among these, we can count the work of Jean-Baptiste Tavernier, Samuel Baron, William Dampier, and others.[5] These traveling reports about a fascinating kingdom of two kings (a *vua* and a *chúa*)

---

the Representatives of the Four Religions,'" in *Beyond Conversion and Syncretism: Indigenous Encounters with Missionary Christianity, 1800–2000*, ed. D. Lindenfeld and M. Richardson (New York: Berghahn Books, 2012), 167–94.

4. See the bibliography for full reference of their works. Rhodes had lived for a total of seven years in Tonkin and Cochinchina (1627–30, 1640–45), Marini for twelve years; Tissanier came to Tonkin in 1658 and lived through a chaotic time there. Another missionary description of Tonkin is also found in the report by Cristoforro Borri (1631), although he was never in Tonkin.

5. Again, see the bibliography for full reference of their work. Tavernier's account must be used with care, since he never set foot in Tonkin. His information mainly came from his brother, Daniel Tavernier, who worked briefly for the Dutch in Tonkin between 1639 and 1645, and the

were collected, translated, and reprinted in later collections. They were combinations of geographical reports, notes on fauna and flora, descriptions of people and customs, and any information that was deemed useful to other missionaries and traders. Until the mid-nineteenth century, these accounts were valuable sources of information on Tonkin.

Unearthing a Treasure

This book intends to contribute to the historical study of traditional Vietnamese religions by introducing, translating, and evaluating a never-before-published eighteenth-century manuscript entitled *Tam Giáo Chư Vọng* (Errors of the Three Religions). How I found this text is purely coincidental. Back in 2004, while doing research in the archives of the Foreign Mission Society of Paris (AMEP), particularly to trace the sources of the *Conference of the Four Religions*, I encountered a 1750 Latin treatise on Vietnamese religions entitled *Opusculum de sectis apud Sinenses et Tunkinenses* (A Small Treatise on the Sects among the Chinese and Tonkinese), (henceforth, *Opusculum*). The archivist informed me that a translation of this work was published in English in 2002.[6] As I read the treatise, I noticed similarities among many arguments and issues raised by the *Conference* and *Opusculum*. Their descriptions of Vietnamese religious beliefs and practices are almost identical at places. However, the language and writing styles are different. The *Conference* was written in a dialogical manner and in the demotic Vietnamese script (*chữ Nôm*), and *Opusculum* is a series of essays in Latin with Sino-Vietnamese phrases inserted here and there. In its defense of Christianity and refutation of the *tam giao*, the *Conference* cites many Sino-Vietnamese phrases and expressions from the classics that did not appear in *Opusculum*.

The similarity and yet difference between the two texts led me to believe that the anonymous author of *Conference* might have relied on written source(s) other than *Opusculum* for his citation of the classics. Furthermore, upon reading the preface of the *Opusculum*, I realized that its author, the Augustinian missionary Adriano di Santa Thecla, claimed that his work relied on other written sources for his information on Vietnamese religions. He mentioned in particular two books written in Vietnamese: the *Dị Đoan Chi Giáo* (*The Teaching of Hereterodoxy*) and

---

Tonkinese who traded with him. In fact, Samuel Baron wrote about his experience in Tonkin partly to refute some of Tavernier's claims.

6. Adriano di Santa Thecla, *Opusculum de sectis apud Sinenses et Tonkinenses / A Small Treatise on the Sects among the Chinese and Tonkinese,* trans. Olga Dror as *A Study of Religion in China and North Vietnam in the Eighteenth Century* (Ithaca, NY: Cornell University Press / SEAP, 2002).

the *Đại Học Chi Đạo* (*The Way of Great Learning*) of Hilario Costa, bishop of East Tonkin.[7] Adriano di Santa Thecla's remark piqued my interest in searching for the lost Vietnamese text(s) that could be the source(s) of the *Conference*.

With the help of the late professor Antoine Trần Văn Toàn of the Catholic University of Lille, I discovered a Vietnamese text entitled *Tam Giáo Chư Vọng* from the same archive that houses the *Opusculum*. The text is written in the Romanized Vietnamese script (*chữ quốc-ngữ*) and described the "errors" of the traditional religious practices from a missionary's perspective. The literary affinity between *Opusculum* and *Tam Giáo Chư Vọng* is remarkable. Both texts identify their authors as Italian missionaries evangelizing in Tonkin, and their contents are so similar, even mirroring each other at places, that they could be considered works drawn from the same source of information.[8] After carefully comparing the two texts (see Appendix A), I believe that my discovery is related to the missing text that Adriano refers to in his treatise of Vietnamese religions.

A close reading of this particular Christian text in its historical and cultural contexts will present a valuable case study of Vietnamese religious practices as missionaries and converts encountered them. My study portrays the religious challenges that converts had to face as they sought to establish their Christian identity within their social interactions. To understand the history of Christian missions within its cultural and religious context, the descriptions of religious beliefs and rituals provided by *Errors of the Three Religions* are a valuable source to complement standard accounts of Vietnamese religious culture.

An Outline of This Study

As a study and a translation of the text, this book has two major parts. The first part is a historical study of *Tam Giáo Chư Vọng* or *Errors of the Three Religions* (henceforth, *Errors*) by way of a long contextual introduction distributed in five chapters. The first two chapters cover the religious and literary background of *Errors*. Chapter 1 considers the Catholic presence in Tonkin and its interaction with Vietnamese religions along with a brief description of the effects of the Chinese Rites Controversy in Vietnam. Chapter 2 introduces the text, including the genre, history of composition, structure, content, audience, and authorship of *Errors* as well as its relationship to other Christian texts in Vietnam at that time.

---

7. These works presumably were lost.

8. See Appendix A for a discussion comparing Adriano's *Opusculum* and the *Tam Giáo Chư Vọng*.

The next two chapters focus on significant Vietnamese religious practices described in the text. Since many of the beliefs and rituals described belong to popular religiosity, the "errors" will not be analyzed according to the threefold division of Confucianism, Daoism, and Buddhism. Instead, I will focus on the cultic practices in traditional Vietnam. Chapter 3 analyzes the many religious rites, including the worship of Heaven, nature, spirits, heroes, and religious figures in public cults as well as private rituals. Chapter 4 deals with the afterlife and the cult of the dead, according to both Confucian and Vietnamese folk Buddhist practices; for a comparison, I will also present the Vietnamese Catholic practice of ancestor veneration.

The last chapter evaluates *Errors* from a contemporary perspective. It traces the influence of *Errors* on later Vietnamese Catholic texts of the late eighteenth and nineteenth centuries and appraises its legacy for the understanding of the nature of Vietnamese religions. The significance and limitation of the work in light of contemporary interreligious dialogue and theology of religions will also be discussed.

The second part contains an annotated translation of the original text published here for the first time. It comprises three books; each is divided into a series of dialogues between a Christian priest and a Confucian scholar, explaining and evaluating many religious beliefs, practices, and rituals of the Tonkinese that the author considers problematic or erroneous from a Christian point of view. Issues regarding Confucianism are treated in fifteen articles, Daoism in twelve articles, and Buddhism also in twelve articles. The footnotes of my translation will provide essential references for those interested in the details of Chinese/Vietnamese concepts, historical figures and religious customs.

For interested readers, *Errors* can be considered a snapshot of Vietnam's traditional religious practices. Nevertheless, this rare work is not a survey of Vietnamese religions in general, but rather a Christian presentation of the "errors" (*chư vọng*) of the *tam giáo* in eighteenth-century Tonkin. The author focuses only on popular cults, beliefs, and practices that he considers harmful to the Christian life. Viewed from this perspective, readers should not rush to conclusions about the past or present religious situation in Vietnam based on the text alone, without a deeper understanding of the author's motivation and circumstances. *Errors* helps explain the attitude of the missionaries toward certain religious beliefs and practices that were considered incompatible with Christianity. As elsewhere in East Asia, Christianity is often considered foreign to—and by extension, incompatible with—Vietnamese culture. In *Errors*, the author strives to show that the so-called native religions of Vietnam are in fact Chinese imports, and thus they are no more legitimate than Christianity when it comes to the question of compatibility with the minds and hearts of the people.

In the absence of other comparable works, *Errors* (and *Opusculum*) are the most informative source on traditional Vietnamese religious customs. Taken together, they are the first extant treatments of the Vietnam's religious heritage. Whereas the discussion of Vietnamese beliefs, rituals, and worship in other missionary reports or travelogues are, for the most part, cursory and dismissive, *Errors* and *Opusculum* elaborate and supply the details that other descriptions of Vietnamese religions glossed over. In the aftermath of the Chinese Rites Controversy, they serve as handbooks to explain to Christian converts why certain beliefs and practices of their fellow Vietnamese were incompatible with the Christian faith. The translation, annotation, analysis, and evaluation of an important, hitherto neglected manuscript—*Tam Giáo Chư Vọng*—will be a valuable addition to the corpus of important texts that describe the Christian perception of Vietnamese religious traditions from first-hand observations. By making available an annotated translation of a rare, complex, and important manuscript of the history of Vietnamese Christianity, I hope to encourage the readers to do further studies on similar subjects.

Abbreviations

AMEP	Archives de la Societé des Missions Étrangères de Paris
BEFEO	*Bulletin de l'École Français d'Êxtreme-Orient*
Cathechismus	*Cathechismus pro ijs qui volunt recipere baptismus in octo dies divisus*
Conference	*The Conference of the Four Religions (Hội Đồng Tứ Giáo)*
Cương Mục	*Khâm Định Việt Sử Thông Giám Cương Mục*
DHCJ	*Diccionario Historico de la Compañia de Jesus*
Errors	*Errors of the Three Religions (Tam Giáo Chư Vọng)*
Loại Chí	*Lịch Triều Hiến Chương Loại Chí*
Opusculum	*Opusculum de sectis apud Sinenses et Tunkinenses*
Toàn Thư	*Đại Việt Sử Ký Toàn Thư*

Gods, Heroes, and Ancestors

Introduction

Religions of Traditional Vietnam

The dominant ideology in pre-twentieth-century Vietnam was influenced by the "triple religious tradition" or *tam giáo*—Confucianism, Daoism, and Buddhism. Any serious attempt to understand the history of the development of Christianity in Vietnam had to take into account this religious background.[1] At first glance, a comparative study of Chinese religions can shed light on the Vietnamese *tam giáo*, since it is customary to assume that the cultural heritage of the country is an extension of imperial China.[2] Historically, the area that comprised today's North Vietnam was incorporated into China as a frontier province that lasted until the tenth century.[3] During this long period of Chinese rule, there was a constant influx of Chinese migrants mixing with the indigenous population. As a result, over the centuries, Sino-Viet elements—from writing to religion, customs and laws, architecture and culinary practices—permeated into the population, even long after the Vietnamese people secured their autonomy from Chinese rule

---

1. The best survey on traditional Vietnamese religions today remains Léopold Cadière, *Croyances et pratiques religieuses des Viêtnamiens* (Hanoi, 1944–1956; repr., Paris: École Française d'Extrême-Orient, 1992); and Joseph Nguyen Huy-Lai, *La tradition religieuse, spirituelle et sociale au Viêtnam: Sa confrontation avec le christianism* (Paris: Beauchesne, 1981).

2. Scholars who study Vietnam find themselves vacillating between East Asian and Southeast Asian studies. In the field of Asian studies, it is customary to group Vietnam with China, Japan, and Korea as part of the Sinosphere. Contemporary scholarship, however, classify Vietnam studies as part of Southeast Asian studies.

3. It was called Jiaozhi (交趾) during the Han dynasty and Annam (安南) during the Tang dynasty, among others. For account of the history of Vietnam before the tenth century and its many names, see Keith W. Taylor, *The Birth of Vietnam* (Berkeley: University of California Press, 1983).

and established their own kingdom called Đại Việt (大越) from the eleventh century forward.

Until the twentieth century, the country continued to adopt many facets of the Chinese culture. Since the majority of traditional customs, philosophy, social, and religious institutions in premodern Vietnam were similar to those of the Chinese, it is customary to see them as "copies" of Chinese institutions of the Han, Tang, Song, Ming, and Qing dynasties.[4] In the history of Christian mission, the conflation of China and North Vietnam was also carried over in ecclesiastical policies.[5] During the nearly one-hundred-year debates on the Chinese Rites Controversy (1645–1742), many religious practices of Tonkin were cited as examples of Chinese superstition by those who opposed the Jesuit method of evangelization.[6]

This observation is partially correct. After almost two millennia of Chinese influence, it is difficult to distinguish between which cultural and religious elements are native to Vietnam and which were borrowed from its northern neighbor. Nevertheless, it is insufficient to describe Vietnamese traditional religions through Chinese religious and philosophical texts, for not everything in China was mirrored in Vietnam. In appropriating the religious teachings and practices from China, Vietnamese people also developed their own version of *tam giáo*.

A characteristic of traditional Vietnamese religions was the tendency to harmonize diverse religious beliefs and practices. Endowed with a practical religious sense, people were disposed to welcome and accept the possibility of multiple religious sentiments. The Vietnamese language did not have an equivalent word for the Latin term *religio*. Instead, people referred to religion as "way" (*đạo*) in common speech, or "teaching" (*giáo*) in scholarly writings.

The traditional religions of Vietnam can be a characterized as a blending of both indigenous spiritual cults and the teachings and practices of Chinese religious traditions. According to the noted French missionary Léopold Cadière, the

---

4. See for example, Alexander Woodside, *Vietnam and the Chinese Model* (1971; repr., Cambridge, MA: Harvard University Press, 1988); Stephen O'Harrow, "Men of Hu, Men of Han, Men of Hundred Man: The Biography of Si Nhiep and the Conceptualization of Early Vietnamese Society," *BEFEO* 75 (1986): 249–66; Neil Jamieson, *Understanding Vietnam* (Berkeley: University of California Press, 1993); Liam C. Kelly, *Beyond the Bronze Pillars: Envoy Poetry and the Sino-Vietnamese Relationship* (Honolulu: University of Hawai'i Press, 2005).

5. When Rome appointed François Pallu, MEP (1626–1684) as the first Apostolic Vicar for Tonkin in 1658, he was also put in charge of the vast regions of South China.

6. The footnotes attached to the 1704 and 1715 papal pronouncements against the Chinese Rites mention drawing on the descriptions of the rites by Alexandre de Rhodes and others who labor exclusively in Vietnam.

"true religion of the Viet people is the cult of the spirits."[7] The people venerated elements of the natural world, such as the sun, moon, stars, mountains, streams, rocks, and trees, as well as spirits of deceased ancestors, heroes, and even people who died accidentally. This indigenous form of animism was the foundation on which Confucian ethics, the Buddhist view of the afterlife, and Daoist magical practices were integrated.

The story of the development of the three teachings/religions of traditional Vietnam before the tenth century was shrouded in obscurity. The few surviving records and artifacts make it difficult to delineate the development of these traditions during the early period. It seems like the introduction of these traditions coincided with the greater influx of Chinese migrants in the local population and with the introduction of Chinese civilization to Tonkin during the first millennium of the common era.[8] In the following sections, I will sketch a history of Confucianism, Buddhism, and Daoism from its beginning until the eighteenth century.

Confucianism

Confucianism came to Vietnam along with Chinese customs during the Han dynasty.[9] Early attempts to bring "civilization" to the Viet natives were met with resistance, for the Han officials could not subdue the indigenous population after the annexation of the Nan-yue kingdom in 111 BCE. By the third century of the common era, Shi Xie (Sĩ Nhiếp or Sĩ Tiếp), a learned scholar and a good administrator of the Jiaozhi commandary (r. 187–226), was able to promote

---

7. Cadière, *Croyances et pratiques religieuses des Viêtnamiens*, 1:6.

8. For a general account the development of the Three Religions of traditional Vietnam, I rely on the Vietnamese primary sources which were composed in Sino-Vietnamese: the *Đại Việt Sử Ký Toàn Thư* (Complete Chronicle of the Great Viet), abbreviated as *Toàn Thư*; and the *Khâm Định Việt Sử Thông Giám Cương Mục* (The Imperially Ordered Mirror and Commentary on the History of the Viet), abbreviated as *Cương Mục*. Another important source is the encyclopedia of Phan Huy Chú, the *Lịch Triều Hiến Chương Loại Chí* (Categorized Records of the Institutions of Successive Dynasties), abbreviated as *Loại Chí*. See the bibliography for the full references and translations into Vietnamese of these works.

9. For an introduction to Confucianism in Vietnam, see Nguyen Ngoc Huy, "The Confucian Incursion into Vietnam," in *Confucianism and the Family*, ed. Walter H. Slote and George A. De Vos (Albany: SUNY, 1998), 91–136; Keith Taylor, "Vietnamese Confucian Narratives," in *Rethinking Confucianism: Past and Present in China, Japan, Korea, and Vietnam*, ed. John B. Duncan and Herman Ooms (Los Angeles: University of California Press, 2002), 337–69; Liam C. Kelly, "Confucianism in Vietnam: A State of the Field Essay," *Journal of Vietnamese Studies* 1, nos. 1–2 (2006): 314–70; see also Nguyen Huy-Lai, *La tradition religieuse spirituelle sociale au Viêtnam*, 127–92.

Confucian learning among the natives. For this reason, he was later on credited by the Vietnamese scholars as the "originator of Viet learning" (*nam giao học tổ*) for his efforts to propagate Confucian thought, along with Chinese writings, literature, rites, and customs.[10] Yet, before the eleventh century, the impact of Confucianism on the population, beyond a few people who worked in official capacities, was unknown.

During the early period of independence from China, under the Đinh (968–980) and Early Lê (980–1009) dynasties, Vietnamese rulers often appointed Buddhist monks, the most learned men in the country, as court advisors and chancellors (*quốc sư*). However, a century later, the kings of the Lý dynasty (1009–1225), although Buddhists themselves, realized that they needed a strong sociopolitical system to govern the country and to resist Chinese incursion from the north. They decided to appropriate Confucian statecraft to secure loyalty, establish law and order, and bring stability to society. At the same time, they continued to use Buddhist advisors in their court.[11] With the establishment of the National Academy (Quốc Tử Giám) in 1070, where sons of aristocratic families studied Confucian literature, Confucianism gradually exerted a greater role in the court of independent Đại Việt.

Although most officials were still chosen from military families or Buddhist and Daoist monks, civil-service examinations, first held in 1075, were employed to select competent mandarins to serve the expanding bureaucratic needs.[12] Members of aristocratic families and the monks competed in a wide range of subjects, including the teachings of Confucius, disseminated through the works of Dong Zhongshu and others.[13] The incorporation of Confucianism into the examination curriculum provided a political philosophy and a system of ethics to maintain the social order. Selected elements of Confucian morality and political philosophy were appropriated to construct a practical philosophy for civil life and governance. Through its emphasis on the virtues of filial piety and loyalty

---

10. After his death, various legends and worship were attached to him, especially in *Departed Spirits of Viet Realm* (Việt Điện U Linh Tập); Shi is honored in some temples today as King Sĩ (Sĩ Vương). See Taylor, *The Birth of Vietnam*, 70–80.

11. Keith Taylor, "Authority and Legitimacy in 11th century Vietnam," in *Southeast Asia in the 9th to 14th Centuries*, ed. David C. Marr and A. C. Milner (Singapore: Institute of Southeast Asian Studies, 1986), 139–76.

12. *Toàn Thư*, Bản kỷ, 3:8a (translation, 1: 294); *Loại Chí*, Khoa mục chí, 1 (translation, 2:7–8). During the Lý dynasty, examinations were held in 1086, 1152, 1165, 1185, and 1193. The exact content of these exams were not known, but it was most likely based on similar civil-service examinations of the Tang and Song dynasty.

13. Van Doan Tran, "Confucianism: Vietnam," in *Encyclopedia of Chinese Philosophy*, ed. Antonion S. Cua (New York: Routedge, 2003), 173–74.

and the Three Bonds (*tam cương*), that is, the subordination of wife to husband, children to father, and subject to ruler, Confucianism formed the relational ethics necessary in an agrarian society. The mixing of the pragmatic elements of Confucianism with Buddhist and Daoist metaphysical elements results in a harmonization of the three teachings that, from a Vietnamese perspective, more or less share the same roots, that is, from China. Beginning in 1195 under the reign of Lý Cao Tông, the examination included teachings from the Three Religions, and the practice continued during the Trần dynasty (1225–1400).[14] It provided the kings of Lý and Trần dynasties with the needed institutional framework to run the country and defend it from invasions from the north (China) and the south (Champa and Khmer).[15]

During their brief occupation of Đại Việt (1407–1427), Ming officials launched a project of Sinicization.[16] They established a number of Confucian schools and brought newly edited Confucian classics and Neo-Confucian works.[17] This policy altered the course of Confucianism in Vietnam even long after the Ming had gone. Civil-service examinations that began during the Lý-Trần era were expanded and revised under the Lê dynasty on the basis of the Ming curriculum. Beginning in 1442, civil examinations were organized every three years at three levels: the province (*thi hương*), the national (*thi hội*), and at the imperial courts (*thi đình*) to recruit competent administrators for the kingdom. Examinations at all levels took four days, the first day on the Chinese classics (*kinh nghĩa*), the second day on composition of official writings, petitions, and reports (*chiếu, chế, biểu*), the third day on composition of poetry and prose (*thi phú*), and the fourth day on philosophical, historical, or political essays (*văn sách*). At the province level, successful candidates who passed the first three days of exams were awarded the title learned person (*sinh đồ* or *tú tài*), and those who passed all four exams were entitled recommended scholar (*hương cống* or *cử nhân*). Candidates who passed all four exams at the national level were named

---

14. The examination based on a Three Religions curriculum was first given in 1195, and again in 1227 and 1247. *Loại Chí*, Khoa mục chí 1 (translation, 2:7–9).

15. On Confucianism in the Trần dynasty, see O. W. Wolters, *Two Essays on Đại Việt in the Fourteenth Century* (New Haven, CT: Yale Southeast Asia Studies, 1988).

16. *Toàn Thư*, Bản kỷ, 9:25b (translation, 2:252). Also see John K. Whitmore, "Chiao-chih and Neo-Confucianism: The Ming Attempt to Transform Vietnam," *Ming Studies* 4 (1977): 51–91.

17. *Toàn Thư* records that "[in 1419] the Ming sent officials to bring over the Four Books, Five Classics, *Compendium of Nature and Principle* (Tính Lý Đại Toàn), *On Goodness* (Vi Thiện Âm Chất), and *On True Filial Service* (Hiếu Thuận Sự Thực) to teach Confucianism in all districts, counties, and prefectures." (Bản kỷ, 10:3b; translation, 2: 259). The first three books are mentioned in *Errors of the Three Religions*.

advanced scholar (*tiến sĩ*). A month later, they were qualified to sit for the examination at the imperial palace to be tested by the king himself. Successful candidates were awarded different degrees of honor, the highest being *trạng nguyên*, *bảng nhãn*, and *thám hoa*, or the first-, second-, and third-level laureate. The names of the top three laureates were inscribed in stone tablets and honored at the Temple of Culture in Thăng Long, a practice that lasted until the end of the eighteenth century.[18]

Vietnamese Confucianism, however, never developed to the level of scholarship of contemporary China or Korea.[19] Because of the honor attached to a career in public office, generations of young men would undergo years of study, but without the support of a vigorous academic institution. Most Confucian learnings took place not in the court-academy or provincial institutions but in village schools. Scholars devoted themselves to studying the classics in order to pass the civil-service examinations. They were less interested in philosophical debates than in rules of conduct and correct rituals.[20] As a result, Vietnamese scholars did not leave behind any significant philosophical writings or schools of thought, save a few collections of poetry and books of history and geography. The scholastic learning of the Confucian elites, except for a few prominent scholars like Nguyễn Bỉnh Khiêm (1491–1585) or Lê Quý Đôn (1726–1784), did not equip them to face the societal changes of the seventeenth and eighteenth centuries.

But since both Buddhism and Daoism had no special teachings regarding family organization and statecraft, Confucianism had a primary role in these areas. Central to Vietnamese Confucianism was the emphasis on order and harmony. Confucius saw order in the universe and in human affairs and translated it into the moral bonds and obligations among family members. This emphasis on virtues and moral obligations fit well with the practical mentality of the premodern Vietnamese, who did not much concern themselves with metaphysical questions. Confucianism in Vietnam was reduced to a system of family ethics and a code of social conduct.[21]

---

18. *Loại Chí*, Khoa mục chí 1 (translation, 2:13–25).

19. On Confucianism in the Lê dynasty see, John K. Whitmore, "From Classical Scholarship to Confucian Belief in Vietnam," *Vietnam Forum* 9 (1987): 49–65; and "Literati Culture and Integration in Dai Viet, c. 1430–1840," in *Beyond Binary Histories: Reimagining Eurasia to c. 1830*, ed. Victor Lieberman (Ann Arbor: University of Michigan Press, 1997), 221–43.

20. Alexander Woodside, "Classical Primordialism and Historical Agendas of Vietnamese Confucianism," in *Rethinking Confucianism*, ed. John B. Duncan and Herman Ooms, 116–43.

21. Stephen B. Young, "The Orthodox Chinese Confucian Social Paradigm versus Vietnamese Individualism," in *Confucianism and the Family*, ed. Walter H. Slote and George A. De Vos (Albany: SUNY, 1998), 137–61.

Although Confucianism was favored exclusively by the intellectual elite and political rulers, only basic Confucian ideas—mostly in ethics and rituals—reached the masses. In terms of ritual, the vast majority of the population did not understand Confucianism as a cohesive system. Rather, they appropriated fragments of Confucian ethics and supplemented them with local customs and beliefs. Most people kept their various native cults and continued to seek help from the local spirits in conjunction with Daoist and Buddhist practices. The ruling class adapted to this mentality by appointing a Minister of Rites to be in charge of religious affairs and to certify (*sắc phong*) village gods and deified heroes. In this way, they could control local cults and reduce their subversive potential.

Buddhism

Buddhism also made its way to Tonkin during the latter Han period.[22] In the third century of the common era, Luy Lâu (Bắc Ninh today) was known as a Buddhist center in East Asia, where Indian and Central Asian monks traveling to and from China would stop. Between the fourth and sixth centuries, the arrival of Indian scholars and monks from Southeast Asia, as well as Chinese monks and the founding of various Zen schools, solidified the Buddhist presence.[23] From the extant Buddhist literature, it is clear that by the tenth century Buddhism had developed a close affinity with the indigenous religions of Vietnam. The integration of native deities and local cults into the development of Vietnamese Buddhism was a natural course of development. Early on, when Buddhist temples were few and far between, missionary monks often took up residence in local shrines or temples. Many local spirits and deified heroes were eventually brought within the Buddhist pantheon and transformed into guardians of Buddhism (*hộ pháp*, "protectors of the dharma").[24]

---

22. The history of Buddhism in Vietnam before the twentieth century has not been documented thoroughly. The best account, although dated, remains Trần Văn Giáp, "Le Bouddhisme en Annam des origins au XIIIe siècle," *BEFEO* 32 (1932): 191–268. Other notable works include Nguyễn Lang (Thich Nhat Hanh), *Việt Nam Phật Giáo Sử Luận* [History of Vietnamese Buddhism] (Hanoi: NXB Văn Học, 2000); and Cuong Tu Nguyen, *Zen in Medieval Vietnam* (Honolulu: University of Hawai'i Press, 1997). Nguyễn Lang's work was edited and translated by Nguyễn Tài Thư as *Buddhism in Vietnam* (Hanoi: Thế Giới Publishers, 1993). Hà Văn Tấn's *Buddhist Temples in Vietnam*, rev. ed. (Hanoi: Thế Giới Publishers, 2008) deals with Buddhist architecture and provides useful information on the development of Buddhism in Tonkin.

23. Cuong Tu Nguyen, *Zen in Medieval Vietnam*, 12–13. Prominent among these monks was Kang Senghui, who had become a Buddhist monk in Jiaozhou before moving to China and becoming a leading exponent of Buddhism there. See Thich Nhat Hanh, *Master Tang Hoi: First Zen Teacher in Vietnam and China* (Berkeley: Parallax Press, 2001).

24. Cuong Tu Nguyen, *Zen in Medieval Vietnam*, 14.

During the Đinh, Early Lê, and Lý dynasties, Vietnamese rulers found in Buddhism a cultural force that could help them secure legitimacy. Past interactions with monks from other parts of Asia had contributed to the formation of a clerical class necessary for the development of a newly formed kingdom of Đại Việt. Many prominent Buddhist monks exerted national political influence. At the same time, these monks were hailed in folklore as miracle workers who could use their magical powers to help those in need and ward off troubles. These magical tales reflect the popularity of Buddhism among the common people. The association of Buddhist monks with magical powers might also hint at the presence of Tantric elements in Vietnamese Buddhism.

Buddhism in Vietnam reached its highest development between the eleventh and fourteenth centuries during the Lý and Trần dynasties.[25] The Lý were patrons of Buddhism, but they also practiced a policy of openness and nonexclusivity. Although many kings supported the large-scale construction of Buddhist temples and some became monks after passing on their thrones to successors,[26] the Lý never established Buddhism as a national religion. Instead, these kings saw Buddhism as a major element that could help foster a national culture. Under the Lý patronage, different forms of Buddhism flourished: both the "popular" style, which included tantric, ritual, and devotional elements mixed with indigenous religions, and the "elite" or court-sponsored style modeled after Chinese Zen Buddhism.[27]

The Trần were also powerful Buddhist benefactors, although their costly wars with the Mongols from the north and the Chams from the south prevented them from building as many temples as the Lý did. These wars, however, provoked a national emergency that helped the Trần establish themselves as leaders of the nation. In order to solidify their position, Trần rulers had to rely more and more on Confucianism for statecraft and administration while they tried to maintain the balance of power between members of the Three Religions.[28] For the Trần aristocrats, Buddhism was a religion that provided for the spiritual needs of the individual, while Confucianism was a more effective and suitable system

---

25. Nguyễn Tài Thư, *Buddhism in Vietnam*, 65–122.

26. The *Thiền Uyển Tập Anh* (*Eminent Monks of the Thien Community*) mentions that several Lý monarchs were members of Zen school Thảo Đường (Lý Thánh Tông, r. 1054–1072; Lý Anh Tông, r. 1138–1175; and Lý Cao Tông, r. 1176–1210), but none of the kings became monks. Among the Trần monarchs, Trần Nhân Tông (r. 1279–1293) was the founder of the Zen school Trúc Lâm on Mount Yên Tử.

27. Cuong Tu Nguyen, *Zen in Medieval Vietnam*, 19–20.

28. Cuong Tu Nguyen, *Zen in Medieval Vietnam*, 20–21.

for dealing with worldly affairs. For this reason, after retiring, many Trần kings and nobles withdrew to the mountains to practice Zen Buddhism. Vietnamese Zen (Thiền) reached its peak under the Trần dynasty with the foundation of the Bamboo Grove (Trúc Lâm) school of Zen and the composition of important Zen literature.[29]

In the middle of the fourteenth century, the tide began to turn against Buddhism. The Trần aristocrats who had supported Buddhism lost much of their economic and political power. Mandarins from the Confucian circles began to criticize Buddhism as a burden on society.[30] In 1396, Hồ Quý Ly (1336–1407), the prime minister who served King Trần Nghệ Tông (r. 1370–72) and his successors, issued an order to purge the ranks of Buddhist monks and dissolve many monasteries.[31] Furthermore, a major part of Buddhist literature and other Vietnamese writings composed during Lý and Trần eras was lost during the period of Ming occupation. These events disrupted the continuity of the Buddhism of later centuries with its past.

Buddhism suffered further marginalization when the kings of the Lê dynasty adopted Confucianism as the state ideology. Confucian doctrines replaced the wider teachings of the Three Religions as the main subject of civil examinations. Although it fell out of favor in the royal court, Buddhism strengthened its hold in the villages. Many village temples were built or restored under the Mạc and Lê dynasties, sometimes with contributions from the upper class. Pureland Buddhism spread widely to the general population, where it became a religion of salvation. Belief in paradise and hell shaped the moral behavior of many people. Vietnamese Buddhists prayed to A Di Đà (Amitābha) and Quan Âm (Avalokiteśvara) for deliverance. The cult of Quan Âm blended with the native cult of Mother Goddess (*Mẫu*), turning the bodhisattva of compassion into a goddess of mercy[32]

---

29. On the Zen literature, we can count Trần Thái Tông's *Instruction on Emptiness* (Khoá Hư Lục) and the biographies of famous Zen monks, *Eminent Monks of the Thien Community* (Thiền Uyển Tập Anh). J. C. Cleary, "Buddhism and Popular Religion in Medieval Vietnam," *Journal of American Religion* 59, no. 1 (Spring 1991): 93–118.

30. See, for example, Trương Hán Siêu's and Lê Quát's diatribes recorded in *Toàn Thư*, Bản kỷ, 7:17b, 36a–b (translation, 2:144, 164).

31. *Toàn Thư*, Bản kỷ, 8:26a (translation, 2:201). This is not unlike the great persecution of Buddhism that happened in China in 845 CE where tens of thousands monks were laicized.

32. For a survey of the cult of Quan Âm in Tonkin, see Nguyễn Minh Ngọc, Nguyễn Mạnh Cường and Nguyễn Duy Hinh, *Bồ Tát Quán Thế Âm Trong Các Chùa Vùng Đông Bằng Sông Hồng* [Quan Âm in the Buddhist Temples of the Red River Delta] (Hanoi: NXB Khoa Học Xã Hội, 2004).

By the eighteenth century, Buddhism had largely transformed into a religion of the masses. The doctrines of karma and reincarnation influenced popular piety. The village pagoda became a place of refuge from daily sufferings. Buddhist monks and priests became specialists in funeral ceremonies and other rituals that had little to do with Buddhist doctrines. Attempts to revive Buddhist Zen schools in the seventeenth century did not produce any lasting results.

Daoism

Early Daoist history in Vietnam was shrouded in obscurity, except for the sporadic mention of individual Daoist priests.[33] When the Yellow Turban movement, inspired by Daoist magic, was brutally suppressed in China, many survivors migrated to the South. Daoism gradually spread throughout the land so that in the tenth century, Daoist priests were recognized by a royal ranking alongside Buddhist monks and Confucian scholars. Along with Buddhism, Daoism also enjoyed the patronage of the Lý and the Trần monarchs. The Lý supported the construction or restoration of Daoist temples in addition to Buddhist ones.[34] A number of Daoist temples appeared during the Lý era devoted to the worship of the Heavenly King (Thiên Đế).[35] Other temples were also dedicated to the worship of the Three Venerables (Tam Tôn or Tam Thanh), the highest gods of Chinese Daoism.[36] The Trần monarchs, though Buddhist themselves, also welcomed Daoist priests to the court.[37] Apart from dynastic records, one can find the elusive Daoist presence only in popular legends. The cults and legends recorded

---

33. For example, a certain Daoist named Yên Kỳ Sinh who was supposed to settle in Mount Yên Tử (Quảng Ninh Province) in the fourth century. See Nguyễn Duy Hinh, *Người Việt Nam với Đạo Giáo* [Vietnamese People and Daoism] (Hanoi: NXB Khoa Học Xã Hội, 2003), 353–81.

34. In 1010, Lý Thái Tổ issued a decree calling for the restoration of old Buddhist and Daoist temples in the villages. In 1031, the Daoist priest Trịnh Trí Không petitioned for Daoists to be registered in the temple Thái Thanh, erected by imperial order twenty years earlier. *Toàn Thư*, Bản kỷ, 2:3ab, 20b / translation, 1:250, 267.

35. For example, the *Toàn Thư* mentions that in 1016, the temples Thiên Quang and Thiên Đức were built, and four statues of Thiên Đế were erected (Bản kỷ, 2:7b; translation 1: 254). In 1057, the temples Thiên Phúc and Thiên Thọ were built, and the gold statues of Brahma (Phạm Thiên) and Indra (Đế Thích) were commissioned for worship (Bản kỷ, 3:2a; translation, 1:288).

36. *Toàn Thư* mentions that in 1134, the king visited the Ngũ Nhạc temple and had it restored; the following year he came to venerate the newly cast statues of Tam Tôn (Three Venerables). Bản kỷ, 3:38b (translation, 1:325).

37. For example, a Chinese Daoist named Hứa Tông Đạo, who settled near Thăng Long in 1302, was credited for "spreading the magic" (*Toàn Thư*, Bản kỷ, 6:17a; translation, 2:92). In 1368, Trần Dụ Tông invited the Daoist priest Huyền Vân to the court to ask about Daoist practices (*Toàn Thư*, Bản kỷ, 7:28a; translation, 2:155).

in fourteenth-century collections of tales, such as *Departed Spirits of the Viet Realm* (Việt Điện U Linh Tập) and *Strange Tales from South of the Passes* (Lĩnh Nam Chích Quái), tell of the influence of Daoist concepts of immortality (e.g., the story of Chử Đồng Tử) and magic. But for the most part, their magical feats were attributed to the power of the Buddha.

During the Lê dynasty, there was little record of Daoist activities at the court. The elevation of Confucianism as the orthodox school of thought relegated Daoism to a marginal place. Unlike Buddhism, the presence of Daoism in later centuries cannot be documented with certainty because the common people often confused the two religions. Buddhist temples were also places where Daoist deities were honored, and the few existing Daoist temples could not be distinguished from temples dedicated to non-Daoist spirits.

As in China, Daoism in Vietnam also could be conceived as belonging to two related groups: philosophical Daoism (*đạo gia*) and religious Daoism (*đạo giáo*). Philosophical Daoism, a doctrine based on the classics—*Daodejing*, the books of *Zhuangzi* and *Huainanzi*—provides a worldview based on the natural approach to life. It introduced to the Vietnamese people the concept of *dao*, the theory of yin and yang, the theory of Five Elements, and the ethics of "noncontrivance" (*vô vi*) and "spontaneity" (*tự nhiên*). The interchange between the philosophical Daoist worldview and the Confucian rationality gave rise to Neo-Confucian cosmology during the Song dynasty, which was eventually transmitted to Vietnam during the Lê era. The discourses on the Supreme Ultimate (*thái cực*), universal principle (*lý*), vital energy (*khí*), and nature (*tính*) in the works of Song Neo-Confucians were absorbed by Vietnamese intellectuals. Although philosophical Daoism did not extend much outside the literati circle, it allowed one to be closer to nature and free from the constricted life regulated by Confucian rules of conduct.

Religious Daoism, on the other hand, was a religion with very complex origins that came to prominence with the Yellow Turban movement in the Han era.[38] It brought together the ancient cults of spirits, the use of amulets and charms, the search for longevity and immortality, and Laozi's philosophy of detachment and simplicity, among other elements. With its practices of spiritual healings, magic,

---

38. In the second-century CE, a Daoist named Zhang Jiao (or Zhang Jue) started a sect called Taiping dao (Way of Great Peace). By using magic and spiritual healings, he attracted a great number of people from all over the country. In 184, the followers of Taiping dao revolted against the corrupted officials of the Han dynasty, in a movement known as the Yellow Turban rebellion. For a summary, see Barbara Hendrische, *The Scripture on Great Peace: The Taiping jing and the Beginnings of Daoism* (Berkeley: University of California Press, 2006), 1–66; Henri Maspero, *Taoism and Chinese Religions*, trans. Frank A. Kierman. Jr. (Amherst: the University of Massachussetts Press, 1981), 25–31.

alchemy, and divination, religious Daoism gained popularity among Vietnamese people because it blended in seamlessly with the native religious sentiments. Daoist rites of purification and incantations to manipulate natural forces or control spirits to ward off evils and cure sickness appealed greatly to the people. The search for longevity and immortality through Daoist breathing and meditating techniques, alchemy, and dietary practices were popular among the upper classes and the literati.[39]

In Vietnam, Daoism did not take an institutional form, as it did in China. Although there were Daoist priests and temples, there were no Daoist schools or lineages. Daoist temples (*đạo quán*) were places to worship the immortals and genies rather than monasteries to train monks and priests. Foremost among the Daoist deities is the Jade Emperor (Ngọc Hoàng), who was assisted by two ministers, Nam Tào (*Southern Constellation*) and Bắc Đẩu (*Northern Constellation*), who are in charge of life and death respectively. Other deities and spirits, including the immortals, make up the Vietnamese Daoist pantheons. Vietnamese Daoists worship immortals both of Chinese and Vietnamese origins. Among the Vietnamese immortals were Chử Đồng Tử, the Mountain Spirit of Tản Viên, Thánh Gióng of Sóc Sơn, and Princess Liễu Hạnh.[40] The cult of Chư Vị (the Honored Ones) was a Daoist adaptation of the worship of nature, also known as the cult of Tam Phủ (*Three Palaces*) or Tứ Phủ (*Four Palaces*). The followers of this cult worshipped the goddesses who governs the three worlds of heaven, earth, and water (or four worlds, if you add the forest). These goddesses included the Princess Liễu Hạnh (*Mother of the Sky*), Mẫu Thượng Ngàn (*Mother of the Earth*), Mẫu Thoải/Thủy (*Mother of the Sea*), and Mẫu Nhạc Phủ (*Mother of the Forest*).[41] The national hero, Trần Hưng Đạo, who saved the country from the Mongols' invasions, although not an immortal, also had his own Daoist cult.[42] Particular to Vietnamese Daoism is the use of mediums (*đồng nhân*) to communicate between the living and the spirit world. The use of mediums was popular even at temples of non-Daoist origins (e.g., Princess Liễu Hạnh, General Trần

---

39. On Vietnamese religious Daoism, see Nguyen Huy Lai, *La tradition religieuse spirituelle sociale au Viêtnam*, 251–86.

40. On the cult of immortals, see Nguyen Van Huyen, *Le culte des immortels en Annam* (Hanoi, 1944).

41. On the cults of Mother Goddesses, see Ngô Đức Thịnh, *Đạo Mẫu Việt Nam* [Goddess Worship in Vietnam] (Hanoi: NXB Tôn Giáo, 2009); Olga Dror, *Cult, Culture and Authority: Princess Liễu Hạnh in Vietnamese History* (Honolulu: University of Hawai'i Press, 2007).

42. On the cult of Trần Hưng Đạo, see Phạm Quỳnh Phương, *Hero and Deity: Tran Hung Dao and the Resurgence of Popular Religion in Vietnam* (Bangkok: Mekong Press, 2009).

Hưng Đạo). The Daoist practices blended so seamlessly with shamanist rituals that even their practitioners could not always tell the difference.[43]

On the popular level, the Vietnamese were more attracted to esoteric Daoism (*nội đạo*), whose practioners were various lay specialists who might not be attached to any Daoist temple. These "masters" (*thầy*) functioned like shamans, who would act as intermediates between humans and spirits by performing cultic healing rituals or magic for those who sought their assistance. Masters of the amulets (*Thầy bùa*) would create the amulets by writing special characters or pictographs on pieces of paper, which were either worn or consumed by the patients to protect themselves from the bad spirits. Magician healers (*Thầy pháp*) would perform a number of rituals to expel or appease the bad spirits that brought illness or misfortunes. Sacrificers (*Thầy cúng*) would make ritual offers, especially at funerals. Soothsayers (*Thầy bói*) would interpret the signs and dreams to predict the future. Sorcerers (*Thầy bói tuy* or *thầy phù thủy*) would control the spirits to obtain the favors sought by the petitioner. Geomancers (*Thầy địa lý*) would give advice on *feng shui* in regards to finding a suitable burial plot. Vietnamese Daoism remained largely a folk practice with many magical and shamanic elements.[44]

The Triple Religions in Practice

The brief account of the Three Religions in Vietnam was to demonstrate that through much of its history, the basic teachings of the three religions were blended together without the need for differentiation or critical comparison. Vietnamese intellectuals combined Buddhist worldviews, Confucian ethics, and Daoist cosmology into the practice of *tam giáo* without maintaining any distinction between them.[45] These teachings offered moral and practical guidance linking personal, family, and social levels of existence. The Confucian concepts of humanness and righteousness were seen as compatible with the Buddhist

---

43. On Vietnamese mediumship, see Maurice Durand, *Technique et pantheon des mediums viêtnamiens* (1955; repr., Paris: École Française d'Extrême-Orient, 1992). Contemporary studies include Karen Fjelstad and Nguyen Thi Hien, *Possessed by the Spirits: Mediumship in Contemporary Vietnamese Communities* (Ithaca, NY: Cornell-SEAP, 2006); Barley Norton, *Songs for the Spirits: Music and Mediums in Modern Vietnam* (Chicago: University of Illinois, 2009); Kristen Endres, *Performing the Divine: Medium, Market and Modernity in Urban Vietnam* (Copenhagen: Nordic Institute of Asian Studies, 2011).

44. Nguyen Huy Lai, *La tradition religieuse spirituelle sociale au Viêtnam*, 268–83.

45. See, for example, the 1578 inscription of a stele at a Buddhist temple at Cao Dương by the famous Confucian scholar Nguyễn Bỉnh Khiêm (1491–1585) on the compatibility of the Three Religions in *Sources of Vietnamese Tradition*, ed. George Dutton, Jaynes S. Werner, and John K. Whitmore (New York: Columbia University, 2012), 114–15.

doctrine of compassion. The Daoist notions of purity and tranquility were linked to the Zen idea of emptying the mind.[46] However, the integration of the Three Religions in Vietnam never materialized into any single system as it did in Ming China. Even though they advocated for a common source of the Three Teachings, Vietnamese literati of this era, like Ngô Thì Sĩ (1726–1780) and Phan Huy Ích (1750–1822), appropriated elements of Buddhist and Daoist teachings to demonstrate the universality of Confucianism and to protect its hegemony.[47]

In the early twentieth century, the French missionary Léopold Cadière, after many years studying the religious mentality of the Vietnamese, summarized the religious situation of traditional Vietnam as follows:

> [The Vietnamese] have two religions: one principal, the religion of the spirits, which has a double object: its cult is addressed both to the personified forces of nature and to the souls of the dead, the latter includes the cult of heroes, the cult of abandoned souls, and the cult of ancestors. This religion also has a double mode of exercise: religious in Confucianism and magical in Taoism. Beside this principal religion, there is a secondary religion, and that is Buddhism.[48]

The classification of religions in Vietnam into the Three Teachings is somewhat arbitrary, as we have seen. This "harmony" of religions was not free from competition or from political maneuvering at different times in Vietnamese history. Yet a clear distinction between the religions did not exist in premodern Vietnam. For the common people, "all religions were good," since their concern was promoting their own well-being. This lack of distinction, however, did not mean that there was religious indifference in the Tonkinese culture. On the contrary, people took their religion and the spirit world for granted, as essential parts of their lives. In traditional Vietnam, as in other parts of the premodern world, the divine presence was felt everywhere. Everyone believed in some supernatural powers that were thought to be capable of helping individuals and their families in their times of need.

---

46. Duong Ngoc Dung, "An Exploration of Vietnamese Confucian Spirituality: The Idea of the Unity of the Three Teachings," in *Confucian Spirituality*, ed. Tu Weiming and Mary Evelyn Tucker (New York: Crossroad Press, 2004), 2:300–301

47. Nguyễn Kim Sơn, "Về Nho Học và Nho Giáo Việt Nam Thế Kỷ XVIII—Đầu Thế Kỷ XIX" [Confucian Studies and Vietnamese Confucianism in the Eighteenth and Early Nineteenth Centuries], in *Một Số Vấn Đề về Nho Giáo Việt Nam* [Issues on Vietnamese Confucianism], ed. Phan Đại Doãn (Hanoi: NXB Chính Trị Quốc Gia, 1998), 49–96.

48. Cadière, *Croyances et pratiques religieuses des Viêtnamiens*, 1:31–32.

The Vietnamese people had the ability to integrate newer traditions into their existing belief systems, blending traditions together without seeing them as contradictory. They freely took values and practices from different religious traditions and incorporated them into their own religious practices and worship. Both in public cults and private devotion, various religious practices were mixed together without paying attention to idiosyncrasy. The layout of many Buddhist temples in Tonkin reflected the principle of "buddhas in the front and former worthies in the back" (*tiên phật hậu thánh*), regardless of the deity's religious background. On the temple grounds were multiple shrines, side chapels, and altars in honor of different deities and spirits of whom different favors were requested.[49]

The Vietnamese took this multireligious identity for granted. This attitude toward religion was instrumental in helping individuals cope with the inevitable crises of life. Life for the Tonkinese peasants was hard. In addition to frequent natural disasters, including flood, typhoons, droughts, plagues, and famines, they had to deal with corrupt officials, heavy taxes, and forced labor. Frequent riots and rebellions compounded economic crises and destabilized the population. This vulnerability may account for the popularity of the many magical and folk practices of the Tonkinese.[50]

To understand the religious background of *Errors of the Three Religions*, let us turn to some observations by a contemporary author, Samuel Baron's description of the religions of Tonkin.[51] Born of a Dutch merchant and a Vietnamese woman, Baron lived in Thăng Long until 1659, before he was sent by his father to Europe to learn the trade. For Baron, the Tonkinese were quite religious, for there were "many sects among the people." And yet, there were two chief "sects": that of Confucius and that of the Buddha.

Of Confucianism, Baron saw it as a "moral philosophy" comparable to those of the Greeks and Romans. On a basic level, followers of Confucianism "acknowledge a supreme deity, and that all terrestrial things are directed, governed, and preserved by him." But these people also "venerate and pay a kind of adoration to spirits. They expect a reward for good deeds and punishment for evil." They believed in "immortality of the soul, and pray for the deceased," and they believed

---

49. For an illustrated description of Vietnamese traditional temples, see Ann Helen Unger and Walter Unger, *Pagodas, Gods, and Spirits of Vietnam* (London: Thames and Hudson, 1997).

50. A. Terry Rambo, "Religion and Society in Vietnam" (1977), repr. in *Searching for Vietnam: Selected Writings on Vietnamese Culture and Society* (Kyoto: Kyoto University Press, 2005), 71–79.

51. Samuel Baron, "Of the Sects, Idols, Worship, Superstition, and Pagodas or Temples of the Tonqueenese (Tonkinese)," in *A Description of the Kingdom of Tonqueen* (1685), repr. in *Views of Seventeenth-Century Vietnam*, ed. Dror and Taylor, 277–81.

that "the air is full of malignant spirits" and that "those spirits are continually at variance with the living."[52]

Baron saw in the Tonkinese a strong commitment to performing rituals to honor deceased friends and parents, not because they believed that "the dead stand in need of victuals"; rather, "they do it for no other reason, than to demonstrate their love and respect to the deceased parents; and withal to teach their own children and friends thereby, how to honor them when they shall be no more." Confucianism according to Baron had neither a particular worship place, nor priests to preach and propagate their doctrine, nor a "due form commanded or observed," and yet "it has their kings, princes, grandees, and the learned men of the kingdom for its followers."[53]

While Baron held Confucianism in high esteem, his description of Buddhism of the seventeenth century was bleak: "The second sect is called *Boot* [Buddha], which signifies the worship of idols or images, and is generally followed by the ignorant, vulgar, and simple sort of people, and more especially the women." Buddhists were seen as idol worshippers and believers in transmigration: "they made an offer to the devil, that he may not hurt them." With regard to the Buddhist clergy, Baron noticed that they "impose a cloister and retired life, and think their works can be meritorious, and the wicked suffered torments together." The Buddhists have "no priest" to preach and propagate their doctrine; "all they have are their *Sayes* [sãi], or Bonzes" and some nuns also. These monks and nuns lived in their own homes, or sometimes, in pagodas. They were often "invited to celebrate their funerals with their drums, trumpets, and other musick [*sic*]: they subsist for the most part by alms and the charity of the people."[54] From Baron's descriptions, many Buddhist monks and nuns acted as funeral ritualists, which is the main religious performance known among Vietnamese Buddhists, even of today.

With regard to the "sect of Lanzo [Laozi]" Baron noted that its many magicians and necromancers were "in great esteem with the princes, and respected by the vulgar so that they are consulted by both in their most weighty occasion; and they receive their opinions and false predictions as very oracles, believing they speak by divine inspiration, and have the fore-knowledge of future events."[55] Baron explained the reason for the proliferation of "conjurers and fortune-tellers."

---

52. Baron, *A Description of the Kingdom of Tonqueen*, 277.

53. Baron, *A Description of the Kingdom of Tonqueen*, 278.

54. Baron, *A Description of the Kingdom of Tonqueen*, 279.

55. Baron, *A Description of the Kingdom of Tonqueen*, 280.

In his observation, the Tonkinese were "very credulous" and superstitious: "They will not undertake any voyages or journey, nor build houses, cultivate grounds, nor bargain for anything considerable; nor even will they attempt, on ominous days, to cure the sick, bury their dead, nor in a manner, transact anything without the advice of their soothsayers and blind wizards."[56] Baron next described at length the activities of the "pretended conjurers [who] are much observed and venerated by the deluded people," in particular, of how *Thay-Boo* [*thầy bùa*, masters of amulets], *Thay Boo-Twe* [*thầy phù thủy*, sorcerers], and *Thay-de-Lie* [*thầy địa lý*, geomancers] make money on their clients.

Descriptions of the religious life of Tonkin by Samuel Baron and others were not free of prejudices. However, in the absence of contrary evidence, they indicate that the people of Tonkin in the seventeenth and eighteenth centuries were open and welcomed any kind of religious and spiritual activity, regardless of origin, that met their daily needs. Openness and natural curiosity were factors that led to the Vietnamese people's welcoming of Christianity.

---

56. Baron, *A Description of the Kingdom of Tonqueen*, 281.

PART ONE

Errors of the Three Religions in Context

I

When the Cross Met the Lotus

CATHOLIC MISSION IN TONKIN DURING THE SEVENTEENTH AND EIGHTEENTH CENTURIES

DURING MAY 1630, Alexandre de Rhodes (1593–1660)[1] and his Jesuit companions received an order of deportation from Lord Trịnh Tráng (r. 1623–1654), who had welcomed them to the capital three years earlier. The charge against them was being spies of Cochinchina. The Jesuit missionaries tried to defend themselves, but they could not persuade the lord of Tonkin. Consequently, they were banished from the capital and exiled to the most southern part of Tonkin, waiting for a Portuguese ship from Macau to pick them up. The nascent Catholic mission in Tonkin almost perished with their departure. The story of Catholicism in Tonkin, entangled in civil and ecclesial politics, as well as the tension between a new religion and the native religious traditions and beliefs, provides the necessary background to understand our text in discussion—*Errors of the Three Religions*.

Tonkin of the Seventeenth and Eighteenth Century
In the Land of Two Kings

During the seventeenth and eighteenth centuries, Đại Việt, known to the outside world as Annam, existed as two political entities or "kingdoms," each with its own

---

1. Born in Avignon, Alexandre de Rhodes joined the Jesuits in 1612 and was ordained in 1618. He was missioned to Cochinchina from 1624 to 1626, again from 1640 to 1645, and to Tonkin from 1627 to 1630. Later on, he was missioned to Isfahan, Persia, in 1654, and died there six years later. See a summary of his biography in *Diccionario Historico de la Compañia de Jesus* (abbreviated *DHCJ*), ed. Charles O'Neill and Joaquin Dominguez (Rome: Institutum Historicum Societatis Iesu, 2001), 4:3242–43. For an account of Rhodes's life and work, see Peter Phan, *Mission and Catechesis: Alexandre Rhodes and Inculturation in Seventeenth-Century Vietnam* (Maryknoll: Orbis, 1998).

court.² The southern region was known to the West as "Cochinchina," a name given by Portuguese navigators to distinguish it from the other Portuguese port, Cochin of India.³ The northern one was called "Tonkin," a transliteration of the Vietnamese name Đông Kinh [Eastern Capital], by Western traders.⁴ Tonkin was ruled under a dual governance of *Vua* [King] Lê and *Chúa* [Lord] Trịnh, a system not significantly different than what was done in the Tokugawa Japan. The king, a descendant of the Lê dynasty, was a nominal figurehead. Real power was concentrated in the Trịnh's house, the real hediatary ruler of Tonkin. The story of how Tonkin was formed can be traced to the civil wars of the sixteenth and seventh centuries.

After reaching a climax under the reign of Lê Thánh Tông (r. 1442–1497), Đại Việt began to suffer civil unrest.⁵ The Lê kings of the sixteenth century were weak and incompetent rulers, who failed to reinvigorate the monarchy and balance the interests of competing military families. The disintegration of the kingdom began when Mạc Đăng Dung (1483–1541) usurped the throne in 1527 and founded the Mạc dynasty (1527–1592). Opposition from the Lê's supporters in the south led by Nguyễn Kim and his son-in-law Trịnh Kiểm was immediate. The Trịnh-Nguyễn alliance installed a descendant of the Lê as the king, moved the court to Thanh Hoá, the old base of the Lê, and began to fight against the Mạc.

When Nguyễn Kim died on the battlefield, Trịnh Kiểm and his son Trịnh Tùng assumed political and military powers. Nguyễn Kim's descendants moved southward in 1558 and started building their domain in the faraway territory near

---

2. In early Western accounts, the word "kingdom" (*reigno, royaume*) appears before Cochinchina or Tonkin. For an example of early Western accounts of these "kingdoms," see Olga Dror and Keith Taylor, *Views of Seventeenth-Century Vietnam: Cristoforo Borri on Cochinchina and Samuel Baron on Tonkin* (Ithaca, NY: Cornell University Press / SEAP, 2006).

3. Cochinchina was the name that Portuguese gave to the country south of China in their sixteenth-century maps. At first it referred to the whole of Annam. Later on, as they started trading with both the Nguyễn and the Trịnh court, Cochinchina refers to the southern state, which geographically is equivalent to central Vietnam today. See Dror and Taylor, *Views of Seventeenth-Century Vietnam*, 15–22.

4. During the fight against the Mạc, the troops loyal to the former Lê dynasty referred to the old capital Thăng Long (modern-day Hanoi) as Đông Kinh (Eastern Capital) to distinguish it from their base, the Tây Đô (Western Capital)—hence the name "Tonkin" in Western accounts.

5. For works on Vietnamese history from the fifteenth to the eighteenth centuries, see Keith W. Taylor, *A History of the Vietnamese* (Cambridge: Cambridge University Press, 2013), 165–393; George Dutton, Jaynes S. Werner, and John K. Whitmore, *Sources of Vietnamese Tradition* (New York: Columbia University Press, 2012), 89–252; Victor Lieberman, "The Least Coherent Territory in the World," in *Strange Parallels: Southeast Asia in Global Context, c. 800–1830*, Vol. 1, *Integration on the Mainland* (New York: Cambridge University Press, 2003), 338–456.

today's Huế.[6] In 1592, the Trịnh defeated the Mạc, captured Thăng Long, and gained control over the majority of the Red River delta. The descendants of the Mạc eventually retreated to the uppermost province of Cao Bằng, where they survived until 1667. As the Trịnh grew more powerful, they set up a parallel court and appointed their own ministers, including military commanders as provincial governors. Calling themselves "lords" or "princes" (officially *Vương*, popularly *Chúa*), the Trịnh assumed control over all practical matters, from military to economic and political affairs, including choosing the successor to the throne.[7]

When the Trịnh turned their ambition toward the south, the Nguyễn refused to relinquish their domain. Nguyễn Phúc Nguyên (r. 1613–1635) declared independence from the Trịnh, and thus began the civil war between the two families in 1627. After a series of failed military expeditions against the Nguyễn over the next forty-five years, the Trịnh gave up their drive to take control of the South. Both sides declared a ceasefire in 1672, taking the Gianh River as their border. The "Outer Region" (Đàng Ngoài) or Tonkin was governed by the Lê-Trịnh, while the "Inner Region" (Đàng Trong) or Cochinchina was governed by the Nguyễn, with a nominal recognition by the Lê kings. For the next hundred years, the Trịnh and the Nguyễn maintained peace and concentrated on developing their respective territories. The country known to the outside world as Annam now existed as two political entities: Tonkin and Cochinchina.

Merchants and Missionaries

By the middle of the sixteenth century, Portuguese traders in Macau had already made contact with the court of Tonkin. In the North, the Mạc (and later the Trịnh) engaged in foreign trading to secure firearms and other goods for their warfare. Sections of Thăng Long were planned for commercial purposes, earning the capital the nickname Kẻ Chợ (the market place).[8] By the 1600s, Phố Hiến was a bustling port for Chinese junks and Portuguese ships. Kẻ Chợ or Thăng Long became the second port in Tonkin. The Portuguese traded with both Tonkin and

---

6. Keith W. Taylor, "Nguyen Hoang and the Beginning of Vietnam's Southward Expansion," in *Southeast Asia in the Early Modern Era: Trade, Power and Belief*, ed. Anthony Reid (Ithaca, NY: Cornell University Press, 1993), 42–65; Tana Li, *Nguyễn Cochinchina: Southern Vietnam in the Seventeenth and Eighteenth Centuries* (Ithaca, NY: Cornell University Press / SEAP, 1998).

7. In 1599, Trịnh Tùng forced the king to confer upon him the title Đô Nguyên Soái Tổng Quốc Chính (Military Chief and General Governor), which enabled him to officially run the country as a viceroy. *Toàn Thư*, Bản kỷ, 17:72b–73a (translation, 3:211).

8. On seventeenth- and eighteenth-century Western maps, the name is variously spelled as Chece, Ketcho, or Cacho.

Cochinchina. In the South, they set up commercial exchanges with the Nguyễn at the ports of Faifo and Tourane. To avoid direct pressure from the lords from both sides, the Portuguese used local Japanese and Chinese traders to run their businesses.

From their base in Java, the Dutch first came to Cochinchina in the early 1620s, before they traded with Tonkin. By 1632, they moved their trading office from Phố Hiến to Thăng Long. The Trịnh demanded an alliance in their military expeditions against the Nguyễn, and when the Dutch lost the 1643 naval battle against Cochinchina, the Trịnh's confidence in them waned. Judging that their business in Tonkin was too hazardous, the Dutch began to pull out and finally quit Tonkin altogether in 1699.[9]

Missionaries, following the trade routes to Southeast Asia, had also attempted to evangelize in Tonkin. The Imperially Ordered Mirror and Commentary on History of the Viet (*Khâm Định Việt Sử Thông Giám Cương Mục*) recorded that around 1533 a certain Westerner named "I-nhi-khu" (Ignacio?) had secretly introduced the "Gia-tô [Jesus] religion" in several villages along the coast of Tonkin.[10] In the latter half of the sixteenth century, Franciscan, Augustinian, and Dominican missionaries from Malacca and Manila came to evangelize in Tonkin.[11] Although their missionary enterprises were sporadic and not organized, there are records of a few conversions.[12] Catholicism, however, took a firm root in Vietnam with the Jesuit missions of the seventeenth century.[13]

---

9. The British and French also established trading posts in Tonkin, but they were not as successful as the Portuguese or Dutch. For a summary of Western involvement in Tonkin and Cochinchina during the seventeenth and eighteenth centuries, see Charles Maybon, *Histoire moderne du pays d'Annam* (Paris: Plon Nourrit, 1919), esp. chap. 1, "Européens en le pays Annam"; "Une factorerie anglaise au Tonkin au XVIIe siècle (1672–1697)," *BEFEO* 10 (1910): 169–204; Donald F. Lach and Edwin J. Van Kley, *Asia in the Making of Europe* (Chicago: University of Chicago Press, 1993), 3:1248–99.

10. *Cương Mục*, Chính biên, 33:6 (translation, 2:301). This information is given in connection with an interdiction against Christianity issued in 1663.

11. Tara Alberts, *Conflict and Conversion: Catholicism in Southeast Asia, 1500–1700* (Oxford: Oxford University Press, 2013), 70–85.

12. The first convert might have been Đỗ Hưng Viễn, the son of a court official under King Lê Anh Tông (r. 1556–1573). Ordonnez de Cevallos claimed to have converted a sister of King Lê Thế Tông (r. 1573–1599), Princess Mai Hoa (Maria Flora), and other nobles in his *Voyage of the World*, but many historians doubt his account, especially his baptizing of Lord Nguyễn Hoàng.

13. No comprehensive history of the Jesuit activities in Vietnam is yet available in English. Much of the early data remains scattered in various archives in Lisbon, Madrid, Paris, and Rome. Recent works using Jesuit archival sources include Đỗ Quang Chính, *Dòng Tên trong*

The Development of Catholicism in Tonkin
The Jesuit Missions

Following a relatively successful mission in Cochinchina, the Jesuits sent an envoy to Tonkin in 1626 to explore the possibility of establishing a mission there.[14] When receiving the news that missionaries would be welcomed because the Lord of Tonkin wanted to establish trading with the Portuguese, the Jesuit superior in Macau decided to send Alexandre de Rhodes and Pedro Marques, former missionaries of Cochinchina, to Tonkin. After landing in Thanh Hoá province on March 19, 1627, they were favorably received by Lord Trịnh Tráng, who allowed them to settle in the capital to evangelize. Already learning the language in Cochinchina several years earlier, Rhodes and Marques preached the Christian doctrines to the native people without the need for interpreters. The mission grew quickly. By the end of 1627, they had baptized more than 1,200 people, including the Lord's mother and one of his sisters.[15] Two more Jesuits arrived with Portuguese traders in July of 1629.

The Trịnh initially welcomed the missionaries for political and commercial reasons. Because of their language skills, Jesuits could act as interpreters and intermediaries for trade with Macau. When trading failed, however, the Trịnh became indifferent toward the missionaries. Furthermore, rumors that the Jesuits were also working for the Nguyen in Cochinchina raised Trịnh Tráng's suspicion of the missionaries' motivation. In May 1630, he ordered the four Jesuits to return to Macau with the Portuguese merchants. Before departure, however, Rhodes gathered some of his closest lay collaborators into the Institute of Catechists, a lay brotherhood, to continue evangelization, to baptize, to teach the faith, and to maintain the community in the Jesuits' absence.[16]

Xã Hội Đại Việt, 1615–1773 [The Jesuits in Vietnamese Society, 1615–1773] (Hochiminh City: Antôn & Đuốc Sáng, 2007); Roland Jacques, *Les missionnaires portugais et les débuts de l'Église catholique au Viêt-nam* (Reichstett: Đinh Hướng, 2004); J. Ruiz-de-Medina and F. Gomez, "Vietnam," in *DHCJ*, ed. O'Neill and Dominguez, 4:3953–69.

14. The Jesuits first came to Cochinchina in 1615 at the request of Portuguese traders to provide spiritual care for them and minister to the Japanese Catholics in exile. By 1617, they had set up a mission station in Faifo, and two more within the next five years.

15. Đỗ Quang Chính, *Dòng Tên trong Xã Hội Đại Việt*, 141–42.

16. The first catechists were former Buddhist monks who converted in 1627: Francis Đức, Andrew Tri, and Ignatius Nhuận. On April 27, 1630, these three men placed their hands on the Book of Gospels and made the following vows: (1) to be celibate until the missionaries returned; (2) to keep a common purse; and (3) to obey a leader appointed by the missionaries. See Đỗ Quang Chính, *Dòng Tên trong Xã Hội Đại Việt*, 149.

Despite the absence of Rhodes and confrères, the mission of Tonkin was far from over. Other Jesuits continued to arrive with Portuguese traders whenever the political climate allowed them to do so. The growth of the Church, however, was largely in the hands of the lay leaders, who actively evangelized among their people, even when the missionaries were subjected to periods of expulsion. According to missionary reports, the number of Christians in Tonkin increased from 5,600 in 1630 to about 100,000 by 1640 and triple that number twenty years later.[17] During this period, with the assistance of lay converts, the Jesuits alphabetized the Vietnamese written language into a new writing system, which eventually came to be known as the *quốc-ngữ* script (romanized Vietnamese). This was the first step toward using the native language as a medium of religious instruction.

French Missionaries and the Establishment of the Vicariates in Annam

Back in Macau, Rhodes spent the next ten years teaching theology while waiting for the opportunity to return to Annam. Eventually, Rhodes was able to enter Cochinchina again in 1640. But the opposition was fierce. Rhodes shuttled between Macau and Cochinchina four times between 1640 and 1645 before finally being deported from the country under the threat of death. After returning to Macau, Rhodes was sent to Europe to find ways to support the growing missions in Tonkin and Cochinchina. To make the situation better known, he published his writings on Tonkin, as well as giving reports on missionary activities. Given the growing Catholic community in both parts of Annam, Rhodes petitioned the Holy See to send more missionaries. He also advocated the need to appoint bishops if the churches in Annam were to survive and develop. Although his grand vision did not materialize until two decades later, it nevertheless altered the history of the mission in Asia.[18]

---

17. Rhodes himself claimed to have baptized 6,700 people by 1630 (*Divers voyages et missions*, 95). Thirty years later, Jesuit missionary Joseph Tissanier claimed there were about 300,000 Christians in Tonkin by 1660. See Joseph Tissanier, *Relation du voyage du P. Joseph Tissanier de la Compagnie de Jésus. Depuis la France, jusqu' au Royaume de Tunquin. Avec ce qui s'est passé de plus mémorable dans cette Mission, durant les années 1658, 1659, & 1660*, repr. in *Mission de la Cochinchine et du Tonkin*, ed. Fortuné de Montézon and Edmond Estève (Paris: C. Douniol, 1868), 143, 159. While we cannot verify the actual numbers, it had to be significant enough for Rome to respond with the appointment of two apostolic vicars for Tonkin and Cochinchina in 1659.

18. Rhodes seems to be at odds with the general tendency of missionaries of this period, which was not to ordain new converts to the priesthood. On this tendency, see Horacio de la Costa,

Because his progress was slow in Rome, Rhodes went to France to campaign among the French clergy. While more Jesuits volunteered for the Annam missions, the French church also established the Foreign Mission Society of Paris (*Société des missions étrangères de Paris*, or MEP) to support missionary activities in East Asia.[19] This newly established missionary society was placed under the control of the Congregation for Evangelization (Propaganda Fide). It was the first step toward changing the way mission work had been carried out in the Far East.[20] Since its foundation in 1622, Propaganda Fide sought ways to take direct charge of foreign missions, which, until this time, were exclusively an operation from Goa and Macau under the patronage of Portuguese authorities (*padroado*), who appointed all missionaries, regardless of their nationality.[21]

In 1659, Pope Alexandre VII (r. 1655–1667) appointed Francois Pallu (1626–1684) apostolic vicar for Tonkin, Laos, and South China, and his friend, Pierre Lambert de la Motte (1624–1679), vicar for Cochinchina and Cambodia. The appointment did not go into effect until several years later. While they were in Siam, waiting for the opportunity to enter Tonkin and Cochinchina, Pallu and de la Motte organized a seminary to train indigenous clergy. When circumstances prevented Pallu from entering Tonkin, Lambert de la Motte acted on Pallu's behalf and organized the church in Tonkin.[22] The first four Vietnamese seminarians, who formerly belonged to the Institute of Catechists, were ordained to the priesthood in 1668, followed by another seven in 1670.[23]

The Jesuits in the Philippines: 1581–1768 (Cambridge, MA: Harvard University Press, 1967), 233–34; Nicholas Standaert, ed., *Handbook of Christianity in China* (Leiden: Brill, 2001), 1:462.

19. The Société des missions étrangères de Paris (MEP) was established in 1659; however, official recognition did not come until 1664. See Adrien Launay, *Histoire générale de la Société des Missions Étrangères* (Paris, 1894), vol. 1, chaps. 1–3.

20. On the work of the French Missionaries in Annam, see Adrien Launay, *Histoire de la mission de la Cochinchine: Documents historiques*, vol. 1, *1658–1728* (Paris, 1923), vol. 2, *1728–1771* (Paris, 1924), vol. 3, *1771–1823* (Paris, 1925); *Histoire de la mission du Tonkin 1658–1717: Documents historiques* (Paris, 1927). A recent account is Alain Forest, *Les missionaires français au Tonkin et au Siam XVIIe–XVIIIe siècles: Analyse comparée d'un relative succès et d'un total échec* (Paris: L'Harmattan, 1998), esp. vol. 2, *Histoires du Tonkin*, and vol. 3, *Organizer une Église convertir les infidèles*.

21. This privilege was confirmed by Popes Leo X (in 1514 and 1516), Paul III (1539), Gregory XIII (1575), and Paul V (1616). See Launay, *Histoire générale de la Société des Missions Étrangères*, 1:17.

22. In their lifetimes, Pallu never came to Tonkin, and de la Motte went back and forth between Siam and Cochinchina. From Siam, they ran the Church in Annam by letters and occasional visits. François Deydier (1634–1693) was the first French missionary who set foot in Tonkin in 1666.

23. Bento Thiện, John Huệ (1668); Martin Mát, Simon Kiên, Anton Quế, Philip Nhân, James Chiêu, Leo Trông, and Vito Trí (1670). For information on the Tonkinese priests, see

When the Holy See appointed these Frenchmen to be apostolic vicars of the lands that the Portuguese considered their mission fields, the authorities in Macau did not give up their control without a fight, and some Jesuits refused to recognize the authority of the apostolic vicars.[24] With the establishment of the vicariates in Tonkin and Cochinchina, the Church in Annam went through a new phase. It no longer depended solely on the *padroado* system of the Portuguese crown and the Jesuit monopoly. The opening of the mission field for other missionary orders in Tonkin—the MEP, Dominicans, and later the Discalced Augustinians—forced the Jesuits to accept the new arrangement.

Dominican and Augustinian Missions

Already in the latter half of the sixteenth century, Augustinian and Dominican missionaries from Malacca and Manila were present at the courts of Cochinchina and Tonkin.[25] However, lack of personnel and resources prevented them from establishing a stable mission. When Pallu and Lambert de la Motte were put in charge of the missions in Annam, they invited the Spanish Dominicans from Manila to help with evangelization.[26] This invitation was meant to balance out the mission field that so far had been in the hands of the Jesuits and, more importantly, to dispel any suspicion that the MEP wanted to replace Portuguese dominance with the French presence. The first Spanish friars, Juan de Santa Cruz (1645–1721) and Juan de Arjona, arrived in July 1676.[27] Territorial disputes with

---

André Marillier, *Nos pères dans la foi: notes sur le clergé catholique du Tonkin de 1666 à 1765* (Paris: Eglise d'Asie, 1995), 2:7–15.

24. The "disobedience of the Jesuits" caused a scandal among the faithful, and at least several of them were recalled to Macau in 1680 (e.g., Giuseppe Candone and Bartolomeo D'Acosta in Cochinchina; Dominico Fuciti and Emmanuel Ferreya in Tonkin). The matter was finally settled in the 1690s. See Forest, *Les missionaires Français au Tonkin et au Siam XVII*ᵉ*-XVIII*ᵉ *siècles*, 2:152–53, 161–67.

25. For example, Bartolome Ruiz, OFM (1584–1586), Ordonnez de Cevallos (1590), Alonso Ximenez, OP (1596), Rafael da Madre de Deus and Miguel dos Santos, OSA (1595).

26. Compared to the Jesuit and MEP, the Dominican mission in Tonkin is understudied, especially if one takes into account that the eastern part of Tonkin was continuously under their pastoral care from 1679 to 1954. More research is needed in various archives in Avila and Manila. For a standard account of the Dominicans in Vietnam, consult Marcos Gispert, *Historia de las Misiones Dominicanas en el Tungkin* (Avila, 1928); Bùi Đức Sinh, *Dòng Đa Minh trên Đất Việt* [Dominicans in Vietnam] (Saigon: Chân Lý, 1972).

27. After a year, the two Dominicans left the mission, but Juan de Santa Cruz returned two years later and stayed in Tonkin until he died in 1721. In 1716 he was appointed the apostolic vicar of East Tonkin. For his biography, see Marillier, *Nos pères dans la foi*, 2:111–12.

the MEP priests almost eliminated the Dominican presence in Tonkin. The Dominicans only returned after they had secured a promise that they would be free to evangelize in the coastal areas.[28]

The next phase of Dominican presence in Tonkin was filled with conflict. When a rival MEP priest, François Deydier (1637–1693), was put in charge of the newly formed vicariate of East Tonkin in 1679, the Spanish Dominicans refused to submit to his authority. After Deydier's death, both the French and Spanish wanted to take control of vacated vicariate of East Tonkin. Eventually, a compromise was made. In 1698, the Italian Raimondo Lezzoli (1655–1706), one of the two senior Dominican missionaries (the other was the Spanish Juan de Santa Cruz), was appointed an apostolic vicar.[29] When Lezzoli died in 1706, the vicariate remained vacant for ten years, until it was filled by Juan de Santa Cruz as the apostolic vicar; but Rome also appointed the Italian Tommaso a Sestri Bottaro (1664–1737) as his coadjutor. When Sestri became the apostolic vicar in 1721,[30] he was opposed by many Spanish Dominicans, who believed he granted too many favors to his compatriots, especially when he gave a mission territory that previously belonged to the Spaniards to a new group of Italian missionaries—the Discalced Augustinians.

The Italian Augustinians came to Tonkin from China in 1701 and faced opposition from the Spanish Dominicans.[31] The resentment of the Dominicans escalated when a member of the Augustinians, Hilario Costa (1696–1754), better known by his religious name Hilario di Gesù, was consecrated by Sestri to be his successor in 1736.[32] Hilario di Gesù Costa was a wise man and a capable pastor. Still, the Spanish Dominicans begrudged a non-Dominican, non-Spanish bishop and complained to Rome. The situation got worse when Hilario died in March 1754 and another Italian, Adriano di Santa Thecla (1667–1765), took temporary charge of the vicariate of East Tonkin.[33] The long struggle between the Dominicans and the Augustinians ended only with the appointment of another Spaniard Dominican, Santiago Hernandez (1723–1777), to govern the missions

---

28. Forest, *Les missionaries français au Tonkin et au Siam XVII*^e*–XVIII*^e *siècles*, 2:153–55.

29. He was the only Italian among the six Dominican missionaries in Tonkin at the time. For his biography, see Marillier, *Nos pères dans la foi*, 2:112–13.

30. For his biography, see Marillier, *Nos pères dans la foi*, 2:113–14.

31. On the activities of the Discalced Augustinians in Tonkin, see Ignacio Barbagallo and Gabriele M. Raimondo, *Gli Agostiniani Scalzi nel Vietnam e nella Cina* (Rome: Edizioni Presenza Agostiniana, 1997); for a summary see Dror, *A Study of Religion*, 22–25.

32. For his biography see Marillier, *Nos pères dans la foi*, 2:124–26.

33. For his biography see Marillier, *Nos pères dans la foi*, 2:126–27.

in East Tonkin.[34] In 1763, the Italian Augustinians were given a choice of either submitting to Spanish authority or leaving the country. The last Augustinian in East Tonkin was Adriano di Santa Thecla, who remained in Tonkin until his death in 1765.

The brief account of missionary activities in Tonkin during the seventeenth and eighteenth centuries provides the ecclesial context to understand the polemical context of our text in the discussion. The competition between different missionary groups—Jesuits versus MEP priests, Dominicans versus Augustinians—for the souls of converts was intense. Their missionary strategies, especially regarding the accommodation to Vietnamese traditional cultures and religions, varied according to their interpretations of the instructions from Rome, especially in the Chinese Rites Controversial context, which I will discuss in a later section.

Reception of Christianity in Tonkin
Social Impacts of Christianity

Since its inception in Tonkin, Christianity quickly became a popular movement among the masses, who were tired of warfare and chaos. The new religion was able to fill the spiritual and moral vacuum by responding effectively to the needs of the suffering masses. The Jesuit missionaries found in the native culture favorable conditions for planting the new faith. These conditions—the traditional worship of Heaven, strong family and communal bonds, an ethics compatible with the Ten Commandments, a spirit of devotion, an emphasis on rituals, and a belief in the afterlife and karma (e.g., cosmic reward and punishment)—were all seen as congruent with the Gospel message. However, the traditional religions also carried elements incompatible with Christian monotheism. Jesuit missionaries carefully distinguished between superstitious practices (e.g., geomancy to select a burial spot, burning paper money, divination for an "auspicious" time and date for marriage, starting a business, etc.) and legitimate cultural ceremonies (e.g., honoring the deceased, marriage customs, etc.).

Despite the early success of Jesuit missions among the Tonkinese peasants, the new religion was viewed cautiously by the ruling authorities. At first, the Confucian ruling elite approached Christianity with curiosity. Unlike the masses, they were neither attracted to nor repulsed by this new teaching. The Jesuits were successful in converting several prominent members of the ruling households but in far smaller proportion than the peasants and the lower-ranking members of the literati. The Trịnh lords were more fascinated by the missionaries' gifts than

---

34. For his biography see Marillier, *Nos pères dans la foi*, 2:118–19.

by their religious teaching. Unlike in Cochinchina, the missionaries in Tonkin did not win a royal appointment, despite the fact that they were drawn from the same pool of highly educated Jesuit missionaries sent to East Asia, and many had served in China and elsewhere.[35] Somehow the court of Tonkin did not have any use for Jesuit scientists. The presence of missionaries and their freedom to propagate the Christian religion were tolerated to suit the Trịnh's political purpose of securing military and commercial trading with the West.

Central to Confucian orthodoxy are the relational ethics of Three Bonds and Five Norms.[36] These norms were seen as foundational to social stability. Any new school of thought or religion had to be measured against them. Since Christian missionaries insisted on monogamy, concubinage was forbidden. This caused resentment among the upper classes, especially among the strict adherents of Confucianism. Polygamy was permitted in Confucianism because it was considered a moral duty to have a male heir in order to continue ancestor worship. If a wife failed to produce a son, the husband was free (or morally obligated) to take a second (or third) wife. When Christian converts were asked to let go of wives other than their first one, the ruling class saw it as a challenge to their Confucian norm.

The Christian emphasis on monotheism was interpreted as disruptive of community bonds. Christian missionaries advocated devotion to a single God to the exclusion of national and local deities. This attitude was contrary to the village norms that expected everyone to participate in the religious activities of the village. Central to the religious life of the village was the cult of *thành hoàng*, the village protectors. Just as every village had to have its leader, it also had to have its spirit-protectors. When Christian converts refused to participate in village ceremonies and held separate liturgies and customs, they were seen as undermining social harmony.

---

35. While no Jesuits in Tonkin served in the Lê's or the Trịnh's courts, at least a dozen Jesuits had served the Nguyễn in Cochinchina between 1673 and 1773: Bartholomeu da Costa (physician, 1673–1695); Juan Antonio de Arnedo (mathematician, 1699–1712); Giambattista Sanna (physician, 1724); Sebastiao Pires (physician, 1720–?); Francisco de Lima (1720–?); Francisco da Costa (1738–1750); Johann Siebert (physician and astronomer, 1738–1745); Josef Neugebauer (astronomer, 1740–1749); Johann Koffler (physician and astronomer, 1741–1755); Xavier de Monteiro (mathematician, 1742–1750, 1752, 1760–1776); and Joaõ de Loureiro (physician and mathematician, 1742–1750, 1752–1778). See Đỗ Quang Chính, *Dòng Tên trong Xã Hội Đại Việt*, 536–46.

36. The Three Bonds (*tam cương*) are the social obligations between ruler and subject, father and son, and husband and wife. The Five Norms (*ngũ thường*) can either refer to (1) Five Moral Relations (*ngũ luân*) to be maintained, i.e., proper behaviors between ruler and subject, father and son, husband and wife, older and younger brothers, and between friends; or (2) Five Moral Virtues (*ngũ đức*): humaneness, righteousness, propriety, wisdom, and trustworthiness. The classics contain grounds for both interpretations, although the latter is more common.

The issues surrounding the cult of ancestors were more complicated. Everyone had to practice the way of filiality (*đạo hiếu*), which was considered a basic social and religious duty of all Vietnamese regardless of class or religious orientation. The elaborate funeral rituals and memorial services were seen as expressions of this filiality. Like their confrères in China, the Jesuits in both parts of Annam quickly recognized the important place of the cult of ancestors among the people. The missionaries were willing to modify the traditional practices of funerals and memorial services, purging them of their "superstitious elements" and replacing them with Christian practices.

With the arrival of MEP and Dominican missionaries to Vietnam after 1664, ancestor worship became a religious and theological bone of contention. These later missionaries considered the cult of ancestors to be acts of idolatry and superstition. The offering of food on the altar of the deceased and prostrations before this altar were prohibited by these zealous missionaries. In extreme cases, the converts were instructed to destroy ancestral tablets. The ban on expressing filial piety before the altar of the ancestors caused intense anxiety. The failure to practice filiality was one of the ten major crimes specified in the Lê Code and could inflict a penalty from caning to execution, depending on the level of the offense.[37] The so-called Rites Controversy started in Annam within forty years of the Jesuit arrival in Tonkin. The Confucian elite, trying to defend the traditional way of life, saw the absence of ancestral tablets in Christian homes as the ultimate betrayal of Vietnamese culture.

Relationship with the Ruling Authority

The association of Christianity with a foreign power also aroused the concern of the ruling classes. Various economic and political concerns prompted the Trịnh of Tonkin and the Nguyễn of Cochinchina to suspect that the missionaries were working for their enemies.[38] Rumors that Vietnamese Catholics were more loyal to the missionaries than to their own lord aroused suspicion among the ruling class. Unable to distinguish between different countries of the West, and more importantly the difference between spiritual and political allegiances, the ruling

---

37. Nguyen Ngoc Huy, Ta Van Tai, and Tran Van Liem, *The Lê Code: Law in Traditional Vietnam* (Athens: Ohio University Press, 1987), Article 2, 110.

38. Rhodes recounts that once Trịnh Tráng recognized that the Portuguese could not abandon their long relationship with the people in Cochinchina, his early toleration waned. *Histoire du royaume de Tunquin*, chap. 10, 189.

authorities considered Catholic Christianity the "religion of the Portuguese" (*đạo Hoa Lang*) and the Roman Pontiff was "the king of Portugal."[39] Also, since both the Trịnh and Nguyễn needed the missionaries to be liaisons for foreign trade, and especially for firearms, the fate of missionaries depended on how successful they were in procuring trade. When the rulers did not get what they needed, they forbade the "religion of the Portuguese" and expelled its missionaries.

Motivated by factors such as religious jealousy, political rivalry, and fear of national instability and foreign influence, Tonkinese rulers repeatedly issued edicts against Christianity in the seventeenth and eighteenth centuries.[40] The Trịnh acted against the missionaries as early as 1628, isolating them from the believers, then expelling them the following year.[41] In 1650, Trịnh Tạc issued an edict prohibiting foreigners from mingling with Vietnamese. He also forbade missionary activities and ordered the destruction of Christian churches and religious books.[42] Before the end of the seventeenth century, there were sporadic proscriptions of Christianity in Thăng Long and Phố Hiến, depending on the attitude of the Trịnh toward Westerners. These persecutions were, however, not serious because the Trịnh still needed the missionaries as liaisons with merchants. The first serious interdiction was an imperial edict in 1663, ordering the expulsion of all missionaries and prohibiting Christians from practicing their religion.[43]

---

39. Rhodes himself tried to dispel any connection between the new religion and Portugal in his 1651 catechism. He wrote, "Do not say that this law (religion) is the law of the Portuguese. The holy law of the Lord of Heaven is a light greater and older than the light of the sun itself. . . . The holy law (religion) of God, though it has appeared to other kingdoms first, should not be seen as belonging to this or that kingdom, but as the holy law of God, the Lord of all things. It is a law nobler and older than any kingdom whatsoever." (*Cathechismus*, First day). Phan, *Mission and Catechesis*, 233.

40. A rare work in English on this subject is John R. Shortland, *The Persecutions of Annam: A History of Christianity in CochinChina and Tonking* (London: Burns and Oates, 1875). See also Adrien Launay, *Les Missionaires Français au Tonkin* (Paris, 1900). These two works, however, focused more on the events of the nineteenth century than on the earlier persecutions in the seventeenth and eighteenth centuries.

41. Rhodes, *Histoire du royaume de Tunquin*, 211, 213–15, 221–22. Fortunately, a Portuguese ship showed up in 1629 and brought Rhodes and Marques back to Thang Long. However, they had to leave Tonkin the following year.

42. This is recorded in *Quốc Triều Chiếu Lịnh Thiện Chính* [A Collection of Imperial Decrees and Regulations: 1619–1705]. See Deloustal Raymond, "La justice dans l'ancien Annam. Traduction et commentaire du Code des Lê," *BEFEO* 13, no. 5 (1913): 55–56.

43. *Cương Mục*, Chính biên, 33:5–6 (translation, 2:300); *Toàn Thư*, Bản kỷ tục biên, 19:4a–4b (translation, 3:269).

Although this ban was reiterated in 1669,[44] it did not take effect because it was not really enforced until 1696.[45]

The political climate changed in the eighteenth century, however. Since most Western commercial companies had left Tonkin by the 1690s, missionaries were no longer useful as mediators for trade with the West. Their presence in Tonkin was seen as subversive to the state, especially after the Trịnh found out that French missionaries were involved in a plot against the king of Siam in 1685.[46] Consequently, earlier Christian prohibitions were reiterated and enforced. At first, the punishment was expelling the missionaries and caning the converts. However, after seeing that missionaries still tried to come back to Tonkin and carry out clandestine activities, the court had them and their collaborators executed.[47] In 1712 the Trịnh began systematically suppressing Christianity.[48] Missionaries reported that Christian persecutions in Tonkin increased in frequency and severity, especially in 1723, 1736–1737, 1741, 1745, 1754, 1773, 1775, and 1778–1779. During this period, missionaries and Vietnamese Christians were killed.[49] Since many uprisings broke out across Tonkin during the same period, the Trịnh tried to eliminate any subversive element.

The number of Tonkinese Christians rose and fell with the periodic anti-Christian raids, but they continued to survive and grow in the rural areas. An optimistic estimation from the early 1660s by the Jesuits placed the number of baptized people at 300,000.[50] A century later, at the height of the persecution, the Church in Tonkin already had two vicariates with a combination of twenty-one

---

44. Launay, *Histoire de la mission du Tonkin*, 60, 66–67.

45. *Cương Mục*, Chính biên, 34:35 (translation, 2:373). Also see Launay, *Histoire de la mission du Tonkin*, 401–2.

46. George Dutton, *The Tây Sơn Uprising: Society and Rebellion in Eighteenth-Century Vietnam* (Honolulu: University of Hawai'i, 2006), 177.

47. Seven Jesuits were martyred for their faith in the years of 1723 and 1737 (Đỗ Quang Chính, *Dòng Tên trong Xã Hội Đại Việt*, 401–16). A number of Dominicans were put on trial and executed in 1745 and 1773.

48. The 1712 imperial edict stipulated that Christians were to be tattooed on the face with four words "học Hoa Lang đạo" (followers of the Portuguese religion). *Cương Mục*, Chính biên, 35:10–11 (translation, 2:400).

49. While figures for missionaries executed are well recorded, the number of locals is less well known. For a listing of Christians killed in both Cochinchina and Tonkin from 1630 to 1858, see De Montézon and Estève, *Mission de la Cochinchine et du Tonquin*, 399–407.

50. See Letter of November 20, 1660 of Tissanier to Cazré (ARSI, Jap-Sin 80, fol. 151); and De Montézon and Estève, *Mission de la Cochinchine et du Tonquin*, 143, 159.

missionaries, forty-six indigenous clergies, a handful of catechists,[51] and a conservative estimation of 30,000 to 40,000 Christians in 1754.[52] Thirty years later, a 1784 count placed the number of Christians once again at between 350,000 and 400,000.[53] In the eighteenth century, Christians constituted a visible minority in a Tonkinese population that ranged between 5.5 and 8 million.[54]

Confucianism versus Christianity

Although state security and public order triggered a number of Christian repressions in the late seventeenth and early eighteenth centuries, many more were carried out in part because Vietnamese rulers, both in Tonkin and Cochinchina, saw in the new religion a threat to the established social and moral norms derived from Confucianism. To the Confucian rulers, Christians were separatists, and their doctrines and practices were a threat to society, and therefore they ought to be banned. The reason given in many of the edicts against Christianity was that this "religion of the Portuguese," or *đạo Hoa Lang*, was incompatible with traditional morality. Of course, the new religion also threatened the interests of some groups—magicians, monks, concubines, and mandarins—who did not hesitate to use their influence and slander to persuade the Confucian rulers to prohibit Christianity and expel its missionaries. However, one of the main concerns was to preserve Confucian morality. Trịnh Tạc (r. 1657–1682) was a devout Confucian, and so were his successors, Trịnh Căn (r. 1683–1708) and Trịnh Cương (r. 1709–1729). Consequently, they felt obligated to protect the people from being corrupted by the "barbaric" customs of the new religion.

To understand the Confucian anxiety about Christianity, it would be helpful to examine the comments of the official history, Complete Chronicle of the Great Viet (*Đại Việt Sử Ký Toàn Thư*), on the 1663 decree against Christianity:

---

51. André Marillier, *Nos pères dans la foi*, 3:149–51.

52. Meyere to Lacere, June 9, 1754 (AMEP, vol. 700, fols. 221–222). Cited by George Dutton in *The Tây Sơn Uprising*, 179n25. Dutton suggests that the number reflects perhaps a century of active proscription against Christianity and a more strict definition of who could count as a Christian. Data for the eighteenth century was notoriously unreliable because there was a considerable debate between different missionaries about the inclusion of lapsed or uncommitted Christians during the persecutions.

53. La Mothe to Deson, June 15, 1784 (AMEP, vol. 700, fol.1208). Cited by Dutton, *The Tây Sơn Uprising*, 179n26.

54. Tana Li estimates a population of 5.6 million for Tonkin in 1750 (*Nguyễn Cochinchina*, 171). Alain Forest, based on MEP accounts, gives a higher estimation, about 8 million in 1766 (*Les missionaires Français au Tonkin et au Siam XVIIe–XVIIIe siècles*, 2:56).

> In the tenth month [of the year *quý-mão* (1663)] an edict was issued prohibiting the people of our country from following the Western religion [*đạo Hoa Lang*]. In the past, a Westerner came to our country to establish this strange religion to deceive naïve people. Many stupid men and women followed it. In their schools (i.e., churches), people mingle together; there is no separation between men and women. We have driven out their religious teachers, but since their religious books and schools (churches) still remain, their bad customs have not changed. Now it must be prohibited.[55]

Thus, besides political motives, the ban on Christianity reflected a clash between Christian morality and the Vietnamese culture. There appears to be a causal link between preserving the interests of orthodox Confucianism and the repression of Christianity. In eighteenth-century Tonkin, Confucian thinkers and officials advocated the harmony of the Three Religions, and, even if they did not personally like Buddhists and Daoists, they did not persecute them. While there is some evidence for the purging of Buddhism and Daoism of what were regarded as superstitious elements in the seventeenth and eighteenth centuries, the Confucian elite never viewed these religions as a threat to their own hegemony. Christian converts, on the other hand, seemed to be willing to let go of rituals and social practices that had been cherished by generations of Confucians. When Christianity, with its link to foreign powers and its defiance of Confucian social practices, became a competing voice in society, its suppression by the political authorities was inevitable.[56]

The Rites Controversy and Its Impact in Vietnam

One of the biggest challenges for Christianity in Asia was how to accommodate to the local cultures. When European missionaries came to Asia, they faced ancient civilizations and religious traditions that were older and more established than Christianity. The missionaries could not afford to disregard local customs. In the history of Christian evangelization in Asia, the so-called Chinese Rites Controversy (1645–1939)[57] represented a tragic clash of religious cultures—a clash that still has repercussions for East Asian Christians today. The events are

---

55. *Toàn Thư*, Bản kỷ, 19:4a–4b; my translation.

56. Ta Van Tai, *The Vietnamese Tradition of Human Rights* (Berkeley: University of California, Institute of East Asian Studies, 1988), 146–76.

57. While the Controversy certainly started before 1645 (and continued after 1939 in some parts of Asia), the given dates mark the official ecclesiatiscal responses to the Controversy.

well documented, but there is no consensus on how to interpret them.[58] In essence, the Controversy concerns three separate but related issues: (1) the proper names for God—the so-called term question; (2) the rites of veneration to Confucius and the ancestors; and (3) the participation of Christians in "pagan" rites. The "term question" was not a concern for the Chinese; it remained a quarrel mainly among missionaries or European intellectuals.[59] The other two issues, however, affected not only Chinese converts but also how Christianity was received in other parts of Asia. Whereas the veneration of Confucius concerned the literati class almost exclusively, the cult of ancestors had profound consequences on the relationship of Asian converts of all classes to their non-Christian relatives and fellow countrymen.

The details of the Controversy as it played out in China and Europe have been extensively discussed in the history of the development of Christianity in Asia. Here, I will give a summary only of those events and issues that shed light on the attitude of the author of *Errors of the Three Religions* regarding the traditional rites of Vietnam.

The China Mission and Jesuit Accommodation

When Matteo Ricci (1552–1610) and his Jesuit confrères arrived in China during the later years of the Ming dynasty, they found that both a state cult of Confucius and the veneration of ancestors were widely practiced in Chinese society. Knowing that they did not operate in a religious vacuum, the Jesuits could not afford to clash head on with an institution that underlay the social fabric of China. If they were to gain access to the Chinese upper classes, the Jesuits realized that they would have to make accommodations to allow the continuation of these rites.

---

58. Since the eighteenth century, the literature on the Chinese Rites Controversy has grown enormously. For summary of the issues involved, see George Minamiki, *The Chinese Rites Controversy from Its Beginning until Modern Times* (Chicago: Loyola University Press, 1985); D. E. Mungello, ed., *The Chinese Rites Controversy: Its History and Meaning*, Monumenta Serica Monograph Series 30 (Nettetal: Steyler Verlag, 1994). On official documents related to the Controversy, see *100 Roman Documents Concerning the Chinese Rites Controversy (1645–1941)*, ed. Ray R. Noll, trans. Donald St. Sure (San Francisco: The Ricci Institute for Chinese-Western Cultural History, University of San Francisco, 1992). Another important collection of documents is Antonio Rosso, *Apostolic Legations to China in the Eighteenth Century* (South Pasadena: Perkins, 1948).

59. The "term question" started with Charles Maigrot's Mandate of 1693, when he forbade the use of *Tian* or *Shangdi* or *Taiji* to designate God. For Maigrot, only *Tianzhu* was the legitimate Chinese expression of *Deus*; the other terms were to be rejected. His opinion was later upheld by Rome in its 1704, 1715, and 1742 decisions. Maigrot's objection to the use of *Jing Tian* (敬天, Veneration of Heaven) in Christian churches incurred the wrath of emperor Kangxi in 1706.

Not all people agreed with Ricci's norm of accommodation, however. In the aftermath of the Protestant Reformation, Catholicism laid a great emphasis on orthodoxy. What were seen as cultural norms and practices by some Jesuits could be viewed by others as expressions of idolatry or superstition. The Jesuits held a conference in Jiading (Zhejiang province) in 1628 to discuss how much accommodation could be tolerated and specifically what elements could be allowed. The dispute about the rites was not confined to the Jesuits. With the arrival of the Franciscan and Dominican friars to Fujian in 1630, the debate escalated.[60] Besides the rivalry among religious orders, the friars from Manila held a different view of how to deal with Chinese traditional rites. Based on their experience of working with Chinese commoners, the friars were uncompromising in condemning the practice of the Jesuits as yielding to superstition.[61] This negative attitude of the friars resulted in their expulsion from Chinese soil by the local magistrate.[62] Frustrated by what he saw in Fujian, one of the expelled Dominican friars, Juan Baptista Morales (1597–1664), complained to the Jesuit superior in Manila. When Morales did not get any response from the Jesuits, he took his case to Rome, submitting a list of seventeen questions in 1643 challenging the Jesuit missionary practices.[63] This began the long and contentious debates between different religious groups, scholars, and church authorities for the next few centuries.

---

60. Until this time, the China mission was entrusted exclusively to the Jesuits based on the *padroado* system. Following the decision by Clement VIII in 1630 to make the China mission available to the friars, Franciscans were eager to go back to the land where they had labored three hundred years earlier. The Dominicans also wanted to enter China by any means they could. When their attempts to go through Macau were blocked by the Jesuits, the friars had to find other ways into China. See John Willis Jr., "From Manila to Fuan," in *The Chinese Rites Controversy*, ed. D.G. Mungello (Nettetal: Steyler Verlag, 1994), 111–28.

61. See the discussion by J. S. Cummins, "Two Missionary Methods in China: Mendicants and Jesuits," *Archivo ibero-americano* 38 (1978): 33–108. Note that the early members of mendicant orders in China did not show the same spirit of adaptation as their counterparts in Central Asia and America. See also Jean-Paul Wiest, "Learning from the Missionary Past," in *The Catholic Church in Modern China: Perspectives*, ed. Edmond Tang and Jean-Paul Wiest (Maryknoll: Orbis, 1991), 181–98.

62. Eugenio Menegon, "Jesuits, Franciscans and Dominicans in Fujian: The Anti-Christian Incidents of 1637–1638," in *Scholar from the West*, ed. Tizziana Lippielo and Roman Malek (Nettetal: Steyler Verlag, 1997), 219–62.

63. In February 1643, Morales submitted to Propaganda Fide a list of seventeen questions concerning (1) fast, yearly confession and communion, and holidays; (2) sacramentals in administering baptism and extreme unction; (3–5) interest, usury, and usurers; (6) contributions to pagan sacrifices and festivals; (7) the cult of Chenghuang; (8) the cult of Confucius; (9) ancestor worship; (10) serving and feeding the dead as if they were living; (11) the ancestral tablet; (12) funerals; (13) instruction of Catechumens concerning the illicit nature of such rites; (14) the use of the adjective *sheng* (holy); (15) worship and obeisance before the tablet set in honor of the emperor; (16) licitness of prayers and sacrifices for relatives who died as pagans; (17)

At first, the Propaganda Fide issued a decree in 1645 forbidding the Chinese converts to participate in the cults of Confucius and the ancestors.[64] These cults were judged to be religious ceremonies incompatible with the Catholic faith. Alarmed by the news of this condemnation of the Chinese rites, the Jesuits appealed to the Holy Office in Rome to defend their practices. In 1656, the Holy Office issued another decree allowing Chinese Catholics to participate in the rites "as long as they are not doing anything superstitious."[65] This new decree reversed the prohibitions but did not nullify the 1645 decree. As a result, nothing was decided, and the matter was by default left to the consciences of the missionaries. Back in China, the issue became contentious between two missionary methods: Ricci's accommodation and its alternative.

Rome was aware of the delicate nature of the issue. Three years later, Propaganda Fide issued an instruction to the newly appointed apostolic vicars of South China, Tonkin, and Cochinchina. The 1659 instruction asked the missionaries not to force Christian converts to abandon traditional rites and customs unless these practices were openly contrary to Catholic faith and morals. In effect, the instruction stipulated that missionaries must accommodate the native practices, not judge or condemn them blindly, and not change what is not contrary to the faith, for nothing causes more hatred and alienation than changing customs of a country.[66] Nevertheless, this guidance did not solve the Rites questions because it was up to the individual missionary's interpretation of the nature of these rites.

When questioned by the Dominicans regarding whether the decree of 1656 nullified the earlier ruling of 1645, the Holy Office issued a notice in 1669 affirming both decrees as valid and maintaining that they had to be observed "according to the questions, circumstances, and everything set down in them."[67] This showed the reluctance and ambivalence on the part of the Roman authorities to take sides on such complex interpretations of the Chinese rites.

Caught between Church and State Politics

In 1693, Charles Maigrot, MEP (1652–1730), the new apostolic vicar of Fujian, was determined to put an end to the different opinions on the rites in his mission field. By requiring all missionaries in his vicariate to affirm the 1645 prohibitions of the rites of

---

preaching Christ crucified. See Rosso, *Apostolic Legations to China*, 111–12; Cummins, "Two Missionary Methods in China," 55–57.

64. See the text of the decree in *100 Roman Documents* (Document #1), 1–5.

65. *100 Roman Documents* (Document #2), 6.

66. *100 Roman Documents* (Document #3), 6–7.

67. *100 Roman Documents* (Document #4), 7.

Confucius and ancestors, the matter moved from a theological dispute to a juridical affair.[68] Maigrot's unilateral decision, without any consultation with the local clergy, caused a great storm among Chinese Christians and reopened the case in Europe. In reaction, the Beijing Jesuits drew support from Emperor Kangxi (r. 1662–1722). They petitioned the emperor to issue a clarification of the rites. In 1700 Kangxi issued an imperial edict affirming that the rites had only a civil and not a religious meaning.[69] After a prolonged investigation, Rome made up its mind. But by the time Kangxi's declaration reached Rome, it was too late to change the course of events.

In 1704, the Holy Office issued a ruling (with the approval of Pope Clement XI) condemning the traditional rites because of their essentially religious nature. They were seen as "tainted with superstition."[70] Briefly, the 1704 decree stipulated the following:

(1) Christians may not "preside, serve, or be present" at solemn rites for Confucius, nor may they participate in rites on full and new moons, nor when officials receive titles and offices, nor when successful candidates receive degrees.

(2) Christians may not "perform, serve, or be present" at the oblation, rites, and ceremonies before spirit tablets, whether at home or at graves, whether in the company of non-Christians or separately, because "all these things are inseparable from superstition."

(3) However, Christians are allowed "mere material presence or participation" provided they do not give approval to the ceremonies, and where hostility to the faith may result if they fail to attend.

(4) Ceremonies on behalf of the dead are not to be condemned where there is no real superstition and ceremonies are "within limits of civil and political rites."

(5) The local church authorities should determine which ceremonies are permissible and under what conditions and should strive to replace pagan practices with those of the Church.

(6) The spirit tablets are permitted in the home only when nothing on them suggests that the souls of the departed reside in them and when an expression of the Christian belief regarding the dead and Christian piety toward deceased parents and ancestors are displayed.[71]

---

68. For a translation of this Mandate (March 26, 1693), see Claudia von Collani, "Charles Maigrot's Role in the Chinese Rites Controversy," in *The Chinese Rites Controversy*, 152–54. It is also incorporated as the first part of the 1704 response from Rome, see *100 Documents* (Document #6), 8–9.

69. For the full text, see Rosso, *Apostolic Legations to China*, 138–40; Minamiki, *The Chinese Rites Controversy from Its Beginnings to Modern Times*, 40–41.

70. *100 Roman Documents* (Document #6, Article 4), 21.

71. *100 Roman Documents* (Document #6, Article 5), 21–22.

The pope appointed Charles Thomas Maillard de Tournon (1668–1710) the papal legate and sent him to Asia to enforce the decree. Upon hearing of de Tournon's arrival, Kangxi granted him an audience, for he was eager to find out Rome's reaction. De Tournon was evasive on the matter, for he realized that he did not have all the facts at hand. When pressed by Kangxi, de Tournon sent Maigrot, who was supposed to be the expert on Chinese religions, to discuss the matter with the emperor. Kangxi examined Maigrot's knowledge of Confucius's teaching, the rites, and the Chinese language, and decided that Maigrot was ignorant on Chinese matters, and thus his opposition to the Jesuit method had no ground. The emperor then decreed that beginning in 1706, any missionary who wanted to work in China must have a "certificate" (*piao*) issued by the imperial court and must promise to follow Ricci's accommodating practices.

De Tournon's mission to China was a failure. It polarized the missionary community and solidified dissension among them. Determined to put an end to all the quarrels, Clement XI reaffirmed the 1704 ruling in 1710, and again in the papal bull *Ex Illa Die* on March 19, 1715. This document rehearses the arguments for condemning the Chinese rites in no uncertain terms and demands complete obedience from all missionaries and clergy in China on pain of suspension, interdiction, and excommunication. When the decrees were promulgated in Beijing in 1716, all missionaries and local clergy were required to swear obedience to Clement XI's decision as a condition of their apostolate.[72] When Emperor Kangxi found out about this decision, he was indignant. He sent the bishop of Beijing out to collect all copies of the decrees and send them back to the pope.[73]

Concerned that China would face mass apostasy, Clement XI sent another legation to the court of Beijing, this time led by the papal envoy, Carlo Ambrogio Mezzabarba (1685–1741), to ask the emperor permission for missionaries to preach an "unadulterated faith" (i.e., without any accommodation). After arriving in China in 1720, Mezzabarba was given an audience with Kangxi, but he could not change the emperor's mind. As a compromise, before leaving China Mezzabarba wrote a pastoral letter to all bishops, apostolic vicars, and missionaries in China, allowing the following Eight Permissions, which he felt Christians could in good conscience observe:

(1) Christians may have funeral tablets inscribed with the names of the deceased, provided that the Christian view of death was made clear and all proper measures were taken to avoid scandals.

---

72. Since the texts of 1704 and 1710 were included in the 1715 bull and were not promulgated until its appearance, it is probable that most missionaries did not know about them except through the interpretation of Tournon. For these texts, see *100 Roman Documents* (Document #24), 50–54.

73. Minamiki, *The Chinese Rites Controversy from Its Beginning until Modern Times*, 56.

(2) Civil ceremonies for the dead are permitted if devoid of superstition.//
(3) The civil cult to Confucius and the tablet in his honor, with the burning of incense and placing foods before the tablet, is permitted if devoid of superstitious inscriptions and accompanied by a declaration of faith.
(4) Candles and incense are permitted at funerals if explanations are given in writing.
(5) Genuflections and prostrations are allowed before a "corrected tablet" and before the coffin.
(6) Foods may be placed on the tables in front of the coffin with the corrected tablet, provided there is an adequate explanation that all this is done to show piety and respect for the deceased.
(7) "Kowtow" is permitted before corrected tablets on the Chinese New Year as well as at other times.
(8) Candles and incense may be used before tombs and corrected tablets with necessary precaution.[74]

These permissions caused confusion because each local church interpreted them differently. The bishop of Beijing followed suit with his pastoral letter, allowing certain practices in the spirit of the Eight Permissions. Fearing that these practices would undermine the papal position, Clement XII revoked the Eight Permissions in 1735. His successor Benedict XIV forbade further discussions concerning the rites in the papal bull *Ex Quo Singulari*, issued on July 11, 1742. All missionaries were required to take an oath of submission to the papal decree, promising never to allow the Chinese rites and ceremonies to be practiced by the people under their care.[75]

The Rites Controversy in Vietnam

The aftermath of the Chinese Rites Controversy forced the missionaries as well as the native clergy to rethink what was superstitious and what was an acceptable practice, even in something as sacred to the Vietnamese as funeral rites. Of

---

74. For the listing, see *100 Documents* (Document #24), 55–56; Minamiki, *The Chinese Rites Controversy from Its Beginnings to Modern Times*, 64–65.

75. For the text of the oath, see *100 Documents* (Document # 24), 53. Two centuries later, the Holy See reversed its position. The decree *Plane Compertum Est*, issued on December 8, 1939, declares that rites to Confucius and by extension to the ancestors are "civil" in nature and acceptable to Catholics. Catholic magistrates and students are permitted passively to attend public ceremonies honoring Confucius and national heroes. Furthermore, it is licit and unobjectionable to bow or show other manifestations of civil observance, for example, offering incense before the deceased or their images.

all the issues regarding the Chinese Rites Controversy, only three concerned Vietnam: offerings to ancestors, worship in front of ancestral tablets, and sacrifices to Confucius and the village gods (*thành hoàng*). The absolute prohibitions on ancestor worship have had tremendous repercussions in Vietnam. It put Catholics in direct confrontation with the laws and customs of the land and was partly responsible for feeding the anti-Christian sentiment that resulted in the execution of thousands of believers.

The practice of filial piety is characteristic of Vietnamese religious and ethical duty. It was considered the foundational virtue for maintaining harmony within society. Thus, no one, from the king to his lowliest subject, wanted to be accused of being unfilial. Being filial was important when one's parents were alive, but it was even more important to remember and serve them after their death. To a Vietnamese observer, Catholics appeared not to have honored their parents because they failed to make offerings and sacrifices or maintain external signs of mourning, such as prostrating in front of the deceased and partaking in memorial banquets. When other Vietnamese saw that Catholic converts did not observe traditional expressions of filial duty, especially the rituals in honor of the dead, they accused them of having abandoned the traditions. Consequently, political authorities viewed Christians as betrayers of their cultural heritage, or worse, as followers of a "false religion" that had to be prohibited. Christians were accused of being unfilial and disloyal—a serious charge that still has repercussions today.

The Lê Code, the law that governed Đại Việt from the fifteenth to the eighteenth centuries, prescribed specific filial obligations and severe punishment for failure to observe them. Among these obligations were rituals honoring the dead in funeral and memorial services; these procedures were spelled out in detail. Realizing that these customs were important to the Vietnamese, early Jesuit missionaries allowed their converts to honor the dead according to the local customs but with modifications to ensure that only God was worshipped.

As an indication of how seriously the Jesuits took this issue, Alexandre de Rhodes devoted five chapters of his *Histoire du royaume de Tunquin* to describing the customs and rites in honor of the dead, including royal funerals.[76] While praising the seriousness and solemnity of funeral and memorial services in Tonkin,[77] de Rhodes regarded certain customs in the memorial banquet, such as the invitation to

---

76. Alexandre de Rhode, *Histoire du royaume de Tunquin*, part 1, chaps. 22 to 26, 77–92.

77. He wrote in *Histoire du royaume de Tunquin*, 86, "There is perhaps no other nation on this inhabited earth that honors and venerates the souls and bodies of the dead more than the people of Tonkin."

the deceased to partake in the food and wine, or the burning of paper money and paper goods, as nothing but "foolishness" and "superstition."[78] However, as to the rites to honor the ancestors as a whole, de Rhodes judged, "[While] truly there are some customs that Christians cannot practice without sin, for the most part, they are innocent and we have judged that they can retain them without interfering with the Holy Religion."[79]

While many Dominicans and MEP missionaries found the Jesuits' strategy of accommodation unacceptable in China, they thought that the situation in Tonkin warranted a different approach. As the Dominicans took over mission work in the coastal areas, they were faced with customs and rites of which the superstitious nature was ambiguous. They took note of them and sent a list of 274 questions to their headquarters in Manila to be discussed by the theologians and missionaries there. In 1680, the Dominican theologian Juan de la Paz responded to the questions in a book, later followed by two more.[80] For the most part, la Paz thought that the customs described in these questions were not of religious but rather of a civil and political nature, and thus acceptable even under a strict understanding.[81]

Even after the papal decree *Ex Illa Die* was promulgated in Annam, questions about whether certain practices were permissible to Christians continued to haunt missionaries. The prohibitions of (1) sacrifices to Confucius and the ancestors on solemn days, (2) sacrifices to Confucius as thanksgiving for passing civil examinations, (3) sacrifices to the ancestors in the ancestral temple, (4) sacrifices to the ancestors on the home altar and at burial sites, and (5) the use of ancestral tablets did not solve problems but made the situation worse. The decree was not promulgated openly in Cochinchina for fear of civil repression. The Eight Permissions allowed by Mezzabarba were welcomed in both parts of Annam, but not for long.[82]

---

78. Rhodes, *Histoire du royaume de Tunquin*, 84–92.

79. Rhodes, *Divers voyages et missions*, 77.

80. Juan de la Paz, *Opusculum in quo ducenta et septuagina quarttuor quaesita a RR. PP. Missionaris Regini Tunkini proposita totidemque Responsiones ad ipsa continentur, experditae per Adm R. P. Fr Joannem de Paz* (Manila, 1680); *Respuesta à 274 questiones de los Missioneros de Tunquin* (1687); *Diversas cartas del estado de la Iglesia de Tunquin donde era vicarisimo* (1718).

81. The MEP bishop Marin Labbé of Cochinchina (1704–1723) praised these works and used them to justify certain practices in Cochinchina. Launay, *Histoire de la mission de Cochinchine*, 1:608–9.

82. We do not know when this papal decree was promulgated in Tonkin, but we can assume that it took effect at about the same time. Launay, *Histoire de la mission de Cochinchine*, 1:601–9.

The final decree, *Ex Quo Singulari* (1742), was meant to end all discussion and debate about the rites under pain of excommunication. The initial reaction of the faithful in Tonkin was obedience to Rome. Under the leadership of the MEP bishop Louis Néez (1680–1784), the clergy of the Vicariate of West Tonkin seemed to comply with the papal bulls of 1715 and 1742.[83] The bishop himself wrote a pastoral letter to his priests and faithful in 1755, in which he approved prostration in front of the coffin and certain practices of funeral rites. He allowed Christians to venerate the dead, provided there were no spirit tablets or any hint of superstition.[84]

While the decrees obliged missionaries and the local clergy to take an oath of obedience to the Holy See's decision on the Rites, they could not stop the discussion. It appeared that each priest interpreted this decision differently, confusing the faithful. In 1753, the apostolic vicar of East Tonkin asked Propaganda Fide if certain practices honoring the dead could be considered civil acts and therefore permissible in the spirit of the Eight Permissions.[85] Another letter from Tonkin to the Holy Office in 1757 asked about the appropriateness of genuflection and the lighting of candles and incense-burning in front of the coffin, provided that anything suggesting superstition was avoided.[86] Again, in 1773, more questions were raised by East Tonkin on whether it was appropriate to prostrate in front of the bier, provided that a crucifix was nearby and there was no hint of superstition.[87] The answers to these questions were negative, citing the previous decrees without further explanation. It seemed as if Rome wanted to close the case and move on.

However, the Christian laity did not. Already in 1759, they wrote a petition asking the bishop to forward to Rome their request for permission to prostrate in front of the deceased. They explained that prostration in front of another human being, living or dead, was a Vietnamese custom of honoring that person. They explained that when the clergy forbade them to venerate their deceased parents in this manner, non-Christians would accuse them of being unfilial; uncommitted Christians would waver in their faith, and faithful Christians would face hostility from their non-Christian relatives.[88]

---

83. In the Archives of the MEP, there is a copy of an oath signed by Peter Triêm, priest of the West Tonkin Vicariate. AMEP, vol. 688, fol. 506.

84. See AMEP, vol. 688, fols. 5–10.

85. *100 Roman Documents* (Document #29), 62.

86. *100 Roman Documents* (Document #30), 62.

87. *100 Roman Documents* (Document #36), 64–65.

88. AMEP, vol. 689, fols. 261–62.

For the next hundred years until the end of the nineteenth century, questions were repeatedly sent to the Holy Office with regard to the rites in Tonkin: in 1783, 1785, 1820, 1837, 1840, 1841, 1843, 1851, 1855, 1856, 1879, and 1889.[89] The frequency and urgency of these questions show that the issues surrounding the rites to the ancestors (such as prostration and the offering of incense to the deceased) were still debated by the people and perhaps the native clergy far more than Rome could imagine. The funeral practices in Vietnam were not a matter of personal choice but public acts that had social and legal consequences. Thousands of Christians paid with their lives while their MEP and Dominican bishops tried to figure out how to walk the narrow line between what was acceptable and what was not.[90]

The situation of Christianity in Tonkin certainly contributed to the defensive tone of *Errors of the Three Religions*. Writing in the aftermath of the Chinese Rites Controversy and amid various persecutions of Christianity, the author intends to explain to his fellow believers the reasons behind the Christian rejection of traditional customs and rites. As we will see, he attempts to justify the Christian stance by arguing against the Confucian position on Christianity. From the Confucian perspective, Christianity is considered an "alien doctrine" or "heterodox way" (*đạo dị đoan*) because its followers deviate from traditional practices. However, the author argues that in reality Christianity is as orthodox as Confucianism, if not more orthodox, since it is not corrupted by Buddhist and Daoist practices like the Confucianism of his day. The text's defensiveness against Confucianism and disdain for Buddhism and Daoism, as we shall see, reflects an apologetic stance that was characteristic of most Christian writings of this era. This tendency was prevalent not only in Vietnam but also in China and Japan, where Christianity existed as a marginal and persecuted religion.

---

89. See the summary of these questions and responses in *100 Roman Documents*, documents #41, 42, 44, 45, 60, 67, 69, 70, 71, 72, 79, 82, 86, 87, 92, and 93. Together with two documents from Cochinchina (#66 and 91) and the three documents cited above, it is amazing that the MEP and Dominican bishops sent these questions to Rome twenty-one times after the promulgation of *Ex Quo Singularis*, which was supposed to stop all discussions.

90. Many MEP priests were convinced that the rites in Vietnam were more of a civil act than religious, but they could not disobey Rome. Launay, *Histoire de la Mission de Cochinchine*, 3:320–36.

2

Text and Context

ERRORS OF THE THREE RELIGIONS

IN 2009, IN a small room at 128 Rue du Bac, Paris, the curator at the archives of the Missions Étrangères de Paris (AMEP) handed me a small folder with a simple marking V-1098. Inside the folder was a small notebook—10 by 15 cm, to be exact. Having tried to locate ancient Vietnamese writings in various European depositories, I was eager to read anything available in the archives of a missionary order that was present in Vietnam for more than three hundred years. On the first page, the words "Tam Giáo chư vaọng" [Errors of the Three Religions] declared the title of the book (see figure 2.1). Questions came to my mind as I flipped through the pages. Who wrote this little book? What were the author's intentions? When was it written? And for whom? The writing style was simple and conversational. Slowly I realized that in my hands was one of the first extended descriptions of the religious customs and rituals of the Tonkinese, many of which I can still recognize today. In the pages, past beliefs and cultic practices came back alive in the dialogues between a Christian teacher and a native scholar.

By the time I finished reading it, I realized that it was a Christian apologetic work. The book's title suggests the polemics within: *Errors* promises to address what it considers errors in the native religions. The situation of Christianity in Tonkin certainly contributed to the defensive tone of *Errors of the Three Religions*. It reflects an apologetic stance that was characteristic of most Catholic writings in East Asia, where Christianity existed as a marginal and persecuted religion. Writing in the aftermath of the Chinese Rites Controversy and amid various waves of persecution of Christianity in Tonkin, the author of *Errors* intended to explain to his fellow converts and opponents the reasons behind the Christian rejection of traditional customs and rites. The author clearly wanted to defend Christian monotheism from what he considered the superstitious ideas and idolatrous practices of nonbelievers. In the following sections, I will discuss its literary context before proceeding to an examination of the text itself.

Defending the True Faith
Apologetic Writings as a Theological Genre

Errors belongs to the type of Christian literature called *apologetic writings* (from the Greek *apologia*, "defense").[1] This theological genre arises from the need of individuals or groups who feel misunderstood and marginalized by the larger society. Its writers seek to harmonize their beliefs and practices with the broader culture and serve to strengthen the convictions of the believers themselves and to convince others of their validity. Apologists provide believers, often neophytes, with ways to explain and justify their beliefs and practices against their detractors and opponents.

Depending on the context, we can speak of apologetic writings in two senses. Positive apologetics make use of the common cultural and philosophical expressions of a particular society to describe the beliefs and practices of a religion in order to persuade outsiders of their legitimacy. Negative apologetics, on the other hand, attack the beliefs and/or practices deemed to be harmful to one's religion by exposing their weaknesses and contradictions, or by demonstrating the inadequacy of the arguments advanced against one's religion. Since apologetic materials are driven by the social and political struggles of individuals and groups, they cannot be understood apart from that surrounding context. Given the hostile environment toward Christianity in eighteenth-century Tonkin, it is natural to see apologetic writings such as *Errors* begin to appear.

Errors stands in continuity with early Christian apologetic writings, which were composed to construct the new Christian identity, and distinguish it from Judaism and Greco-Roman religions.[2] With regard to their environment, the emerging Christian community adopted Greek philosophical concepts into its theology but distanced itself from the religious and ritual practices of the Romans and Greeks. As Christianity spread among non-Jews and gained influence throughout the Roman empire, many people felt attracted to the new religion.

---

[1]. The literature on Christian apologetics is extensive. For a standard survey, see Avery Dulles, *A History of Apologetics* (Philadelphia: Westminter, 1971). For an anthology of selected apologetic texts from the first century until the Middle Ages, see William Edgar and K. Scott Oliphint, *Christian Apologetics Past and Present: A Primary Source Reader* (Wheaton: Crossway Books, 2009).

[2]. See Judith M. Lieu, *Neither Jew nor Greek? Constructing Early Christianity* (Edinburgh: T & T Clark, 2002); also her *Christian Identity in the Jewish and Graeco-Roman World* (Oxford: Oxford University Press, 2004).

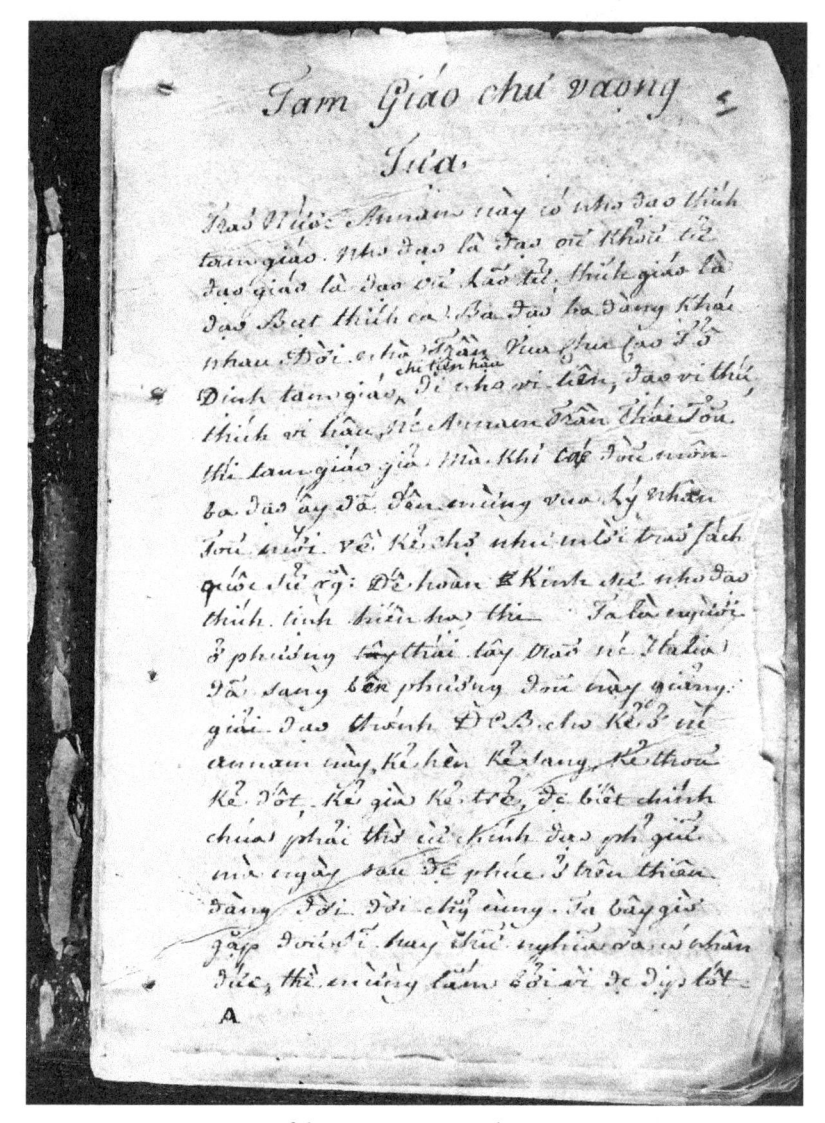

FIGURE 2.1 The First Page of the Text *Tam Giáo Chư Vọng*

Others, however, perceived it to be socially offensive, politically subversive, or intellectually absurd.[3] Hostility toward Christians, which resulted in a number of local and state-sponsored persecutions from the end of the first century to the first decades of the fourth century, naturally led to the development of apologetic

---

3. See Robert Louis Wilken, *The Christians as the Romans Saw Them* (1984; repr., New Haven, CT: Yale University, 2003).

literature against paganism and in defense of the legitimacy of Christianity in the Greco-Roman world.[4] At a time when Christianity was both attractive and repulsive to many people, defending Christian beliefs and practices from the enmity of Roman society was not only a task to protect Christians from popular violence and political repression, but also to uphold the credibility of Christian beliefs.[5] The uneasy relationship between Christianity, as a minority religion, and its surrounding culture was mirrored in what Christian converts in Tonkin were experiencing.

In the Christianized Roman Empire, apologetic writings did not diminish but transformed into new arguments for the superiority of Christianity. Having no fear of being seriously challenged, Christian apologists continued to attack Roman paganism with increased boldness. In contrast to the pagans and barbarians, the Church appeared as the bearer of civilization and culture. To reject the Christian message was to go back to an inferior state of mind. Consequently, the missionary outreach to non-Christians took a form of positive apologetics. Attempts were made to convince them of the ineffective power of their gods and the greatness of the Creator God who sent his Son to save the human race. Consequently, they were exhorted to accept the Christian message, renounce their gods, receive baptism, and live according to the pattern set out by the missionaries.[6]

Faith and Reason

The religious challenge to the Christian Church in the Middle Ages came from unconverted Jews and Muslims. Unlike the pagans and barbarians, these people had a rich cultural heritage themselves and were unlikely to be persuaded

---

4. Antipagan apologetics is already found in the New Testament, for example in Paul's writings and speeches (cf. Romans 1, Corinthians 3, Acts 17), but it appeared in full form in the second and third century in works such as *Epistle to Diognetus*, Justin Martyr's *Apology*, Tatian's *Oration to the Greeks*, Tertulian's *Apology*, Clement of Alexandria's *Exhortation to the Greeks* (*Protrepticus*), and Origen's *Against Celsus*.

5. For a survey of primary sources on various issues that arose between Christians and non-Christians in the early Church, see Ramsay MacMullen and Eugene N. Lane, eds., *Paganism and Christianity, 100–425 C.E.: A Source Book* (Minneapolis: Fortress, 1992). For an overview of apologetics in the Roman world, see Mark Edwards, Martin Goodman, Simon Price, and Chris Rowland, eds., *Apologetics in the Roman Empire: Pagans, Jews, Christians* (Oxford: Oxford University, 1999), especially the introduction and chapters 5 (Greek apologists) and 6 (Latin apologists).

6. On the relationship between Christianity and paganism in the late antiquity, see Maijastina Kahlos, *Debate and Dialogue: Christian and Pagan Cultures c. 360–430* (Burlington, VT: Ashgate, 2007).

by Christian appeals. Hence, in their disputes with Jews and Muslims, medieval theologians felt the need to stress the rational grounds of the Christian faith. The idea of defending the Christian faith as the only "true religion" (*religio vera*) was born out of these disputes. From the twelfth to the fifteenth centuries, there was a surge of apologetic works to deal with objections from Jews and Muslims.[7] To the unbelievers and skeptics, Christian doctrines could not be taken on faith alone. Scholastic theology was developed to give demonstrative reasons for the central mysteries of the Christian faith.

By the late Middle Ages, there already existed two types of writing that explained and defended the Christian religion against nonbelievers: the *catechismus*[8] and the *doctrina christiana*. The former is a type of apologetic based on natural theology, dealing with philosophical topics such as the existence, nature, and attributes of God, the creation of the world, and the problem of evil. *Doctrina christiana*, on the other hand, is a kind of handbook focusing more specifically on Catholic beliefs and practices like the Apostles' Creed, the Ten Commandments, the Seven Sacraments, the basic prayers (e.g., *Pater Noster* and *Ave Maria*), the works of mercy, the seven capital sins and their opposing virtues, laws and precepts, and the "four last things."[9] The book was usually given to catechumens and the newly baptized to aid their memorization of the essential doctrines and precepts of the Catholic faith.

When European missionaries came in contact with the people of East Asia, natural theology was a practical method to gain entry into the hearts and minds of the people to be evangelized. Included among the many themes treated in this genre are the distinction between true and false religions, the history of salvation, and the life of Christ, as in the works by Matteo Ricci and Alexandre de Rhodes. Different audiences are targeted by the two kinds of works in this genre. *Catechismus* was addressed to nonbelievers in order to defend the credibility of

---

7. Works such as Peter Alphonsi's *Dialogue with the Jew Moses*, Peter the Venerable's *Against the Inveterate Obstinacy of the Jews* and *A Book against the Sect or Heresy of the Saracens*, or Peter of Blois's *Against the Perfidy of the Jews* were often polemical. Not all Christian authors engaged in polemics, however. For example, Peter Abelard's *A Dialogue between a Philosopher, a Jew and a Christian*, Thomas Aquinas's *Summa contra gentiles*, and Raymond Lull's *Book of the Gentile and the Three Wise Men* and *Book of the Tartar and the Christian* represent the efforts to use reason as a common ground in dialogue with other believers. See Dulles, *A History of Apologetics*, 81–110.

8. The *Catechismus* of this era was primarily a pre-evangelization work; it did not function as the modern "catechism," which was known at that time as *Doctrina Christiana*.

9. The "four last things" refer to Catholic doctrines regarding death and the afterlife; they include (1) particular and general judgments, (2) heaven, (3) hell and purgatory, and (4) the resurrection of the body.

the Christian message, whereas the aim of *doctrina christiana* was to teach the neophytes about the faith of the Church.[10] The distinction between these two types of writings is not always clear, for the needs of the audience sometimes required including or omitting certain items. In many cases, a missionary would first compose a *doctrina christiana* before acquiring sufficient knowledge of the local language and cultural expression to compose a *catechismus* proper. St Francis Xavier's catechism can serve as an example.

Experiments with Presenting the Faith

When Francis Xavier (1506–1552) arrived in Goa in 1542, he first composed a short catechism, followed by a set of instructions for Jesuit catechists in 1545.[11] However, when he came to Japan a few years later, Xavier had to change his evangelizing method, since the Japanese were a people who "have a high opinion of themselves ... [and] have little esteem for all other foreign races."[12] Through his debates with Japanese monks, Xavier formed a catechetical method for his Japanese audience. Constructing a kind of natural theology, he argued first that the universe is created and ordered by a Creator; that it is not eternal; that the heavenly bodies and natural objects are not living creatures; that God creates the human immortal soul; and that the Buddhist teachings on the above-mentioned points are erroneous.[13] Then he narrates the Christian story, including the creation of the world, the fall of the angels, the creation and subsequent fall of humanity, the flood and the confusion

---

10. This type of material was known among the Chinese as *Tianzhu Jiaoyao* (Essential Teachings of the Lord of Heaven) or *Shengjiao Yaoli* (Essential doctrines of the Holy Religion), and in Vietnam by similar names. For a list of Chinese works in the genre of *Doctrina Christiana*, see Nicholas Standaert, *Handbook of Christianity in China*, vol 1., *To 1800* (Leiden: Brill, 2001), 609–11. In Vietnam, we can cite Girolamo Majorica, *Thiên Chúa Thánh Giáo Khải Mông* [Introduction to the Holy Religion of the Lord of Heaven] (ca. 1630s) (N.p., 2003).

11. The work contains an exposition of the Creed, the *Pater Noster*, the *Ave Maria*, the Ten Commandments, the precepts of the Church, the *Salve Regina*, the *Confiteor*, the seven capital sins and their opposing virtues, the theological and cardinal virtues, the corporal and spiritual works of mercy, prayers before the Eucharist and blessings at meals, and other prayers for the deliverance from sins and protection from evils. For the full text of this brief catechism, see *The Letters and Instructions of Francis Xavier*, trans. M. Joseph Costello (St Louis: the Institute of Jesuit Sources, 1992), Doc. #14, 41–45. In his *Instruction for the Catechists of the Society of Jesus* given in 1545, we see a similar approach, except that it takes the form of questions and answers; see *The Letters and Instructions of Francis Xavier*, Doc. #53, 131–33.

12. Xavier's letter to his confrères from Cochin, January 29, 1552. For the full text, see Costello, *Letters and Instructions of Francis Xavier*, Doc. #96, 326–43.

13. Costello, *The Letters and Instructions of Francis Xavier*, 333–35.

of tongues after the fall of Babel, which gave rise to idolatry, the history of salvation in Israel, the mysteries of the life of Jesus, and finally, the four last things.[14] In addition, the Christian convert also learned the sign of the cross, the Apostles' Creed, the basic prayers, and other Catholic materials translated into Japanese from his 1542 catechism.[15]

Here we see the beginning of a missionary strategy. First, reason is used to refute potential converts of their beliefs about the universe and the human soul, and then persuade them to worship the one true God and his Son, Jesus Christ, and so attain the eternal bliss of paradise instead of suffering the eternal torments of hell. After their conversion and baptism, they would be taught the Christian doctrines. This method would be used again and again by later missionaries.

In a similar approach, the Jesuit head of the East Asia mission, Alessandro Valignano, stressed a gradual approach to evangelization.[16] Valignano believed that the most effective method involves studying the uniqueness of the people, especially their language, customs, cultures, and beliefs. He chose to approach the Japanese mind with persuasion rather than force and depth instead of superficiality. To realize this end, Valignano invited local experts in Japanese religions to help him compose a catechism to aid his fellow missionaries and local coworkers in their presentation of the Christian doctrines and to engage with Japanese Buddhism. In his experience, the Japanese Buddhists struggled with similar issues, namely how to explain divine nature, divine communication, life after death, moral reward and punishment, and so forth. Consequently, Valignano's *Catechismus Christianae Fidei* is divided into two parts: the first part deals with topics of Christian teachings, such as natural religious truths and revealed truths; the second part deals with topics of Christian living, such as the Ten Commandments, the sacraments, and the last things.[17] This two-step catechetical method advocated by Valignano set the tone for the later Jesuit approach to catechesis.

---

14. Georg Schurhammer, *Francis Xavier: His Life and Times*, vol. 4, *Japan and China 1549–1552* (Rome: The Jesuit Historical Institute, 1982), 106–10.

15. Costello, *The Letters and Instructions of Francis Xavier*, Doc. #96, 341.

16. See Josef Franz Schutte, *Valignano's Mission Principles for Japan 1573–1582*, trans. John J. Coyne (St. Louis: The Institute of Jesuit Sources, 1980–1985).

17. Valignano's work was published in 1586 and entitled *Catechismus christianae fidei in quo Veritas nostrae religionis ostenditur et sectae Japonenses confutantur* (A Catechism of Christian Faith to Demonstrate the Truth of our Religion and to Refute the Japanese Sects). For the common people, Valignano composed a catechism in Japanese, *Dochirina Kirishitan*, which resembles a standard catechism (explanations of Christian prayers, the Creed, the Ten Commandments and the precepts of the Church, the seven mortal sins, the sacraments,

The situation in China followed a similar pattern. No Jesuit missionary had been able to set foot inside China, due to both language barriers and the political situation. The Chinese authorities were watchful of foreigners. The Portuguese were allowed to set-up a trading post in the tiny peninsula Macau, the southern tip of Guangdong province, but they could not advance further. After spending nine months in Macau in 1577, Valignano realized the depth of the problem. If Christianity had any chance of penetrating into China, the missionaries had to learn the local language and culture. Furthermore, they had to make friends with the intellectuals of the society and enlist their help in preaching the Gospel. Michele Ruggieri and Matteo Ricci would be the first two Jesuit missionaries to China to follow this directive. At first, the two missionaries shaved their heads and wore grey robes like Buddhist monks to emphasize the religious character of their mission. Within a few years, Ricci realized that Buddhism was not held in high esteem in China. From 1592 onward, the missionaries would no longer be identified as "monks of India" but as "scholars from the West." They would adopt the gowns of the Confucian literati, make friends with them, learn Chinese literature, and begin to compose works in the Chinese language.[18]

The first book of Christian doctrine to appear in Chinese was a "catechism" by Ruggieri entitled *True Record of the Lord of Heaven* (Tianzhu Shilu) with the collaboration of Ricci. Written as a dialogue between a European (Ruggieri) and a Chinese scholar about Christian faith, it presents arguments from the order of nature that should lead a person to God. At that early stage of their work, the two missionaries struggled with finding the proper terminology for their Christian vocabulary. *True Record* was the first written presentation of the Christian faith for a Chinese audience, and it was quite successful. With Valignano's encouragement, after several drafts, Ruggeri finally published it in

---

etc.). See Josef F. Schütte, *Valignano's Mission Principles for Japan*, vol 1, part 2 (Anand, India: Gujarat Sahitya Prakash, 1983), 67–89; Nicholas Standaert, "Responses & Reflections," in *Christianity and Cultures: Japan and China in Comparison 1543–1644*, ed. Antoni M. Üçerler (Rome: Institutum Historicum Societatis Iesu, 2009), 61–64.

18. On the Jesuit mission in China, see George Dunne, *Generation of Giants: The Story of the Jesuits in China in the Last Decades of the Ming Dynasty* (Notre Dame: Notre Dame University Press, 1962); Liam Matthew Brockey, *The Jesuit Mission to China, 1579–1724* (Cambridge, MA: Belknap Press, 2007). On Ricci's work in China, see R. Po-chia Hsia, *A Jesuit in the Forbidden City, Matteo Ricci, 1552–1610* (New York: Oxford, 2010); Mary Laven, *Mission to China: Matteo Ricci and the Jesuit Encounter with the East* (London: Faber & Faber, 2011). Ricci's writings have been collected and reprinted in many anthologies, notably Pasquale d'Elia, ed., *Fonti Ricciane: documenti originali concernenti Matteo Ricci e la storia delle prime relazioni tra l'Europa e la Cina* (1579–1615), 3 vols (Rome: La Liberia dello Stato, 1942–49).

Canton in 1584.[19] This was the missionaries' first experience with communicating Christian doctrines in the Chinese language.[20]

Matteo Ricci's Catechism

In 1603, a work entitled *True Meaning of the Lord of Heaven* (Tianzhu Shiyi) by Matteo Ricci was printed in Beijing with a preface by the Chinese scholar Feng Yingqing. The book was hailed to be as excellent as if it had been written by a Chinese Christian author and quickly became a best-seller.[21] Upon its publication, the Jesuit superiors decided that it would replace Ruggieri's work as the definitive *catechismus* in Chinese.[22] *True Meaning* was also popular outside of China. It was translated into Japanese, Korean, Mongolian, and Manchurian.[23]

---

19. It has sixteen chapters dealing with the following themes: (1) existence of a true God; (2) God's nature and attributes; (3) human knowledge of God; (4) creation of everything by God; (5) angels and the first parents; (6) the immortality of the human soul; (7) life after death; (8) promulgation of God's law in three phrases: natural law, the Mosaic law, and the law of the Gospel; (9) the incarnation of the Son of God; (10) the nature of the law of the Gospel; (11) the mysteries of faith; (12) the Ten Commandments in general; (13) the first three commandments; (14) the last seven commandments; (15) religious life; and (16) baptism. See Leon Wieger, "Notes sur la première catéchèse écrite en chinois 1582–1584," *AHSI* 1 (1932): 72–84; Joseph Shih, *Le Père Ruggieri et le problème de l'évangélisation en Chine* (Rome: Pontificia Universitas Gregoriana, 1964).

20. The catechism, however, did not show any adaptation to the Chinese context, save some terminology such as *Tianzhu* (Lord of heaven) for God, *sheng'en* (sacred favor) for grace, *tiantang* (heavenly palace) for heaven, *linghun* (spirit) for soul, etc., which seemed to borrow from existing religious vocabulary of the Chinese. Gianni Criveller, *Preaching Christ in Late Ming China. The Jesuit Presentation of Christ from Matteo Ricci to Giulio Aleni* (Taipei: Ricci Institute for Chinese Studies, 1997), 95–96.

21. It went through several reprinting within a few years: Beijing, 1603; Canton, 1605; Hangzhou, 1607; subsequently it was reissued by Li Zhicao (1565–1630), in a 1629 collection of early Jesuit Chinese writings, *Tianxue Chuhan* (Primary Basket of the Study of Heaven). For a chronology of its composition and printing, see Douglas Lancashire and Peter Hu Kuo-Chen, trans. and ed., *The True Meaning of the Lord of Heaven (T'ien-chu Shih-i)* (St. Louis: The Institute of Jesuit Source, 1985), 19–21.

22. Ruggieri's work was withdrawn from circulation, and preserved in the Roman archives of the Society of Jesus (ARSI). It is now available in *Chinese Christian Texts from the Roman Archives of the Society of Jesus*, ed. Nicholas Standaert and Adrian Dudink (Rome: Procura Generaliza della Compagnia Di Gesù, 2002), 1:1–80.

23. Citing the *Fonti Ricciane*, George Dunne (*Generation of Giants*, 96) mentions a Vietnamese translation, but I do not find any evidence of a Vietnamese (*nôm*) translation of the *True Meaning*. According to Louis Pfister, the Japanese translation appeared in 1604. A Korean translation appeared much later, perhaps in the early eighteenth century. A Manchurian translation was produced under the reign of Kangxi, as the emperor took delight in this book. See Pfister, *Notices*, 35.

In *True Meaning*, Ricci offered an original method of evangelization. He presented Christian teachings by blending Thomistic theology with the Chinese philosophical tradition, using the Socratic method of question and answer. Structured as a long dialogue between a Chinese scholar and a "Western Scholar" (Christian missionary), the book is divided into eight chapters, presenting various themes of the Christian faith. Ricci's *catechismus* represents the culmination of an intercultural dialogue between Ricci and his Chinese friends.[24] *True Meaning* is not simply a Western philosophical inquiry dressed up in a Chinese gown; it also took Chinese thought into account to explain Christian doctrines. To achieve this, Ricci had to learn the Confucian classics in depth during his early years in China.

True Meaning is substantially a refutation of what Ricci considered deviations from the true worship of Heaven found in ancient China. Ricci's agenda is well expressed in the preface to the book written by his collaborator Li Zhicao:

> In this book, [Ricci] says that men know to serve their parents but do not know that the Lord of Heaven is the parent of all. Men know that a nation must have a rightful ruler but do not know that the Lord, who alone "governs Heaven," is the rightful ruler at all. A man who does not serve his parents cannot be a (true) son; a man who does not know the rightful ruler cannot be a (true) minister; a man who does not serve the Lord of Heaven cannot be a (true) man.... The general purpose of the book is to make men repent their transgressions and pursue righteousness, curb their passions, and be benevolent toward all. It reminds men of their origin from above so as to make them fear lest they fall down into the place of punishment; it makes them consider the awful consequences and hasten to cleanse themselves of all sin. Thus they might not be guilty of any offense against the Great Heavenly Lord Above.[25]

---

24. In his study of the Confucian *Four Books*, Ricci frequently discussed their contents with his Chinese friends, and these conversations inspired him to write another presentation of the Christian doctrines, which would appeal to the Confucian intellectual. Around the year 1595 or 1596, Ricci began writing a new catechism with terms and quotations taken from the Confucian texts. In 1597, a Latin translation was submitted for official approval. The text subsequently was revised as Ricci incorporated many suggestions of his growing number of friends, especially the Confucian scholars in Beijing.

25. Li Zhicao's preface to *Tianzhu Shiyi*, in *Tianxue Chuhan* (1629), trans. David Mungello, in *Sources of Chinese Tradition*, vol 2. *From 1600 to the Twentieth Century*, comp. Wm Theodore de Bary and Richard Lufrano (New York: Columbia University Press, 2000), 145–46.

Ricci regarded contemporary religious thoughts, namely Neo-Confucianism and Buddhism, as departures from the pristine truths of ancient China. Thus he set out to correct these errors by teaching people the truths and saving them from ignorance and sin.

True Meaning represents the mature fruits of Ricci's reflections and debates with the Neo-Confucians and the Buddhists of his time. In the Latin summary attached to the first edition of *True Meaning*, Ricci presents its structure and main contents.[26] Choosing natural theology as a starting point, Ricci explains his strategy:

> This [catechism] does not treat all the mystery of our holy faith, which need be explained only to catechumens and Christians, but only certain principles, especially such as can be proved and understood by the light of natural reason.... It treats of such truths as there is in the universe a God, who has created all things and continually conserves them in being; that the soul of man is immortal, and will receive from God in the next life remuneration for its good and evil works; that the transmigration of souls into the bodies of other men and of animals is false, and similar things....
> *If it does not propose to refute directly all the errors of the sects in China, it destroys at the roots, with irrefragable arguments, the opinions of the Chinese which contradict those truths.*[27]

Ricci's aim was to knock down the old beliefs to make room for the new ones. This polemical tendency is quite strong and can be felt throughout the text. Nevertheless, *True Meaning* is an attempt to construct a dialogue between the

---

26. See the text in Lancashire and Hu, *True Meaning*, 460–72. Here is my quick summary of the eight chapters: Chapter 1 discusses the Lord of Heaven (God) as the creator of the universe and the ruler of all things in it. Chapter 2 offers answers to some of the mistaken views concerning God as presented in contemporary Chinese thought, including the Daoist concept of "non-being" (*wu*), the Buddhist concept of "emptiness" (*kong*), and the Neo-Confucian concept of "Supreme Ultimate" (*taiji*) as sources of creation. Chapter 3 offers arguments for the spiritual and imperishable nature of the human soul and connects them to the moral life. Chapter 4 continues the discussion on the human soul and its spiritual nature, and makes a clear distinction between the creation and its Creator. Chapter 5 defends Ricci's view of the human soul by attacking the Buddhist teaching of the transmigration of souls. Chapter 6 presents a moral theory focusing on the connection between action, motivation, and the afterlife of reward and punishment. Chapter 7 affirms the fundamental goodness of human nature and connects it with the life of virtue. Chapter 8 answers objections against certain Western customs, especially clerical celibacy on the ground of filial piety. At the end, Ricci briefly talks about the saving work of God through Jesus and encourages the reader to join the Church.

27. D'Elia, *Fonti Ricciane*, 2:292–96, trans. George Dunne, *Generation of Giants*, 96–97; emphasis added.

Christian West and the Chinese tradition in order to present the reasonableness of Christianity to his audience. To achieve this purpose, Ricci used Chinese classical texts, historical examples, and arguments from Western scholastic and humanist philosophy, not only to explain Christian doctrines but also to evaluate Chinese ideas under discussion.

The influence of *True Meaning* on later catechisms and apologetic works in Tonkin (such as *Errors*) is quite obvious. Since its publication in 1603, it is possible that more than one copy of *True Meaning* was available in Tonkin. In his memoir, Alexandre de Rhodes recounted the story of how he stumbled upon a Christian book that "had been brought from China and was a work authored by one of our Fathers."[28] Rhodes recognized the book right away, since he had used a number of Chinese religious texts in his evangelization. Later on, when Rhodes composed his catechism during 1636–1645 in Macau and Cochinchina, he seems to have incorporated many of Ricci's teachings into his work.[29]

Alexandre de Rhodes's Catechism

In 1651, Propaganda Fide published a bilingual catechism written by Alexandre de Rhodes. The work was printed in two columns with the full title *Cathechismvs [sic] pro ijs, qui volunt suscipere Baptismvm in Octo dies divisus* in Latin and *Phép giảng tám ngày cho kẻ muấn chịu phép rửa tọi, ma beào đạo thánh đức Chúa blòi* in romanized Vietnamese script (Catechism for those who want to receive Baptism divided into eight days).[30] This is the first extant systematic work that presents the Christian faith to a Vietnamese audience.

The significance of this work on Vietnamese Catholicism is twofold. First, it is the first published book in the native language using a new script, later called the "national script" (*chữ quốc-ngữ*). It is the distinctive medium for Christian missionaries to communicate with the local people, and it facilitated the development of a Vietnamese Christian literature. Second, the book represents an early attempt at inculturating the Christian message. Prior to the publication of this catechism, other treatises on the Christian faith had been circulated among the

---

28. See the story in Rhodes, *Histoire du royaume de Tunquin*, 180–81. English translation is from Phan, *Mission and Catechesis*, 116–17.

29. See the comparison between the *True Meaning* and *Cathechismus* in Phan, *Mission and Catechesis*, 119–21.

30. See a facsimile reprint of this work together with a French translation in Alexandre de Rhodes, *Phép Giảng Tám Ngày / Cathechismus in octo dies divisus*, introduced by Nguyễn Khắc Xuyên (Hochiminh City: Tủ Sách Đại Kết, 1993). For a full English translation, see Peter Phan, *Mission and Catechesis*, 211–315.

Tonkinese, for example, Introduction to the Holy Teachings of the Lord of Heaven (*Thiên Chúa Thánh Giáo Khải Mông*)[31] written by Girolamo Majorica around 1635–1640. Majorica's work, however, belongs to the genre of *doctrina christiana*; in fact, it is an annotated translation and adaptation of Robert Bellarmine's catechism.[32]

In a sense, Rhodes's catechism is a follow-up to Ricci's *True Meaning*. But unlike Ricci, who focused on "pre-evangelization" through the use of natural theology, Rhodes devoted nearly half of his work to discussing the mysteries and doctrines of the Christian faith, following Xavier's approach. The objective of the book is made clear by its title: it is directed "to those who want to receive baptism" (*pro ijs qui volunt suscipere baptismum*). Like Xavier and Valignano to the Japanese and Ruggieri and Ricci to the Chinese, Rhodes found the Vietnamese were fond of a rational approach to Christian doctrines. Hence, Rhodes stated in his catechism, "[T]he true law [religion] is the law of reason, the law of right order. If our actions conform to reason, we earn merit; if they are contrary to reason, we fall into sin."[33]

Using reason as his principle of engaging the Vietnamese mind, Rhodes commented on his method:

> [Those who are interested in the faith] were all delighted when I pointed out to them how our religion conforms to right reason, and they admired above all God's Ten Commandments, finding that nothing more reasonable could be uttered or more worthy of being laid down by the Supreme Ruler of the world. My favorite method was to propose to them the immortality of the soul and the afterlife. From thence I went on to prove God's existence and providence. Advancing thus from one degree to the next, we gradually came to the more difficult mysteries. Experience has shown us that this way of instructing the pagans is very useful.[34]

---

31. The manuscript is preserved in the Bibliothèque Nationale in Paris. It was transliterated into *quốc-ngữ* script by Võ Long Tê in 1988 and published by the Catholic Hán-Nôm Translation Group of Saigon Archdiocese in 2003. The book is divided into six sections: (1) Introduction; (2) On the sign of the cross; (3) On the twelve points of the Creed; (4) On the *Pater Noster*; (5) On the *Ave Maria*; (6) On the Ten Commandments. The manuscript is incomplete, missing the part on the sacraments.

32. We do not know whether Majorica's catechism bears any resemblance to another book with the same title that appeared in China, the *Tianzhu Shengjiao Qimeng* by Joaõ da Rocha (1566–1623). According to Pfister, the Chinese work is a translation of a Portuguese catechism. See Pfister, *Notices*, 69. In any case, both belong to the genre of *doctrina christiana* rather than *catechismus*.

33. Cited by Phan, *Mission and Catechesis*, 218.

34. Rhodes, *Divers voyages et missions*, 96. Translation is adapted from Phan, *Mission and Catechesis*, 128–29.

His catechetical method was discussed at length in *Histoire du royaume de Tunquin*. First, he took issue with those who proposed a *tabula rasa* approach. Some missionaries believed that "it is necessary first to destroy the errors of paganism and disabuse the minds of pagans of these erroneous views before establishing and teaching the doctrines and principles of the Christian religion."[35] For Rhodes, this is not a wise approach, for if people's beliefs are attacked, their hearts might be hardened and not open to hearing the truth. Second, he also objected to the proposal to explain only certain mysteries of Christianity and not the Trinity to those who were about to receive baptism "in order to avoid troubling their minds with doubts which this most sublime and ineffable mystery might induce."[36]

From his own experience, Rhodes found a "third way," more appropriate to the Vietnamese. This consists of a three-step program. First, he would speak about the truths that the mind can comprehend, for example, that there is order in the universe, that God is the creator and ruler of the universe, and that there is an obligation of the human person to know, love, and serve God to attain eternal life. Only after these truths have been accepted would he proceed to discuss the "errors of paganism" that turn a person away from the worship of the true God. In Rhodes's words,

> This method requires that one not attack the errors of the Tonkinese sects before establishing the truths knowable by the light of natural reason, such as the creation of the world, the end for which the sovereign Principle of created things has made and ordered the rational creatures, the obligations incumbent upon them to know and serve God. The goal is to build in the hearers' minds a sort of firm foundation on which the rest of their faith can be supported and not to turn them off, which often happens, by our rebutting and ridiculing their devotions, false though they are, and their superstitious observances.
>
> I have often been more successful, as far as I can tell, in impressing upon them feelings of piety and natural love toward the Creator and the First Principle of their being. Then, by means of a narrative of the history of the universal flood and the confusion of languages, I inspire in them a sense of fear of God whom they must fear and adore. Then follows a refutation of the idolatry which, incidentally, the devil himself has not introduced into the world until after the flood.[37]

---

35. Rhodes, *Histoire du royaume de Tunquin*, 175.

36. Ibid.

37. Rhodes, *Histoire du royaume de Tunquin*, 176. Translation by Phan, *Mission and Catechesis*, 127.

Here Rhodes was in agreement with other missionaries who insisted that the mysteries of the Christian faith could not be explained without first dislodging the erroneous concepts of pagan about God and their superstitions.

In the final step, Rhodes moves to an exposition of the mysteries of the Christian faith: the Holy Trinity, the Incarnation, and the Passion and Resurrection of Christ. More than trying to explain these doctrines, Rhodes sought to connect the Christian doctrines with devotion and moral life in order to foster the love of God and the practice of virtues. For Rhodes, the catechetical instruction is meant to lead a person from right beliefs to correct practices. Rhodes's catechetical method can be seen from the following outline of the *Cathechismus*: the first part, consisting of the first four days, is devoted to explaining a natural theology about God; the second part, from the fifth day to the seventh day, presents the life of Christ in detail; the third part, the last day, is an exposition of the moral life and an instruction for baptism.[38]

In terms of method, Rhodes avoids lengthy philosophical discussions of the Riccian style, and he does not quote extensively from Chinese or Western sources. In the first two chapters, he uses Vietnamese proverbs and sayings to build his case. In latter chapters, he entices his audience with biblical stories and analogies to explain the finer points of doctrines. Rhodes's approach is different from the fourfold exposition of the Apostles' Creed, the Ten Commandments, the sacraments, and the basic prayers that are common to *doctrina christiana*.

The brief survey of apologetic literature from early Christianity to the beginning of Christian missions to East Asia demonstrates that works like *Errors* belong to the genre of Christian apologetics, especially in their negative attitude toward non-Christian religions. Like the early Christian apologists who lived in a society that considered Christianity harmful and its teachings absurd, the author of *Errors* also lived in a time when Christianity

---

38. The *first day* discusses the purpose of the present life, true and false worship, God as the ruler and supreme Father, right worship that is due to God, and eternal reward and punishment. The *second day* discusses the nature of God as the origin of all things, the attributes of God, and the call to respond to God. The *third day* discusses the story of creation, of angels and their fall, of the universe and of Adam and Eve, and the fall of humanity. The *fourth day* continues the biblical history of humanity from Adam's descendants to Noah. Next, Rhodes turns to the discussion on the origins of the "false" Chinese sects (Buddhism, Daoism, Confucianism) and their doctrines, the cult of spirits among the Vietnamese, and the "true" religion of Abraham and his descendants. There is also a discussion on the human soul. The *fifth day* discusses the basic mysteries of the Christian faith: the Holy Trinity and the Incarnation. The veneration of Mary is also explained. The *sixth* day presents the life of Christ from his infancy to the public ministry. The *seventh day* presents the passion narratives of Christ, his crucifixion and death, followed by his resurrection and ascension, and the descent of the Holy Spirit. The *eighth day* discusses the final destiny of humanity, the Ten Commandments, and preparation for baptism.

was prohibited and Christians were persecuted. The nonconformist attitude and the refusal of Vietnamese Christians to participate in common rituals were questioned by many of their fellow citizens, and the legitimacy of Christianity as a true religion was doubted. The author of *Errors* had to explain why Christians worship God exclusively, and he did it by repudiating the traditional rituals.

The Text: History, Content, and Method
The Manuscript

The manuscript of *Errors* is kept in a folder with a numeration AMEP volume 1098. The bound volume is comprised of 104 sheets of thin paper with Vietnamese script written on both sides. The paper was fragile and needed to be handled with care. The first two pages are numbered in lowercase roman numerals, and the rest of the manuscript in Arabic numerals. The numeration is out of sequence between pages 66 and 77, and again from page 121 until the end.[39] The last sheet is unnumbered; it may have been intended as an insert for the missing information at the end of page 74. Most of the pages are written on in their entirety, except pages 70, 71, and 74.[40] If one includes the blank pages and inserts in the final tally, the manuscript runs to a total of 208 pages.

The document contains neither the author's name nor the date of composition. It is written in *quốc-ngữ* script—the romanized script devised by Jesuit missionaries in the seventeenth century. When comparing this text with other eighteenth-century manuscripts preserved in the archives of the Missions Étrangères de Paris (AMEP), we can accurately date the style of *quốc-ngữ* to eighteenth-century orthography.[41] The spelling and usage of the *quốc-ngữ* in this manuscript exhibits features of an intermediate stage between the first two dictionaries of the Vietnamese language:[42] the 1651 *Dictionarium*

---

[39]. In the manuscript the numeration is as follows: 1–66, 69–76, 67, 68, 77, 78–120, 211–95, where it should be 1–66, 67–77, 78–120, and 121–205. Apparently the scribe got a bit mix up and jumped from 120 to 211 instead of 121. In the transcription and translation of the text, I renumber the incorrect pages accordingly.

[40]. The last four lines of page 70 (page 69 of the manuscript) and the entire page 71 are blank, as if the copyist would fill up the information later. The second half of page 74 (page 76 in the manuscript) is also left blank.

[41]. A small collection has recently been published by Đoàn Thiện Thuật, *Chữ Quốc Ngữ Thế Kỷ XVIII* [*Quốc-ngữ* of the eighteenth century] (Hanoi: NXB Giáo Dục, 2008).

[42]. For example, the double consonants "bl" and "ml" are still retained. The ending "ng," abbreviated by the tilde, "~," still appears in the combinations of "ữ" (ung), "uõ" (uông), and "oũ"

Annamiticum, Lusitanum, et Latinum[43] and the 1838 *Dictionarium Annamitico Latinum*.[44]

The handwriting is clear and fairly legible, although it is hard to decipher the letters in some places because of corrections. The text appears to be copied from another manuscript, since there are occasional duplicate phrases being crossed out and written over. According to the archivist of the AMEP, Fr. Gérard Moussay, this particular text is not the original but one of the copies sent to the archives by Bishop Louis Néez (1650–1764), the vicar apostolic of West Tonkin.[45] The most challenging issue for the scholar is deciphering the meanings of the Sino-Vietnamese phrases embedded in the text. Since the Sino-Vietnamese words and phrases are written in their Romanized forms rather than in Chinese characters, the meanings of these phrases cannot be ascertained with accuracy. A further challenge is that many of the Sino-Vietnamese words do not seem to make sense, due to misspelling, or orthographic variation, or possible copyist's errors.

Structure and Content

After a two-page introduction stating its purpose, the text is divided into three books corresponding to the "errors" of Confucianism, Daoism, and Buddhism, respectively. Each book begins on a new page with a preface and a table of contents and is divided into articles. Each article is a series of dialogues between a "Western Scholar" and an "Eastern Scholar" in the style of Matteo Ricci's *True Meaning of the Lord of Heaven*. This dialogical approach reflects a pedagogical and rhetorical device, which enables the author to introduce, explain, and evaluate the teachings of other religions. This method is common in the Western tradition, for example, in the works of Plato, Anselm, and others, as well as in the Confucian tradition of *Analects* and *Mencius*.

The treatment of the subject matter under the threefold category of Confucianism, Daoism, and Buddhism is rather artificial, serving the author's

---

(ông). But there are already alternative spellings of "ư" and "ương" and "aõ" and "aong" (ong). Abbreviations are used with consistency throughout (e.g., "s.le" for "song le," "l.hôn" for "linh hôn," "ng`ta"for "người ta," "n'c" for "nước," "ph?" for "phải," etc.).

43. Alexandre de Rhodes, *Dictionarium Annamiticum, Lusitanum, et Latinum* (Rome, 1651).

44. Jean Louis Taberd, *Dictionarium Annamitico Latinum* (Serampore, 1838).

45. Louis Néez, MEP, came to Tonkin in 1715 and became vicar apostolic of West Tonkin in 1740. He was on a friendly terms with the Dominicans, Augustinians, and Jesuits. For his biography, see André Marillier, *Nos pères dans la foi: notes sur le clergé catholique du Tonkin de 1666 à 1765* (Paris: Église d'Asie, 1995), 2:81–82.

apologetic interests rather than offering a comprehensive and scholarly exposition of these religions. Some of the issues discussed do not fit comfortably into the book's thematic division. A glance at its table of contents will show that author is more interested in the practices and rituals of the religions in question than in their doctrines. For instance, ten of the fifteen articles in Book 1 (Articles 6–15) discuss and evaluate the various cults and ceremonies to the spirits, domestic and public deities, cultural or military heroes, and honors to the ancestors. Nine of the eleven articles in Book 2 (Articles 3–11) are devoted to exposing the "superstitious" acts, rituals, and beliefs associated with religious Daoism. Four of the twelve articles in Book 3 (Articles 8–11) deal with Buddhist funeral practices. In addition to reporting on religious practices, the author also sets out to correct those beliefs of these three religions that he judges to be false. He is particularly interested in refuting the Neo-Confucian and "Buddhist" accounts of the origin of the universe[46] as well as correcting some of the popular myths.[47]

Literary Sources

The author of *Errors* drew on a number Chinese and Vietnamese writings in his composition. The author demonstrated quite an extensive knowledge of Chinese and Vietnamese history. He often drew examples from Chinese historical chronicles, such as Sima Qian's *Records of the Grand Historian* (Shiji), Pan Gu's *History of the Han Dynasty* (Hanshu), Sima Guang's *Comprehensive Mirror for Aid in Government* (Zizhi Tongjian), and the petitions against Buddhism by Fu Yi and Han Yu of the Tang dynasty. In discussing Vietnamese figures, he relied mainly on Ngô Sĩ Liên's *Complete Chronicle of the Great Viet* (Đại Việt Sử Ký Toàn Thư), and to a lesser extent on Lý Tế Xuyên's *Departed Spirits of Viet Realm* (Việt Điện U Linh Tập) and Trần Thế Pháp's *Strange Tales from South of the Passes* (Lĩnh Nam Chích Quái). The breadth and wealth of cited sources, sometimes in lengthy quotation, demonstrated that the author had a good understanding of the standard literature available to a member of the Vietnamese literati class.

---

46. In the first five articles of Book 1 and Articles 4–5 of Book 3, the author presents and refutes the other alternatives to God as the Creator.

47. For example the myth of Pangu as the creator of the world (Book 1, Article 2), the great flood that occurred in Emperor Yao's time (Book 1, Article 5), or the nature of solar and lunar eclipses (Book 1, Article 12).

In terms of Confucian canonical text, the Four Books and the Five Classics were the most cited.⁴⁸ He also quoted from or referred to other texts that had circulated in Vietnam since the Lê dynasty, such as *Discourses of the Confucian School* (Kongzi Jiayu), Zhu Xi's *Outline of the Comprehensive Mirror* (Tongjian Gangmu), Hu Guang's *Compedium of Nature and Principle* (Xingli Daquan), Yuan Liaofan's *Collated Annals of the Mirror of Law* (Gangjian Hebian), and the commentaries on the classics by Dong Zhongshu, Zhu Xi, Cheng Yi, and other Confucian masters. In terms of ritual prescription, he relied on *Record of Rites* (Liji) and Zhu Xi's *Family Rituals* (Jiali).⁴⁹ These sources were common materials for civil-service examinations in Tonkin between the fifteenth and eighteenth centuries.

In contrast to his knowledge of the Confucian literature, the author was much less familiar with Daoist and Buddhist canonical works, and instead relied on secondary sources for an explanation of Daoist or Buddhist beliefs. In his discussion of Daoism, he made reference to a single chapter in the *Daodejing* and nothing from *Zhuangzi*. Likewise, his main Buddhist source was the *Sutra of Forty-Two Sections* (Tứ Thập Nhị Chương Kinh).

His information on Daoist and Buddhist beliefs and practices primarily came from lesser-known texts, such as the Daoist manual *Book of Hồng Lục* (Hồng Lục Thư)⁵⁰ and the pseudo-Buddhist texts *Lamp of the Mind* (Tâm Đăng),⁵¹ *Esoteric Branches* (Bí Chi),⁵² and *Hoàng Đồ Vĩnh*.⁵³ It is possible that the author did not have much contact with Buddhists or Daoists, so he did not get access to their literature, and instead, he relied on secondary information channeled by Confucian scholars.

---

48. Four Books refers to the Confucian books collated by Zhu Xi: the *Analects*, the *Great Learning*, the *Doctrine of the Mean*, and the *Mencius*. Five Classics refers to the books that traditionally were collected and edited by Confucius: the *Classic of Odes*, the *Classic of Documents*, the *Classic of Changes*, the *Record of Rites*, and the *Annals of Spring and Autumn*.

49. Since there were a few ritual manuals circulating in Vietnam at the time, I am not sure which version the author had used for his text. Nevertheless, the Confucian rituals in Vietnam were modeled after Chinese rituals of the Song and Ming, notably the customs set by Zhu Xi.

50. I have no information on this text except its title mentioned in *Errors*.

51. The *Lamp of the Mind* (Tâm Đăng 心燈) seems to be the work of a Daoist and Buddhist syncretistic sect, since its content and language incorporate elements from both traditions. A survival copy is preserved at the Institute of Hán Nôm Studies in Hanoi, catalogue A2481.

52. This book has been lost.

53. This book *Hoàng Đồ Vĩnh* is unidentifiable since the title seems to be incomplete. The phrase literally means "let the fortune of the emperor be eternal," and is often found in title pages of texts written during the Lê dynasty. Cf. Dror, *A Study of Religion*, 207n159.

With regard to Christian writings, the author incorporated materials from Matteo Ricci's *True Meaning* and Alexandre Rhodes's *Cathechismus*. The influence of Ricci's *True Meaning* is undeniable: even a casual reader will readily recognize that the author imitated the style of Ricci's dialogues between a Western Scholar and an Eastern Scholar. Furthermore, our author's agenda was the same as Ricci's, namely, to establish the truth of the Christian worship of God as the sole creator and benefactor of all things and to present a rational refutation of what its author perceived to be errors in the Vietnamese religions.

The influence of Ricci's *True Meaning* on *Errors* is evident on the following points. First, in terms of method, *Errors* uses the Confucian classics, historical examples, and reason as proofs of his arguments. Second, like Ricci, our author was eager to refute the errors of Neo-Confucianism, Daoism, and Buddhism. In addition, our author was polemical when discussing Buddhist doctrines. He also employed Ricci's strategy of "complementing Confucianism for repudiating Buddhism" (*buru paifo* 補儒排佛) by citing anti-Buddhist arguments written by Chinese and Vietnamese Confucians to buttress his case.

The main difference between the two works is their target audience and approach. *True Meaning* was mainly addressed to Chinese intellectuals who were well versed in philosophical discussions, and consequently, it had a more theoretical nature. *Errors* was aimed at potential Vietnamese converts and neophytes who needed to examine the merits of certain common beliefs and religious practices, and thus it was of a more practical bent. The arguments of *Errors*, even on themes similar to those of *True Meaning*—for example, concerning the Supreme Ultimate, the Sovereign on High, the goodness of human nature, the doctrine of transmigration of the soul—were philosophically unsophisticated, and instead, *Errors* was filled with concrete examples and analogies.

In terms of content, Alexandre de Rhodes's *Cathechismus* also influenced the reasoning of *Errors*. At times the author of *Errors* seemed to do nothing more than give fuller expositions and explanations of what Rhodes presented in the first four days of his catechism. A quick comparison of the main points of refutation by the author of *Errors* shows that he was heavily relying on Rhodes's work:

(1) Usage of the arguments from design to prove that the universe cannot come into existence by itself (cf. *Cathechimus*, Day 1);
(2) Homage to Heaven without worshipping the "Lord of Heaven" (God) is insufficient (Day 1);
(3) The Lord of Heaven is the sole source, the first cause of heaven, earth, and all things (Day 2);
(4) The Lord of Heaven is an all-powerful, all-knowing, all-benevolent, and all-just deity who rewards the good and punishes the wicked (Day 2);

(5) It is our duty to worship the Lord of Heaven above everything else (Day 2);
(6) The Lord of Heaven created this universe and the first human beings (Day 3);
(7) A great flood happened in the time of Noah; afterward, his descendants migrated all over the world (Day 4);
(8) There are two kinds of Buddhist teachings: external (public) and internal (esoteric), which propagate many errors (Day 4);
(9) China (and by extension Annam) were misled into following Buddhism by the error of the Chinese emperor Han Mingdi, who mistook it for the true religion of the West (Day 4);
(10) Laozi taught the false doctrine that "nothingness and emptiness make up the first principle called the great *dao*" (Day 4);
(11) The worship of Confucius is futile, for he cannot grant any favor (Day 4);
(12) The doctrine of transmigration of the soul is contrary to reason (Day 4);
(13) It is wasteful to make elaborate offerings to the deceased because they can no longer use the food and drink as if they were alive; burning paper money and offering other goods to the dead are futile (Day 4).

In addition, the author of *Errors* followed Rhodes's style of using historical figures and narratives to prove his points. The main difference between them was their sources: while Rhodes used examples from the Bible, the author of *Errors* referred to Chinese and Vietnamese historical figures. On this approach, the author of *Errors* was closer to Ricci than to Rhodes.

Genre and Intended Audience

Errors, as evidenced by the title and contents of the text, was intended as a work in the apologetic tradition. The author presented himself as a seeker of the truth who wanted to "examine and discuss the doctrines [*lẽ dạo*]" of the Three Religions "in order to better understand their errors."[54] But that is not the author's only intention. He was also interested in learning from his dialogue partner what the traditional religions had taught. He was on a quest for the "truth" as he understood it. He was convinced that once his interlocutor was exposed to the same truth, the latter would turn away from the errors of the traditional religions to embrace the worship of the true God. In the preface, the author clearly presented his agenda:

---

54. *Errors*, Preface, i. The page number of *Errors* refers to the annotated manuscript numeration (see my translation in Part II of this book).

From Italy of the Western world, I have come to the East to preach the holy way of the Lord of Heaven to the people of Annam—to the lowly and the noble, to the learned and the ignorant, to the old and the young. My goal is to introduce them to the true Lord, worship him, and follow the true way, so that after death they may attain the blessing of eternal paradise. I am now very pleased to meet a learned and virtuous Eastern Scholar. This is a good opportunity for me to learn about the three religions more fully as well as to discuss the truths concerning them.... According to *Great Learning*, "when things are examined, knowledge is reached." Therefore, this Western Scholar[55] is requesting to have a conversation with the Eastern Scholar to examine and discuss the doctrines of those three religions to better understand their errors.[56]

The target audiences were educated members of the Christian community. However, being a manuscript rather than a printed text, the book's distribution was rather limited. Given fact that this work was written in *quốc-ngữ*—the roman alphabet invented by Jesuit missionaries to communicate with their local coworkers—suggests that it was likely an internal document intended to aid the native clergy and catechists in evangelization.[57] Many learned members of the Christian communities, including catechists, seminarians, and priests, were proficient in writing this script as early as 1659.[58] They used it to write reports and letters to missionaries. Written communication for a wider audience in Tonkin before the twentieth century would require Chinese characters or the demotic Vietnamese script (*nôm*).[59]

---

55. "Western Scholar" is the form of self-reference used by Matteo Ricci in his *True Meaning of the Lord of Heaven*.

56. *Errors*, Preface, i–ii.

57. Until 1865, *quốc-ngữ* was not popular outside of Christian circles. When the French colonized the Southern part of Vietnam, they instituted programs to spread this writing style in public school as a stepping stone for the natives to learn French, and for the colonizers to learn Vietnamese.

58. In the Roman Archives of the Society of Jesus (ARSI), there is a letter by Igesico Van Tin to Giovanni Filippo de Marini, dated September 12, 1659 (ARSI Jap-Sin 81, fol. 247), and another letter by Bento Thien also addressed to Marini dated October 25, 1659 (ARSI Jap-Sin 81, fol. 246). Bento Thien also wrote a small booklet entitled "History of Annam in 1659" (ARSI, Jap-Sin 81, fols. 254–59).

59. The persistent use of *nôm* in religious and other writings among Catholics was continued until the early decades of the twentieth century. Between 1915 and 1930, *quốc-ngữ* quickly became prominent because it was used in the newspaper, magazines, and modern literature. By 1945, it virtually replaced *nôm* as the official script of Vietnam.

A secondary target of the book seems to be potential converts, especially those from the class of the literati. In the preface of Book 1, we read,

> I [the Western Scholar] deeply respect and admire Confucianism because it wisely teaches correct truths about the Five Virtues and the Five Relations. However, Confucianism not only teaches the truths; it also contains errors and falsehoods that contradict the holy way of the Lord of Heaven, which is the great and most righteous way that people everywhere must believe and follow to attain peace.
>
> Therefore, I invite the Confucian scholar to discuss and analyze with me the errors that are intermingled with Confucian truths. If during the discussion, you find that I defame Confucianism, I will take the blame; but if I speak the truth, you must agree and follow me along the same path. In doing so, you will follow the example of many other Confucian scholars who have surrendered to the truth and turned to the holy way of the Lord of Heaven—the way that has brought the people of this world to the path that leads to the most valuable and everlasting blessings.[60]

Thus, the book serves a dual purpose. For Christians, it is an apologetic manual, equipping them with arguments against the religious practices of the pagans. At the same time, the author tries to reach out to the Confucian class, attempting to reason with them regarding the "truth" that they should follow. This deliberate choice of style was no doubt modeled more on the dialogues of the more famous work, Ricci's *True Meaning*, rather than the prose style of Rhodes's *Cathechismus*. This imitation of the Riccian style speaks of the author's hope of reaching an audience similar to Ricci's, an audience consisting of the learned members of the Christian community as well as potential converts.

Errors was to help the native believers and converts to resolve the questions concerning their attitudes toward certain traditional rituals and customs. Because of the social context in which Christianity found itself a minority religion, its members were alienated from and often misunderstood by the larger society for not participating in the "common" rituals. Thus, it is not surprising that Christians and their converts felt a need to understand why Christianity rejected certain customs and religious practices. The need to defend themselves from the Confucian charge of being "unreasonable" and "ignorant" was a common concern for Vietnamese Catholics.

---

60. *Errors*, Book 1, Preface, 2.

Date and Authorship

On the basis of the information provided in the text, our author is a man "from Italy in the Western world, [who] has come to the East to preach the holy way of the Lord of Heaven to the people of Annam."[61] In other words, he was an Italian missionary who had labored in Tonkin at the time of the composition.

When attempting to date the text, we find a small reference where the author notes that "the present year [is] *nhâm-thân*, which is the thirteenth year of Cảnh Hưng's reign."[62] This allows us to date the manuscript to the year 1752. A piece of external evidence that may shed light on our inquiry is another manuscript from the same archive, entitled *Opusculum de sectis apud Sinenses et Tunkinenses*. This manuscript, written in Latin by the Italian missionary Adriano di Santa Thecla in 1750,[63] was another treatise on Tonkinese religions. After closely examining this work (which I will present in a later section) and comparing it with our present manuscript, we can conclude that the two are contemporary.

Using these data, we can begin to consider possible candidates for authorship. In the eighteenth century, Italian missionaries in Tonkin were laboring only in the vicariate of East Tonkin. If the manuscript were written by one of them, its author would have had to arrive in Tonkin at least a few years before 1752, in order to master the language and culture to the extent that he would have been able to produce such a work. Another the important datum is that the manuscript mentions the worship at the Temple of the Military, which, according to imperial record, was only established in 1740.[64] This brings us closer to the range of composition: 1740–1752.

Was the author Jesuit, Dominican, or Augustinian? In the period of 1740–1750, there were only a few Jesuits and Dominicans of Italian origin who labored in Tonkin, and none of them was reported to have left behind any religious writings.[65]

---

61. *Errors*, Preface, i.

62. *Errors*, Book 1, Article 5, 29.

63. Adriano di Santa Thecla, *Opusculum de sectis apud Sinenses et Tunkinenses / A Small Treatise on the Sects among the Chinese and Tonkinese*. Annotated, translated, and introduced by Olgar Dror, as *A Study of Religion in China and North Vietnam in the Eighteenth Century* (Ithaca, NY: Cornell University Press / SEAP, 2002).

64. *Cương Mục*, Chính biên, 38:33–34 (translation 2:529).

65. The two Jesuits were Isidoro Luci (from 1694 to 1719) and Francesco-Maria Buctharelli (from 1715 to 1723), and the two Dominicans were Raymond Lezoli (from 1681 to 1706) and Thomas de Sextri (from 1701 to 1737). Data on these missionaries are drawn from Marillier, *Nos pères dans la foi*, 2:99–100, 102, and 112–14, respectively.

The largest number of Italian missionaries during this period was a group of Discalced Augustinians who evangelized in East Tonkin for nearly sixty years (1701–1759). They were a small group, totaling thirteen to seventeen Italians[66] and six Vietnamese[67] who served in Kẻ Sặt and Kẻ Vân near Hải Dương. Despite their small number, there were several prominent writers among them. The first was Hilario Costa, better known by his religious name Hilario di Gesù (1696–1754), who arrived in 1723 at the young age of twenty-seven.[68] Hilario di Gesù (henceforth, Hilario) had a talent for language and was respected by many missionaries and native priests as a prolific writer,[69] authoring at least a dozen different works in Vietnamese, including the *Dị Đoan Chi Giáo* (Superstitious Teachings), *Đại Học Chi Đạo* (Path to Great Learning), and *Index historicus*.[70] Another prominent Augustinian missionary was Adriano di Santa Thecla (1697–1764), who arrived in 1738.[71] Adriano di Santa Thecla (henceforth, Adriano), the author of the aforementioned *Opusculum de sectis* (1750), was a close associate of Hilario and was appointed by the latter to be the vicar general of the vicariate in 1749. The third Italian, Domenico di San Martino (1703–1741), who arrived together with Adriano in the same year, was known to be the author of the two-volume work *Chinese Superstitions and Rites*.[72] Other Augustinians did not leave

---

66. On these Italian Augustinian missionaries, see Marillier, *Nos pères dans la foi*, 2:123–27. According to the list compiled by Gabriele M. Raimondo, seventeen Augustinian missionaries went to Tonkin altogether; four were not listed in Marillier's account of the clergy in Tonkin. See Gli Agostiniani Scalzi nel Vietnam e nella Cina, 39–48.

67. On these Vietnamese Augustinians, see Marillier, *Nos pères dans la foi*, 2:63–64.

68. Hilario di Gesù became bishop of Core (or Corycus) and coadjutor of East Tonkin in 1736 and took over the administration of the vicariate the following years. He was the papal visitor to settle the dispute among the clergy in Cochinchina in 1750s. During his episcopacy, he ordained a number of Vietnamese, both secular and religious, to the priesthood (six in 1739, three in 1741, two in 1744, three in 1748, four in 1749, four in 1750, and two in 1751). Source: Marillier, *Nos pères dans la foi*, 2:124–26, Barbagallo and Raimondo, *Gli Agostiniani Scalzi nel Vietnam e nella Cina*, 42–43. His letters are collected in *Epistolario III°: Lettere di P. Ilario Costa di Gesù*, ed. Pietro Scalia (Rome: Edizione Presenza Agostiniana, 2000).

69. As described in the words of the contemporary MEP priest (and later bishop) Louis Néez, "He has a wonderful talent for writing. Because of him, the mission in Tonkin has quite a few books, which he has written not only for the use of his religious brothers but also for the whole Christian population in his vicariate." Marillier, *Nos pères dans la foi*, 2:124.

70. These works were acknowledged by Adriano di Santa Thecla (henceforth, Adriano) in his preface to the *Opusculum de sectis*. A list of Hilario di Gesù's work is found in Adriano's *Life of Hilario* composed after the bishop's death. Scalia, *Epistolario III°*, 307–339, esp. 335.

71. See his biography in Marillier, *Nos pères dans la foi*, 2:126–27; and Dror, *A Study of Religion*, 27–29.

72. Barbagallo and Raimondo, *Gli Agostiniani Scalzi nel Vietnam e nella Cina*, 44.

behind any writings. In all likelihood, the author of *Errors* must be one or more of these three missionaries.

A Hypothesis of Authorship and History of Composition

Although the exact date of composition of *Errors* and its author remain a mystery, my hypothesis is that Hiliario di Gesù was the main author of this work. After becoming a bishop in 1736, Hilario was concerned about the formation of indigenous clergy. Thus he might have begun composing religious materials in Vietnamese for his catechists and priests to use. Then he had to deal with the aftermath of the Rites Controversy when the papal bull *Ex Quo Singulari* (1742) explicitly forbade the concessions to local customs, including the cult to Confucius, to *Thành Hoàng* and other national spirits, and to the ancestors. Hilario might have composed the *Dị Đoan Chi Giáo* (Superstitious Teachings) in the mid-1640s to help his indigenous priests and catechists cope with the issues. Later, Hilario, with some assistance from the literati, also expanded the *Dị Đoan Chi Giáo*, renaming it *Tam Giáo Chư Vọng* in 1752.

My hypothesis that the vicar apostolic of East Tonkin, Hilario di Gesù, is the main author of *Errors* is highly probable. Of all the missionaries living in the second quarter of the eighteenth century, none surpassed him in the knowledge of the religions in Tonkin. In all likelihood, Hilario was working with his close associates, not excluding Adriano. The fact that *Errors* is preserved in the archives of the MEP points to the esteem and friendship that Louis Néez, the vicar apostolic of West Tonkin, had for Hilario and his writings. If this work had not been written by Hilario or in his name, it probably would not have survived to make an impact on later Christian apologetic works of the eighteenth and nineteenth centuries.

In addition, given the extensive knowledge of Confucian literature and Vietnamese history displayed by the composer of the text, we cannot rule out that *Errors* could also be a composite work by multiple authors, including Vietnamese priests and/or the Christian members of the literati. Given the fact that missionary works in Tonkin during the eighteenth century were clandestine activities only, tolerated at times by the ruling authorities, it is unlikely that a single Western missionary at this time could have sufficient time to acquire such an in-depth knowledge of Confucianism and Vietnamese history. He had to rely on his Vietnamese associates to supply the necessary information.[73]

---

73. Even the most prominent MEP bishop of Cochinchina, Pierre Pigneau de Béhaine (1741–1799), did not exhibit in his writings such a mastery of Confucian texts and Vietnamese history as the author(s) of *Errors* did, despite the bishop's claim that "with the help of God, I have

In terms of composition and authorship, the author of *Errors* displays a comprehensive knowledge of Chinese and Vietnamese written sources. He also was well acquainted with the rituals and customs among the Tonkinese of his time, an acquaintance due most likely to direct observation. If the author had not identified himself as an Italian missionary in the preface, the work could have been understood to have been written by any Tonkinese catechist or priest.

Refutation as a Method of Defending Christian Practice

Errors of the Three Religions is a conversation between a Western (Christian) scholar and his Eastern (Confucian) counterpart on selected religious topics of the three traditional religions. The Western Scholar usually begins the conversation with an observation, which he then invites his interlocutor, the Eastern Scholar, to explain and clarify, and concludes by giving his own thoughts on the issue at hand. Though the title of the work is the "errors" of the Three Religions, the fact is, for both the author and his interlocutor, the most important task is the search for religious truth. Since the author is convinced that his religion is "the holy way of the Lord of Heaven, which is the great and most righteous way"[74] for all people everywhere, he will judge the other's position by the Christian perspective.

To legitimate his position, the author employs several strategies for his arguments. First, he appeals to history, using both historical examples from China and Vietnam to show that most of the customs under discussion are of late origin, and therefore not as indispensable as one might think. Secondly, he appeals to reason as a means to examine the issues at hand, to see whether they are true or false, rather than accepting them merely because of tradition. In order to refute the traditional beliefs and long-held customs, he uses reason to expose the internal inconsistency, especially regarding those he feels are irrational, such as the doctrine of transmigration, the custom of burning joss paper, and the popular practices of divination and fortune-telling.

In the process, he quotes extensively from Confucian texts as well as books of history to support or refute a case, but everything must be evaluated in the light of reason. Here the author applied the exact same method of investigation as any Confucian scholar would follow: examine the data, interpret it, and use his

---

been studying Chinese and Vietnamese [*nôm*] writing systems in the past seven years. I am proficient enough to read and understand their books with ease." Quoted in Adrien Launay, *Histoire de la mission de la Cochinchine: Documents historiques* (Paris, 1927), 3:7.

74. *Errors*, Book 1, Preface, 1.

reason to find the truth in it. His extensive use of the classical texts and historical figures intends to show that his arguments are to be taken seriously and that *Errors* can be an aid for native priests and catechists in reaching out to a wider audience. In doing so, he continued the path set down by Ricci in sixteenth-century China and Rhodes in seventeenth-century Vietnam.

The use of reason is important in these works. This is a heritage of the emphasis on using reason to explain the Christian faith. Since the Confucian gentry of China and Vietnam were intellectuals, the use of reason is an important method of dialogue with which to engage their interests. Ricci, Rhodes, and the author of *Errors* all wanted to demonstrate the harmony between reason and Christian faith and argued that the new faith they tried to introduce to the people of China and Vietnam does not contain absurd and irrational teachings.

The classification of issues into three categories, the "errors" of Confucianism, Daoism, and Buddhism, may strike the reader as arbitrary because, at times, the issue under discussion has nothing to do with the religion in question. For example, when discussing funeral rites, the author strives to distinguish between Confucian rites (which he sees as legitimate) and the Buddhist rites (which he sees as superstitious). He links the practice of burning paper money and paper goods to Buddhism, but this practice was of Chinese origin and was not a Buddhist custom. In another example, he classifies geomancy as a Confucian practice, whereas it belongs to popular religion. The mixture of cults and religious practices reflects a reality of eighteenth-century Vietnam in which rituals and beliefs were observed without concern for their origin. However, one must remember that the work was composed at a time when missionary activities in Tonkin were illegal. Under these circumstances, the author of *Errors* might not have had the proper time or the adequate resources to investigate the traditional religions thoroughly by studying their sacred texts and rituals and discussing them with their representatives. Most information presented in the book was likely to have been supplied by his Vietnamese converts, some of whom might have been former Daoist or Buddhist ritualists.

Errors follows both *True Meaning* and *Cathechismus* in regarding Daoism as superstitious and Buddhism as evil. With regard to Confucianism, like Ricci and Rhodes, the author of *Errors* was more nuanced and careful in his criticism because he did not want to alienate the ruling class, which was dominated by Confucians. The strategy of using original Confucian classics to refute Neo-Confucianism and to use the Confucian arguments against Buddhism conforms with Ricci's principle of "complimenting Confucianism to repudiate Buddhism" (*buru paifo*). In this sense, *Errors* is essentially a selective text that deals with certain religious aspects of Vietnamese traditional religions. Despite these weaknesses, the reader still encounters an author who is open-minded and fair enough to willingly enter into dialogue with members of another religious tradition.

3

Of Gods and Heroes

WORSHIP IN TRADITIONAL VIETNAM

WESTERN TRAVELERS TO Tonkin in the seventeenth and eighteenth centuries, whether missionaries or traders, noted an active religious life there. Temples and shrines existed in every village and district. Various feasts were held throughout the year, and elaborate funerals and ceremonies were part of their ancestral piety.[1] These visitors could not avoid the syncretistic and eclectic character of the traditional cultic practice of Vietnam. There was no real sense of separation between the sacred and secular, or between the religious and civil. On the one hand, they observed the high ceremonies performed by kings and officers; on the other hand, they also saw the same people petitioning various spirits to meet their needs. Vietnamese people believed in and worshipped all visible and invisible powers.

The Three Religions were recognized throughout the country, but none gained a distinct body of adherents in the general public. A person worshipped indiscriminately at a pagoda or temple, praying to various deities at his or her convenience. It was not rare to find images of the buddhas and bodhisattvas as well as statues of other spirits, sages, and eminent heroes side by side on the same altar. The rituals performed toward these beings, specified in rites manuals, were almost the same for the public and private worship, whether they were for the spirits, deified heroes, or exemplary figures. The distinctiveness of these rites—Confucianist, Buddhist, or Daoist—was not a matter of concern when it came to

---

1. See a 1659 description by Bento Thien in his "History of Annam" about the various festivals in Tonkin, trans. George Dutton, in Dutton, Werner, and Whitmore, *Sources of Vietnamese Tradition*, 223–26.

the powers of these gods and spirits to procure material blessings and protection from harm. Efficacy was all that mattered.[2]

Of all the issues discussed in *Errors*, that which most sustains the interest of the author concerns the worship to many spirits, deified heroes, and religious figures in Tonkin. Given that Christian converts had to live among their neighbors and relatives who believed in the power of these figures, the main concern of the author of *Errors* is to refute the many forms of non-Christian worship that were prevalent. From a Christian monotheistic perspective, the worship of other gods and spirits is strictly forbidden.

In discussing the many cults and religious customs, the author often starts out with a description of the rite or cult, its origin, and how it is practiced before giving his assessment of the merit of the rite or cult in question. In the following sections, I also use a similar approach to provide the modern audience with a sense of traditional Vietnamese cults in the court, in the village community, at home, and in a religious setting.

An Overview of Traditional Vietnamese Worship
Spirits, Heaven, and the Ancestors

Underlying Vietnamese religious observances was a basic belief in the communication between the spirits and humans. As Léopold Cadière observed, the "true religion" of the Viet people was the cult of spirits.[3] The innumerable spirits were either deities or spiritual beings (*thần*) that were to be honored, or ghosts (*ma*) and demons (*quỷ*) that were to be feared. *Thần* included past heroes, immortals, or people who had made great contributions to the village or nation. They also included benevolent and malicious spirits who inhabited rocks, trees, animals, and the rest of the natural world. People made offerings to them to avoid disasters and obtain success. Ghosts and demons included the wandering souls (*cô hồn*) and wicked spirits who sought to harm people. They were appeased by making offerings or neutralized with the help of magicians and sorcerers.

August Heaven (*ông Trời*) is a supreme deity of the Vietnamese pantheon, although it is not clear whether this deity is indigenous to Vietnam or an import of the sky god of the Zhou. He is conceived anthropomorphically as a being—a creative source, supreme ruler, and moral judge—who enabled people to live according to his will: to do good and avoid evil. Since he is

---

2. For a solid introduction to the cultic life in traditional Vietnam, see Léopold Cadière, "La religion des Annamites," in *Croyances et pratiques religieuses*, 1:1–23.

3. Cadière, *Croyances et pratiques*, 1:6.

in charge of the whole cosmos, August Heaven, like an earthly king, would appoint numerous spiritual assistants to help him govern the natural world and human affairs.

The belief in Heaven in traditional Vietnam was never formalized into an organized religion: there were no sacred scriptures, images, temples, prayers, and no special class of priest or minister. There were only believers and prayers. All worship to Heaven was done outdoors at an open altar. Although everybody believed in Heaven, only the king could perform the solemn worship of Heaven (*tế Giao*), a rite borrowed from the Chinese, to legitimize the king's ruling as the "son of Heaven." Acting on behalf of his people, the king prayed to Heaven for good weather and protection from plagues and disasters. In addition, the king or his representative performed other official sacrifices that were regulated by the Minister of the Rites, who followed the customs laid down by ancient ritual manuals.

While the official worship of Heaven is a privilege reserved for the king, the common people turned to lesser spirits and especially to their ancestors. At the communal level, every village had its own guardian spirits, called Thành Hoàng, who resided in the main altar in the community hall (*đình*). The cult of the village gods was important for the local religious life. In exchange for the villagers' veneration, the guardian spirits were expected to protect the village from disasters and harm, ensure the villagers' health and prosperity, and maintain harmony. Ceremonial feasts honoring the village gods were carried out at regular intervals and were celebrations of the communal life of the village. Although some spirits were venerated locally, other spirits of deified heroes were also worshipped in different villages. The royal court devised a system that ranked the spirits to be worshipped in three grades: supreme, middle, the lower.[4] Supremely ranked spirits were usually national heroes, whose deeds were retold in well-known hagiographies and who were worshipped in more than one locale. The other two classes of spirits consisted of less well-known figures, and they were only venerated locally.

Domestically, the ancestors are the most important spirits because of their relationships with their living descendants. Whether or not one believed in the ability of the ancestors to bless their descendants and save them from troubles, the cult of the ancestors was the public expression of the virtue of filiality and family etiquette. These memorial observances included any dead member of the family across generations, even a child. The unmarried deceased of the family

---

4. The process is called "establishing the rank and promotion of the spirits" (*tạo khoa bạt thần*), and is described in *Errors*, Book 1, Article 9.

were particularly cherished, since they had no direct descendant to remember them. Acting upon the Confucian principle "to serve the dead as if they were alive" (*sự tử như sự sinh*), people offered food and drink, fruits and flowers, and burned incense to the ancestors at special times of the year, and especially on their death anniversaries when memorial banquets were held. Important events in the family (e.g., birth, marriage, death) were communicated to the ancestors as if they were still present. Thus, the cult of the ancestors was common to Vietnamese of all religious persuasions, for it kept the memory of the ancestors alive and strengthened the familial bonds. Many large families contributed to the building and maintenance of a common ancestral hall (*từ đường*), where the tablets or pictures of the deceased from the past five generations—from one's great-great-grandparents down to one's deceased parents—were placed on the family altars. The details of the ancestral rites will be discussed in the next chapter.

People of a particular trade or craft also worshipped the founder of their trade or craft (*tổ sư*) on the family altar. In Vietnamese homes, there might also be the worship of spirits that protect and bring prosperity, such as the Local God (*thổ địa*), the Kitchen God (*táo quân*), or other guardian spirits. Unlike the ancestors, these lesser spirits did not have special rites dedicated to them, nor did they require a space in the family altar. Rather, a simple offering of incense and foods was enough to appease them.[5]

Temples and Rites

Traditional places of worship in Vietnam were both indoors and outdoors. Indoor structures included a number of different types of buildings. The *đình* was a communal house, a place of gathering for the community, in which the back chamber sometimes was reserved to worship the tutelary deity of the village.[6] The *đền* was a regional or national temple erected in honor of a king, a deity, or a famous person who acquired merit among the people. A *đền* of a female goddess was sometimes called a *phủ*, and a *đền* of a Daoist deity was called a *điện*. The *chùa* was a Buddhist pagoda or temple; it was called an *am* if there was no resident monk or nun. The *miếu* or shrine was in the form of a small temple. The *văn miếu* was a *đền* dedicated to Confucius and his disciples in the capital or at

---

5. See a description in *Errors*, Book 1, Article 11. For a survey of popular Guild Founders, see Nguyễn Vinh Phúc and Nguyễn Duy Hinh, *Các Thành Hoàng & Tín Ngưỡng Thăng Long* [The Guardian Spirits and Their Cults in Hanoi] (Hanoi: NXB Lao Động, 2009), 132–49.

6. Not every village has its guardian spirit worshipped in its *đình*, especially if there is a temple dedicated to that deity in the vicinity.

the headquarters of the provinces. At the country or district level, it was called the *văn chỉ*, while at the ward or village level it was called *từ chỉ*. The outdoor worship had no permanent structure but took place mostly at the *đàn* or temporary earthen platforms built for sacrificial purposes.

With the exception of Buddhist or Daoist ritual masters who conducted religious ceremonies, there was no separate class of clergy to celebrate most of the public rituals. In a family, the head of the household led the ceremonies, sometimes with the assistance of a Confucian scholar if the head were illiterate. At the village and district levels, appointed officers conducted the ceremonies, while at the state level the king himself or his surrogate acted as the minister of the rites. The Confucian literati, although not trained as ritual specialists, were usually educated enough to be the de facto masters of ceremony in both public rituals and private devotions.

Because the Vietnamese were supposed to honor the living and the dead through rituals, they made offerings (*cúng*) or solemn sacrifices (*tế*). *Cúng* entail presenting the dead and the spirits with materials that express the devotion of the living. These offerings might be useful to the spirits and might include food, wine, fruits, and flowers. In the act of *cúng*, the offerings were placed on a table and incense was burned. Sometimes, the worshippers would say a short intercessory prayer was said (*khấn*), either aloud or silently. They would offer gestures of honor called *vái/bái* (bowing) or *lạy* (deep bowing) in front of a spirit tablet or statue. *Tế*, a word borrowed from the Confucian tradition, expressed a more solemn form of *cúng*. It was used in conjunction with imperial cults where the rubrics of the rites were stipulated by ritual manuals. In Vietnamese tradition, *cúng* and *tế* together were the external expressions of gratitude and honor toward those who were deemed worthy of respect. They were different only in degree and were used to remind the living of the merit and power of the dead.

Official Cultic Rituals

According to the *Record of Rites*, ancient kings sacrificed to the gods and spirits that governed the natural and human worlds. Rituals of imperial China and Vietnam could be systematized into a three-tiered hierarchy. The emperor presided at the solemn sacrifices to the most exalted gods in and around the capital. High-ranking ministers performed the middle sacrifices to the lesser gods and spirits. Local officials offered regular sacrifices at the county level. All sacrifices were performed according to specific rites on particular days determined by the Minister of Rites. The cultic life of the Lê-Trịnh era (1599–1786) followed customs set by the Ming court and codified in imperial protocols such as the

Collected Regulations in the Lê Dynasty (Lê Triều Hội Điển),[7] and Phan Huy Chú's *Categorized Records of the Institutions of Successive Dynasties* (Lịch Triều Hiến Chương Loại Chí).[8]

The official rituals venerated the gods and spirits, not for personal blessings for the one who made the offering, but rather, for the sake of the people within his responsibility or care. Acting on behalf of his community, the official who offered sacrifice exercised the governance of his domain—a world including humans, gods, and spirits. These cults acted as points of contact and methods of maintaining harmony between the human world and the spirit world. They nurtured the gods and enhanced their power while simultaneously fostering the well-being of the patron. Still, the sacrifices were not a means to appease the gods and spirits with worldly materials; the efficacy of these rites depended on the celebrant's sincerity and reverence.

Sacrifices to Heaven and Earth

The annual sacrifices to Heaven and Earth that were to be performed at the beginning of the year by kings and emperors were the most solemn rites of the official religion. During the Lê-Trịnh era, the royal processions to and from the platform of sacrifice (*nam giao*) were scenes of great pomp, with elephants, horses, soldiers, mandarins, officers, and a great number of attendants.[9] Westerners who lived in Thăng Long at the time took notice of this elaborate ceremony, although they themselves were not allowed to attend. While Samuel Baron called it the "Ceremony of the King's Blessing of the Country,"[10]

---

7. Institute of Hán Nôm, ms. A 52; translated by Trần thị Kim Anh in *Một Số Điển Chế và Văn Bản Pháp Luật Việt Nam: từ thế kỷ XV đến XVIII* [An Anthology of Ancient Vietnamese Regulations and Legal Codes: From the Fifteenth to the Eighteenth Century], ed. Nguyễn Ngọc Nhuận (Hanoi: NXB Khoa Học Xã Hội, 2009), 2:12–218; on the regulation of the rites and ceremonies, see 2:151–218.

8. This book is a nineteenth-century encyclopedia of imperial Vietnam. It is divided into ten books, which cover (1) Vietnamese geography, (2) biographies of famous people, (3) offices and officials, (4) rites and ceremonies, (5) civil examinations and their laureates, (6) economy and taxation, (7) laws and regulations, (8) the military, (9) literature, and (10) international relations. Information on traditional ceremonies is found in Book 4.

9. Phan Huy Chú, *Loại Chí*, Lễ nghi chí 1 (translation, 1:722–23. Also see a contemporary discussion of this ritual for venerating heaven by Phạm Đình Hổ, ca. 1790s, trans. George Dutton and Matthew Cochran in Dutton, Werner, and Whitmore, *Sources of Vietnamese Tradition*, 186–88.

10. Samuel Baron, "On the Ceremony of the King's Blessing the Country, Vulgarly amongst Them, Called Boua-dee-yaw, or According to Their Characters, Can-ja," chap. 14 in *A Description of the Kingdom of Tonqueen*, in Dror and Taylor, *Views of Seventeenth-Century Vietnam*, 259–61.

Alexander de Rhodes more accurately described it as "offering the sacrifice to the Supreme Ruler."[11]

The sacrifices to the spirits of Heaven and Earth originated in China in the Zhou dynasty. According to the regulations of the *Zhou Book of Rites* (Chu Lễ), the sacrifice to "August Heaven Supreme Sovereign" (*Hạo Thiên Thượng Đế*) took place on the winter solstice in an outdoor enclosure planted with trees situated in the southern suburbs of the capital. The altar of heaven, a round, three-tiered platform, was erected in the middle of this suburban enclosure (*giao*). It was here that the king or emperor prostrated himself and made his offerings on behalf of the people, praying for the blessings of heaven. The sacrifice to "August Earth" (*Hoàng Địa Kỳ*), which was enacted for the sake of symbolic symmetry, took place on the summer solstice on a two-tiered square platform in the northern suburbs of the capital (*xã*). The ceremony was similar to that to Heaven, but it was simpler. The shape of the platforms reflected the common belief in a round heaven and a square earth. Of the two cults, the sacrifice to Heaven was far more important and dominated the official cultic life. Still, because Heaven needs the nurture of the Earth to sustain life, the cult of Earth was needed. Eventually, the cult of Earth was absorbed into the cult of Heaven, and its sacrifice was performed at the *giao*.

The first recorded sacrifice to Heaven in Vietnam happened under the reign of King Lý Anh Tông (1138–1175), who built a round platform in 1153 to perform sacrifices to Heaven every three years.[12] The Trần dynasty, however, did not follow the practice. After more than two hundred years of neglect, the rite was restored under the reign of King Lê Thánh Tông. In 1462, the king decreed an annual sacrifice to Heaven and Earth to take place on the first day of spring. Three earthen platforms for the purpose of imperial sacrifice were built in the southern suburb of Thăng Long. The main one was for the sacrifice to Heaven and Earth, while the left and right platforms were for the sacrifices to the stars and the spirits of mountains and rivers.[13] The sacrifice at *nam giao* was interrupted during the Mạc era and was restored under the Trịnh. However, it underwent significant changes during the seventeenth century. In 1600, General Trịnh Tùng began to make to sacrifice to Heaven together with the king, effectively making himself a coruler.[14] This practice was maintained by

---

11. We do not know if Rhodes ever witnessed it, but he discussed it in his catechism (*Catechismus*, Day 1). See Phan, *Mission and Catechesis*, 221–22.

12. *Cương Mục*, Chính biên, 5:6 (translation, 1:387).

13. *Cương Mục*, Chính biên, 19:17 (translation, 1: 962).

14. *Cương Mục*, Chính biên, 31:1–2 (translation, 2:225–26).

the Trịnh until the end of the eighteenth century. The Trịnh also enlarged the sacrificial platform and built a permanent structure with a roof and pillars on the principal platform in 1663.[15]

The sacrifice to Heaven (*tế giao*) during this period can be briefly described as follows.[16] To prepare for the ceremony, the king fasted for two days prior to the actual celebration, while the altars and the sacrifices were prepared. On the day of the ceremony, the king wore a black robe, and, seated in a carriage, he led the procession from his palace to the *giao*. Upon arrival, he went through the third-level gate into the left pavilion and changed into a ceremonial robe. The lord of Tonkin did the same in the pavilion on the right. Then the king, assisted by his attendants, washed his hands before proceeding to the first-level gate that led to the altars. The lord did the same, while the mandarins and military officers remained outside at the second-level gate.

The master of ceremonies announced each step that the king and his officers were to follow. First, the king went to his position before the altars (*bái vị*), where he bowed to the spirit tablets of "August Heaven Supreme Sovereign" (*Hạo Thiên Thượng Đế*) and "August Earth" (*Hoàng Địa Kỳ*). Next, an assistant made the blood offering of the sacrificial animals (*ế mao huyết*). Then, the king washed (*quán tẩy*) and dried (*thuế cân*) his hands. Next, the king knelt and offered incense to Heaven (*thượng hương*), after which a designated mandarin read a written prayer (*độc chúc*) aloud. After the prayer, all prostrated themselves (*phủ phục*) in silence. Then on their knees, they bowed four times before standing up again (*cúc cung bái*). Music accompanied every step. At the end, the master of ceremonies announced the completion of the ceremony (*lễ tất*). Afterward, the king and lord re-entered their pavilions to change clothing again and returned to the palace.[17]

---

15. *Toàn Thư*, Bản kỷ, 19:4a (translation, 3:269). This structure was a casualty of war during the Tây Sơn era. When the Nguyễn dynasty established its capital in Huế, it built a new and elaborate three-tiered square platform with a round platform on the top in the south of the capital to sacrifice to Heaven and Earth. The sacrifice was performed here on a regular basis (though not annually from the 1880s) until 1943. For a description of the place, see Cadière, "Le sacrifice du Nam Giao," in *Croyances et pratiques réligieuses*, 1:91–101.

16. See the description of *Yết Giao* (Giao Ceremony) in the chapter "Lễ Thuộc" [On the Rites] of *Lê Triều Hội Điển* in Nguyễn Ngọc Nhuận, *Một Số Điển Chế và Văn Bản Pháp Luật Việt Nam*, 2:183–85; "Lễ Tế Trời Đất" [Sacrifice to Heaven and Earth] in *Loại Chí*, Lễ nghi chí 2 (translation, 1:732–38).

17. In the sacrifice of *giao* during the Lê dynasty, only incense was offered. The sacrifice was expanded to include meat, wine, a piece of silk, and a piece of jade in the manner of sacrifices to the spirits during the Nguyễn dynasty. For the *giao* ceremonies under the Nguyễn dynasty (1802–1945), see Cadière, *Croyances et pratiques réligieuses*, 1:102–28.

Curiously, this most important religious ceremony of the imperial times was only briefly discussed in *Errors*, even though it was mentioned extentively in Rhodes's catechism and Baron's description of Tonkin.[18] The reason might be twofold. First, because it was designated to honor Heaven, it was not an "error" to be refuted. And second, since it was an exclusively royal function that had little effect on the Christians, the author might have felt it unnecessary to elaborate on it. On the other hand, although described by the author of *Errors*, the sacrifices to spirits of nature such as the sun, the moon, the stars, the spirits of flood and drought, mountain and rivers,[19] and so on, played a subsidiary role in traditional Vietnamese cultic life.[20] They were seen as extensions of the more general cult of Heaven and Earth rather than possessing their own cultic status. Offerings were made to them in conjunction with other ceremonies.

Sacrifices to the Divine Farmer and Other Spirits of Nature

Another important official cult was the sacrifice to the God of Grain or Thần Hậu Tắc, personified as the Divine Farmer or Thần Nông, for a good harvest. In Vietnam, the sacrifices to the God of Soil (*xã*) and the God of Grain (*tắc*) were performed together beginning with the Lý dynasty.[21] In 1484, King Lê Thánh Tông dedicated a platform in Hồng Mai village, Thanh Đàm district, to the sacrifice to the Divine Farmer.[22]

As in the other solemn sacrifices, the king had to fast for one day to prepare himself while the altars and sacrifices were arranged on a raised platform (*đàn*). On the day of the sacrifice, the king and his mandarins proceeded from his palace to the platform. He first stopped to wash and change into a ceremonial robe before ascending the platform to make the sacrifices. The actual celebration followed a pattern of prescribed steps for a solemn sacrifice in the ritual manual.[23]

---

18. See Rhodes, Catechismus, Day 1 (Phan, Mission and Catechesis, 221–22); Baron, *A Description of the Kingdom of Tonqueen*, chap. 14 (Dror and Taylor, *Views on Seventeenth-Century Vietnam*, 259–61).

19. See *Errors*, Book 1, Article 6. Cf. *Opusculum*, Chapter 1, Article 3.

20. Phan Huy Chú only makes brief mention of the sacrifices to the spirits of Wind, Thunder, Cloud, and Rain together "according to rites of the Ming." *Loại Chí*, Lễ nghi chí 6 (translation,1:872).

21. *Cương Mục*, Chính biên, 3:14 (translation,1:313) records that "[in 1048] platforms were built to perform sacrifices to the God of Soil (*xã*) and the God of Grain (*tắc*)."

22. *Cương Mục*, Chính biên, 23:43 (translation,1:1124). Nowadays, it is the Bạch Mai ward in the Hai Bà Trưng district of Hanoi.

23. It consists of the following steps: gathering and going into position (*tựu bái vị*); bowing to the spirit tablets (*bái*); standing up (*hưng, bình thân*); burying the blood and hair of the

After the sacrifice, the king went down to a reserved field and ploughed a couple lines before handing the task to officers who one by one followed suit (*lễ tịch điền*). This ceremonial ploughing was meant to emphasize the importance of agricultural work that even the king could not neglect. In the Lê-Trịnh era, the sacrifice to the Divine Farmer was performed by the lord of Tonkin rather than the king himself, and the ceremonial ploughing of the field was delegated to the mayor of Thăng Long.[24]

According to information given in *Errors*, the sacrifice to the Divine Farmer also took place in villages. Offerings were made to the Divine Farmer several times annually at the Hạ Điền (Coming down to the field) and Thượng Điền (Going up from the field) planting ceremonies, and also at the Thường Tân (New Crop) ceremony during the harvest. The author of *Errors* articulates his mixed feelings about this rite. He writes,

> To remember and praise the merit of the Divine Farmer for teaching people how to farm is appropriate.... [I]t is not appropriate, simply for the sake of honoring him, to consider him a holy being with the power to help people cultivate and to bless them with good harvests and other good things. There is only one Lord of Heaven who endows people with all kinds of skills, giving them the five kinds of grains in the field, possessions in the home, and peace in the village. For that reason, do not put your trust in the Divine Farmer and offer sacrifices to him.[25]

Since the cult's primary function was to honor the Divine Farmer for teaching people agriculture, the author wants to affirm the positive value of this rite but feels that it contradicts his belief in the exclusive devotion to God.

---

sacrificial animals (*ế mao huyết*); welcoming the spirit (*nghinh thần*); washing the hands (*quán tẩy*); offering incense (*thượng hương*); offering a piece of silk (*điện bạch*); offering of a wine and meat libation (*sơ hiến lễ*); kneeling and prostrating (*quỵ, phủ phục*); proclaiming the prayer (*độc chúc*); kneeling and prostrating (*quỵ, phủ phục*), bowing two times (*bái*); sometimes a second and third round of wine libation were also offered (*á hiến lễ*); drinking the blessed wine (*ẩm phúc*); bidding farewell to the spirit (*từ thần*). After the master of ceremonies burned the piece of silk and the prayer paper, he announced the completion of the ceremony (*lễ tất*). See Phan Huy Chú, *Loại Chí*, Lễ nghi chí 6 (translation, 1:873).

24. Phan Huy Chú complained about this, saying, "In the ancient times, the kings went to *nam giao* on the first day of the year to sacrifice to Heaven, and he also sacrificed to the Spirit of the Rice (thần Hậu Tắc) for a good harvest.... Now, since the time of the restored Lê, the Lord Trịnh went to sacrifice on behalf of the king, and the ploughing of the field was delegated to the mayor of the capital. Alas, they only did it to keep the form but not the essence of the rites as the ancient kings did." *Loại Chí*, Lễ nghi chí 6 (translation, 1:874).

25. *Errors*, Book 1, Article 7, 45.

Sacrifice to the Imperial Ancestors

The cult of the imperial ancestors also held exalted status among the official rituals. In essence, it was not different from the regular cult of ancestors, which I will discuss in the next chapter. However, the rituals were much more elaborate than what a commoner could afford. Five times a year, at the beginning of each season and on the anniversaries of the deaths of imperial ancestors, the king offered a carefully prepared feast of meat, wine, rice and other material objects to his forebears. Imperial ancestors were treated like demigods. Being omnipresent, they were expected to exert auspicious power over the throne. The sacrifice to the deceased kings—up to nine degrees of the king's ancestors—took place at the imperial ancestral shrine (*thái miếu*) inside the imperial palace. During the Lê-Trịnh era, the Trịnh lords also erected their own Ancestral Shrine and made offerings to their ancestors in a similar manner, although with slightly less solemnity than those of the king. In addition, the deceased kings and lords shared a portion of the ritual feasts offered at the altar of Heaven and at the Sacrifice to the Chief's Banner. These will be discussed later.

Cult of Confucius

Strictly speaking, the cult of Confucius was not a religious ceremony but a civic cult sanctioned by the state in both China and Vietnam. After his death, Confucius's disciples and descendants continued honoring his memory through annual memorial sacrifices at his tomb at Qufu in Shandong province. The actual cult of Confucius, however, began with the sacrifice to Confucius and his disciples in the capital's imperial academy in 241 CE, during the Three Kingdom Era.[26] This marks the first recorded official celebration of the cult outside of his hometown. The court extended a similar honor to the Duke of Zhou, a towering figure in Chinese civilization, who was much admired by Confucius himself. They were venerated together until the middle of the seventh century during the Tang dynasty, when the Duke of Zhou was honored in the temple reserved for the Zhou kings, while Confucius had his own cult at the Temple of Literature (*wenmiao*). In 739, Confucius was elevated to the Exalted King of Culture (*Wenxuan wang*). Other honorific titles were later granted to him by the Song, Yuan, Ming, and Qing emperors.[27] The Tang codes

---

26. For the development of the cult of Confucius in China, see Thomas A. Wilson, ed., *On Sacred Grounds: Culture, Society, Politics, and the Formation of the Cult of Confucius* (Cambridge, MA: Harvard University Press, 2002).

27. In 1008, the word "Profound Sage" (*xuansheng* 玄聖) was added to the title "Exalted King of Culture"; in 1013 the title was changed to "Ultimate Sage, Exalted King of Culture"

for sacrifices to Confucius established much of the ritual subsequently used through imperial times.

As Confucianism regained its official status at the court, the cult centered on Confucius expanded to include his disciples and followers. When the Four Books were added to the Five Classics as canonical texts, their alleged authors were subsequently honored in Confucian temples.[28] Yan Hui, Zengzi (Zeng Shen), Zisi, and Mencius came to be seen as "orthodox successors" of Confucius, and together they formed the Four Associates (*tứ phối*) whose statues stand to the right and left of Confucius's figure in Confucian temples. Other Confucian scholars, ten or twelve sages and seventy-two worthies, were also honored throughout the ages, though the list of their names varied from place to place.[29]

According to tradition, the veneration of Confucius began in Đại Việt during the Lý dynasty when a shrine was erected in 1070 to honor Confucius. The shrine also functioned as an academy for the Lý princes.[30] As Confucianism gained more currency at court, Confucian scholars petitioned the king to have Confucius honored in a "Confucius's Temple" (*Khổng miếu*), similar to those of the Tang and Song dynasties.[31] The Duke of Zhou, Confucius, and Mencius, and other famous Confucian scholars were honored separately in the second imperial academy (*Quốc học viện*), built in 1135 to conduct the

---

(*zhisheng wenxuanwang* 至聖文宣王) to be followed by "Ultimate Sage of Great Perfection, Exalted King of Culture" (*dachengzhisheng wenxuanwang* 大成至聖文宣王) in 1307. In 1530, the Ming emperor Jiajing (嘉靖, 1522–1566 CE) simplified it to "Ultimate Sage, Primary Sage Master Kong" (*zhishengxianshi Kongzi* 至聖先師孔子). In the Qing dynasty, the honorific title of Confucius was changed two more times, to "Ultimate Sage of Great Perfection, Exalted First Master of Culture" (*dachengzhisheng wenxuanxianshi* 大成至聖文宣先師) in 1645, and finally to the simpler Ultimate Sage, First Master (*zhishengxianshi* 至聖先師) in 1657. Wilson, *On Sacred Ground*, 50–57.

28. The Four Associates are Yan Hui (顏回), who did not leave any writing, but was considered the primary disciple of Confucius; Zeng Shen (曾參), the author of the *Great Learning*; Confucius's grandson Zisi (子思) or Kong Ji (孔伋), the author of the *Doctrine of the Mean*; and Zisi's student Mencius (孟子) or Meng Ke (孟轲), the author of a book by the same name, the *Mencius*.

29. For a list of these Confucian scholars or sages, see Thomas Wilson, *Genealogy of the Way: The Construction and Uses of the Confucian Tradition in Late Imperial China* (Standford, CA: Stanford University Press, 1995), Appendix A.

30. *Toàn Thư*, Bản kỷ, 3:5a (translation, 1:291); *Cương Mục*, Chính biên, 3:29–30 (translation, 1:327). Although the traditional date 1070 was given as the establishment of a Temple of Literature, archeological excavations in the areas of the present Temple of Literature and National Academy in Hanoi have not yielded any artifact older than the fifteenth century. It is possible that the shrine was not a separate temple but a part of the imperial school.

31. *Toàn Thư*, Bản kỷ, 4:12b (translation, 1:342); *Cương Mục*, Chính biên, 5:8–9 (translation, 1:389).

study of Confucian canon.[32] Still, prior to the Lê dynasty, the honors accorded Confucius were more of a memorial nature; there was no evidence of a religious rite to Confucius.

The National Academy (*Quốc tử giám* or *Thái học viện*), with students drawn from all ranks of society, was established in 1428. It was built next to the restored Temple of Literature, which was now dedicated not only to Confucius but also his chief disciples and successors (e.g., the Four Associates and Ten Philosophers).[33] Actual sacrifice to Confucius began in 1435 under the reign of Lê Thái Tông (r. 1434–1442). The king, following the custom of the Tang dynasty, ordered the offering of wine (*thích điện*) to Confucius during the first weeks of the second and eighth months,[34] thus beginning the semiannual sacrifices to Confucius in the Lê dynasty. In addition, beginning in 1442, the laureates who passed the highest level of the civil examination were honored with their names inscribed on stone tablets erected at the National Academy. Consequently, scholars who passed the civil examinations and newly appointed mandarins were required to offer sacrifices to Confucius at the Temple of Literature as a gesture of thanksgiving. In addition, secondary temples and shrines of culture (*văn chỉ, văn từ*) were established in every district and in major villages. These temples and shrines functioned as places to honor both Confucius and the local laureates. They were symbols of the commitment to a Confucian education, which continued until the early twentieth century.

Errors devotes an article to the cult of Confucius, including a description of a solemn sacrifice to Confucius in Tonkin.[35] In the sacrifice, the general pattern of Confucian worship followed that of the other imperial cults. Our author agrees that Confucian scholars should honor their Supreme Teacher. However, since making offerings and prayers to Confucius is ineffective, Christian scholars should not adopt them. Not only was Confucius a mortal who had no power to grant success in examination; he was also a recipient of the blessings granted by the Lord of Heaven, who alone has the authority and power to give "fame and prosperity to anyone he wishes."[36]

---

32. *Toàn Thư*, Bản kỷ, 5:19a (translation, 2:26); *Cương Mục*, Chính biên, 6:35 (translation, 1:455).

33. For a study of this Confucian temple, see Tran Ham Tan, "Étude sur le Văn-miêu de Hanoi (Temple de la Littérature)," *BEFEO* 45, no. 1 (1951): 89–118.

34. *Toàn Thư*, Bản kỷ, 9:25b (translation, 2:252); *Cương Mục*, Chính biên, 16:24 (translation, 1:865).

35. *Errors*, Book 1, Article 12. Cf. *Opusculum*, Chapter 1, Articles 4–5.

36. *Errors*, Book 1, Article 12, 71–72.

Cult of the Military

In 1721, the Trịnh established a military academy for the study of martial arts and military strategy. They also organized martial arts competitions and tactical examinations that were to be held every three years.[37] The patronage of the military by the Trịnh might have led to the establishment of a Temple of the Military in Thăng Long by 1740.[38] The Trịnh also promoted a cult of the military to display their power and prominence at the court. This was symbolized through rituals including the Oath-Taking Ceremony (Hội Minh), the Veneration of the Chief's Banner (tế Kỳ Đạo), and the worship at the Military Temple (Võ Miếu). These cults were described in both *Errors* and *Opusculum de sectis*, which points to their prominence in the Lê-Trịnh era. The specifics of these particular historical cults will be discussed in the following sections.

THE OATH-TAKING CEREMONY

The Oath-Taking Ceremony, called Hội Minh or Minh Thệ, began in 1028 during the reign of Lý Thái Tông (r. 1028–1054) as the ceremony of pledging loyalty to the king. The spirit of Mount Đồng Cổ was alleged to have warned the king in a dream of a plot against his life. After he suppressed the rebellion, the king mandated that a temple would be built in honor of the spirit Đồng Cổ. Every year, all mandarins and nobles had to gather at the temple and take an oath of loyalty and drink a cup of wine mixed with a drop of their blood to seal the oaths.[39]

---

37. Candidates were examined on basic knowledge of the Sunzi's *Art of War*. If they passed the exam, they were required to demonstrate their fighting skills while riding a horse as well as on the ground with swords, lance, and other long weapons. If they passed this level, they would then be examined on battle tactics. Whoever passed all three levels would have an oral exam with the lord, and be appointed to a military rank. In 1731, the examination was revised to add an archery competition. The first two steps of the test were reversed, that is, the practical examination took place before the theoretical part. See *Cương Mục*, Chính biên, 35:36–37 and 37:20–21 (translation, 2:424–25, 482–83).

38. We do not know when the Temple of the Military was first erected, but according to an entry in the imperial record *Cương Mục*, a decree was issued in 1740 for the worship at the Temple of the Military: "The main chamber of the temple is dedicated to the 'Accomplished King of Military, the Great Duke [Lü] Wang.' Other military figures such as Sun Wuzi, Guan Zhong and 18 other generals are worshipped in the eastern and western side chambers. General Trần Hưng Đạo should also be worshipped at the Temple of the Military. General Guan Yu of the Han dynasty, on the other hand, should have his own temple. Twice a year offerings should be made in the first weeks of spring and autumn." *Cương Mục*, Chính biên, 38:33–34 (translation, 2:529).

39. *Cương Mục*, Chính biên, 2:29–30 (translation, 1: 285–86). The oath-taking ceremony also took place at the royal palace from time to time when the Lý king needed to affirm their authority. Cf. *Cương Mục*, Chính biên, 4:22–23, 34 (translation, 1:363–64, 374). Still, the Lý lost their thrones to the Trần in 1226.

The custom was followed by subsequent Trần kings until it was suppressed in 1399 by Hồ Quý Ly (1336–?), a contender to the throne of the Trần.[40]

When King Lê Thái Tông ascended to the throne in 1434, he restored the custom with a significant change. The annual ceremony no longer took place in a temple but on a spacious plot in the capital. Similar pledges of loyalty to the king were also made in every prefecture of the country.[41] After defeating the Mạc, forces loyal to the Lê gathered at the southern gate of the capital to take the oath.[42] This again became a regular event during the seventeenth and eighteenth centuries, when the Trịnh used this ceremony to test the loyalty of their subjects.

The Oath-Taking Ceremony was a requirement for every officer, civil or military, to pledge allegiance to the ruling authority. In the ceremony, the blood of a freshly killed chicken was drained into cups of wine and placed on the altar. Then, calling the names of Heaven and Earth to be his witness, the oath-taker knelt in front of the altar and recited the oath formula in these words:

> I bow to King of Heaven and Queen of Earth. I come from such prefecture, district, and village. I am [name], and I was born in a such and such year. I swear my complete loyalty to King [name] and Lord [name]. If I do not remain loyal after I drink from this cup of wine and blood, may Heaven and Earth and all the spirits strike me down and kill me.[43]

After professing the oath, he drank the wine mixed with blood to prove his sincerity.

In the politically volatile atmosphere of Tonkin of the Lê-Trịnh era, this ceremony was invoked more frequently, in both the capital as well as all the prefectures, as a way for the Trịnh to maintain their power. All nobles, civil and military officials, and their families had to renew their vows of loyalty to the king and the lord on the three last days of the year. They were also required to report any information they had that could be harmful to the rulers. The heads of prefectures, as well as local officials, also compelled their subjects to take the oath.[44] In some cases, it was even required of foreigners living in Tonkin. When the Jesuit

---

40. *Cương Mục*, Chính biên, 6:5 (translation, 1:427). The oath ceremony was suspended in 1399 after an attempt on Hồ Quý Ly's life by forces loyal to the Trần.

41. *Cương Mục*, Chính biên, 16:3 (translation, 1:843); *Loại Chí*, Lễ nghi chí 6, 2:879–80.

42. *Cương Mục*, Chính biên, 30:11 (translation, 2:208).

43. *Errors*, Book 1, Article 8, 47.

44. Adriano di Santa Thecla gives a detailed discussion of this special ceremony in *Opusculum*, Chapter 2, Article 5.

Of Gods and Heroes 91

missionary Giulio Baldinotti was charged with spying for Cochinchina in 1626, the entire Portuguese crew on his ship had to take the oath of loyalty to the Lord of Tonkin as proof of their innocence.[45]

THE VENERATION OF THE CHIEF'S BANNER

In *Errors*, there is a short description of another military cult called the Veneration of the Chief's Banner, or *Tế Cờ (Kỳ) Đạo*.[46] This rite, an adaptation of Song and Ming military customs, only existed in Vietnam between the fifteenth and eighteenth centuries and functioned like a modern military parade.[47] Since it was an affair conducted by the military officers to honor the Trịnh lord, only he and not the king was present at the ceremony. The day before the ceremony, offerings were made at various shrines dedicated to the spirits of former generals and shrines dedicated to weapons (e.g., bow, crossbow, cannon, musket, and lance) and animals (e.g., elephant and horse) used in a battle. On the day of the sacrifice, all of the officers gathered with their troops at the sites to perform the rites, while the lord rode an elephant from his palace to a tower near the platforms to observe it. The sacrifices were performed on three separate platforms, the first of which was dedicated to Heaven and Earth, the second to the saints and heroes, and the third to the protecting spirits of the banners or flags of the general. The rites followed a procedure similar to the sacrifice to the god of Agriculture. During the ceremonies, the troops fired their cannons and muskets and waved their flags and weapons.[48] After the ceremony, they competed in archery, shooting, and wrestling.

The ceremony was a display of military power, and it impressed foreigners such as Samuel Baron, who interpreted this ceremony as "purging the country from all malevolent spirits."[49] Baron described the rite as a mock battle between

---

45. Giulio Baldinotti, "La relation sur le Tonkin du P. Baldinotti (1626)" *BEFEO* 3 (1903): 71–78.

46. *Errors*, Book 1, Article 8, 49.

47. For a description of the procedure see Phan Huy Chú, *Loại Chí*, Lễ nghi chí 6 (translation,1:875–77).

48. *Loại Chí*, Binh chế chí 3 (translation, 2:371–73).

49. According to Baron, "The *Theckydaw* (*Tế Kỳ Đạo*) is observed commonly once every year, especially if there (is to) be a great mortality amongst the men, elephants, or horses of the general's stables, or the cattle of the country. The cause of which they attribute to the malicious spirits of such men as have been put to death for treason, rebellion, and conspiring the death of the king, generals or princes, and that in revenge of the punishment they have suffer'd, they are bent to destroy every thing, and commit horrible violence. To prevent which, their superstition has suggested to them the institution of this *Theckydaw*, as a proper means to drive the devil away, and purge the country of evil spirits." See Dror and Taylor, *Views of Seventeenth-Century Vietnam*, 263.

the soldiers of the Trịnh and the evil spirits, complete with artillery, knights on elephants and horses, and foot soldiers who brandished weapons while running through the streets and over platforms chasing the evil spirits.

THE TEMPLE OF THE MILITARY

The rituals of the cult of the military that took place in the Temple of the Military (*Võ Miếu*) paralleled the civil rites to Confucius and the literary sages in the Temple of Literature (*Văn Miếu*). This rite originated in the Tang dynasty in China when powerful military clans based along China's northwestern frontier overshadowed the influence of civil officials at the court. In an attempt to appeal to these warriors, the Tang court founded a military cult centered on Lü Wang, a famous military strategist, during the reign of Tang Zuzong (799–805). By conferring on Lü the honorific title "Accomplished King of the Military" (*Wucheng wang*), they echoed the title that was given to Confucius. If the civil officials were to have their "exalted king of culture," the military also had to have their own "accomplished king of the military."

This cult fell into obscurity in China after the Tang dynasty, but it was adopted by the Trịnh in Tonkin as a way to honor their military members. According to the information in *Errors*, the Great Duke Lü Wang, his Two Associates, and the Twelve Generals were venerated at the Temple of the Military so as to mirror Confucius, his Four Associates, and the Ten Philosophers of the Temple of Literature.[50] "Offerings were sacrificed to them on the first week of the second and eighth months in the same manner as to Confucius."[51] Of the generals who were worshipped at the Temple of the Military, all but one were famous Chinese generals from the Warring States to the Song era. The only Vietnamese figure honored there was General Trần Hưng Đạo (d. 1300), the military hero who already had a separate cult devoted to him.[52]

In his assessment of the cult, the author of *Errors* shared a similar sentiment regarding the efficacy of making offerings to generals at the Temple of the Military as he did with the rite to Confucius. Military commanders performed

---

50. See *Errors*, Book 1, Article 13. This fact provides another internal datum for the dating of the manuscript. Given that the sacrifice to the military figure was established in 1740, *Errors* could not have been written before that time.

51. *Errors*, Book 1, Article 13, 74.

52. In Vietnam, there was a separate cult centered on Trần Hưng Đạo that has lasted until today. Like the cult of Guan Yu in China, his cult thrived because he enjoyed popular support as the patron saint of many groups. For a modern study of the cult, see Phạm Quỳnh Phương, *Hero and Deity: Tran Hung Dao and the Resurgence of Popular Religion in Vietnam* (Bangkok: Mekong Press, 2009).

the sacrifices to these past heroes in order to procure victory. However, our author considers it a futile task to make such offerings, since these figures themselves were not able to determine the outcome of a battle. Making religious sacrifices to the generals does not guarantee a favorable outcome: "many who worship these generals have lost battles and the generals could not help them at all."[53]

The military cults floundered as the Trịnh fell from power and finally disappeared during the Tây Sơn occupation of Tonkin (1786–1802). As the center of imperial power moved to Hue, the Temple of the Military in Thăng Long was abandoned in the nineteenth century, and the military cults were no longer maintained by the subsequent Nguyễn dynasty.

Worship in the Villages

A visitor to premodern Vietnam could see shrines and temples in every conceivable corner, in villages, on roads, on river banks, or at the bases of hills. The spirits commonly worshipped in Tonkin may be divided into three types. The first type of spirit is made up of legendary figures whose cults were followed in their respective temples. The second type of spirit is that of nature, such as the spirit of a tree, a rock, a stream, a river or lake, a mountain, an animal, a bird, or a fish. These spirits had no regular cults or rituals attached to them. Offerings were made to them mostly to ward off evil when necessary. The third type of spirit, that of deified humans, makes up the majority of the spirits worshipped in traditional Vietnam. They are the spirits of legendary heroes and heroines, kings and queens, military figures, cultural figures, and arts-and-crafts founders, among others. The cults devoted to them followed the general pattern of ritual worship specified in ritual manuals. Most of these human spirits came to be the tutelary divinities or guardian spirits of a particular village or district.

The Ranking and Promotion of the Spirits

The royal court established a ranking system for the spirits as an instrument to maintain imperial control over the local cults. Depending on the spirits' merits and powers, the court issued a certificate ranking them in one of three classes. The first-class spirits were venerated at famous temples and shrines in multiple locations, while spirits of the second class were venerated in local temples or shrines. Spirits of the third class often did not have a temple dedicated to them but were worshipped along with other spirits.

---

53. *Errors*, Book 1, Article 13, 75.

The spirits of the supreme rank (*thượng đẳng thần*) were those whose names and actions were famous. They could be the personalized spirits of important mountains and rivers, such as the spirit of Mount Tản Viên[54] or of the Tô Lịch river, or they could be legendary figures, such as Đổng Thiên Vương,[55] Chử Đồng Tử,[56] and Princess Liễu Hạnh, whose lives had supernatural elements (*linh dị*) and efficacious powers (*thiêng*).[57] They could also be historical heroes or heroines, such as Lý Ông Trọng, the Trưng Sisters, Trần Hưng Đạo, Lý Thường Kiệt, and others whose virtues and deeds were worthy of imitation. Their stories were told in the earliest hagiographies or "lives of the spirits" (*thần tích*).

The spirits of middle rank (*trung đẳng thần*) were those who had been worshipped in local villages. Their deeds might not have been well known, but they might have displayed magical powers or benefited the local people. The spirits of the lower rank (*hạ đẳng thần*) were those whose deeds had been forgotten. They were often worshipped in groups. Outside of these rankings were those spirits who were worshipped out of superstition. They were frequently characterized by the court as false spirits (*tà thần*), demonic spirits (*yêu thần*), or base spirits (*dê tiện thần*). These spirits were often of animals, rocks, trees, or people who died unnatural deaths.

The process of ranking the spirits was called "establishing the ranks and promotions of the spirits" (*tạo khoa bạt thần*). Besides the obvious examination of the record of its merits, the spirit under consideration needed to display its power to work miracles. According to *Errors*, the test to determine whether a spirit deserved the honor of being certified took place as follows:

> When the villagers petition a spirit to become their village god, they bring a buffalo to the official and write the spirit on the animal's head. The official commands the spirit to strike the designated buffalo dead if the spirit accepts the rank. If the buffalo is stricken dead before everyone present, the spirit receives the royal certification for becoming a *thần* [deity] and is registered in the official record of the spirits.[58]

---

54. See the story "Núi Tản Viên," in Trần Thế Pháp, *Lĩnh Nam Chích Quái*, trans. Lê Hữu Mục (Saigon: Khai Trí, 1960), 77–78; *Toàn Thư*, Ngoại kỷ, 1:4a–5b (translation, 1:130–31).

55. See the story "Đổng Thiên Vương," in Trần Thế Pháp, *Lĩnh Nam Chích Quái*, 55–57; *Toàn Thư*, Ngoại kỷ, 1:3b–4a (translation, 1:130). For a modern discussion of his cult, see Tran Quoc Vuong, "The Legend of Ông Dóng," in *Essays into Vietnamese Pasts*, ed. Keith Taylor and John Whitmore (Ithaca, NY: Cornell University Press / SEAP, 1995), 13–41.

56. See the story "Đầm Nhất Dạ," in Trần Thế Pháp, *Lĩnh Nam Chích Quái*, 51–54.

57. *Errors* discusses the stories of Đổng Thiên Vương, Lý Ông Trọng, and Liễu Hạnh in Book 1, Article 10.

58. *Errors*, Book 1, Article 9, 53.

The process of ranking the spirits seemed arbitrary to our author. However, to be fair to the procedure, this is not unlike the process of canonization in the Catholic church, when miracles are required as proof of sainthood.

The Cult of the Village Deity

The cult of *Thành Hoàng* or the Guardian Deity was essential for community life in traditional Vietnam.[59] Every village was to have its patron deity, called Phúc Thần (Deity of Fortune) or Thành Hoàng (Deity of Moat and Ditch). Originally, the name Thành Hoàng (Chinese: *Chenghuang*) was used to indicate the guardian spirit of a city that was surrounded by walls and ditches in ancient China. Only the capital and major cities, not the villages, had temples dedicated to *Chenghuang*. City officials made regular sacrifices to their *Chenghuang* for protection from wars and natural disasters.

The first known Thành Hoàng of Vietnam was the spirit of the Tô Lịch river, which was honored by Gao Pian as the protector of the citadel Đại La (modern day Hanoi) in the ninth century. After Lý Thái Tổ moved his capital to Đại La and renamed it Thăng Long (Ascending Dragon) in 1010, he continued to honor the spirit of the Tô Lịch river as the capital's guardian spirit. In 1189, King Lý Cao Tông travelled widely, and whenever he encountered a sacred place, he conferred upon the spirit of that locality a title and allowed a temple to be built in its honor.[60] However, the cult of Thành Hoàng was not under imperial control until the thirteenth century.[61]

In contrast to China, the cult of Thành Hoàng in Vietnam centered on the villages. Perhaps because cities were few and far between in traditional Vietnam, the cult was developed in rural areas where the villages had been the main units of social organization. As their number multiplied, the local cults of spirits could not be ignored by the court, and efforts were made to include

---

59. On the cult of Thành Hoàng, the major study remains Nguyen Van Khoan, "Essai sur le '*Dinh*' et le culte du deity tutélaire des villages au Tonkin," *BEFEO* 30 (1930): 107–39. See also Paul Giran, *Magie & religion annamites; introduction à une philosophie de la civilisation du peuple d'Annam* (Paris: A. Challamel, 1912); Phan Kế Bính, *Việt Nam Phong Tục* [Customs of Vietnam] (1915; repr., Saigon: Khai Trí, 1973); Nguyen Van Huyen, "Contribution a l'étude d'un génie tutélaire annamite Li-phuc-man," *BEFEO* 38 (1938): 1–110; Đào Duy Anh, *Việt Nam Văn Hoá Sử Cương* [An Outline History of Vietnamese Culture] (Hue, 1938). For a recent study, see Nguyễn Vinh Phúc and Nguyễn Duy Hinh, *Các Thành Hoàng & Tín Ngưỡng Thăng Long—Hà Nội* [The Guardian Spirits and Their Cults in Hanoi] (Hanoi: NXB Lao Động, 2009).

60. *Toàn Thư*, Bản kỷ, 4:21a (translation, 1:352).

61. According to the stories in *Việt Điện U Linh Tập*, in the years 1285 1287, 1312, and 1313, the Trần kings certified a number of Guardian Deities, and at the same time they ordered temples and shrines dedicated to the "unworthy" spirits to be destroyed.

them in the national hierarchy. In the Lê dynasty, villages were compelled to submit the names of their local deities for court examination and registration. As the custom of ranking the spirits became popular during the Lê dynasty, every village wanted to have its deity honored as a certified spirit. The movement toward having a village protector was to legitimize the spirits that had already been worshipped in the village.[62]

The number and quality of these guardian spirits varied from village to village. Most of the time it was the spirit of a person who had great merit in the eyes of the villagers. Other times it was a spirit from nature that was to be worshipped to ward off the plague, disaster, or a spirit that displayed some strange power. There were cases in which people worshipped thieves, soil collectors, or others whose morals were questionable. Regardless of their backgrounds, the spirits to be worshipped had proven themselves responsive to the prayers of the people in their time of need. Since not all the deities worshipped in a village were heroes or famous people, the villagers adopted a certified spirit to be their Thành Hoàng. Thus a village could have more than one Guardian Deity. If they could afford it, the villagers built a temple dedicated to that spirit, or they simply worshipped their Guardian Deity in the communal house.

From the fifteenth century onward, the back chamber of the *đình* was reserved to worship Thành Hoàng in the communal house. In this chamber, a spirit tablet inscribed with the name and title of the deity was placed on a throne or ritual bed. The royal certificate (*sắc*) was kept in a special box in front of the throne. A written booklet of the spirit's hagiography (*thần tích*) was also kept there. Some villages had coffers holding the costumes and headpieces "worn" by Thành Hoàng during festivals. In front of the ceremonial throne was an altar for articles of worship, such as incense burners, vases, and candle stands. To the sides of this altar were other worship objects made of wood, including banners, flags, ritual weapons, carriages, and sometimes a life-sized horse.

The hagiographies of the Thành Hoàng followed a legendary pattern similar to those written in the *Việt Điện U Linh Tập* and *Lĩnh Nam Chích Quái*, the two earliest collections of Vietnamese hagiography. For example, they had an unusual birth; their physical features were different; they possessed excellent virtues or

---

62. In the fourteenth century, according to the *Lĩnh Nam Chích Quái*, only 24 spirits were certified in the whole country. The number increased to hundreds in the following centuries. In the villages surrounding Thăng Long alone, there were at least 110 spirits worshipped as their guardian deities by the early twentieth century. Nguyễn Vinh Phúc and Nguyễn Duy Hinh, *Các Thành Hoàng*, Tables 1–5, 13–47.

unsurpassed talents; they had done great deeds that benefited the nation, the people, or the village; their deaths were also out of the ordinary; they displayed powers after death and helped the living; and they were remembered by the people and certified by the court. The spirits of the lower ranks and the "unworthy" or "false" spirits had no biography.

The ritual feasts to the Village Deity were communal affairs that occurred according to the seasonal celebrations. Offerings were made regularly on the first and full moon, and at special times of the year: in the ceremony of supplication for tranquility (*Kỳ An*), in the ceremony of offering of new crops (*Thường Tân*), in the ceremony of supplication for blessings (*Kỳ Phúc*), and other seasonal festivals. No doubt, the most celebrated ceremony of the cult was the anniversary feast of the Guardian Deity himself. On this special occasion, the whole village was involved in preparing the ritual feasts. Solemn sacrifices were made according to ritual protocols in a manner similar to that of the Divine Farmer or Confucius, and the celebration could last several days.[63] It was also an opportunity for social gathering; the occasion called for a village festival (*hội*) replete with feasting and entertainment. *Errors* mentions that during this time, "each day they offer sacrifices, then sing songs throughout the day and night, and compete in games like wrestling, stick-fighting, or cricket." Only during a mourning period for a ruler were all forms of entertainment prohibited. Sacrifices were also made to the Guardian Deity when the villagers needed to pray for rain (*đảo vũ*) or to dispel a plague or disaster (*tống ách*).[64]

The author of *Errors* recognized the importance of this cult in the social life of the Vietnamese, prompting a sympathetic comment on the rites:

> It is fitting to venerate and trust in a guardian deity as the protector of the village. However, one must choose a spirit who truly has the merit and virtues befitting veneration. One must not choose a false spirit who has no merit and power. One must choose a being among those in heaven—being favored by the Lord of Heaven—because they are worthy of our total reverence and trust.[65]

---

63. According to the descriptions given by Phan Kế Bính as well as by Nguyen Van Khoan, the rite itself was a complex ritual of many steps. See Phan Kế Bính, *Việt Nam Phong Tục*, 81–85; Nguyen Van Khoan, "Essai sur le '*Dinh*,'" 127–30.

64. *Errors*, Book 1, Article 9, 52–53.

65. *Errors*, Book 1, Article 9, 54.

It is compelling that he made a connection between the veneration of Thành Hoàng and the Catholic concept of the patron saints: "The followers of our religion in all places often choose a holy man or woman—the 'patron saint' of their village—to protect the people who live in that area."[66]

More than a religious rite, the cult of Thành Hoàng helped foster communal identity. The Village Deity represented the village's common history, customs, morality, and rules. The social bond among the villagers was fostered and a common identity was created in his cult. A French colonial scholar best captured the essence of this cult:

> The protective deity represents an appreciable amount of common memories, common aspirations. He embodies the rule, custom, morality, and at the same time, the penalty. He will punish or reward according to whether his laws were violated or observed. He is ultimately the personification of this higher authority, which has its source and strength from the same society. Moreover, he forms a link among all community members; he makes a block, a sort of moral personality in which all the essential attributes are found in each individual.[67]

The fact remains that, for Vietnamese Catholics, the prohibition against participating in the local cult of Thành Hoàng, if they happened to live in a non-Catholic village, caused tremendous social repercussions. As Catholic families were broken up and forced to live among non-Catholics as part of the court policy of "eliminating separatists" (*phân sáp*) during the nineteenth century, the question of Catholic involvement in the local cults and festivals became more acute, as evident in the repeated concerns and questions sent to Rome by missionary bishops.

Domestic Cults

Among the spirits that were worshipped at home, three stood out as typical in a household: Táo Quân or the Kitchen God; Thổ Công or the Household Guardian; and Tiên Sư or the Guild Founder. They were described both in Book 1, Article 11 of *Errors* and mentioned by Tavernier, Baron, and Tissanier. The following is a brief description of these spirits.

---

66. *Errors*, Book 1, Article 9, 55.

67. My translation. Paul Giran, *Magie et religion annamite*, 334–35, cited in Nguyen Van Khoan, "Essai sur le '*Dinh*,'" 112.

Kitchen God

In traditional Vietnam, Táo Quân or the "Lord of Hearth" is in charge of both the kitchen and family affairs. He was assigned by Heaven to help members of the household live in harmony. Every year he went to heaven on the twenty-third day of the last lunar month to report on the affairs of the family during the year. He returned on New Year's Eve with heaven's judgment. The coming year's heavenly reward or punishment depended upon the family's moral behavior during the present year. Therefore, the most important feast day of Táo Quân was the date of his departure to heaven, the time when solemn offerings were made.

In *Errors*, the story of Táo Quân, popularly called the Kitchen God (*vua bếp*), is recounted in verses and can be summarized as follows. Once upon a time, there was a couple named Trọng Cao and Thị Nhi. They often quarreled over domestic affairs. One day the husband beat his wife. Thị Nhi ran away from home and became homeless. Eventually, she met a man named Phạm Lang and married him. In the meantime, Trọng Cao lost his fortune and became a beggar. One day he came to beg at the house of Phạm Lang. The lady of the house recognized him as her former husband and gave him food and drink. While they were talking over old times, Phạm Lang returned from a hunting trip. Afraid that Phạm Lang would misunderstand, Thị Nhi hid her former husband in the haystack. Phạm Lang had brought back some game meats and burned the haystack to roast them. He unwittingly burned Trọng Cao before Thị Nhi could explain the situation. Thị Nhi realized her mistake and jumped into the burning haystack to die with her former husband. Because he loved his wife, Phạm Lang also leapt into the flames to be with her. Thus, all three died in the fire.[68]

Subsequently, the Jade Emperor, upon hearing their tragic story, appointed them to be the three-in-one Kitchen God but each with a different responsibility: Phạm Lang was to be Thổ Công (Duke of the Soil), caring for the kitchen; Trọng Cao was to be Thổ Địa (Earth Deity), caring for the home; and Thị Nhi was to be Thổ Kỳ (Local Guard), caring for the household transactions. This cult of the Kitchen God was apparently a mixture of different traditions. Somehow, the worship the Hearth Spirit, one of the five major household spirits stipulated in the chapter "Monthly Proceeding" of the *Record of Rites*,[69] was adapted into a popular devotion. This story of Trọng Cao and Thị Nhi undoubtedly aroused the popular imagination and thus helped spread the cult of Táo Quân.

---

68. *Errors*, Book 1, Article 11, 61–62.

69. See *Errors*, Book 5, Article 7, 40, 42.

Household Guardian

Thổ Công, or the "God of Soil," was the guardian spirit of the household. He was also called variously Thổ Địa [Earth Deity] or Thổ Chủ [Lord of Soil]. He was in charge of protecting the members of the household from harmful spirits, watching over their daily affairs, and bringing blessings to the household. Popular belief sometimes conflated the cult of the Kitchen God with the cult of the Household Guardian. Since the two shared similar functions, they were worshipped together at the same altar in many homes. The spirit tablets of the Thổ Công on the altar were inscribed with the three titles: *Thổ địa long mạch tôn thần* (the guardian spirit of the earth); *Ngũ phương ngũ thổ Phúc đức chính thần* (the spirit who brings blessings from all directions); and *Đông trù tư mệnh Táo phủ thần quân* (the lord of the hearth who guards the kitchen). The offerings to Thổ Công were made regularly on the first and full moon. In addition, whenever offerings were made to the ancestors on memorial feasts (*giỗ*) or festivals (*tết*), a portion was also offered to Thổ Công. On the feast day of Táo Quân at the end of the year, a new spirit tablet for Thổ Công was made and the old one was burned.

The cult of Thổ Công seems to have evolved from the common belief that every locality had its guardian spirits, from the river, the road, and the land. There were many legendary accounts of Thổ Công or Thổ Chủ, two of which were recounted in *Errors*. One involved the five brothers of the Lê family, who were credited with killing a ferocious tiger, and the other was about a certain wood gatherer named Vương Chất. These accounts were later repeated in other Vietnamese apologetic works.

The Guild Founder

Westerners who travelled to Tonkin in the past centuries all agreed that the cult of Tiên Sư [Ancient Teacher] or Tổ Sư [Original Teacher] was prominent in Tonkinese households.[70] Tiên Sư or the Guild Founder was the inventor or founder of a particular art or trade. Since he or she taught the art or trade to others, he or she was honored by later generations as their Tổ Sư or "Original Teacher." Each trade guild also had its own founder to be honored and worshipped.[71]

---

70. Rhodes, *Histoire du royaume de Tunquin*, book 1, chapter 29:106–7. According to Rhodes's experience, this veneration of Tiên Sư or *nos anciens maîtres* was the most persistent cult, and it prevented people from converting to Christianity. He also held a negative view on the cult of Thành Hoàng and called it "the most foolish superstition" (*la plus folle superstition*) (107). Tissanier also had a similar observation.

71. For example, since the seventh century, the brothers Trần Hoà, Trần Điền, and Trần Điện of Đình Công Village in Hà Đông were credited with teaching the art and trade of silversmithing; since the tenth century, Phạm Đôn of Thanh Nhạn Village in Phúc Yên was credited with the art of straw-mat weaving; since the thirteenth century, the monk Không Lộ and his

Artisans set up an altar in their household to remember those who taught them the arts. The altar dedicated to their Primary Teacher was either on the left or the right of the main altar to the ancestors, where a spirit tablet and/or an image of the Teacher was placed. On the first and full moons and at other festivals, people made offerings to their First Teacher in the same manner as the offerings to their ancestors. On the anniversaries of the Teacher's birth and death, members of the same line of art or trade would gather to publicly honor their "patron saints." The cult of the Guild Founder demonstrated the gratitude of later generations toward their ancestors in the trade for providing them a means of living. Because Thăng Long of the seventeenth and eighteenth centuries was a gathering place for traders and artisans, it was not unusual to see many households displaying the altar of their Tiên Sư.

Cults of Religious Figures

The Mother Goddess Cult

Within the traditional cult of spirits, goddess worship (*đạo Mẫu*) was also quite popular and had a long history.[72] The cult of the goddess existed in different parts of Vietnam and found a way into the ranks of Buddhist and Daoist deities. The earliest Buddhist figures venerated in Vietnam were the female personifications of the natural forces: Dharma Cloud (Pháp Vân), Dharma Rain (Pháp Vũ), Dharma Thunder (Pháp Lôi), and Dharma Lightning (Pháp Điện).[73] The rulers of the four realms (*tứ phủ*)—sky, land, forest, and water—were said to be female.[74] Even Avalokiteśvara,

---

disciples were credited with the art of casting copper; since the sixteenth century, the scholar Phùng Khắc Khoan, who went to China to learn the art of making silk, was considered the founder of this art in Tonkin.

72. For a general introduction to the cult of goddess in traditional Vietnam, see Ngô Đức Thịnh, *Đạo Mẫu Việt Nam* [Goddess Worship in Vietnam] (Hanoi: NXB Tôn Giáo, 2009). For some recent studies, see Olgar Dror, *Cult, Culture and Authority: Princess Liễu Hạnh in Vietnamese History* (Honolulu: University of Hawai'i Press, 2007); Karen Fjelstad and Nguyen Thi Hien, eds., *Possessed by the Spirits: Mediumship in Contemporary Vietnamese Communities* (Ithaca, NY: Cornell University Press / SEAP, 2006); Philip Tayloy, *Goddess on the Rise: Pilgrimage and Popular Religion in Vietnam* (Honolulu: University of Hawai'i Press, 2004).

73. The tradition about the origin of these deities came from the story "Man Nương" in Trần Thế Pháp, *Lĩnh Nam Chích Quái*. For a discussion of the story, see Cuong Tu Nguyen, *Zen in Medieval Vietnam*, 70, 332–34n10.

74. See Peter Simon and Ida Simon-Baroudh, "Les Génies des Quatre Palais," *L'Homme* 10, no. 4 (1970): 81–101.

the boddhisattva of compassion, was turned into a goddess in Vietnamese devotion.[75]

Among the spirits of supreme rank in traditional Vietnam was a woman by the name of "Princess" Liễu Hạnh. She was considered the principal deity of the goddess cult in traditional Vietnam, a cult that was connected with female mediums. Her cult became popular in the eighteenth century when the poetess Đoàn Thị Điểm (1705–1748) composed her hagiography.[76] Even though Liễu Hạnh was never a member of the royal family, she was given the title of "princess" (*công chúa*) or "noble lady" (*bà chúa*) by the court. The listing of Liễu Hạnh as one of the Four Immortals of Vietnamese pantheon bespoke the popularity of this deity.[77] It also had a strong connection with another indigenous Daoist cult called Chư Vị (the Honored Ones), which included Liễu Hạnh in their pantheon as well as other spirits that were worshipped by Vietnamese shamans.

There are two accounts of this goddess retold in *Errors*: the first one seems to draw from a Confucian source in a matter-of-fact style,[78] and the second is identified as bearing Daoist imagery.[79] The two accounts exhibit differences in tone toward the cult of Liễu Hạnh. The Confucian account portrays her as an impure goddess who is playful but not harmful, whereas the Daoist account portrays her as a powerful goddess who inspires a home cult. The author of *Errors* had nothing but contempt for Liễu Hạnh's cult, which he thought should be destroyed. This was an unusual reaction toward Liễu Hạnh in comparison to the author's response to other spirits.

> Liễu Hạnh is a demon, not a being from heaven. A celestial being is chaste and does not engage in seducing scholars and men as she did. She surely

---

75. One can argue that the influence of the native cult of Mother Goddess was so strong in Vietnam that it even affected the mainline religions. For example, in many Buddhist homes, the Goddess of Mercy often was the only venerated figure on the altar. One can make a similar observation about the devotion to the Blessed Virgin Mary in many Catholic homes in Vietnam.

76. For a major study of Liễu Hạnh, see Olga Dror, *Cult, Culture, and Authority: Princess Liễu Hạnh in Vietnamese History* (Honolulu: University of Hawai'i Press, 2007).

77. According to Vietnamese tradition, the Four Immortals (Tứ Bất Tử) are (1) Thánh Dóng or Phù Đổng Thiên Vương, the legendary child hero who rode his horse to heaven after driving the enemy out of the country during the legendary reign of King Hùng; (2) Sơn Tinh or Tản Viên Sơn Thần, the legendary spirit of Mount Tản Viên who married the daughter of King Hùng the Eighteenth; (3) Chử Đồng Tử, the pauper turned prince-consort who possessed the power of immortality at the time of King Hùng; (4) and Liễu Hạnh, the alleged daughter of Indra who lived for a short time during the Lê dynasty.

78. *Errors*, Book 1, Article 10, 59.

79. *Errors*, Book 2, Article 7, 123–24.

is a goddess of lust, and her temple is a temple of lust. We must practice scholar Hồ Dĩnh's advice that whenever one passes a temple of lust one should burn it down.[80]

This negative attitude to the cult of Liễu Hạnh was also shared by Adriano di Santa Thecla.[81] Apparently, the cult's connection to mediumship was associated with demonic activity.

Lady Buddha of Compassion

The cult to Avalokiteśvara, known in Vietnam as Quan Âm or Phật Bà (Lady Buddha), has been a prominent feature of Vietnamese Buddhism at least since the eleventh century. The iconography of Quan Âm in Vietnam was exclusively that of a female, sometimes dressed in a white robe while at other times depicted with multiple arms and eyes. [82] These forms representing Guanyin (Quan Âm) emerged in China between the tenth and eleventh centuries.[83] Moreover, the popular story about Quan Âm as Princess Diệu Thiện or Mẩu Thiện (Miaoshan

---

80. *Errors*, Book 2, Article 7, 124.

81. The account given by Adriano di Santa Thecla (*Opusculum*, 46–47) is similar to the Confucian account: "A famous woman named Lady Liễu Hạnh is added to [the most prominent spirits]. She was born in Thiên Bản district of the southern province. Since she had sung, as they say, disgracefully and impudently, people, being jealous, killed her and threw her into the river. The Devil took her shape and name and introduced, developed, and secured her cult in many provinces. She is worshipped mainly in Quỳnh Lưu district in Cửa Tuần village of Nghệ An province. Her temple, or miếu, is built there, where two girls attend on her. When one of them leaves another is put in her place. The girls are selected from all the girls of that district by Lady Liễu Hạnh herself or by a demon with her name. The one selected is assigned to serve as one of the two attendants or zealous servants. She is expected to speak when possessed by Liễu Hạnh or by the demon. The girl, upon leaving the temple, is paid a considerable amount of money, according to the way of life she chooses." Dror, *A Study of Religion*, 145.

82. For a description of the devotion to Quan Âm in Vietnam, see Nguyễn Minh Ngọc, Nguyễn Mạnh Cường, and Nguyễn Duy Hinh, *Bồ Tát Quán Thế Âm Trong Các Chùa Vùng Đồng Bằng Sông Hồng* [Quan Âm in theBuddhist Temples of the Red River Delta] (Hanoi: NXB Khoa Học Xã Hội, 2004); Trịnh Thị Dung, *Hình Tượng Bồ Tát Quan Âm Trong Phật Giáo Việt Nam* [Image of Avalokiteśvara in Vietnamese Buddhism] (Hanoi: NXB Tôn Giáo, 2012).

83. The literature on the cult of Guanyin is enormous. For recent works on the subject, see Sandy Boucher, *Discovering Kwan Yin, Buddhist Goddess of Compassion* (Boston: Beacon Press, 1999); Gil Farrer-Halls, *The Feminine Face of Buddhism* (Wheaton: Quest, 2002); Martin Palmer and Jay Ramsay, with Man-Ho Kwok, *Kuan Yin Myths and Prophecies of the Chinese Goddess of Compassion* (Charlottesville: Hampton Roads Publishing, 2009); Chun-Fang Yü, *Kuan Yin: The Chinese Transformation of Avalokiteshvara* (New York: Columbia University Press, 2001).

in Chinese), which originated in China around the twelfth century, was the main source of the Vietnamese legends regarding her.[84]

According to the account given in *Errors*, the princess Diệu Thiện was a former life of Quan Âm. Diệu Thiện was the third daughter of King Diệu Trang (Miaozhuang). Unlike her sisters, she refused to get married. For this reason, she took refuge in a Buddhist monastery. After many failed attempts to force her to change her mind, the king, in his anger, burnt down the entire monastery. Because of her magical powers, Diệu Thiện could escape harm.[85]

As in China, the bodhisattva of compassion, who originally was a male in the Indian tradition, was transformed in Vietnamese Buddhism into a goddess of mercy. The cult of Quan Âm developed out of the Pure Land tradition in seventh century China. In chapter 25 of the *Lotus Sutra*, Avalokiteśvara promised that those who believed in her would be saved from evils and harm. Since the cult appeared in Vietnam, it has fit well within the indigenous tradition of goddess worship (*đạo Mẫu*). According to *Errors*, the popularity of her cult was due to the belief that she "has more power to save people than any other buddhas."[86] In the popular imagination, she was known as an all-knowing and all-powerful being who could save people from all kinds of trouble and even prevent them from falling into hell. She was sometimes depicted as a lady crossing the South China Sea, other times as a lady holding a child.[87]

---

84. See Glen Dudbridge, *The Legend of Miaoshan* (1978; repr., Oxford: Oxford University Press, 2004).

85. The story told by the author of *Errors* is incomplete. The legend of Diệu Thiện claims that after the fire, she escaped to a cave on Perfume Mountain (Hương Sơn) and continued her monastic practice there. When, as the result of bad karma, the king was struck with an incurable disease, Diệu Thiện returned to visit her father in disguise. She secretly offered her hands and eyes to be made into medicines for her father. Cured of the disease, the king and his family wanted to find the anonymous donor. Upon discovering that the benefactor was his daughter, the king, the queen, and the two remaining sisters converted to Buddhism. See the complete versions in Dudbridge, *The Legend of Miaoshan*, 25–34.

86. *Errors*, Book 3, Article 11, 200.

87. This form of Quan Âm comes from a sixteenth- or seventeenth-century story of Quan Âm Thị Kính, or the Child-Giving Guanyin. The tale describes a devout Thị Kính reluctantly marrying a son of a wealthy, influentual Sùng family, and becoming a devoted wife. Soon after her marriage, she was accused of the attempted murder of her husband, Thiện Sĩ, after which she was banished from the village. She took refuge in a Buddhist temple, disguised as a male novice named Kính Tâm. There, she was accused of impregnating Thị Mầu, a daughter of a local weathy man. Kính Tâm was innocent but could not tell "his" secret, so "he" had to move out of the temple. Finding the baby abandoned, Kính Tâm raised the child as "his" own, and endured local derision for the child's sake. When the child was three years old, Kính Tâm developed a terminal disease. Knowing that she was dying, she left a letter detailing the trials

Influenced by Buddhist tantrism, Vietnamese iconography of Quan Âm during the Lê-Trịnh era often displayed her as sitting on a lotus throne with multiple arms reaching out and blessing people.[88] The image of Quan Âm as having a thousand eyes in a thousand hands dominated many prominent Buddhist temples in Tonkin.[89] Because the author of *Errors* was probably unfamiliar with the tantric form of Quan Âm, he thought of her as a "demon in disguise" since "no human being can have multiple heads and arms."[90]

Jade Emperor

The cult of Jade Emperor (Ngọc Hoàng), a favorite god in the Chinese pantheon, did not seem to gain much currency in traditional Vietnam outside of the Daoist circle. Nevertheless, the cult attracted enough followers to be mentioned by Christian apologetic writings from the seventeenth to the nineteenth centuries. In *Errors*, our author discusses the cult of Jade Emperor by demythologizing the figure. He gave two accounts of the historical origins of this deity.

One story holds that Jade Emperor was a man named Zhang Yi, the grandson of the famous Han general Zhang Liang; he learned Daoist magic and became immortal. Centuries later, Zhang Yi appeared to Emperor Huizong of the Song dynasty in a dream to help him fight the rebels. The emperor considered Zhang Yi a god and conferred upon him the title "Jade Emperor the Supreme Sovereign" (Ngọc Hoàng Thượng Đế).[91] Another account mentions that he was the son of King Guang Yan of the Miao Le kingdom, whose wife was barren. One night, Queen Bao Yueguang dreamt that the Daoist god Yuanshi brought her a boy. Upon waking, the queen became pregnant and gave birth to a son the following year. Since he was a precious gift from the god, she named him "Jade Emperor."[92]

---

and tribulations she endured. After his death, the villagers discovered she was a woman and was falsely accused. Thị Kính's story so moved the emperor that he elevated her to the rank of divinity with the tile "Quan Âm the Compassion Protector of Children." There are many variations of this story, one of which can be found in Dutton, *Sources of Vietnamese Tradition*, 180–86. This story, however, did not appear in *Errors*.

88. This particular form of Quan Âm (with multiple arms and hands) has fallen out of favor today; instead, the white-robed-standing Quan Âm, somewhat like the Blessed Virgin Mary of Lourdes or Fatima, became more popular in the twentieth century.

89. See examples in Bảo Sơn Temple, Đại Dương Temple in Hanoi; Kim Tưởng Temple in Cổ Loa (Hanoi); Hiếu Temple, Mễ Sở Temple in Hưng Yên; Bút Tháp Temple, Tiêu Sơn Temple in Bắc Ninh; and Huyền Kỳ Temple in Hà Tây. Nguyễn Minh Ngọc, Nguyễn Mạnh Cường, and Nguyễn Duy Hinh, *Bồ Tát Quán Thế Âm*, 307–83.

90. *Errors*, Book 3, Article 11, 201.

91. *Errors*, Book 2, Article 2, 101.

92. *Errors*, Book 2, Article 2, 102.

This account was repeated in Catholic works of apologetics of the nineteenth century.

The author of *Errors* finds the two accounts contradictory. If Jade Emperor were a historical figure, he could not have been the son of a fictitious king from a fictitious kingdom. The apparent contradiction between the two accounts was enough for the author to dismiss the figure of Jade Emperor as someone worthy of worship.

A Christian Evaluation of Traditional Worship

The usual approach of our Christian author to the worship of spirits was to demythologize them. First, the author sought to provide a historical account of the spirits to demonstrate their human origin. The biographical details of Confucius, Laozi, Sakyamuni Buddha, Quan Âm, Jade Emperor, and other spirits made the case that as human beings, these figures did not possess the power to grant blessings and protect people from harm. Second, by claiming that powers are granted from God alone, the author of *Errors* argued that the worship of these spirits was ineffective, and therefore, a waste of resources.

The general Christian opposition to traditional Vietnamese cults is related to the Western interpretation of words and concepts such as *thờ, cúng,* or *tế*. The term *thờ* was translated by missionaries as *adorare* or worship, which, according to Catholic theology, must be reserved solely for God. In contrast, for the Vietnamese, *thờ* is more inclusive. It is a word indicating honor and service that applies to both the living and the dead, to humans and gods. Vietnamese "worship" or serve their parents (*thờ cha kính mẹ*), ancestors (*thờ ông bà tổ tiên*), their kings (*thờ vua*), and their heroes (*thờ thánh*), as well as heaven (*thờ trời*) or the Buddha (*thờ Phật*). *Thờ*, therefore, has only a generic sense of honoring, a devotional act, which is directed toward anyone (or anything) worthy of respect. It is the semantic equivalent of the Sino-Vietnamese words *kính* (respect/honor) or *sự* (serve), which are found in the Confucian maxims "honor the spirits as if they are present" (*kính thần như thần tại*) and "serve the dead as when they were alive" (*sự tử như sự sinh*).

Cúng (offering) and *tế* (sacrifice) were acts of honoring the spirits somewhat analogous to the offerings and sacrifices in ancient Israel. The sacrifice to Heaven in traditional Vietnam was different in degree but not in kind from the sacrifices to other spirits and to one's own ancestors. In some cases, *cúng* and *tế* were meant to appease evil or troubled spirits, but for the most part, they were expressions of honor, respect, and gratitude that one felt toward the sages and heroes of the past—those deified beings who dominated the Vietnamese pantheon. This is a point of contention for the Christian that is repeated throughout *Errors*—that is, that devotion and honor should be reserved for God alone. Traditional Vietnamese thinking could not accept the reason for this exclusive worship, which led to the Confucian rejection and persecution of Christianity in the seventeenth and eighteenth centuries.

From a Christian perspective, the Vietnamese cults of spirits can be mixed with "superstitious" practices. But, in essence, they are no different than the cults of saints in Catholicism. If one takes a survey of the spirits (*thần*) who were worshipped in Tonkin, the majority were of human origin rather than celestial beings, deified animals, or natural objects and phenomena. They were heroes and heroines, teachers and inventors, kings and generals, scholars and nobles whose deeds were worth remembering. By "worshipping" them, later generations were able to learn of their virtues and merits. In this view, the cults of spirits were an extension of the cult of ancestors, which was and remains at the heart of Vietnamese religious expression, our topic of discussion in the next chapter.

In *Errors*' assessment of the cult of Thành Hoàng (Guardian Deity), for example, we can see that tension play out. On the one hand, the author could see the benefit of honoring deified heroes. On the other hand, he could not accept the cult of Thành Hoàng wholesale, because it had been explicitly forbidden by Rome as superstitious. His pejorative assessment of Vietnamese deities as "rebels against the Lord of Heaven" or "demons in disguise" should be read with care. These terms were less an actual judgment on the merits of particular deities than the reflection of a general bias that was characteristic of missionary thinking of this era; that is, paganism had nothing positive to offer to the Christians.

4

In the Realm of the Dead

FILIAL PIETY AND ANCESTRAL WORSHIP

OF ALL THE issues that characterized the tension Catholics had in traditional Vietnamese society, none surpassed the matters of "ancestral worship"—the most important religious and social expression of the Vietnamese people. The public display of filial virtue (*hiếu*) was the foundation of all morals and customs. Regardless of religious background or personal belief, the practice of honoring one's ancestors was expected of everyone. The solemnity with which Vietnamese expressed their respect for their ancestors left lasting impressions on Westerners. In the seventeenth century, Alexandre de Rhodes made a rather sweeping assessment: "There is perhaps no other nation on this inhabited earth that honors and venerates the souls and bodies of the dead more than the people of Tonkin."[1] Hence, the longest articles in *Errors* focus on the funeral and memorial practices of the Tonkinese—both in Book One and again in Book Three. To provide the reader with a context to understand the related issues, I will describe the background of the rites to the ancestors, and then give a Christian evaluation of these rites.

Vietnamese Anthropology and Ancestral Worship

The cult of the ancestors, found in many ancient cultures, is based on the fundamental belief that death is not the end of a person's existence but rather his or her transformation into a privileged place in the family hierarchy. As the deceased are remembered and honored collectively as ancestors, their virtues are exemplified while past wrongs are forgiven. Regardless of the merits acquired or

---

1. Rhodes, *Histoire du royaume de Tunquin*, part 1, chap. 23, 80.

transgressions committed during their lifetimes, the ancestors take on new personas as spiritual members of the family who can influence the material world. It is believed that deceased family members retain both an interest in, and the ability to affect, their living relatives.

Fundamental Characteristics

The practice of ancestor veneration is based on several basic premises: (1) a belief that the dead survive in another realm or spiritual reality; (2) a notion of family as a corporate body that includes the dead and the living; (3) an understanding that the dead and the living mutually depend on and benefit each other; and (4) the use of rituals as the mode of communication between the living and the dead that bonds family members within and across generations.[2]

First, in Vietnamese cosmology, death is a doorway to another world called *âm phủ* or "the palace of the dead." In *âm phủ*, the dead continue their lives in a manner similar to the *dương gian* or the world of the living. They continue to engage in similar activities and still need material assistance, including shelter, clothing, food and drink, utensils, and money. If they do not receive the needed support, the spirits of the dead return to disturb the living.[3]

Second, traditional societies, including the Vietnamese, have an extended notion of the family that includes the dead and the living. Underlying this notion is the belief that the bond between the dead and their surviving relatives is not severed at death. The deceased continue to be present to and take an interest in the affairs of their living family members in some metaphysical form. In traditional Vietnamese society, "the dead rule the living," and the result can be either positive or negative. On the positive side, ancestors are credited with the ability to cure illness, ward off plagues, avert disaster, promote fertility, or promote the well-being of family members. They can also be advocates to the higher deities and powerful spirits on behalf of their families. On the negative side, ancestors can be a chastising force, causing illness or trouble when they are displeased. In either case, the ancestors are supernatural beings who are concerned for and interact with their surviving family members. They act as social controllers who reward the deserving and punish the delinquent.

---

[2]. The best study on this theme remains Léopold Cadière, "La famille et la religion en pays annamites," in *Croyances et pratiques réligieuses*, 1:33–84.

[3]. Similar concepts existed in ancient Egypt, China, India, and other cultures, hence the custom of burying goods and animals, and in extreme cases, other human beings with the dead.

Third, the relationship between the dead and the living is interdependent. All family members are mutually interdependent, with reciprocal duties and obligations. Parents care and provide for their children in their infancy and youth. In turn, adult children provide for their parents in their old age. The cult of the ancestors is a ritualized extension of this moral obligation. A person making offerings to his ancestral spirits is merely acting according to the prescribed social order: the old are to be supported and treated with special reverence. Ritual sacrifices are performed to provide the ancestors with food and other means of self-sustenance. If they do not receive sacrifices, the ancestral spirits become "hungry ghosts" or "lost souls" (*cô hồn*) and may become malicious. The principle of interdependence also demands that the deceased help the living. Since all family members are to contribute to the common well-being and the spirits are thought to have resources beyond those of living members, the ancestors are expected to help the family in critical times. By rectifying bad luck, providing good fortune, and giving advice, the ancestors assist the family in its struggle against shifting fortunes. The ancestors thus function as a safety net in times of serious threat.

Fourth, the relationship between people is established and maintained through communication. Family members share their opinions, desires, hopes, and fears with one another. Communication between the living and the dead can be expressed through rituals such as offerings, prayers, and, if needed, divination. Petitions from the living to the spirits are made through direct prayers (*khấn*) or written orations (*văn tế*). Letters to the spirits are burnt so as to send the messages to the spirit realm by way of smoke.

Communication from the dead to the living is more challenging. Dreams are viewed as the ordinary mode of communication from the spirits. Ancestors appear to descendants in dreams to reveal their needs or intentions. However, dreams can have multiple meanings and oftentimes require interpretation, so for many people, the most straightforward way to interpret the messages from an ancestor is through divination. While there are many forms of divination, the simplest method is that of casting coins, called *xin âm dương*. The person prays to the ancestors and asks for their approval on the issue in question, then takes two coins and casts them on a plate. If one coin is a head and the other a tail, this is *yang*, a sign of the ancestor's approval; if both coins are heads or tails, this is *yin*, an unfavorable answer. The process can be repeated three times to ensure a valid response. In general, this practice is sufficient for simple confirmation from the world beyond. More complicated situations demanding longer or more precise messages may require a medium or sorcerer to communicate the will of the ancestor(s).

A Display of Confucian Filial Piety

Although rituals honoring the dead and their spirits have existed since prehistoric times, the Confucian tradition linked the practice with filial piety. In Confucian social ethics, filial piety (*hiếu*, Chinese: *xiao*) has been considered the most important virtue. Under this paramount virtue, all other ethical qualities derive their import: humaneness (*nhân*, Chinese: *ren*) and righteousness (*nghĩa*, Chinese: *yi*), core values of Confucianism, are seen as its extensions. Filial piety grounds all interactions in familial relationships.

The social function of ancestor worship, therefore, is to cultivate kinship values such as filial piety, family loyalty, and continuity of the family lineage. The key to understanding the rites to the ancestors is expressed in a teaching by Confucius: "When parents are alive, serve them according to ritual. When they die, bury them according to ritual and sacrifice to them according to ritual."[4] Ancestral rites were performed to express one's sincerity and reverence toward one's parents. They were used primarily to instruct the living on social conduct rather than to appease or request favors from the dead. In performing these rites, the basic lesson of gratitude is taught to the younger generations. The living pay respect and homage to the dead to "repay the debts" that they owe to the ones who brought them into the world and raised them to adulthood. They worship and honor their ancestors, and they will be worshipped and honored in turn by their descendants.

The concept of "serving the dead as if one serves the living"[5] is the heart of the Confucian interpretation of the ancestral rites. One can interpret the meaning of sacrifice to the dead espoused by the *Record of Rites* as primarily a ritual of remembrance. This is primarily the position of the Confucian literati, those who have to uphold the social norms. The ancestral rites are public expressions of filial piety. When a person abandons these rites, he cannot defend his conduct as being filial.

Concepts of the Soul and the Afterlife

Foundational to the cult of the ancestors is the doctrine of the immortality of the soul. The Vietnamese concept of the human person maintains that humans are made of material and nonmaterial substances. The material components

---

4. *Analects*, 11:5. Since there are many translations of Confucius' *Analects*, I will give reference to the standard way of referencing the Chinese text by chapter and verse.

5. Cf. *Doctrine of the Mean*, chap. 19. Since there are many editions and translations of this classic, I will give reference to the standard way of referencing the Chinese text by chapter (and verse when needed).

of the body are flesh, muscle, bone, and the vital organs. But they cannot function without the immaterial driving force called *khí* (Chinese: *qi*), the vital energy that shows the sign of life. Originally a term to depict vapor or breath, *khí* signifies the animating force that makes an animal or a person a living being.

Another immaterial component of the human person is the pair of souls called *hồn* and *phách* (or *vía*). All humans are said to possess three *hồn* (the spiritual soul), whereas there are seven *phách* (the material soul) for a man but nine *phách* for a woman.[6] The spiritual souls are said to originate in heaven and enter the body at birth; the material souls come from the earth and are generated during the development of the fetus. At death, the spiritual souls ascend to heaven, and the material souls return to the earth.[7]

Confucianism, Daoism, and Buddhism modified the basic belief in the immortality of the soul and the concept of an underworld. Because of its focus on human affairs and conduct in this world, Confucianism does not concern itself with what happens after death. It takes the existence of the world of spirits and the dead for granted but does not develop theories of the human soul or the afterlife. Neo-Confucians, who adhered to a materialist and rationalist view of a person, equated the souls (*hồn* and *phách*) with the vital force (*khí*), which perishes after death. When the vital energy gathers, there is life; when it disperses, there is death. The fate of humans is no different than that of animals. Confucian offerings to the dead are made not so much to sustain them as to honor them and keep their memory alive.

With its concern for prolonging life, Daoism has no theory about the human soul and its fate after death. Daoists seek immortality through the practice of alchemy and techniques of health preservation. Those who attain the secret of

---

6. The three *hồn* are the vegetative soul, the emotional soul, and the rational soul. There is no explanation why there are seven *phách* for man and nine for woman. I think it might have some connection to different orifices of the body, traditionally seven for man (i.e., two eyes, two ears, nose, mouth, and the anus), and nine for woman (the seven plus the urinal orifice and the vagina). Alexandre de Rhodes has an interesting explanation for the number of *phách* or *vía*. He writes, "There are seven more spirits which also reside in the same body.... They do not have names for each but collectively call them *bảy vía* [seven spirits]. When someone is suddenly frightened in an accident, they say he lost a spirit or *mất vía*. And since women are more easily frightened than men, they assign them nine spirits called *chín vía*. There is another reason to give women more *vía*; it is for their preservation, for women often live longer than men, old ladies more than old men." He also recounts how every year the Lord of Tonkin received another *vía* to replace his weary one. This event is celebrated in an elaborate ceremony. See Rhodes, *Histoire du royaume de Tunquin*, part 1, chap. 26, 93–94.

7. Cadière, "La religion des Annamites," in *Croyances et pratiques réligieuses*, 1:17.

life are transformed into immortals (*tiên*) without ever going to another world. Although Daoists believe in a world of spirits and ghosts that one can control by amulets and magic, they have not developed a distinctive rite for the dead. Most Daoist worship derives from popular customs and in imitation of Buddhist rituals.

Buddhism also does not have a clear theory about the human soul. To Buddhists, the human person is made up of different aggregates that disintegrate after death, when the present life vanishes and people are reborn with new identities. Depending on their *karma*, or the merits of past deeds, they are reborn into one of the six paths that belong to the realm of desire.[8] Eventually one will escape the cycle of birth and death altogether once one reaches nirvana. Strictly speaking, the doctrine of transmigration does not concern itself with offerings to the dead. The dead and the living cannot influence one another; each has to live with his own *karma*.

Vietnamese Buddhists did not strictly follow this doctrine. Instead, they believed in the three realms of existence: paradise, earth, and hell. Paradise or "land of the Buddha" is the popular conception of Amida's Pure Land, where the soul enjoys a blessed afterlife with the bodhisattvas and Buddhist saints. The earth is the visible world of human beings and animals as well as the invisible world of the spirits and ghosts. Hell is a place with multiple levels of imprisonment and punishment, governed by the Ten Kings of Hell. However, all three realms are only transient stages.

The Ancestral Rites in Practice

To the individual Vietnamese, deceased ancestors are not supernatural beings but familial spirits who continue to live and share in the joys and sorrows of the family. They are to be remembered individually—at least back to five generations—before being honored collectively as the ancestors. Through simple prayers, the ancestors are informed of the happy occasions—marriage, childbirth, a new home, new business, passing a major exam, taking an office, to name a few—or of sad events—incurring a serious illness, losing property, or the death of a member of the family. More solemn rituals take place at the family altar or in the ancestral

---

8. They include the world of the gods (*deva*), titans (*asura*), humans, animals, suffering ghosts (*preta*), and hell (*naraka*). According to Buddhist cosmology, if one practices Buddhism diligently, one can be born into the higher realms of form (*rūpadhātu*) and formlessness (*ārūpyadhātu*). Buddhist cosmology is quite complex. For an introduction to this subject, see Akira Sadakata, *Buddhist Cosmology: Philosophy and Origin*, trans. Gaynor Sekimori (Tokyo: Kosei Publishing Co., 1997).

hall on New Year's Eve and, in particular, on the anniversaries of the deaths of the parents and grandparents. No family member can be absent on these occasions. Such an offense may be liable to legal punishment.

On the day of the ceremony, before the assembled family, the head of the family enacts a carefully prescribed ritual. Putting on his best robes, he lights the candles and lamps on the altar decorated with flowers and incense. He makes the food offering, pours the wine libations, says the prayers, and prostrates himself before the altar. The rest of the family follows suit, standing, kneeling, and bowing accordingly. Everyone present must endeavor to think that he or she is in the presence of the ancestors who have come to the altar to take part in the family banquet. Every step of the rites is performed with precision because the rites themselves embody the virtue of filial piety.

Traditional Funeral Rites and Memorials

The standard form of the ancestral rites was derived from Zhu Xi's *Family Rituals*,[9] or *Văn Công Gia Lễ*, a manual of Confucian ceremonies and etiquette, which was introduced to Vietnam in the fifteenth century.[10] The increasing need for proper ritual guidance at home prompted Vietnamese Confucians to compose their own ritual books modeled after Zhu Xi's manual. These manuals of rites were briefer than the original and accommodated popular customs. One such manual is *Family Rituals by Thọ Mai* (Thọ Mai Gia Lễ) by the mandarin Hồ Sĩ Tân (1690–1738).[11] Written for the use of his family, it nevertheless became a popular guide to the funeral practices in Tonkin up to the twentieth century.[12]

---

9. For an English translation of this important manual, see Patricia B. Ebrey, *Chu Hsi's Family Rituals: A Twelfth-Century Chinese Manual for the Performance of Cappings, Weddings, Funerals, and Ancestral Rites* (Princeton, NJ: Princeton University Press, 1991). For a study on its history and influence, see her *Confucianism and Family Rituals in Imperial China: A Social History of Writing about Rites* (Princeton, NJ: Princeton University Press, 1991).

10. The scarcity of extant records does not permit us to examine the traditional cults of the ancestors prior to the Lê dynasty. Imperial sources such as the Lê Codes and *Collection of Customs of the Lê Dynasty* (Lê Triều Hội Điển) mention the ancestor rites as they apply to the imperial household but do not contain much on the rites at the family level.

11. Hồ Sỹ Tân (ca. 1690–1738), style name Thọ Mai from Quỳnh Lưu District, passed his doctoral examination in 1721 and became a mandarin. His *Family Rituals* was partly based on a work by his grand-uncle, the mandarin Hồ Sỹ Dương (1621–1681) entitled *Hồ Thượng Thư Gia Lễ* [Family Rituals by the Great Official Ho]. Both Hồ Sĩ Dương and Hồ Sĩ Tân have been honored at the Temple of Culture in Hanoi.

12. A nineteenth-century French translation was done by E. C. Lesserteur, entitled *Ritual domestiques des funérailles en Annam* (Paris: Imprimerie Chaix, 1885).

Vietnamese Buddhists also adapted Confucian rites and produced their own ritual book.

The author of *Errors* gives us a brief but fairly complete description of traditional Confucian funeral rites and memorials. His description is based on a number of guides, among which *Correct Practices of the Family Rituals* (Gia Lễ Chính Hành)[13] and *Updated Family Rituals* (Gia Lễ Tiếp Kinh)[14] are mentioned by name. Every step was to be followed with utmost care. To give a reader a sense of Tonkinese eighteenth-century funeral practices, I am going to describe the traditional rituals for the dead using the information given in *Errors* and supplement them with data from Zhu Xi's and Thọ Mai's manuals wherever appropriate.[15]

Before the Burial

The beginning of the end: When an illness becomes acute, the dying person is moved to the main room, and a three-yard-long piece of white silk is placed on his chest. Everyone must be quiet awaiting his last breath, when *khí*, the vital energy, finally exits. Some Buddhists have a custom of inviting monks to recite the prayer "Protection for the Journey" (*kinh bảo đảng*) to guide the dying person on his journey to the netherworld. When death is confirmed, a piece of paper is placed on the face of the deceased. The body is "brought down to the ground" (*hạ thổ*) and laid there for a while before being brought back to the bed, as a way of saying that, coming from the earth, the body now returns to the earth.

The rite of "calling the soul back" (phục hồn): To prevent the deceased from becoming a wandering soul, a family member (ordinarily the eldest son) climbs up on the roof of the house and invites him or her to return home. Holding an outer garment of the deceased, he shouts three times, "The three *hồn* and seven *viá* of my father (or nine *viá* of my mother)! Please come home." When finished, he rolls up the garment, comes down, and places it on the body. Then everyone may make gestures of mourning.

Making the soul cloth: As soon as the person is dead, the white silk cloth is removed from the chest and is knotted into a human figurine to make a "soul

---

13. This 1599 work by Peng Bin is cited by Patricia Ebrey as one of the adaptations of Zhu Xi's *Family Rituals*. I do not know if the edition used by the author of *Errors* is the same as this work or a Vietnamese work of the same title.

14. According to the information in Thọ Mai's *Family Rituals*, the Confucian scholar Ngô Sĩ Bình of Tam Sơn commune in Đông Ngàn district composed and printed this book in 1707. An incomplete copy of the *Family Rituals* (catalogue number AM 572/MF 963) is preserved in the Institute of Hán-Nôm Studies in Hanoi.

15. See also Rhodes, *Histoire du royaume de Tunquin*, part 1, chaps. 23 and 24 for a description of these rites in seventeenth-century Tonkin.

cloth" (*hồn bạch*). A temporary home for the deceased, it is placed on a small table called the "soul seat" (*linh tọa*), where the soul will enjoy the oblation offered to it. From this moment on, the soul cloth is treated like the actual presence of the deceased until it is replaced after the burial by the "spirit tablet" (*thần vị* or *thần chủ*) to be worshipped at the family altar or at the ancestral hall.[16]

Selecting the master of ceremonies and assistants: The eldest son (if he does not survive, then his eldest son) is automatically established as the principal mourner (*tang chủ*).[17] Several close male family members are chosen to plan and assist in the oftentimes elaborate and time-consuming funeral. Their functions include those of the funeral director (*hộ tang*), the letter recorder (*tư thư*), and the gift recorder (*tư hoá*). As signs of mourning, everyone fasts and alters his or her hair and clothes. Death announcements are sent to relatives, colleagues, and friends.

Washing and dressing the body (mộc dục): The body is removed from the deathbed and washed with water boiled with fragrant herbs. Fingernails and toenails are cut. The hair is washed, dried, combed, and pulled up into a knot. Sons and daughters (or daughters-in-laws) are to wash and enshroud the deceased themselves. In the meantime, the burial clothes are prepared and laid out on a table, including a head wrap, earplugs, eye covers, a face cover, gloves, shoes, robe, belt, undergarments, trousers, and socks. Then the body is shrouded and placed on a bed in the center of the hall.

Preparation of the coffin: The coffin should be made from straight planks of good-quality wood, the head end large and the foot end small. Several inches of ashes are poured into the coffin and a piece of paper placed on the ashes for padding.[18] This is covered with a board with seven star-like holes resembling the Ursa Minor constellation (*thất tinh*); then a mattress, cushion, and pillow are placed inside the coffin. When everything is ready, the body is transferred to the coffin. Before putting the body into the coffin, a ritual called "expelling the wood demon" (*phạt mộc*) is sometimes performed.[19] Afterward, a "name banner" (*minh*

---

16. Nowadays, both the soul cloth and the spirit tablet are replaced by a picture of the deceased.

17. If the husband or father is alive at the time of the funeral of a wife or unmarried daughter, he takes the role of the presiding mourner. The wife of the deceased or the wife of the principal mourner can lead the mourning if there is no male principal mourner; otherwise she is the copresiding mourner (*phụ tang chủ*).

18. The ashes absorb the bodily secretions as the corpse decomposes. Rich families may substitute dry tea leaves for the ashes.

19. It is believed that, since trees have live spirits inside them, when a tree is chopped down to make a coffin, an exorcism must be performed to "send the evil spirits off to their places and prevent them from harming the soul of the deceased." After making the sacrifices to the various spirits, a monk or priest takes a knife and strikes at the coffin three times to expel the demons. This custom is not mentioned in the Zhu Xi's or Thọ Mai's rituals.

tinh) is made by writing the title, the family name, the posthumous name, and the social position of the deceased on a large red banner, then hanging it on a pole to the left side of the coffin.[20]

The rite of "putting rice into the mouth" (phạn hàm): Before the coffin is closed, the master of ceremonies puts a pinch of rice and three new coins into the mouth of the deceased so that the soul will not be hungry. Wealthy families substitute pearls and three pieces of gold for the rice and coins. The face is then covered, the shroud is placed on the body, and the coffin is closed.

Daily rituals: The mourners wait for three days for a return to life before declaring their loved one has departed them forever. Each morning of the three days, the principal mourner brings water, a towel, and a comb to the soul bed to "wake up" the deceased (who is supposed to reside in the soul cloth) for the morning hygiene practices. Then they carry the soul cloth on the ritual chair to the offering table to take the morning, midday, and evening meals. At the end of the day, the ritual chair is carried back to the soul bed to rest. This custom re-enacts the daily activities of the deceased when he or she was alive.

The rite of "putting on the mourning garments" (thành phục): The official mourning period begins on the fourth day. An oblation and a prayer are said before everyone dons their white mourning garments, which differ in quality and design according to the degree of relationship. Ritual books specify the style, material, and measurements for each type of mourning garment for male and female mourners.[21] Because these garments are public displays of the filial virtue, wearing the correct garment at the funeral and during the mourning period is a serious obligation.[22]

---

20. The size of the banner is specified according to the ranking of the public office that the deceased held. A high-ranking officer, for example, might have his name banner of 9 *thước* (3.6 meters) long. A lower-ranking officer has a shorter banner. A commoner usually has a 5-*thước* (2-meter) banner.

21. There are at least five degrees of mourning and corresponding garments. The first type is called "untrimmed sackcloth" (*trảm thôi*), reserved for mourning the father and husband, or main-line grandson and his wife as double heirs for their grandfather; the mourners wear it for three years. The second type is "even sackcloth" (*tế thôi*), reserved for mourning the mother, main-line grandson, and his wife as double heirs for their grandmother; the mourners also wear it for three years. A son of a single mother can wear the "untrimmed sackcloth" to mourn his mother. Other types of mourning garments are specified for mourning siblings and relatives. The "remembrance cloth" (*cơ niên* or *mộ phục*) entails a one-year period of mourning; the "greater processed cloth" (*đại công*) a nine-month; the "lesser processed cloth" (*tiểu công*) a five-month; and the "fine hemp" (*ty ma*) a three-month period of mourning.

22. Imperial regulations such as the Lê Codes specify the duration of mourning, which is dependent on the degree of kinship with the deceased as well as the punishment for those who fail to observe the custom.

Besides wearing the customary mourning garments like those specified in the *Family Rituals*, some Buddhists have their hair cut by a monk (*thế phát*) as an additional sign of mourning. This practice is shunned by strict Confucians, who believe that one should let the hair grow uncombed as a sign of mourning.

The Burial Process

Opening the grave (khai huyệt): According to custom, the person should be buried within three months from the day of death.[23] When a suitable burial place has been selected, the funeral director chooses a day to make offerings to the god of the earth (*hậu thổ*) before the attendants can dig the grave. On the night before the burial, an outdoor oblation is made to the spirits of the roads (*tế đạo lộ*) for a propitious funeral procession.

Presenting to the ancestors (yết tổ): On the day of the burial, the soul cloth is first taken to the ancestral hall (*từ đường*) to greet the ancestors. At the ancestral hall, the head of the clan announces to the ancestors that the deceased will soon join them. Then the soul cloth is carried back home again to accompany the coffin.

The rite of "moving the coffin" (chuyển cữu): At the proper time, the funeral director summons the workers to tie the coffin on the catafalque (*đại dư*) with its head to the front. Then they rotate it around a turn as if the deceased were at the house one more time before departing. A sending-away oblation (*tế chuyển cữu*) is made before moving the coffin out of the house. The soul cloth now is transferred to a "chariot of the soul" (*linh xa*), which will precede the coffin in the funeral procession.

Purchase of a funeral house: The author of *Errors* mentions this custom, which does not appear in Zhu Xi's or Thọ Mai's *Family Rituals*, as an act of filial piety. A life-size and often decorated house made of paper is constructed and purchased to accompany the deceased to the gravesite. It is carried in front of the catafalque during the funeral procession and burned after the burial.

Funeral procession: Before departing for the gravesite, more oblations are made to the spirit of the funeral carriage (*dư thần*) and the spirit of the road, praying for a safe journey that will not be disturbed by demons. The order of procession is as follows: the announcers proceed first, followed by the carriers of the incense burner, the name banner, the soul carriage, the food carriage, the

---

23. Most people were buried as soon as all the burial preparation was completed unless there was a grave reason to delay the burial (e.g., the children or close relatives were living far away; the deceased died away from home and needed to be transported back to his or her native place for burial; kings, nobilities, or famous persons who might require elaborate funerals that need longer preparation and mourning, etc.).

underworld furnishings, and the catafalque. The principal mourners walk behind the coffin wailing, followed by relatives and guests. If the coffin is carried by boat, an oblation is made to the spirit of the river. An oblation is made whenever the procession rests during the journey or making a turn at a three-way crossroads.[24]

At the gravesite: The name banner is spread on the casket before it is lowered into the grave. When the coffin is halfway down into the grave, an offering is made to the god of the earth on the right side of the grave. Another offering is made after covering the grave with dirt.

The rite of "inscribing the tablet" (đề chủ): After washing his hand and offering incense, the ritualist writes the deceased's posthumous name, title, and rank in society on the front side of the tablet, and the dates of birth and death on the reverse side. Then the tablet is placed on the altar with the soul cloth behind it. An oblation is made, asking the deceased to leave the soul cloth and come into the spirit tablet. Then the spirit tablet is carried home to be placed on the family altar.

After the Burial

The rite of "pacifying the soul" (tế ngu): The first three days after burial are considered a sacred time. The mourners visit the gravesite twice a day in the morning and the evening. An oblation called "pacifying the soul" (*ngu*) is made each day during these three days to ensure that the deceased will be comfortable in his or her new environment.[25] People believe that although the body is already at rest under the ground, the soul is still wandering around trying to find its home. Thus one must plan to welcome the soul to its new residence in the spirit tablet by making the offerings. After the rite of pacification, the soul cloth is buried in a clean plot of land.

Mourning period: From that time on, food oblations are made to the spirit tablet. The "morning oblation" (*triêu điện*) must be offered on the new and full moon for the next three months. Buddhists make additional offerings on the seventh, thirtieth, and fiftieth days after death.[26] At the end of the hundredth day

---

24. This allowed the coffin carriers and the mourners to rest and take refreshment on the way, since the walk to the burial site was often long.

25. Léopold Cadière reports that the rite of pacifying the soul (*tế ngu*) is performed on the hundredth day after death. "La famille et la religion annamites," in *Croyances et pratiques réligieuse*, 1:37. This contradicts both Zhu Xi's and Thọ Mai's family rituals, which specify that the rite is to be done in the three days after burial. Is it a possibility that there is another "pacifying the soul" after three months? Or might he have confused the rite of "cessation of wailing" (*tốt khốc*) with *tế ngu*?

26. The one-week, one-month, and seven-week memorial offerings were influenced by Buddhist practices. Zhu Xi's and other books of *Family Rituals* do not mention this custom.

of mourning, there is an oblation called "cessation of wailing" (*tốt khốc*). From this day forward, memorial sacrifices replace the funerary sacrifices during the seasonal rituals like the New Year, the Clear and Bright Festival (*thanh minh*), the Middle Period Festival (*trung nguyên*), and on the anniversary of death.

Veneration of the ancestors: Many large families built an ancestral hall (*từ đường*) to house the spirit tablets of the ancestors up to five generations. Once an ancestor has passed the fifth generation, his or her spirit tablet is removed from the altar, and the memorial feast is no longer required for that ancestor. In the case of the proto-ancestor, his descendants must worship him forever without ever removing his tablets. Regular worship of ancestors occurs in these halls at various times of the year. The spirit tablets of one's immediate parents and paternal grandparents are usually kept on the family altar. The eldest son of the main line is charged with performing sacrifices to all direct ancestors as well as caring for their tombs and the ancestral hall. A special plot of land is set aside as the inheritance field (*hương hoả*) to provide the means for the eldest son (and his main-line descendants) to carry out these duties.

Although the Confucian literati wanted to maintain time-honored customs and traditions, popular religiosity added other customs to the rites for the dead. Because most of these customs were of late origin, particularly from the Tang period (sixth to tenth centuries) in China, they were viewed by the literati as "superstitious" and thus did not appear in any Confucian ritual manual. Since some of these customs have been quite popular in Tonkin and discussed by the author of *Errors*, they are included here for the sake of completeness.[27]

Exhumation and Reburial

Three years after burial, the corpse is exhumed, the bones are cleaned, and then they are reburied in a new vault. There are many reasons for this practice: reburial in the case of a poor or haphazard one necessitated by plague or war; reburial in the native place of an ancestor buried away from home; burial in a more auspicious plot for those whose belief in geomancy suggested a better future for the living if ancestors were reburied there; to assuage ancestral displeasure as interpreted through illness or misfortune striking the family. Not everyone could afford to follow this custom of reburial, however, especially if there was no discernible trouble in the household. Although not discussed in *Errors*, the custom

---

27. It is still practiced by many North Vietnamese today, even within my family.

was widely practiced in many regions of Tonkin.[28] The custom of reburial is linked closely with the practice of geomantic divination, which is discussed below.

GEOMANTIC DIVINATION

Chinese geomancy (*fengshui*) is the art of spatial arrangement based on the theories of yin-yang, the five elements, and observations of the features of the land and course of water in order to find a location with a high concentration of vital energy (*khí*).[29] It is believed that an auspicious plot can bring vital energy to benefit the person who lives there, or their descendants if an ancestor is buried there.[30] In premodern Vietnam, almost every construction project of importance—mansions, temples, or palaces—was done according to geomantic principles. Thus people searched for an auspicious burial plot for their ancestors because they believed that by doing so, they would have wealth, honor, many children, good fortune, and longevity. The search was often conducted with the help of a geomancer (*thầy địa lý*), who would find the right time or the right direction to bury or rebury the ancestors.[31] Not everyone could master this esoteric and difficult art, and charlatanry was rampant.

---

28. Alexandre de Rhodes describes this practice in his *Histoire du royaume de Tunquin*, chap. 23, 83–84. The custom is still being practiced today, although in much more limited circumstances. After my grandfather died in Saigon in 1974, he was exhumed and brought back to his native village in North Vietnam, for a reburial in 1980. As recently as 2008, an aunt of mine died in Hanoi and was buried temporarily in a cemetery in view of an eventual relocation to a "better spot" within three to five years.

29. Geomantic divination or Chinese geomancy is a general term for what the Chinese call *fengshui* [wind and water] and the Vietnamese call *địa lý* [terrestrial measurement]. Unlike the art of *feng shui* that focuses on spatial arrangements in the world of the living (*yang*) and the dead (*yin*), Vietnamese masters of *địa lý* focus their attention on finding an auspicious plot for burial.

30. The art of geomancy originated among the non-Confucian schools of the late Zhou period and was later on adopted by religious Daoism. A school of diviners and geomancers existed during the Han dynasty, although not much is known about them before the Tang dynasty, when the first geomantic manual was supposed to be compiled by Liao Yu. For a description of the Chinese geomancy up to the nineteenth century, see J. J. M. de Groot, *The Religious System of China*, vol. 3, chap. 12 (1882; repr., Taipei: Ch'eng Wen Publishing, 1976).

31. Vietnamese geomancers trace the origin of their esoteric art to two seventeenth-century scholars, Nguyễn Đức Huyên and Hoà Chính. The first was better known as Master Tả Ao, a name taken from his village. After learning from the best geomancers in China, he helped to spread the art in Tonkin by composing a manual of geomantic divination bearing his name, the *Geomancy by Tả Ao* (Tả Ao Địa Lý). The different schools of geomancy can be divided into three main branches: those specializing in calculating the auspicious time based on astrology; those specializing in identifying features of the land and bodies of water; and those specializing in navigating a divination compass. A good master is said to know all three branches. Phan Kế Bính, *Việt Nam Phong Tục*, part 3, chap. 22, 279–82.

BURNING OF JOSS PAPER

Because of the belief that the deceased still need material assistance in the netherworld, money and other paper goods were sent to them through burning at the gravesite or at home during holidays and memorial services. They would be transformed into real money and objects for the dead to use in the afterlife. Burning spirit money and other paper objects is an expression of honoring and caring for the ancestors in the afterlife, guaranteeing their well-being and a positive disposition toward the living. Spirit money or joss paper (*vàng mã*) was also burned during a temple service to procure a favor from the spirit. The ritual is also used to pay the ancestor's spiritual debts, thus allowing them to be released from the underworld prison.

This custom has a long history in China. Like other ancient cultures, the Chinese of the Zhou period had a custom of burying goods with the dead. Following the invention of paper, people realized that paper would make a cheaper substitute for real or mock objects made out of other materials. Wang Yu of the Tang dynasty was credited with originating the use of paper money for imperial sacrifice. The custom has prevailed among the Chinese and Vietnamese since then.[32] Not originally a Buddhist practice, it has been nevertheless widely practiced by Buddhists in Tonkin, especially in their funeral and memorial services and on the feast of Ulambana, the Buddhist "Day of the Dead."

According to traditional beliefs, a person who dies without an heir may turn into a lost soul if there is no one making offerings to him or her. Orphaned spirits lacking a family to offer sacrifices may become malicious. Such unhappy spirits cannot simply be ignored. Offerings for these destitute beings are made by cooking rice broth on the first and full moon, then sprinkling it on leaves for the soul to consume.[33] The appeasing of the lost souls is particularly done on the full moon of the seventh month, popularly known as "the day of the dead," when all souls are allowed back to this world to be with their families; those orphaned spirits will leave the living undisturbed if they are fed.

---

32. For a contemporary study of the burning of paper good, see Janet Lee Scott, *For Gods, Ghost and Ancestors: The Chinese Tradition of Paper Offerings* (Seattle: University of Washington Press, 2007).

33. According to popular beliefs, "these wandering souls have skinny legs and thin necks, so they cannot walk firmly on the ground, and stay on tree branches [like birds]; since they cannot eat rice (or solid food), people cook rice porridge and sprinkle the soup on the leaves so that they can eat." *Errors*, Book 3, Article 11, 202.

Folk Buddhism and the Afterlife

The author of *Errors* discusses features of Buddhism as it was practiced in the eighteenth-century Tonkin. Some beliefs and customs could be recognized as Buddhist, whereas others were a mixture of Daoist or folk beliefs. In the absence of other sources to the contrary, however, the descriptions regarding the Buddhist approach to the afterlife can be seen as a window into folk Buddhism in Tonkin.

The Doctrine of Transmigration of Souls

One of the major features of the Buddhist teachings on death and dying is the doctrine of transmigration, or what is popularly called "rebirth" (*luân hồi*).[34] Buddhism teaches that after death, people journey on one of the six paths of rebirth (*lục đạo*). Those who accumulated merit will be reborn in the worlds of the gods, the titans, or humans. Those with bad *karma* will be reborn as animals, suffering ghosts, or, worst of all, hell-beings. The latter are called the three wicked paths (*tam đồ ác lộ*). Vietnamese Buddhists believe that if one kills an animal, bird, or sea creature, "one will become the same creature in the next life and will eventually be killed by another. Furthermore, anyone who does not kill will die only once and will never have to be reborn again in the cycle of birth and death, or at the least, the person will gain enough merit to be reborn as a human and not as an animal."[35] This explanation is given to deter the killing of animals and to foster vegetarianism.

On the surface, the doctrine of transmigration contradicts the Confucian filial sense and seems to go against the practice of ancestor worship. If one is to be reborn as another person or other life form, the familial connection between generations is severed, making the practice of ancestor worship useless. This has been a point of doctrinal contention between Buddhism and Confucianism for centuries. The author of *Errors* simply repeats the Confucian arguments against this doctrine and brands it as ridiculous, inconsistent, and unfilial, calling it a "false and empty teaching that Buddhism has made up."[36]

Another version of rebirth was conceived by the followers of the "Inner Way" (*nội đạo*), a Daoist-Buddhist sect in Tonkin, a group that might include the authors of the esoteric manuals called Esoteric Branches (*Bí Chi*) and Lamp of the Mind

---

34. For an introduction to Buddhist view on death and the afterlife, see Carl Becker, *Breaking the Circle: Death and the Afterlife in Buddhism* (Carbondale: Southern Illinois University Press, 1993).

35. *Errors*, Book 3, Article 7, 179.

36. *Errors*, Book 3, Article 6, 182.

(*Tâm Đăng*). This group interpreted the teachings on rebirth or "returning in cycle" (*luân hồi*) in physiological terms. According to this school, the transmigration or rebirth in another realm after death is only a metaphor rather than a reality.[37]

Buddhist Hell

Before they can be reborn into another form of being, wicked people with bad karma must undergo punishment in a place of torment called "hell," or, literally, "terrestrial prison" (*địa ngục*). It is worth noting that prior to the seventh century, the concept of "hell" as the place of punishment for the various sins one committed during one's lifetime did not exist in China. In the older view, the world of the dead or *âm phủ* was very much like this world, where both joy and suffering coexist. Medieval Chinese Buddhist rites for the dead gave rise to the popular concept of hell.[38] In Chinese Buddhism, hell is a system of multilevel prisons, governed by the ten kings, in which the deceased undergo a trial administered by one of these kings every seventh day after death. The soul is sent to the next level after each trial until the seventh week.

Although the concept of forty-nine days of trial and punishment also existed in other Mahayana Buddhist traditions, the next three levels of the trial were a Chinese Buddhist innovation to accord with their traditional memorial services. The eighth trial begins on the hundredth day after death, the ninth in the first month after the first year, and the tenth during the third year. The condemned soul is imprisoned in one of many prisons of hell between trials and suffers the appropriate punishment for his transgressions. The concept of a dreadful place of afterlife punishment captured the popular imagination and served as a powerful motivation for people to do good and avoid evil. But it is not a place without hope. People can pray to the compassionate bodhisattva Ksitigarbha (Chinese: Dizang wang) to help their loved ones evade the trials of the ten kings.[39]

Vietnamese Buddhists inherited this concept of hell and also the practice of seven-week sacrifices from the Chinese. On the seventh day of each week after death, the family asks Buddhist monks to perform prayer services and make offerings to spirits to help "speed" their loved ones through the underworld

---

37. *Errors*, Book 3, Article 6, 264.

38. Stephen F. Teiser, *The Ghost Festival in Medieval China* (Princeton, NJ: Princeton University Press, 1988); *Scripture on the Ten Kings and the Making of Purgatory in Medieval Chinese Buddhism* (Honolulu: University of Hawai'i Press, 1994). For a pictorial presentation of Chinese hell, see Anne Swan Goodrich, *The Chinese Hells: The Peking Temple of Eighteen Hells and Chinese Conceptions of Hell* (St. Augustin: Monumenta Serica, 1981).

39. Teiser, *Scripture on the Ten Kings*, 1–6.

trials. Devout Buddhists also follow a calendar to pray for a particular buddha or bodhisattva on a different day of the month to redeem their ancestors from suffering. On the specified day, the person must abstain from meat and recite the name of the buddha or bodhisattva a thousand times.[40] For the living, this practice of reciting the name of the Buddha is also a means to insure for themselves a safe journey to the "Buddha's land" after death.

In *Errors*, we find a description of a particular rite of atonement called "breaking the prison" (*phá ngục*) to release the soul from hell. Although hell in Buddhism is a temporary stage of existence, still it is full of enough suffering that one wishes to release beloved ancestors from it and expedite the rebirth process. This special rite was to be performed in an elaborate ritual, described in detail by the author of *Errors*, involving the construction and tearing down of a paper prison, after chanting Buddhist prayers and making solemn offerings to the guardian spirits of the dead.[41]

The Buddha's Land

Many Vietnamese Buddhists also believe in a "paradise", called the "Pure Land" (*tịnh thổ*) or "the Buddha's land." This is the "land of bliss" or *sukhāvatī* mentioned in the scriptures of Pure Land Buddhism.[42] According to the *Larger Pure Land Sutra*, the monk Dharmakara vowed to save all beings in a pure Buddha land. He was determined to use his stored merits from many aeons (*kalpas*) and his meditative powers of image projection to create a Pure Land. At the completion of his endeavors, Dharmakara became the ruler of a Buddha field called "the land of bliss." He became known as the "Buddha of limitless life" (Amitāyus) and the "Buddha of limitless light" (Amitābha), or Amida Buddha. The Pure Land of Amida Buddha is another realm of existence, an alternative to the three worlds of desire, form, and formlessness of Indian Buddhism. For the common Buddhists in Vietnam, the goal is to reach this Buddha's land after death. One does so by diligently meditating or reciting the name of Amida, hundreds or thousands of

---

40. The book *Lamp of the Mind* gives a list of these days. For example, on the first day of the month, one prays "*Namo* [homage to] *Dīpankara Buddha*"; on the full moon: "*Namo Amitābha Buddha*"; on the thirtieth day: "*Namo Śākyamuni Buddha*," and so forth. *Errors*, Book 3, Article 10, 189.

41. *Errors*, Book 3, Article 10, 185–86. Cf. Adriano di Santa Thecla, *Opusculum*, 104–6.

42. The concept is rooted in the Mahayana idea of a Buddha field (*buddhaksetra*) that is formed through the merits of high-level buddhas and bodhisattvas. Scriptural authority for the Pure Land is found in the *Larger* and *Smaller Pure Land Sutras* (*Sukhāvatī-vyuha sūtras*), of which Sanskrit, Tibetan, and Chinese versions are available. See Hisao Inagaki, *The Three Pure Land Sutras: A Study and Translation from Chinese* (Berkeley: Numata Center for Buddhist Translation and Research, 1995).

times each day, with the aid of a rosary-like ring of wooden beads. Amida promises to deliver his devout followers, protect them from falling into the three wicked ways, and bring them to his land for a blissful afterlife.

A lifelong devotion to Amida might not have been enough without a proper guidance at the moment of death. The journey to the Buddha's land described in *Errors* is a long and arduous one with twists and turns. Hence, a Buddhist monk was called in to help the dying get oriented in the afterlife by reciting the prayer "Protection for the Journey" (*bảo đàng*). As the soul travels in the netherworld, it should follow the step-by-step instructions given in the prayer; otherwise, it will get lost and never reach its destiny.[43]

A Christian Interpretation of the Cult of the Ancestors

The main objection of the author of *Errors* concerning the traditional funeral rites and memorial services was the food oblation. He considered any offering to the dead an act of ignorance and a mockery of true filial piety. The dead now belong to the spiritual world, and they no longer need material sustenance. His view was expressed in the following comment:

> People make such offerings to their parents and ancestors because they believe that the souls of their ancestors reside in the soul cloth or spirit tablet and enjoy the food offerings. However, it is impossible for a deceased person to return to consume food and wine offerings from their descendants. Food and drink sustain the bodies of the living. But once the souls of the dead leave their bodies, they have no bodies to sustain. The human soul has a spiritual character; it is the most spiritual entity among all creatures. It does not depend on the body to live but has a life of its own. Therefore, when it leaves the body, the soul does not need food or drink as a living person does. Moreover, when the soul is one with the body, it does not need food. Food is needed only to sustain the life of the body. If you believe that the soul needs food to sustain itself, then it must have food twice a day. But if the soul is offered food only once a year during its memorial feast, how can it sustain itself? A dead body no longer needs food. When one offers food to the soul, one insults the soul, for the soul does not eat or drink. Such an act is merely mocking the soul, making it angry and sad. Therefore, those who make offerings to their ancestors are

---

43. *Errors*, Book 3, Article 8, 173–77.

not being filial; they are proving, rather, to be truly unfilial. Food offerings are for the living; the soul does not consume them at all. Alas, those who make such offerings are profoundly ignorant.[44]

The author of *Errors* was well aware of the emphasis on filial piety among Vietnamese. In his view, people put filial piety in the wrong place for the wrong reason. By making offerings to ancestors so that the deceased can bring material benefits to the living, the latter have erred greatly:

It is the duty of the living to help the dead, not the duty of the dead to help the living. A descendant's duty to arrange solemn funerals for their ancestors is simply repaying a filial debt to those who gave birth to them. This is a great debt that no one can ever repay sufficiently. If descendants believe that their ancestors will reward their efforts with wealth, honor, and longevity, they are gravely mistaken.[45]

Our author's comment on ancestral sacrifices echoes the view of Alexandre de Rhodes. In his memoir on Tonkin, Rhodes discussed the memorial banquets that he attended on several occasions.[46] While admiring Vietnamese piety toward the ancestors, he pointed out three "gross errors" in this practice, which, according to him, led to "superstition." The first error is the "belief that the souls of the deceased parents can freely come and go as they please or when invited, not knowing that there are permanent barriers separating them from us." The second is the "foolish supposition that the deceased also can consume meat and wine at our banquet." The third, a "more absurd error than the other two," presumes that "life, health, the well-being of the family and all the material prosperity of the household depend on their deceased parents."

The Christian Concept of the Afterlife

The Christian objection to ancestral sacrifices results from a different concept of the afterlife than that of the Vietnamese. Christians believe that the soul faces judgment immediately after death. Depending on its merit or sin, it will go to heaven, where the soul enjoys the presence of God, or hell, the eternal punishment for the unrepentant. Catholic theology also speaks of an intermediate place

---

44. *Errors*, Book 1, Article 14, 83–84.

45. *Errors*, Book 1, Article 14, 90.

46. Rhodes, *Histoire du royaume de Tunquin*, part 1, chap. 24, 84–85.

or stage of purification called purgatory, reserved for those who had not accumulated enough merit to enter heaven immediately. In addition, medieval Catholic doctrine included a permanent state of bliss called "limbo," where the unbaptized infants (and good pagans) lived without suffering but also without the joy of being with God.[47]

The realms of heaven, hell, purgatory (and limbo) are considered to be permanently separated from this world. There is no communication across worlds, except through prayer. Catholics believe that the best way to remember and honor their ancestors is by praying for them and performing acts of charity on their behalf, so that they may enjoy everlasting life. Once they get to heaven, they, in turn, will pray for the living. This view is expressed in the comment by the Christian Scholar in *Errors*:

> The Lord of Heaven has sent them, as living souls, to live in a place of reward or punishment from whence they are unable to return. If they are still in purgatory, we ask a priest to offer Masses for them. We gather the relatives to pray that the souls of our ancestors will soon ascend to paradise to enjoy eternal blessings. These ritual practices bring actual benefit to the ancestors. Why would one expend resources on conventional rituals that bring no real benefit to the soul, simply to be extolled for fulfilling filial duties? Such behaviors are foolish and futile. Moreover, using sustenance for the body and offering it up to the soul is an act of contempt. Those practicing such rituals are in fact unfilial.[48]

Accordingly, true filial piety toward the ancestors must bring real benefits to them rather than empty rituals.

Some Confucians would agree with the Christian position. They do not believe that the dead actually can come back to this world and eat the offered foods, but they consider it a significant moral act that forms a basic attitude of gratitude toward one's family (and by extension to the country). An example from Vietnamese history can illustrate this point. In the late eighteenth century, Cochinchina fell into the hands of the Tây Sơn, who drove the Nguyễn into exile. While on the run, Prince Nguyễn Phúc-Ánh

---

47. The teaching on limbo is a theological solution for the problem that infants cannot be condemned to hell because they have not sinned but they cannot enter heaven because they had not been baptized. Some theologians extended limbo for "good" pagans, who through no fault of their own did not receive baptism, the necessary condition to enter heaven according to Christian theology. This teaching was discontinued after 1965.

48. *Errors*, Book 1, Article 14, 89.

was befriended by Bishop Pigneau de Béhaine. Although favorably disposed toward Christianity, the prince explained to the bishop that he could not be a Christian convert because it would mean he would have to abandon ancestor worship:

> I know that my ancestors are no longer with me. I also know that whatever I do for them (e.g., ritual worship) does not really benefit either them or me. But [I have to perform these rites because] I want to show everyone that I do not forget my ancestors, and I want to demonstrate a good example of filial piety to my subjects.... In my view, there is no other real obstacle to prevent my whole kingdom from converting to Christianity.... I have prohibited acts of sorcery and divination; I wholly consider the cult of the spirits wrong and ridiculous. But I have determined to keep ancestor worship for the reasons above because I consider it to be one of the most essential foundations of our moral formation.[49]

For the prince, ancestral worship was a civic duty, to be practiced by all, regardless of their religious persuasion. This view echoed the verdict by Emperor Kangxi in China at the height of the Chinese Rites Controversy. The Chinese and Vietnamese Confucian rulers could not understand why Catholics did not make a concession to the traditional form of ancestral worship like the Buddhists had done.

Vietnamese Catholics and the Cult of the Ancestors

Despite the differences between the Christian and traditional views on the concepts of the human person and the afterlife, Catholic missionaries could not ignore the venerable custom of honoring the ancestors among the Vietnamese. In the first half of the seventeenth century, Jesuit missionaries had found creative ways to modify traditional funeral rites and honor the ancestors. In general, they accepted most of the Confucian rites except acts that were considered superstitious and idolatrous, such as the burning of joss papers and other objects, making food and wine oblations, praying to the various spirits during the funeral procession, or making offerings to the god of earth. Catholics were to give Christian burial with Masses and prayers, and offerings to the dead were limited to flowers and incense. They were allowed to bow before the dead as they did with the living. Instead of burning joss paper, the living were to perform acts of charity

---

49. Launay, *Histoire de la Mission de Cochinchine*, 3:320; translation mine.

to accumulate merits for their loved ones in the world beyond. Most of these acts, however, were thought to affect only the deceased, who were in purgatory. No amount of Masses or prayers could save anyone from the eternal damnation of hell.

Attempts to separate the legitimate practices from the idolatrous did not endure, however. With the arrival of other missionaries groups, the French MEPs and the Spanish Dominicans, whose members became apostolic vicars in Tonkin and Cochinchina, the Catholic Church in Vietnam adopted a stricter policy. Since the traditional form of ancestor worship resembled the worship of spirits, many Western missionaries, uninformed about cultural symbols of these rites, judged them to be idolatrous. Any activities that could be interpreted as superstitious or following "pagan" customs were prohibited. In an attempt to foster a Christian identity, many traditional rites and customs with regard to the veneration of the dead and honoring ancestors were eliminated without consideration. Furthermore, Catholics were not allowed to participate in or contribute to the funeral and memorial services of their non-Catholic relatives or neighbors. This policy caused a lot of pain and the alienation of Catholic members from their non-Catholic relatives. In fact, the clash over the cult of ancestors has been the primary reason why strict Confucians or Buddhists have adamantly refused to allow their children to marry Catholics, for fear that they would not be venerated but would be forgotten after death.

In reality, Catholics were not unfilial sons and daughters who abandoned their parents and loved ones after death. They held Catholic funeral services and burial. They prayed for their ancestors' fate and offered Masses for them. But the failure to publically display what was considered standard custom caused grave consternation among non-Catholics. Catholics no longer offered oblations, used incense, kept a home altar, or kowtowed to the dead or the spirit tablets. The failure of Catholics to explain themselves convincingly to outsiders contributed to the hatred of Catholics that eventually fueled the severe persecutions in the nineteenth century.[50]

---

50. A historical example illustrates the bias against the Catholics as being unfilial. When Prince Nguyễn Phúc Ánh (the future Emperor Gia Long) was living in exile, he entrusted his seven-year-old son to accompany Bishop Pigneau de Béhaine to France in 1787 to seek support for his campaign against the Tây Sơn. When the crown prince came back to Vietnam after twelve years, he refused to kowtow to the spirit tablets of his ancestors. This irreverent act caused a great scandal among the Confucian officials at the court. Fearful of alienating his Confucian supporters, Gia Long (r. 1802–1820) distanced himself from the Catholics. When Minh Mạng (r. 1820–1840), another son of Gia Long, assumed the throne, the new emperor turned hostile to the Christian faith, partially because he believed that Catholics were not filial and, by extension, not trustworthy subjects.

From a cultural point of view, the cult of the ancestors is the ritual manifestation of veneration, gratitude, and honor rendered to the elder members of a family. Children are brought up with the ideal of what is due to their parents in old age as well as after death. The acute cultural observer Matteo Ricci took a careful note of the pedagogy. In his journal, published posthumously in 1615, Ricci makes this observation:

> The most solemn thing among the literati and in use from the king down to the very least being is the offering they annually make to the dead at certain times of the years. . . . In this act, they make the fulfillment of their duty to their relatives, namely to "serve them in death as though they were alive." Nor do they think in this matter that the dead will come to eat the things mentioned or that they might need them; . . . they do this because they know of no other way to show their love and grateful spirit toward them [the dead] . . . the ceremony was begun more for the living than for the dead, that is, to teach the children and the ignorant ones to honor and serve their living relatives . . . since they do not recognize any divinity in these dead ones, nor do they ask or hope for anything from them, all this *stands outside of idolatry*,[51] and also one can say there is *probably no superstition*.[52]

Ricci considered the cult of the ancestors to be essentially nonreligious, that is, a civil act. He was aware of the religious elements in the rites, but for him, these practices were accidental and could be regulated without destroying the essence of the ancestral rites.

The critical issue of our interest is not the religious nature of the Vietnamese cult of the ancestors, but how to interpret them contextually. If we look beyond the forms, the intention of the traditionally prescribed rituals expresses a deep love and respect for the deceased, a fact that no one can deny. Alexandre de Rhodes marveled at the "the extraordinary affection that the Tonkinese give to their deceased parents." Many of them ended up in debt because they spent extravagantly on memorial banquets and other ceremonies, which Rhodes regarded as

---

51. Ricci was told by his Chinese colleagues that the rite had a pedagogical purpose. That was the reason for his qualification of the rites as "probably" (*forse*) being free from superstition. This word "probably" in part is the basis for later attack on Jesuit "probabilism." See Cummins, *A Question of Rites*, 38–41.

52. Quoted by Minamiki, *The Chinese Rites Controversy*, 17–18; italics added. See also Louis J. Gallagher, *China in the Sixteenth Century: The Journals of Matteo Ricci: 1583–1610* (New York: Random House 1953), 96–97.

"useless and frivolous, but they themselves could not disregard because of customs."[53] The author of *Errors* also recognized this point in his long discussion of the funeral rites and memorial services. Within the context of pre-modern Vietnam, these rites were viewed as social functions to serve the good order of society by promoting right relationships in the exercise of filial virtue, which was the core value of Vietnamese family and society.

---

53. Rhodes, *Histoire du royaume de Tunquin*, part 1, chap. 20, 89.

5

Refutation and Dialogue

CHRISTIANITY VIS-À-VIS THE THREE RELIGIONS

AT THE NATIONAL civil exam given in 1463, King Lê Thánh Tông gave the following question:

> When the ancient sages followed the Heavenly will to rule the country, their Way [*đạo*] was pure. Later, after the doctrines of the Buddha and Laozi started, discussion began on the Three Doctrines [*tam giáo*], and thus the way of ruling through the human heart was not as before. I observe that the teachings of the Buddha and Laozi deceive and mislead the people [*hoặc thế vu dân*] leading to the stagnation of the virtues [of humaneness and righteousness] [*sung tắc nhân nghiã*] in society. Their harmful effects have been incalculable, and yet many people still believe in and follow them. The way of the sages in every way—whether keeping the morality of Three Bonds and Five Norms in general or shaping the culture in particular customs—is practical in daily life. Yet, people do not believe in and follow it as they do the Buddhist teachings. Why is it so?[1]

On this question, the laureate Lương Thế Vinh (1441–?), answered,

> [In the ancient days], when the rulers were wise and the people were good, the orthodox way was implemented in the world like the sun and

---

1. See the document in Đinh Khắc Thuân, *Giáo Dục và Khoa Cử Nho Học thời Lê ở Việt Nam qua Tài Liệu Hán Nôm* [Confucian Education and Examination during the Lê Dynasty in Vietnam Through Hán-Nôm Sources] (Hanoi: NXB Khoa Học Xã Hội, 2009): Chinese text, 179, and its Vietnamese translation, 191.

moon brightening the sky; thus how could the heterodox teachings appear? ... From the time of the Han dynasty until now, the Way of the sages has been like a light smoke, and the doctrines of the Buddha and Laozi have developed. The way of the Buddha, which takes the "quiescence" [*tịch diệt*] as its doctrine, came into China from the time of Emperor Han Mingdi. Daoism, which takes "emptiness" [*hư vô*] as its tradition, also originated during the time of the Han dynasty, but it has only grown since the Tang and Song era. After these periods, the doctrine of Three Religions came into existence. Nevertheless, the Way of the sages [Confucianism] is still the orthodox one, and the doctrines of the Buddha and Laozi are false ways. How can the latter doctrines be compared with the former ones to make up the Three Doctrines?

The people of later generations have not critically examined their origin, and therefore they commit errors. For that reason, the way of ruling through the human heart has not been as it was in ancient times. Alas! The doctrines of the Buddha and Laozi resemble the truth but they are in fact contrary to the truth. Thus, the deception of the people that leads to the blockage of the virtues [of humaneness and righteousness] in society is indeed real. ...

If the Way of the sages is from heaven, but it is not understood enough to be able to bring happiness to the people, then the commoners do not follow it. Then the Way of the sages is no different from the heterodox ways. They contrast like yin and yang. When one side prospers the other declines, and vice versa.[2]

Lương Thế Vinh's arguments are echoed in *Errors*. The author of *Errors* blames the decline of Confucianism in Tonkin of his day on the Confucian compromise with Buddhism and Daoism. While not being explicit, he seems to be critical of the idea of "three religions out of the same sources" (*tam giáo đồng nguyên*) advocated by some seventeenth- and eighteenth-century Confucians. The author considers the acceptance of Buddhist and Daoist doctrines by his contemporary Confucians as due to a lack of critical judgment:

When hearing anything, the gentlemen need to examine it thoroughly because no wise person should believe everything he hears. [People of]

---

2. Chinese text in Đinh Khắc Thuân, *Giáo Dục và Khoa Cử Nho Học*, 180, and its Vietnamese translation, 193–94.

this world make up many teachings to make themselves famous rather than paying attention to whether they conform to reason or not. Some people in the past invented a few teachings, and later generations expanded them and turned them into customs. People of today claim that we should take the ancient rules and old customs handed down by our forebears to be the norm; whoever does not follow these norms is branded as guilty and ignorant. In this way, everyone practices [these customs] as habits without understanding their falsehood.[3]

The addition of Catholic Christianity to the three religions of Vietnam created a new relational dynamic among the religions. It challenged the Confucian domination of society. The chief aims of the Confucian literati were to promote harmony in social relations under their leadership. While Buddhism and Daoism during these centuries were controlled and regulated by Confucian authorities, Christianity refused to blend with the Confucian vision of harmony. With its own system of metaphysics, ethics, and religious practices, Christianity competed with Confucianism for the fulfillment of the intellectual and religious needs of the people. In *Errors*, the Christian scholar claims that his religion can correct the deficiency of Confucianism. His attitude reflects the self-confidence of Christians that their religion can overcome the monopoly of Confucianism. Thus, *Errors* is valuable for giving the reader insights into the self-assured attitude of Christians when confronted with Vietnamese Confucians.

Errors was written as a Catholic apologetic work whose purpose was to convince its readers, new or potential converts, to "surrender to the truth and turn to the holy way of the Lord of Heaven."[4] Such a self-assured attitude on the part of the Christian may not be welcomed in today's Vietnamese context of religious pluralism. But a modern reader may be tempted to view this work from the perspective of contemporary interreligious dialogue, rather than examine its merits within its own framework, and thus to dismiss this type of work as a product of an ignorant and intolerant past and therefore not worthy of serious consideration. When apologetic works are studied in their own context, however, a more nuanced critique is in order. In the following sections, I will evaluate the messages and approaches of *Errors* first from a historical and then from a contemporary perspective.

---

3. *Errors*, Book 2, Preface, 95–96.

4. *Errors*, Book 1, Preface, 1.

The Theological Message of Errors

Since the author of *Errors* wished that "[Vietnamese people] know the true Lord, worship him and follow the true way, so that after death they may attain the blessing of dwelling in the eternal paradise,"[5] he set out to expose the "errors and falsehoods that contradict to the holy way to the Lord of Heaven."[6] The errors seen by the author as inhibiting a total devotion to the Lord of Heaven can be divided into three categories: (1) erroneous beliefs; (2) idolatry; and (3) superstitions.

Erroneous Beliefs

The author saw two types of errors of belief among the Vietnamese. First, a mistaken notion of God, which failed to represent him as Creator of this world; and second, false confidence in the power of the spirits to grant blessings and protect against misfortunes.

Mistaken Views of God

The first mistaken view presented in *Errors* concerns the sovereignty of God. For the author, God is the absolute sovereign Being, and no other figure can be equated to him. He is the first cause of the universe and the sustainer of the cosmos in all its life forms. According to the author, a major fault of Confucius was his ignorance of this Creator. It led him to "teach people to worship heaven and earth and all creatures but fail to mention the great Lord who creates heaven, earth, and all things."[7] In the Christian view, equating creatures with their Creator, or pantheism, is a great error.

Another mistaken view concerns the living and intelligent nature of God. The main reason for the author's rejection of the Neo-Confucian concepts of cosmological realities such as Supreme Ultimate and Principle and Energy as divine is that they lack the characteristics of a living being. The author's basic principle is that life begets life. From this perspective, the author urges Confucians to accept God, whom he calls "the Lord of Heaven and Earth," as the first cause. The assertion that "[t]he Lord of Heaven creates the Supreme Ultimate" must be added to the Confucian statement, "The Supreme Ultimate generates the Two Modes; the Two Modes generate the Four Forms; the Four Forms are transformed into

---

5. *Errors*, Preface, i

6. *Errors*, Book 1, Preface, 1.

7. *Errors*, Book 1, Article 4, 21–22

the myriad of things and classified by species and orders,"⁸ in order to make that statement complete and meaningful. Here we see a willingness on the part of the Christian author to use the existing philosophical tradition to explain his theology.

A third mistake in the author's eyes is the identification of the Sovereign-on-High with God. Although "Sovereign-on-High" is the ancient name of the Most High, the author argues that the term has been too tainted by later popular and scholarly traditions to be a suitable name of God. For the author, the Neo-Confucian notion of Sovereign-on-High borders on pantheism because it does not clearly distinguish between the Creator and creation. By not differentiating Sovereign-on-High from the heavens, the Confucian negates the truth that "heaven cannot have the same dignity as its Lord."⁹ *Errors* insists that Christians should use the name "the true Lord of heaven and earth"—and not "Sovereign-on-High"—to express their belief in the One who "creates and rules over heaven, earth, humans, and all things," rather than in One who is identical with heaven.¹⁰

False Beliefs

False beliefs result from wrongly ascribing the power to grant favors and protection from evil to various spirits of nature and mortal beings. Natural objects and phenomena such as the sun, the moon, the stars, and the seasons only are forms of creation that operate according to the laws of nature. They possess neither the consciousness to hear people's petitions nor the power to make things happen. The author presents similar arguments against deified men and women who are honored as gods or spirits (*thần*) by Vietnamese people. The inefficacy of the many figures that Vietnamese worship, be it Shennong, Confucius, Laozi, the Buddha, the Tutelary Genies, or the Kitchen God, to name a few, is argued throughout the text. These gods or spirits are said to have no power of their own to affect the living. As creatures, they are subject to God, who is the absolute ruler of the universe. Thus, whatever power they might possess is ultimately derived from God.

The monotheistic message is clear in the dialogues. People should not mistake any creature for its creator. There is no other being but God who has absolute power over humanity. Only the Lord of heaven and earth "who takes charge of all affairs in heaven and earth to care for human beings in every way" is the worthy object of human hope and trust.¹¹

---

8. *Errors*, Book 1, Article 1, 7.

9. *Errors*, Book 1, Article 3, 15.

10. *Errors*, Book 1, Article 3, 17.

11. *Errors*, Book 1, Article 7, 44.

Idolatry

From the Christian standpoint, *idololatria*—the worship of any creature, natural or spiritual, except God—is a direct violation of the Judeo-Christian First Commandment ("You shall have no other gods beside me"). Catholic theology sees idolatry as a grave sin against faith, since it deprives God of the divine exclusive honor. Nevertheless, the word "idolatry" or false worship (*thờ dối, thờ quấy*) does not appear in *Errors*, as it does in the apologetic works of the nineteenth century. Instead, there are only admonitions that one should not offer sacrifices to popular figures because it is contrary to the way of the Lord of Heaven.

According to the author, mistaken views of God and false beliefs give rise to erroneous worship. The author does not condemn the worship of other spirits as being formally sinful, but he sees it as inculpable ignorance of the true way. Erroneous worship resulted from the corruption of the tradition handed down by the sages and philosophers. People did not understand true worship as it was originally intended by the ancient "sage-kings." Instead, they blindly followed customs invented by later generations. The ancient sage-kings taught true knowledge and worship of God, but people of later generations failed to observe the practices. Because "their minds are clouded" and because they do not know the true God, people are misled by "the demon teaching them to worship the spirits."[12]

Consequently, the author strives to enlighten these erroneous worshippers of the inefficacy of the spirits and to exhort them to abandon futilely worshiping of them:

> Why should one need to offer sacrifices to heaven and earth, deceased rulers, and other spirits? One only needs to offer sacrifices to the true Lord of heaven and earth, who has the power to rule over everything in heaven and on earth, who keeps people from having wayward hearts, and who helps rulers to govern their people justly and peacefully....
>
> Heaven and earth, kings and lords of the past, and spirits do not bring peace and security to this country. Rather, it is the Lord of Heaven, creator of heaven and earth and ruler of everything, who gives peace and security to all. Therefore, you must offer sacrifices only to the Lord of Heaven. Do not continue to offer sacrifices to heaven and earth and to the others.[13]

---

12. *Errors*, Book I, Article 11, 65.

13. *Errors*, Book I, Article 8, 48, 50.

It would be "vain and useless" to offer sacrifices to the spirits and ask for their help; rather, one should return to the true worship due to God.

Superstitions

The third type of error that is condemned in the manuscript involves the beliefs and practices that the author considers superstitious and foolish. A false conception of natural phenomena—such as the movements of stars, thunderstorms, or solar and lunar eclipses—underlies the fear of their powers. The author uses scientific theories to demythologize these phenomena, and consequently, to liberate the minds of Vietnamese people from fear and ignorance. For instance, thunderstorms happen because of the collision of "hot and cold air," not through the action of any thunder god.[14] Solar and lunar eclipses are shadows caused by the regular movements of these heavenly bodies in their orbits, not "the sun and moon eating each other, as people say."[15]

In other cases, the popularity of magical healing, astrology, divination, and physiognomy is traced to the belief in ungodly powers that leads to superstitious practices. Obsession with fate lures people to these practices and diminishes their faith in God's power. To dispel the fear and irrationality of these practices, the author highlights the inconsistency in their results. For example, if offering sacrifices to the stars can help one avoid troubles, then why is it the case that those who do so "still have diseases and trouble, but those who do not are still prosperous and healthy?"[16] If an astral reading is supposed to help predict the outcome of a battle, then why are so many battles lost despite favorable predictions?[17]

With regard to the custom of acting only at favorable times or days, the author urges his audience to trust in God's providence and act morally to ensure good results:

> Why do people need to choose a favorable time to act? Results are good or bad not because of auspicious or inauspicious timing but because people do good and avoid evil. If there are lucky or unlucky days, then why do twins, born of the same mother on the same day and time, end up with

---

14. Cf. *Errors*, Book 2, Article 5, 116–17.

15. *Errors,* Book 2, Article 12, 140.

16. *Errors*, Book 2, Article 5, 116.

17. Cf. *Errors*, Book 2, Article 10, 136.

different fortunes? Why is one wealthy and elegant but the other poor and base? Why does one enjoy longevity but the other a short lifespan? Their fortunes are determined not by timing but by the Lord of Heaven....

Moreover, one should take no heed in one's "day of death" by avoiding going out to work or to conduct business. Life and death are natural phenomena; birth and death occur every day. People die not because of unlucky days but because of other causes. That is why many deaths occur every day. The great Lord in heaven decides how long a person lives; a person will die when his or her date of death arrives.[18]

Prediction of the future is regarded as useless because one's fortune is determined by God, not by any human power. These practices are condemned as foolish and their believers naïve and vulnerable to the predation of magicians, sorcerers, fortune-tellers, and others whom the author considers to be charlatans.

The Legacy of Errors of the Three Religions

Addressed to new and potential converts, *Errors* was preoccupied with distinguishing true belief and worship of Christianity from the "false" ones of the other religions. Such was also the concern of religious literature in Vietnam in the eighteenth and nineteenth centuries. Deeply aware of the pluralistic religious setting of Vietnam, Christian authors strived to make the case for the Christian rejection of certain rites and practices of the Vietnamese general population.

Although *Errors* was circulated in a limited way (we know of only one surviving handwritten copy), its influence reached beyond the original audience. Vietnamese catechisms and apologetic writings of the nineteenth century can be considered adaptations of *Errors* by incorporating its arguments, sources, quotations, and vocabulary. Among these works, two are worthy mentioning: *Phép Giảng Đạo Thật* (Treatise of the True Religion) (ms. 1758, print 1829) and *Hội Đồng Tứ Giáo* (Conference of the Four Religions) (ca. 1780–1830). The number of available editions and printings indicates that *Errors* left a lasting impression on the Christian population.[19] A brief description of each text is presented in the following sections to give readers an overview of *Errors*' legacy.

---

18. *Errors*, Book 2, Article 6, 118–19.

19. According to a catalogue of *nôm* works preserved in the Archives of the Missions Étrangères de Paris (AMEP), the *Treatise on the True Religion*, better known by its Sino-Vietnamese title *Chân Đạo Yếu Lý* [Essentials of the True Religion] had at least four editions in *nôm* script (Cẩm Sơn, 1829; n.p., 1864; Gia Định, 1867; Phát Diệm, 1868); *Conferences of the Four Religions* at least nine editions in *nôm* (n.p., 1864, 1867, 1869; Phát Diệm, 1867, 1869, 1909; Hongkong,

Treatise of the True Religion (1758)

Phép Giảng Đạo Thật (Treatise of the True Religion) (henceforth *Treatise*) is another anonymous work dedicated to the religious education of believers in eighteenth-century Vietnam.[20] This book combines both *catechismus* and *doctrina christiana* traditions, by giving a refutation of the objections to Christianity as well as an exposition of basic Catholic doctrines and practices.[21]

Of interest to us is chapter 2, entitled "On the true and false beliefs about heaven and earth" (*Giảng mlẽ về sự blời đất cùng các tích là thế nào*), which spans 34½ pages (pp. 15–49) of the manuscript. This chapter is a refutation of what the author considers erroneous views on true worship. In chapter 1, the author establishes the existence of the Creator as the "Lord of Heaven and Earth" and the necessity of worshiping him, and chapter 2 can be considered an extension of that discussion, in which the erroneous views of the Creator are explained. This chapter can be divided into three thematic sections.

The first section deals with what the author considered "erroneous beliefs." It is devoted to the exposition of heaven and earth, the Buddha, Mục Mũi,[22] Supreme

---

1897, 1903, 1905), and fourteen *quốc-ngữ* editions. See Chan Ching-ho and Isabelle Landry-Deron, eds., *Mục Lục Thư Tịch Hán Nôm Tàng Trữ Tại Hội Thừa Sai Ba-Lê* [Catalogue of works in Chinese and *nôm* scripts preserved in the archive of the Society of Paris Foreign Missions] (Paris: Église d'Asie, 2004), 17–21.

20. The extant manuscript of *Treatise* is preserved in the AMEP, catalogue number V-1183. The document has 72 sheets of 16 by 22 cm paper, totaling 144 pages, bound into a notebook. Handwritten on both sides of the page in *quốc-ngữ* script, the manuscript has a total of 143 pages of material. The last page is torn at the top, and parts of the first three lines are missing. A loose half sheet, numerated "53 bis," is attached to the first page and bears the title *Catéchisme Raisonné: Tiong Keing* [Analytical Catechism, Tonkin]. The last page ends with a Latin inscription, *Finis. Laus Patris, Deus Filio, honor Sancto Spiritus et Gloria Virgini. MDCCLVIII*. In the early nineteenth century, this catechism was revised and printed in *nôm* scripts. It also was given a Sino-Vietnamese title *Chân Đạo Yếu Lý* (Essentials of the True Religion). The earliest extant printed copy preserved in the AMEP is dated 1829. Later editions include 1864, 1867, and 1868.

21. The catechism is divided in nine chapters: (1) On life and death, body and soul; (2) On the true and false beliefs about heaven and earth; (3) On the doctrine of Three Fatherhoods; (4) On who God is and how He creates the world; (5) On the life of Christ; (6) On the judgment after death, purgatory, heaven and hell; (7) On the four major points (Creed, Lord's Prayer, Sacraments, and Commandments); (8) On the preparation for Baptism; and (9) On the duties of a new believer. From the list of topics, this work functions somewhat like de Rhodes's *Cathechismus*. The *nôm* editions of the nineteenth century were slightly different from the original manuscript. While retaining the content of most chapters, their slants reflect the interests of the nineteenth-century audience, that is, to defend Catholicism from anti-Catholic defamation. The *nôm* editions replace the last two chapters with three new ones: (8) On the witness of the Scriptures; (9) On Catholic morality; and (10) On the defense of anti-Catholic denunciation.

22. Mục Mũi or Mộc Mối was a primordial being defined in Rhodes's catechism as "the created body when the rational soul first entered it as spoken by some idolatrous sect." (*Catechismus*, Second day) in Phan, *Mission and Catechesis*, 255.

Ultimate, Pangu, Laozi, and Jade Emperor (15–23). Following the scholastic style of argument, in each case, the author opens with a rhetorical question: "Is X the first cause of everything?" He then answers with an emphatic "No," then gives the reasons for his response. The arguments are abbreviated versions of what were said about these beings in *Errors*. After the discussion, he concludes with the formula, "Therefore, we must not worship X, because he (or it) is not the first cause of everything." With regards to the Buddha and other deified figures like Laozi and the Jade Emperor, *Treatise* tries to demystify them by giving an account of their lives, using the same materials, almost word for word, taken from the accounts of these figures in *Errors*. Since these figures are mortal, they must be equated to the supreme ruler of heaven. To do so is blasphemous, *Treatise* argues.

In the second section, *Treatise* argues against the worship of various figures and spirits who were popular among the Tonkinese. The refutations are taken from Book 1 and 2 of *Errors*, sometimes verbatim. The gist of the argument is that these figures cannot give blessings to the people and thus should not be worshipped. Exemplary people like Confucius, the Former Teachers, and Guardian Deities (*Thành hoàng*) could be venerated, but being mortal themselves, they are powerless to help their petitioners. Other spirits, like God of Thunder (*Thiên lôi*), Yama Kings of Hell (*Diêm vương*), Household Guardian (*Thổ công*), Land Guardian (*Thổ chủ*), Duke of River (*Hà bá*), Phạm Nhan, Kitchen God (*Vua bếp*), and Wandering Soul (*Cô hồn*), were judged to be either dubious characters or immoral figures who were not worthy of respect and honor. When dealing with these spirits, *Treatise* stresses their powerlessness over human life and that one should not fear them but only the Lord of heaven and earth.

The third section deals with what Christians in general consider superstitious beliefs and practices that go against the exclusive trust in the power of God. These include divination (*bói*), event forecasting (*xem khoa*), fortune telling (*xem số*), the practice of making offerings to change one's fate (*cầu sao đổi số*), physiognomy (*xem tướng*), divination with chicken feet (*xem giò*), astrology and geomancy (*thiên văn địa lý*), and burning joss paper (*vàng mã*). In treating these subjects, the author begins with a question such as, "What is such practice all about? Should we believe in it?," followed by an emphatic "No!" He then gives an account of the origin of the practice in question. The information given in these accounts is largely drawn from Book 2 of *Errors*, which treats these practices as Daoist superstitions. While these practices are considered useless and foolish, other practices such as mediumship (*đồng cốt*) and sorcery (*phù thủy*) are considered demonic, and are strongly condemned by the author.

In short, chapter 2 of *Treatise* can be considered a summary of *Errors*. Even in revised nineteenth-centuries editions of *Treatise*, the second chapter remained almost intact, except for some minor editorial improvements.

Conference of the Four Religions (ca. 1780–1830)

Another important document to the encounter of Christianity and the three religions of Vietnam is *Hội Đồng Tứ Giáo* (Conference of the Four Religions)[23] (henceforth *Conference*). Written by an anonymous author in *nôm* script, this work purported to be a report of three-day debates between a Catholic priest and representatives of the Three Religions that took place in 1773 at the court of Lord Trịnh Sâm, the ruler of Tonkin. The first day was devoted to the question, "What is the origin of humanity and of the cosmos?" The debates on the second day focused on the question, "What should human beings do in this life?" And on the last day, the concern was "Where do humans go after death?" Each day the Christian priest engaged in three rounds of debate, first with a Confucian scholar, then with a Daoist priest, and finally with a Buddhist monk.

The themes and concerns discussed in the debates reflected the complexity of the challenges that Christianity posed to the existing religious beliefs and practices. Unlike *Errors*, which aimed only to expose the errors of the non-Christian religions, *Conference* engaged its reader to debate with a Christian representative. In these debates, the author of *Conference* sought to justify the presence of Catholic Christianity in Vietnam, first by answering criticisms of Christian doctrines and then by refuting errors of the other religions.

The composition of this popular work is obscure. Based on its style and Christian interest, *Conference* was more likely a late eighteenth- or early nineteenth-century catechism for new converts to defend Christian beliefs and practices, rather than a transcript of actual debates.[24] The actuality of a conference between the representatives of the four religions is secondary to the message *Conference* conveys. It addresses three important issues that concern a seeker of truth: the origin, the meaning, and the end of human life in a three-day debate. Non-Christian "errors" are refuted, and Catholic doctrines are presented and

---

23. See my English translation in Anh Tran, "Hội Đồng Tứ Giáo/Conference of the Four Religions: A Christian Encounter of the Three Religions in the Eighteenth-Century Vietnam" (STL thesis, Jesuit School of Theology at Berkeley, 2006), 40–123.

24. The dating of this manuscript is difficult. The earliest known printed copy is an 1864 woodblock-printed edition preserved at Hanoi's Institute of Hán-Nôm Studies (catalogue AB 305), ninety years after the supposed debates took place (1773). However, it is entirely possible that the work might have been composed and circulated in handwritten copies decades before it appeared in print. The text mentioned that it was defending the "religion of the Portuguese" (*đạo Hoa Lang*) from being a "false and harmful religion." *Religion of the Portuguese* was a common Vietnamese name for Catholic Christianity in court documents during the seventeenth and eighteenth centuries. By the third decade of nineteenth century, Christianity was no longer so-called; it was referred to as the "Jesus religion" (*đạo Gia tô*) in imperial edicts. Thus the text might have been composed in the period of 1780–1830.

examined for their merits. The principal criteria for assessing the validity of a position on particular topics are rationality and consistency. The Christian priest wins in every debate, but it is not an easy victory. He must demonstrate the weakness of the other positions and defend his own from reasonable objections of his opponents, especially the Confucian scholar.

In *Conference*, the heart of the matter is "right worship," which occupies the bulk of the discussions. From a literary perspective, the *Conference*'s dialogical style is based on *Errors*, including its use of Chinese texts and historical examples, as well as the content of the arguments. More like a revised and expanded version of *Errors*, *Conference* consists of a series of dialogues between the Western Scholar and the representatives of the Three Religions. Although the Eastern Scholar of *Errors* is now portrayed in three different personas—as the Confucian Scholar, the Daoist Priest, and the Buddhist Monk—his voice still echoes throughout the text. The Confucian Scholar of *Conference*, like his predecessor, the Eastern Scholar in *Errors*, still presumes to be the spokesman for the three traditions. His arguments and ideas are similar to those in *Errors*, at times almost identical in style, word, and thought. A large amount of materials from *Errors* were repeated in *Conference*, pointing to a literary dependence of the latter on the former. Sino-Vietnamese phrases, for examples, were taken from *Errors* and used throughout the work. The insertion of Sino-Vietnamese phrases in a sentence without providing a translation was a deviation from the style of other Christian writings of the nineteenth century. Sometimes *Conference*'s author shortened or expanded *Errors* materials to illustrate his points in the debates.

Conference is not merely an updated version of *Errors*. While *Errors* summarizes information on Vietnamese customs, beliefs, and religious practices that are loosely connected under the schemata of the Three Religions, *Conference* proceeds with a clear and focused agenda of defending Christianity from its opponents. It incorporates materials from other Christian works, perhaps *Treatise* or another catechism available to him. Whereas *Errors* mentions almost nothing about Christian faith and practice, *Conference* integrates Christian beliefs into its arguments. It moves beyond a description of the "errors of the three religions" to an engagement with his opponents. The difference in these two approaches reflects their dissimilar contexts. Unlike *Errors*, arguably an internal document for the training of priests and catechists, *Conference* was written and printed in *Nôm* script to reach a wider audience. Whereas *Errors* focuses on telling his Christian converts the reasons why they should reject their former beliefs and practices, the author of *Conference* expounds on both the whats and the whys of Christian beliefs. It embraces the attitude of the nineteenth-century Vietnamese Christians: they persevered in faith despite the many sufferings and persecutions they had endured. It also expresses the Christian confidence that their religion is as good as, if not better than, the traditional religions.

Meeting the Religious Others
The Development of the Christian Exclusivist Attitude

The view of *Errors* reflects the long-standing position of Christianity vis-à-vis other religions. The assessment of non-Christian religions in *Errors* displays a largely "exclusivist" view of Christian theology toward other faiths.[25] Until Vatican II, the formula *extra ecclesiam nulla salus* (there is no salvation outside of the Church) was used as a principle for missionary work.[26] Catholic missionaries regarded Christianity as either a total "replacement" or "fulfillment" of other religions.[27]

From its beginning, Christianity saw itself as a missionary religion with a mandate to convey God's message to the people of Israel and the Gentiles (cf. Matt. 28:19). Born into a multireligious milieu of the Greco-Roman world, the early Christians developed their identity in that context. In the process, they had to define themselves against both the Jewish community and the larger Greco-Roman culture. Marginalized by the Jewish community, they developed a theology of replacement, which portrays the Church as the New Israel and Christians as the "true" inheritors of Abraham.[28] As inheritors of the monotheism of Israel,

---

25. The categories of exclusivism, inclusivism, and pluralism are first discussed in Alan Race, *Christians and Religious Pluralism: Patterns in the Christian Theology of Religions* (Maryknoll: Orbis, 1983). Since then, there have been variations of these three basic ways of categorizing Christian theology of religious pluralism. For example, Jacques Dupuis uses the categories of ecclesiocentrism, christocentrism, and theocentrism in *Toward a Christian Theology of Religious Pluralism* (Maryknoll: Orbis, 1997); Paul Knitter proposes a fourfold division of replacement, fulfillment, mutuality, and acceptance in *Introducing Theologies of Religions* (Maryknoll: Orbis, 2004).

26. On the history of the exclusivist attitude of the Christian Church, see Francis Sullivan, *Salvation Outside the Church: Tracing the History of the Catholic Response* (New York: Paulist Press, 1992). In recent years, there have been critiques of Christian exclusivism. While these critiques are not necessarily applied to the premodern world, they provide a corrective lens to examine the Christian claims. See, for example, John Hick and Paul Knitter, eds., *The Myth of Christian Uniqueness: Toward a Pluralistic Theology of Religions* (Maryknoll: Orbis, 1987), esp. chaps. 1–6; Paul Knitter, ed., *The Myth of Relgious Superiority: A Multifaith Exploration* (Maryknoll: Orbis, 2005). For a counterview, see Gavin D'Costa, *Christian Uniqueness Reconsidered: The Myth of a Pluralistic Theology of Religion* (Maryknoll: Orbis, 2005).

27. The categories of "replacement" and "fulfillment" are discussed by Paul Knitter in *Introducing Theologies of Religions*, Parts 1 and 2, 19–103.

28. Cf. Gal. 6:16.

the early Christians considered themselves the true keepers of the covenant that had been renewed by Jesus the Messiah.

Whereas the relationship between Christians and Jews during the first few centuries was ambiguous,[29] Christians emphasized the distance between themselves and the practitioners of pagan religions from the beginning.[30] Although Paul and other New Testament writers were disappointed that their fellow Jews did not join them in their commitment to Jesus, they accepted the religious heritage of Israel as their own. The same cannot be said about the early Christian reaction to pagan religions. Here, Christians and Jews were on the same front—they showed the same deep disdain for the idolatry of the Greeks and Romans.[31]

Because they were a small and persecuted minority, Christians had to assert their identity with great zeal and sacrifice. Concern for survival formed a defensive attitude among Christians, especially in matters of orthodoxy and heterodoxy. Absolute claims in faith and morals helped to safeguard Christians from being absorbed by the religious syncretism of the times (e.g., Gnosticism). Early Christian rules of faith were based on the certainty of their beliefs and practices. Any compromise was seen as weakening their unity, threatening their identity, and endangering their survival.[32]

Once the Christians had confidence in their identity as a chosen people and of the universal nature of their religion, they embarked on a mission to evangelize the whole world, seeking to convert pagans to the Christian way of life. From a cultural perspective, Christian evangelization has both confronted and accommodated the cultures it encounters. In the process, Christian missionaries adopted some elements, rejected others, and transformed still other elements into practices acceptable to Christianity. In the battle against Roman and Germanic paganism, religious leaders developed a superior attitude toward non-Christians. By the high Middle Ages, the formula *extra ecclesiam nulla salus* was applied not only to schismatics and heretics but also to people outside of Christianity.

---

29. Stephen G. Wilson, *Related Strangers: Jews and Christians, 70–170 CE* (Minneapolis: Fortress, 1995).

30. See Robert Grant, *Gods and the One God* (Philadelphia: Westminster, 1986); Luke Timothy Johnson, *Among the Gentiles: Greco-Roman Religion and Christianity* (New Haven, CT: Yale University Press, 2009).

31. Paul had a negative view of the Greek and Roman religions. He placed *eidōlolatria* (idolatry) and *pharmakeia* (sorcery) on the same level with other "works of the flesh" such as "fornication, impurity, licentiousness . . . enmities, strife, jealousy, anger, quarrels, dissensions, factions, envy, drunkenness, carousing, and things like these" (Gal. 5:19–21).

32. Henry Chadwick, *Heresy and Orthodoxy in the Early Church* (Brookfield: Variorum, 1991).

Since the late Middle Ages, Western Europe has had only one dominant religion and culture (i.e., Christianity). In addition, unfriendly relations between European Christians, Jews, and Muslims did not foster an acceptance of the followers of other religious traditions as respectable partners in dialogue. Consequently, missionaries were not theologically and culturally prepared to understand and respect believers of other religions. They presented Christianity to the people of East Asia as superior to and more logical than their native religions. Largely out of ignorance and cultural pride, missionaries treated the East Asian religions as wholesale superstition.

A Christian View of the Vietnamese Religions

As we have seen, the author of *Errors* claims that in the "way of the Lord of Heaven" (Christianity) alone can one find fulfillment and salvation. Non-Christians will not attain "eternal happiness" (salvation) unless they believe in and worship the true Lord of Heaven. The view of *Errors* toward the traditional religions of Vietnam reflects the early self-understanding of Christianity within the larger Greco-Roman world. As a minority group, Vietnamese Christians struggled to build their identity amid hostile forces just as their spiritual forebears did in the first few centuries of Christian existence. Just as the early Christians appropriated Greek philosophy but rejected Greek and Roman religions, Vietnamese Christians appropriated Confucian morality but not Confucian rituals. With regard to Daoism and Buddhism, they rejected both of these religions as idolatry and superstition, a similar approach to the attitude of the early Christians toward pagan religions.

The drive to protect a monotheistic belief in and an exclusive worship of God was behind the engagements of the author of *Errors* with the traditional religions of the Vietnamese. His attitudes ranged from dismissive hostility in cases of Daoism and Buddhism to reluctant acceptance of Confucianism. Disdain for Daoism and Buddhism is echoed in the author's refusal to engage their adherents in discussing their beliefs. In his assessment, Daoism is a "heterodox teaching of emptiness," and Buddhism is a "heterodox teaching of extinction."[33] These negative assessments are inadequate and based on the author's limited exposure to popular religious practices of these two religions.

Even Confucianism—accepted by most Vietnamese people and rulers as normative—is portrayed in *Errors* as inferior to the "religion of the Lord of Heaven."[34] While the author views Confucian moral exhortation and

---

33. See the prefaces of Book 2 and Book 3 in *Errors*.

34. Cf. *Errors*, Book 1, Article 4, 21–22.

self-cultivation as praiseworthy and proper, he claims that a moral life alone does not bring eternal reward without knowing and worshipping God. The author sees Christianity as the fulfillment of Confucianism, whereas the Confucianism of his day was judged to have been corrupted by other practices and thus ceased to be a beacon of light to guide people to attain eternal life.

Appraisal of Confucianism

Reading the text, one cannot help but notice the author's favorable attitude toward Confucianism over against Daoism and Buddhism. The main interlocutor of the Christian author is a Confucian Scholar, who assumes the role of a spokesman for all the three religions. The author admits an admiration of Confucian moral teaching because "all noble persons take Confucianism to be the orthodox way and call it the 'way of great learning'":[35]

> Confucianism has many qualities that belong to the true way of the Lord of heaven and earth. It transmits to the human heart the Five Virtues that everyone must keep among the Five Relations. It teaches people to "cultivate themselves, regulate their families, and govern their nation-states until there is peace in the world."[36] Those ideas belong to the way of the Lord of heaven and earth, the way which is instilled in the human heart.[37]

In the author's estimation, Confucianism shares many similar qualities with Christianity. However, he judges Confucianism to be inadequate, because it "has many flawed teachings intermingled with the correct teachings." The "error" of Confucianism is its failure to recognize that there is one Lord and Creator of the universe and that people must render worship to that Lord. Thus, the way of Confucius "partly conforms to the true way of the Lord of Heaven, which resides in the human heart, and partly contradicts it":[38]

> Consider how Confucian scholars teach people to worship heaven and earth and all creatures but fail to mention the great Lord who created heaven, earth, and all things. These scholars teach people to "serve the

---

35. *Errors*, Book 1, Preface, 1.

36. Sino-Vietnamese: 修身,齊家, 治國, 至於平天下 。This idea was taken from the *Great Learning*, where self-cultivation is the heart of Confucian formation.

37. *Errors*, Book 1, Article 4, 21.

38. *Errors*, Book 1, Article 4, 22.

Sovereign on High and to fear the Sovereign on High," but they identify the Sovereign with heaven and do not differentiate him from heaven. They also teach people to worship the deceased as if these people have the power to protect and bestow favor on their descendants.[39]

Like other Western missionaries to China, the author considered the ancient sage-kings of China to have been monotheists and true worshippers of God, and the present state of Confucian worship to be a degeneration of that original orientation toward God. For a Confucian scholar to be true to his tradition, he must accept the Christian message and worship God as well.

Through his dialogue with the Confucian Scholar, the author hopes to convince his audience to rediscover the monotheistic belief in God and to worship God above everything else. The author's approach is straighforward. First, he argues for the recognition of God as the true source of all life. Once one accepts that God is the Creator of heaven and earth and all beings in it, it follows that God is the highest of all spirits and must be worshiped above all things. The author simply challenges the worship of other spirits on the ground of ineffectiveness rather than declaring them as false or evil. True worship and avoidance of superstitious practices are the two constant themes that appear throughout *Errors*, as we have seen.

A Critical View of Daoism and Buddhism

While the author shows respect for Confucianism, he does not share the same attitude toward Daoism and Buddhism. He considers the Confucians learned men but the Daoists and Buddhists ignorant people. He often quotes from the Confucian sources in his arguments, especially from the materials that are familiar to the literati. But he does not exhibit a similar familiarity with Daoist and Buddhist texts, citing only from the Buddhist *Sutra of Forty-two Sections*, the esoteric Buddhist text *Lamp of the Mind*, and a single line from the *Daodejing*. He may have lacked access to texts of the non-Confucian traditions, or he may have deemed that these traditions, as practiced by their adherents, were not worthy of further investigation.

Since orthodox Confucians consider Daoist and Buddhist teachings "alien" (*dị doan*), the author makes extensive use of Confucian diatribes against Daoism and Buddhism. Like the Confucian Scholar, he dismisses "the ways of Laozi and Śākyamuni [Buddha]" as "the heterodox (or alien) teachings of 'emptiness' and

---

39. Ibid.

'quiescence' (*dị đoan hư vô tịch diệt chi giáo*),"[40] which use crafty words that resemble the truth to deceive people. In other words, both are counterfeit religions when viewed through the lens of Confucian orthodoxy. Furthermore, he was fond of using historical examples in both China and Vietnam to dismiss any positive value of these two religions. He cites stories of famous kings and noble persons who were devout Buddhists or Daoists, and yet when calaminites fell upon them, the Buddha and Laozi could not save them from troubles and disasters.

Two reasons seem to explain the author's dismissive attitude toward Buddhism and Daoism. First, he believes that these two religions are dangers to the Christian converts. Second, he attributes the degradation of Confucianism to its corruption by the beliefs and practices of the other two religions. The author worries that the religions of the Buddha and Laozi are seducing Christian converts. Because of their popularity, these religions can mislead simple people, steer them from the truth, and lead them into falsehood through "deceitful magic and divination." Consequently, the converts can fall back to the old ways and "harm themselves in this life and in the next."[41]

Of the two "heterodox ways," Buddhism is presumed to be the more dangerous one because it presents the Buddha as an alternative savior to the Christian God. According to the author, Buddhists claim that the Buddha "possesses power over heaven and earth to grant people wealth, fame, and longevity."[42] With this claim, the Buddha is treated as another divine sovereign who can distract the convert from a wholehearted devotion to God. Furthermore, the author fears that Christian converts would be tricked by Buddhist doctrines, and they would fall into false worship and superstitious practices that would eventually bring them to damnation. He explains,

> Buddhism frequently uses inspiring words to exhort people to practice virtue: words such as "quiescence" [*tịch diệt*], "compassion" [*từ bi*], "purity of mind" [*thanh tịnh*], "merit" [*công đức*], and other similar words. For this reason, people who do not exercise a critical mind take Buddhist teachings to be true and right, and as a result, they have come to believe in Buddhism. Many scholars of the Confucian tradition have also fallen into this wicked way.[43]

---

40. This is a phrase used by Zhu Xi in the preface to his commentary *Great Learning: Chapters and Verses*, and it is often repeated in the Confucian circle.

41. *Errors*, Book 2, Preface, 96.

42. *Errors*, Book 3, Preface, 141.

43. *Errors*, Book 3, Preface, 141–42.

The danger is that people could be misled by these ideas and harm themselves spiritually.

With regard to Daoism, the author considers it a religion of magicians and sorcerers, as did other missionaries.[44] The author of *Errors* dismisses Daoism as an "empty doctrine that contains nothing real and beneficial."[45] In the text, the author claims that Laozi is the originator of sorcery, crediting to him the invention of magic, charms, alchemy, and potions for immortality.[46] The author argues,

> Daoist sorcerers of past and present have always relied on the magic of Laozi. But if their medicine is so effective and if they possess the secret of immortality, why was the medicine not used to save them from death and to prolongue their lives?[47]

Daoist magic and medicine do not seem to be effective after all.

The seduction of Daoism and Buddhism does not only affect the common people, but, as the author sees it, they also have corrupted Confucianism and have led to its downfall. He gives the following reasons:

> These two ways are contrary to morality and cultural norms in every way. They contain nothing good nor anything consistent with the orthodox way [Confucianism], often plotting and scheming against it and telling lies to deceive the ignorant. They also muddy the minds of many gentlemen (*quân tử*) and cause them lose sight of the right and virtuous way. In addition, the deceiver often speaks with charisma, as if he were speaking the truth. In the same way, Daoism and Buddhism frequently use crafty words resembling the truth in order to make people believe. So when a gentleman hears something, he must examine it thoroughly; no wise person should believe everything he hears because people can fabricate

---

44. Adriano di Santa Thecla also calls Daoism "the sect of the magician." Until the twentieth century, the missionary portraits of Daoism in general were negative. Most did not distinguish between Daoist philosophy and Daoist magic and alchemy, conflating the two as Chinese superstitions. Henri Maspero's masterpiece *Le Taoisme et les religions chinois* is an early, serious attempt to understand Daoism as both a philosophy and a religion.

45. *Errors*, Book 2, Article 1, 100–101.

46. *Errors*, Book 2, Article 1, 99. In reality, these practices have nothing to do with Laozi, but they are products of religious Daoism from the Han dynasty onward.

47. *Errors*, Book 2, Article 2, 105.

teachings in hopes of becoming famous. They do not always pay attention to whether these teachings have sound reasoning.[48]

In denouncing Buddhism and Daoism, the author shared the same negative view of these religions that the Confucian elites had held since the fifteenth century. Vietnamese rulers raised Confucianism to the status of the state ideology at the expense of Daoism and Buddhism. Nevertheless, Confucianism, despite its effort to proscribe Daoism and Buddhism, could neither destroy these religions nor prohibit people from following them because it has been infected by their alien doctrines and practices. Thus, rather than being the beacon of truth, according to the author of *Errors*, Confucianism not only failed to correct the errors of the other two religions but had fallen into the same errors it condemned.

A Contemporary Assessment of *Errors*

If *Errors* grows from the thoughts and style of its predecessors—Matteo Ricci's *True Meaning* and Alexandre de Rhodes's *Cathechismus*—it inspires a generation of eighteenth- and nineteenth-century Catholic apologetic writings and catechisms. Although the manuscript of *Errors* (and even the Latin version by Adriano di Santa Thecla) was never published, the voice of its anonymous author was carried through the writings of its successors, and it reached beyond the original Tonkinese audience to many generations of Vietnamese Catholics until the middle of the twentieth century. What insights can be gained from a close reading of *Errors* in terms of its materials on and approach to the traditional religions of Vietnam? The following things strike me as significant.

Contributions

If one looks past the shortcomings of the work, including its polemical language, *Errors* provides many vivid sketches of reality that the broader literature on Vietnamese religions and cultures has overlooked. Invaluable is the vital role of *Errors* in helping us better understand the history of Christian-Vietnamese encounters before the French colonial era. The dialogues in *Errors* are valuable for giving the reader insights into what was at stake for the Christian minority. The disputes represent honest efforts to understand the uneasy interactions between Christianity and Vietnamese religious culture. The existence of

---

48. *Errors*, Book 2, Preface, 95.

Vietnamese Christian apologetic literature should vouchsafe its struggle to integrate Christianity into the Vietnamese culture.

The first is the importance of using reason and history to demonstrate coherent arguments. The central concern is, however, not the rhetorical effectiveness but whether the belief or practice being debated is compatible with the Christian faith. In using rational arguments, the author of *Errors* wants his view to be taken seriously. Since Confucianism also favors reason and debate, the arguments can be an entry for further dialogue and discussion. This strategy of *Errors* provides an opportunity for the Vietnamese readers to critically examine many of the beliefs and practices that they might have taken for granted. Furthermore, the author of *Errors*, even with his limitations and biases, attempts to trace the origin of many beliefs and practices. The book also provides descriptions of certain extinct and forgotten rituals. In the absence of comparable accounts, in many instances, *Errors* and its companion *Opusculum* are the only extant works that provide the valuable information to understand the Vietnamese past.

Finally, in *Errors*, there is an attempt to engage with the local religious culture. A striking feature of *Errors* that sets it apart from other Vietnamese Christian writings is the author's extensive use of the Confucian and Buddhist literature available to him. The sheer volume of citations of these writings in the dialogues reminds the reader of their privileged importance in the debates. In quoting Confucian classics and Vietnamese history rather than Western religious sources, the author of *Errors* shows a willingness to meet his audience on their own cultural terms, and not his. Even though his readings of the Vietnamese religious heritage are rather superficial, the fact that he chooses to engage with his audience in their cultural expressions speaks volumes about his desire to make the Christian faith accessible to a Vietnamese audience. Furthermore, by avoiding lengthy philosophical debates (such as those in Ricci's *True Meaning*) and by using more examples from historical figures and from daily life to refute the "errors" of the Three Religions, he renders the defense of the Christian beliefs and practices accessible to the common people. Although the arguments used by the author seem at times repetitive, unsophisticated, and unconvincing, they help the reader understand and appreciate better the world of those not immersed in a philosophical and theological milieu.

Limitations

Although *Errors* takes the form of a dialogue between a Western (Christian) scholar and an Eastern (Vietnamese) scholar, it is not a work of dialogue. Because of its apologetic agenda, *Errors* suffers from two major deficits that inhibit the potential for a true dialogical encounter: the lack of epistemic humility and cultural empathy.[49]

An exclusivist stance is necessary to safeguard one's religious identity and remind oneself of the importance of truth against religious indifference and relativism. But a lack of humility shown in polemically expressing one's religious convictions can obstruct openness and dialogue. If a believer of one religion (Christian or any other) approaches a believer of another religion with an a priori refutation of the other's beliefs, no real understanding or encounter can take place. Animosities and prejudices fuel intolerant behavior toward other people who do not share the person's views.

Because of its agenda, *Errors* suffers from a lack of objectivity when it describes and evaluates the religions of Vietnam. Written to refute the errors of the traditional religions, the author's Christian biases prevent an appreciation of the values of these religions. In apologetics, what is of ultimate importance is the defense of the faith. The truth of Christianity is the theological lens through which the author viewed and evaluated other religions. Only what fits in with this lens is considered legitimate; what jars with its vision is judged superstitious.

The author of *Errors* was also limited by his theology of revelation. He could not accept the East Asian apophatic approach to God. Abstract and impersonal terms for the primal principle of the universe such as *Dao*, the Supreme Ultimate, nothingness, or emptiness do not make sense to him. For the author, God must be a personal, living, all-knowing, and all-powerful being to be worthy of worship and trust. That God is an absolute sovereign who demands from all human beings total love and service is taken as a self-evident proposition through natural reason. The vindication of Christian beliefs is presumed and not questioned, and this attitude precludes a genuine interreligious dialogue.

The lack of cultural empathy is another impediment to dialogue. For effective dialogue, one must understand the culture and background of one's interlocutors. The world's great religions include many intricate elements involving not only the religious aspect but also the social, political, ethnic, and cultural dimensions of their geographical settings. Failure to be sensitive to the diverse expressions of religious experience in various settings leads to misjudging another religious belief or practice.

Each religious culture has a different set of symbols, languages, and expressions that need to be taken into account. Often the filter of one's own language and cultural or religious background will distort the meaning of the concept to

---

49. These are two of many problems that could inhibit true dialogue. On the topic, see Catherine Cornille, *The Im-possibility of Interreligious Dialogue* (New York: Crossroad Press, 2008).

be understood. Cultural translation is a challenge. For example, when a missionary translates the Vietnamese word *thờ* as "worship" or "adoration," he or she naturally assumes that the Christian connotation of *latria* (the exclusive devotion to God) applies to *thờ*. Likewise, when Vietnamese see sin translated as *tội* (crime), they immediately think of punishment and miss the nuance of a broken relationship between humanity and the divine. Even if they use the same term, different ideas might arise. When Western Christians read, "I bow to Heaven!" (*Tôi lạy Trời*), they might not always recognize it to be a pledge of submission to God, thinking that the Vietnamese worship the material sky.[50] When Vietnamese hear the words *Thiên Chúa* (Lord of Heaven) or *Thượng Đế* (Sovereign-on-High), they might contextualize God in their own understanding of a hierarchy of spirits, whereas God means the Absolute Reality for Christians. Thus, effective interreligious dialogue requires an effort to understand others in their own contexts, rather than simply translating one concept into another by using equivalent terms.

Like other missionaries of his times in Vietnam, the author of *Errors* did not understand the other religions in their proper terms and concepts, especially with regard to their religious practices. Due to a lack of cultural and religious training that were available to the later missionaries such as Léopold Cadière, the author's portrayal of Vietnamese religions was uneven, emphasizing more their superstitious aspects than their cultural values. The failure to connect beliefs and practices through cultural context led to an underappreciation of certain practices such as the cult of Confucius and of ancestors, as I have discussed in the previous chapters.

---

50. This misunderstanding is expressed in the arguments against naming Sovereign-on-High as God in Article 3 of Book 1. Prejudice prevents the author from recognizing the multivalent use of Heaven (to refer to the material sky as well as the creative power behind the cosmos).

Conclusion

LIKE ANY RELIGION, Christianity is situated within its surrounding cultures and interacts with them. Christian missionary activity, from its earliest days, has been confronted with a dilemma. How does Christianity proclaim its message to all nations and peoples while retaining its unique identity? How can Christianity maintain its essence without being absorbed into the dominant culture in which it immerses itself? This dilemma has been resolved in whole or in part through a process called "inculturation" by Catholics[1] (and "indigenization" or "contextualization" by Protestants).

A proper understanding of another faith must be grounded in its own context and not in one's own. Early descriptions of Asian religions by Western missionaries often resulted in gross caricatures because the missionaries attempted to describe other religions in terms of pre-established Christian categories and concerns (e.g., faith, salvation, etc.) rather than allowing them to stand on their own terms and expressions. The soteriological concern expressed in *Errors*, namely, "to attain happiness in paradise," is a Christian agenda. On the contrary, the Vietnamese Confucian concern is to maintain social harmony and to promote well-being in this life, rather than happiness in the afterlife. Unless one understands the presuppositions, concerns, and background of the other, as I have argued, true dialogue cannot happen.

---

1. This term is a Catholic theological expression that describes the interaction or implantation of the Gospel into a particular cultural setting. The term is different from "enculturation," which is used widely in the social sciences. For the relationship between faith and culture in Christian context see Robert Schreiter, *Constructing Local Theologies* (Maryknoll: Orbis, 1985); Michael Paul Gallagher, *Clashing Symbols: An Introduction to Faith and Culture* (London: Dartman, Longmann & Todd, 1997); Peter Schineller, *A Handbook of Inculturation* (New York: Paulist Press, 1990).

Conclusion

The story of Christianity in Vietnam should be seen as the outcome of the insertion of the faith into the land's historical and cultural conditions, and thus must be understood contextually. Despite limited resources, the message of the Gospel was delivered to Vietnamese society as widely as possible. Christian communities were established throughout the coastal areas of Tonkin under the leadership of the missionaries. As Christianity made contact with Vietnamese culture, inculturation did take place, albeit incompletely. It created a Vietnamese Christian culture that is alive and vibrant today. Even if Christian converts at the time never achieved a dominant position in society or exerted influence beyond their villages, their impact on Vietnamese society was felt by the ruling elite. Because of their historical circumstances, Christians were struggling for survival and could not appeal widely to the Vietnamese society of their time. The full synthesis of the Gospel and the Vietnamese culture is still in the making.

Exploring an apologetic work like *Errors* is both rewarding and frustrating. What the author claims about the "errors" of the traditional religions of Vietnam reveals more about his view than about the actual beliefs and practices of the adherents of the Three Religions. Nevertheless, given a reasonable amount of contextual awareness, new insights can be gained. In the study of the early history of Christianity in Vietnam, and of its cultural context, information about the religious situations are deciphered through the writings of foreign missionaries and merchants. Alexandre de Rhodes, Samuel Baron, Adriano di Santa Thecla, and the anonymous author of *Errors*, to name a few, have provided descriptions of the religious environment in Tonkin. Despite their limitations, it is possible to test the accuracy of their accounts through a cross-examination of available Chinese and Vietnamese sources—dynastic records, laws and regulations, and ritual manuals—as I have done. Every recovered bit of information, when used with care, becomes significant in the quest for a more well-rounded understanding of Vietnam's past.

Reviewing the past helps us understand the present. In evaluating such an apologetic work as *Errors*, we must remember the context in which it was composed. A text like *Errors* is typical of certain aspects of the Christian apologetic tradition—the defiant struggle to establish and maintain the uniqueness of Christianity in its religious surroundings. Whether an accurate picture of the religious situations of eighteenth-century Vietnam lies behind this one-sided Christian description is impossible to ascertain, given the scarcity of available materials on the subject. More comparative studies on specific Vietnamese religious practices should be done to provide a corrective lens to the information presented here.

What has been done is a preliminary attempt to provide the reader with an entry into the world of Vietnamese Christian apologetics. This study has explored the issues arising from a Christian encounter with the Vietnamese culture and religions, and it has also examined the interactions with and the attitude toward the religious environment in which Christians found themselves. Hopefully, the translation of *Errors* and the introduction of this work to our contemporary audience will help blaze new trails for further investigation into the cultural and religious tradition of Vietnam.

PART TWO

Errors of the Three Religions

An Annotated Translation of

TAM GIÁO CHƯ VỌNG

Archives des Missions Étrangères de Paris

Vol. 1098
by Anh Q. Tran

Notes on the Translation

This annotated translation adheres to the following conventions:

- All Chinese names have been rendered in Pinyin wherever possible. Their Sino-Vietnamese equivalents will be noted in the Index.
- Chinese and Vietnamese concepts have been translated into English wherever possible. Since some Chinese and Vietnamese words have several meanings, they have been rendered according to the context. For example, *giáo* (Chinese: *jiao*) can be translated as "teaching," "doctrine," or "religion."
- Whenever possible I supply the Chinese characters in the notes, especially for the quotations from the classics.
- The capitalization of translated words depends on the context, as in "heaven" (the world above) and "Heaven" (the divine). Consequently, the divine designation has been rendered as "Lord of Heaven," but when the term refers to the lordship of God, it has been translated as "Lord of heaven (or heaven and earth)."
- The original manuscript number is inserted in the text using a bold-type face, for example, {**p. 99**}.
- Cross-references in the footnotes taken from sources such as the *Toàn Thư*, Adriano's *Opusculum*, and *Hội Đồng Tứ Giáo* follows the pagination of the original texts (in Sino-Vietnamese, Latin or *Nôm* script), the pages from their printed translations will follow in parenthesis as needed.
- Olga Dror's translation of the *Opusculum* will be referred as *A Study of Religion*.
- Due to limited space, the critical transcription and textual analysis of the original Vietnamese manuscript of Tam *Giáo Chư Vọng* will not be printed here. It will be made available to the interested reader upon request

{p. i}

ERRORS OF THE THREE RELIGIONS

Preface

There are three teachings (religions)[1] in Annam[2]: the teachings of *ru*,[3] Laozi, and Śākya[muni].[4] Ru-ism [or Confucianism][5] is the way of Confucius, Daoism is the way of Laozi, and Buddhism is the way of Śākyamuni Buddha. These three teachings represent three different paths. During the reign of the Chen kings [in Southern China], King Zhou Gaozu[6] [of Northern Wei] ranked the three teachings, putting Confucianism first, Daoism second, and Buddhism last. In Annam, the first civil-service examination on the three teachings occurred during the reign of King Trần Thái Tông.[7] When King Lý Nhân Tông returned to Kẻ Chợ,[8] followers of the three teachings came to congratulate him, as

---

1. Throughout this text, the phrases "three teachings," "three doctrines," and "three religions" are used interchangeably as translations of *tam giáo*. Strictly speaking, "religion" is not the best rendering of the Sino-Vietnamese words *giáo* (teaching) or *đạo* (path, way), but it could be understood in this sense.

2. *Annam* (Pacified South) was the common designation of Vietnam among the Chinese and other foreigners from the seventh century until 1945.

3. *Nho* (*ru* 儒) is a class of erudite scholars in imperial China. The term was originally used to designate people who were ritual masters and dancers in the Zhou dynasty. Under Confucius and his successors, the meaning of *ru* was expanded to include the Confucian form of learning; thus, the term has become a synonym for the literati or Confucian scholars.

4. Śākya (Thích ca or Thích già) is the clan name for the historical Buddha. After achieving enlightenment, Siddhartha Gautama was honored as the "sage of the Sakya clan" (Śākyamuni).

5. *Nho giáo* (儒教, the teaching of *ru*) is conventionally rendered as "Confucianism." The Chinese and Vietnamese traditions, however, recognize Confucius only as a great teacher in the *ru* tradition, but not as the founder of a new doctrine or school of thought. When Kang Yuwei attempted to establish a Confucian religion in the early twentieth century, he coined the term *Kongjiao* (孔教, doctrine of Kong), which is the Chinese equivalent of Confucianism. In this translation, "Confucianism" refers to both *Ru* and *Kongjiao*.

6. During the North-South dynasties (fourth to seventh dynasties), China was ruled by different kings. The Chen king referred here was Chen Baxiang (陳霸先) also known posthumously as Chen Wudi (陳武帝) or Chen Gaozu (陳高祖), 503–559 CE, who ruled the Southern kingdom of China. In the North, Yuwen Yong (宇文邕), also known posthumously as Zhou Wudi (周武帝) or Zhou Gaozu (周高祖), 548–578 CE, employed Confucian scholars as court officials. This led to a revival of Confucianism, which had been in decline since the time of the Eastern Han.

7. Examinations of the Three Teachings began in the year đinh-hợi (1227). Cf. *Toàn Thư*, Bản kỷ, 5:4a (translation, 2:10).

8. *Kẻ Chợ* is literally "the market place." This term is used to designate any urban area. From the sixteenth to eighteenth century, it was the vernacular name for Hanoi, while its formal name was Thăng Long.

mentioned in our history book: "When the king returned to the capital, the followers of Confucianism, Daoism, and Buddhism together offered laudatory poems."[9]

From Italy in the Western world I have come to the East to preach the holy way of the Lord of Heaven[10] to the people of Annam—to the lowly and the noble, to the learned and the ignorant, to the old and the young. My goal is to introduce them to the true Lord, worship him, and follow the true way so that after death they may attain the blessing of eternal paradise. I am now very pleased to meet a learned and virtuous Eastern Scholar. This is a good opportunity for me {p. ii} to learn about these three religions more fully as well as discuss the truths concerning them.[11]

A learned person must not only study books but must also examine the arguments contained in them. Since books can teach errors through the use of clever words, a learned person must examine the arguments within these texts to see whether they are true or false. The book *Great Learning* states,[12] "A scholar who cannot utilize his learning cannot be called a learned person."[13] If a scholar cannot distinguish a good argument from a bad one, he should not be called a scholar. Only one who can tell truth from falsehood deserves to be called a learned and wise person. According to *Great Learning*, "When things are examined, knowledge is reached."[14] Therefore, this Western

---

9. From *Toàn Thư*, Bản kỷ, 3:22b (translation, 1:309).

10. "Lord of Heaven" (*Đức Chúa Trời*, Sino-Vietnamese: *Thiên Chúa/Chủ* 天主) is a short abbreviation of the Lord of heaven and earth (*Đức Chúa Trời Đất*, Sino-Vietnamese: *thiên địa chi chủ* 天地之主), a common designation for God among the Vietnamese and Chinese Catholics.

11. *Đạo* (*dao* 道) is translated literally as "way" or "path." Here it is used in the sense of religion.

12. *Great Learning* (*Daxue* 大學) was originally a chapter in the *Book of Rites* (*Liji* 禮記), but Zhu Xi separated it from the main text, and made it one of the four major books of the Confucian canon.

13. This quotation is not found in the original *Great Learning*; it may come from a Vietnamese edition of the book.

14. Sino-Vietnmese: 物格而後知至。See the chapter "Root of Knowledge" (*zhiben* 知本) in the *Great Learning*.

Scholar[15] is requesting a conversation with the Eastern Scholar to examine and discuss the doctrines of the three religions to better understand their errors.[16] Following the same ranking determined by kings of the past, this discussion is divided into three books: the first book discusses the errors of Confucianism, the second the errors of Daoism, and the third the errors of Buddhism.

---

15. "Western Scholar" is the form of self-reference used by Matteo Ricci in his *True Meaning of the Lord of Heaven* (*Tianzhu Shiyi* 天主實義).

16. In the context of the book, "errors" refer to beliefs or practices that are judged to be contrary to the Christian faith.

{p. 1}

BOOK 1: THE ERRORS OF CONFUCIANISM

Preface

ALL NOBLE PERSONS[17] take Confucianism to be the standard and refer to it as "the way of great learning" whose purpose is "to illuminate the illustrious virtue, to renew the people, and to rest only after attaining the highest good."[18] These nobles do so because Confucianism teaches them to cultivate the Five Virtues and to observe the precepts of the Five Relations so that people may become noble and the world be at peace. If I dismiss the teachings and practices of Confucianism as erroneous, either the Eastern Scholar would disagree with me, or accuse me of deliberately defaming Confucianism. No, I deeply respect and admire Confucianism because it wisely teaches correct truths about the Five Virtues and the Five Relations. However, Confucianism not only teaches the truths; it also contains errors and falsehoods that contradict the holy way of the Lord of Heaven, which is the great and most righteous way that people everywhere must believe and follow to attain peace.

{p. 2} Therefore, I invite the Confucian scholar to discuss and analyze with me the errors that are intermingled with Confucian truths. If during the discussion, you find that I defame Confucianism, I will take the blame; but if I speak the truth, you must agree and follow me along the same path. In doing so, you will follow the example of many other Confucian scholars who have surrendered to the truth and turned to the holy way of the Lord of Heaven—the way that has brought the people of this world to the path that leads to the most valuable and everlasting blessings.

---

17. "Noble person" (*junzi* 君子) literally means "son of ruler," a title reserved for the nobility of the Zhou. Confucius expanded the meaning to denote the ideal person.

18. Sino-Vietnamese: 大學之道, 在明明德, 在新民, 在止於至善。 This is the famous opening of the *Great Learning*.

INDEX OF THE ERRORS OF CONFUCIANISM

Article 1:   On How the Supreme Ultimate Created Heaven and Earth
Article 2:   On the Origin of Pangu
Article 3:   On the Sovereign on High
Article 4:   On the Origin of the Right Way
Article 5:   On the Great Flood
Article 6:   On Sacrifices to Heaven, Earth, and the Six Spirits of Nature
Article 7:   On Sacrifices to the Five Emperors and the Five Spirits
Article 8:   On the Oath-Taking Ceremony and the Chief's Banner Celebration
Article 9:   On Thành Hoàng and Other Spirits
Article 10: On King Dóng, King Trèm, King Bạch Mã [and Princess Liễu Hạnh]
Article 11: On the Kitchen God, the Household Guardian, the Land Guardian, and the Guild Founder
Article 12: On the Cult of Confucius and the Great Sages
Article 13: On the Cult of Thái Công and the Mighty Generals
Article 14: On Funeral Rites and the Veneration of Ancestors
Article 15: On Geomancy

{p. 4}

Article 1

On How the Supreme Ultimate Created Heaven and Earth

The Western Scholar says: I have heard that

> The Supreme Ultimate[19] generated the Two Modes;[20]
> The Two Modes generated the Four Forms;[21]
> The Four Forms were transformed into a myriad of things and classified by species and order.[22]

So I ask you: What is the Supreme Ultimate, and how did it generate the Two Modes?

The Eastern Scholar replies: Confucius says, "What is meant by the Supreme Ultimate? The Supreme Ultimate is the Energy [*khí*][23] and the Principle [*lý*]."[24] This means that the Principle is not a thing but the origin of things or the essence of things, just as Master Zhu [Xi][25] says, "The Principle is the origin of things." Therefore, the Energy and the Principle reside within heaven and earth and in all things. According to the book *Nature and Principle*[26]:

---

19. "Supreme Ultimate" (*taiji* 太極) can also be translated as Supreme Polarity.

20. "Two Modes" or "Two Principles" (*liangyi* 兩儀) is the basic division in Chinese cosmology. At the fundamental level, they are yin and yang, or heaven and earth.

21. "Four Forms" (*sixiang* 四象) are further sub-divivisions of yin and yang.

22. Sino-Vietnamese: 太極生兩儀, 兩儀生四象, 四象變化而次類繁矣。 According to Olga Dror (*A Study of Religion*, 97–98nn53, 61), this quotation is from the *Kangjian Hebian* of Yuan Liaofan.

23. *Khí* (*qi* 氣) originally meant "vapor," but its range of meaning includes air, energy, vitality, and spirit. In Neo-Confucianism, it is often paired and contrasted with *Lý* (*li* 理, principle), paralleling the Greek notions of "mater and form," hence my translation of *qi* as "Energy."

24. Since the doctrine of the Supreme Ultimate was formulated by Song Neo-Confucians, this quotation cannot be attributed to Confucius.

25. Master Zhu is the honorific title of Zhu Xi (朱熹), 1120–1200, a famous Neo-Confucian in the Song dynasty.

26. The full title of this book is the *Compendium of Nature and Principle* (Xingli Daquan 性理大全) composed by the scholar Hu Guang (胡廣), published in 1415. It was a standard textbook for civil-service examination in the Ming dynasty.

Book 1: The Errors of Confucianism

The Supreme Ultimate is truly the Principle of heaven, earth, and all things.
Within heaven and earth, there exists the Supreme Ultimate.
Within all things there exists the Supreme Ultimate.[27]

Hence, the Supreme Ultimate did not beget heaven and earth in the same way that parents give birth to children or workers build a house; rather, it begat heaven and earth like the blood of our body giving form to the body, {p. 5} or like the lumber of a house making up the house.

The Western Scholar asks again: You said that the Supreme Ultimate is the Principle and the Energy and that the Supreme Ultimate resides within heaven and earth and makes up heaven and earth. So did the Supreme Ultimate exist before heaven and earth, or did it come into existence with the creation of heaven and earth?

The Eastern Scholar replies: The Supreme Ultimate did not exist before heaven and earth; they both came into existence at the same time. The Supreme Ultimate, as well as heaven and earth, were created by the same source and in the same manner. *Nature and Principle* states:

> Although it is said that the Supreme Ultimate generated the Two Modes,
> The Two Modes generated the Four Forms,
> The Four Forms generated the Eight Trigrams.[28]
> In reality, the Supreme Ultimate and heaven and earth appeared together
>   at the same time.
> Whatever has form has shape;
> When there is One, there is Two;
> When there is Two, there is Three.[29]

Thus, the Supreme Ultimate came into existence at the same time as heaven and earth. And, as I said earlier, the Supreme Ultimate is not a thing but the essence of things, that which makes things. Therefore, the Supreme Ultimate could not have

---

27. Sino-Vietnamese: 太極只是天地萬物之理, 在天地則天地中有太極, 在萬物則萬物中有太極。

28. The "Eight Trigrams" (*bagua* 八卦) are an arrangement of solid (*yang*) and broken (*yin*) lines that are divided into eight groups of three lines each, representing the eight directions.

29. Sino-Vietnamese: 睢為之曰: 太極生兩儀, 兩儀生四象, 四象生八卦, 其實一時具足, 如有形則有影, 有一則有二, 有二則有三 。 This is an oblique reference to *Daodejing* 42: "One" refers to undifferentiated reality, "two" to yin and yang, and "three" refers to the triad of heaven, earth, and human, which gives rise to other phenomena.

existed independently before the formation of the heaven and {p. 6} earth—the two great entities that were born before everything else.

The Western Scholar comments: If the Supreme Ultimate coexisted with heaven and earth, then where did the Supreme Ultimate come from? Was the Supreme Ultimate self-generated or did it come from another source? I believe that the Supreme Ultimate could not self-generate and therefore had to come from another source. If the Supreme Ultimate did not exist, how could it have brought itself into existence? If something does not exist, there must be some sort of pre-existing being that brings it into being. Let us look at all living things—which were all born from existing entities. For example, all humans, birds, and animals must have parents, all fruits must come from trees, and all trees must come from other trees. This also applies to the Supreme Ultimate, whose existence requires another pre-existing source, not self-generation. Since the Supreme Ultimate is not the matter itself but the essence of matter to form a myriad of things, there must have been an all-knowing and all-powerful Being who existed before the Supreme Ultimate and created it. This Being took the Principle and Energy and separated them {p. 7} into heaven and earth, moved them to create yang energy, and then brought them to rest to create yin energy. I have heard that "when the Supreme Ultimate moves, it creates yang; when it rests, it creates yin." This Being took the yin and yang energies to fashion all things.

Therefore, we must not take heaven and earth or the Supreme Ultimate to be the origin of all things. We must consider first and foremost the One who is all-knowing and all-powerful to be the origin of all things. We must place the highest Being before the Supreme Ultimate. We must say:

> The Lord of Heaven created the Supreme Ultimate,
> [Then] the Supreme Ultimate generated the Two Modes,
> The Two Modes generated the Four Forms,
> The Four Forms were transformed into a myriad of things and classified by species and order.

This addition makes the statement complete. It brings out its truth and builds upon everything Confucian scholars have claimed about the power of heaven and earth in generating all things. In the *Classic of Changes*, Confucius says: "The great power of heaven and earth is to produce."[30] Master Zhu Xi explains this: "For the

---

30. Sino-Vietnamese: 天地之大德，曰生。 This quotation is from chapter "Explaining the Diagrams" (Xici 繫辭) of the *Classic of Changes*.

heaven to remain firm from above, for the earth to be populated from below, it is nothing other than generating things. Thus, the *Classic of Changes* claims, 'The great power of heaven and earth is to produce.'"[31] Furthermore, the book *Discourse of the [Confucian] School* says: "The Lord of heaven and earth produces everything."[32] These statements {p. 8} speak the truth when we see heaven and earth as the secondary cause of origin, the Lord of Heaven and Earth being the first.

The Eastern Scholar says: The Supreme Ultimate, together with heaven and earth, did not emerge from a pre-existing being but from the void. Master Cheng[33] states:

> Heaven and earth take "voidness" [*hư*][34] to be their power.
> The ultimate goodness is voidness.
> Voidness is the origin of heaven and earth.
> Heaven and earth emerged from the midst of voidness.[35]

Thus, before heaven and earth existed, their root was in the void. Since their existence began with voidness, their roots are from no other pre-existing entity but emptiness.

The Western Scholar replies: Those who speak like that view nonexistence as existence.[36] If voidness is nothingness, it has no quality. It cannot be a generative power, it cannot be the ultimate good, nor can it be the origin of heaven and earth. Nothingness is on the same order as heaven, earth, and all things. Thus, heaven

---

31. Sino-Vietnamese: 維天則確然於上, 地則薈然於下; 一無所為只以生萬物為事。故易曰: 天地之大德, 曰生。 *Opusculum* has the word *đồi* (頹) in the phrase 地則薈然於下 instead of *hội* (薈), so it can also be alternately translated as "the earth is broken down from below." Cf. Dror, *A Study of Religion*, 99n70.

32. Sino-Vietnamese: 主天地以生萬物。 This quotation cannot be identified from the *Discourse of the Confucian School* (Kongzi Jiayu 孔子家語).

33. Master Cheng refers to Cheng Yi (程頤), 1033–1107 CE. He and his brother Cheng Hao (程灝), 1032–1085 CE, were instrumental in making the "principle" central to neo-Confucian thought.

34. Voidness or emptiness (*xu* 虛) is a Daoist concept. Philosophically, it does not mean nothingness, but rather undifferentiation.

35. Sino-Vietnamese: 天地以虛為德, 至善者虛也, 虛者天地之祖, 天地從虛中來。 I cannot identify the source of this quotation.

36. This can also be translated as "viewing the nonbeing as being."

and earth truly came from nothing. However, we must not view emptiness as the origin of heaven and earth. On the contrary, we must look to a pre-existing Being {**p. 9**}—an infinitely intelligent and powerful Being, who created heaven and earth from nothing. Seen in this way, the above statement that "heaven and earth emerged from the midst of voidness" may be valid.

Moreover, if the Confucian scholar viewed voidness as the generative power and the origin of heaven and earth, he would share the same position as Buddhists[37] and Daoists, for the followers of these two religions often see "nonexistence" [*hư vô*] as the root cause of everything. That is why Master Chen says in his commentary on the *Doctrine of the Mean*, "Buddhists look at 'emptiness' [*không*] as their foundation. Daoists look at 'nonbeing' [*vô*] as their foundation."[38] As a result, Confucian scholars refer to these two religions as "the heterodox teachings of 'nonexistence' [*hư vô*] and 'quiescence'[*tịch diệt*]."[39] Therefore, you Confucian scholars should not take voidness and nothingness to be the generative power, the origin of heaven and earth; otherwise, you will be of the same mind as the followers of Śākyamuni and Laozi, who often take "emptiness," [*không*] "voidness," [*hư*] and "nonbeing" [*vô*] to be the origin of heaven and earth and everything.

---

37. Literally, *đạo bụt* is the "way of the Buddha," but it is often used in a pejorative sense as *secta idolatrum*.

38. Sino-Vietnamese: 釋氏以空為宗, 老子以無為宗. I cannot identify which Master Chen is being referred to here.

39. According to the Confucian view, the doctrines of Daoism and Buddhism are heterodox (*dị doan*) because they are based on the concept *hư vô tịch diệt* (there is no permanence; everything is empty), which is contrary to Confucian realism.

Article 2

On the Origin of Pangu

The Western Scholar says: I have heard that according to history "Pangu[40] was born of the chaos following the separation of heaven and earth."[41] Now I ask you: "Did Pangu come into existence at that moment, or did he exist before heaven and earth and only emerge at that time of chaos"?

The Eastern Scholar replies: It is not possible that Pangu existed before heaven and earth because when there was no heaven {p. 10} or earth, there was no place for him to live. Therefore, Pangu could only have come into being after heaven and earth were created.

The Western Scholar asks again: When Pangu came into being, to whom did he owe his existence? To himself or to another being?

The Eastern Scholar replies: Pangu came into being by the power of heaven and earth, because:

> The Supreme Ultimate generated the Two Modes;
> The Two Modes generated the Four Forms;
> The Four Forms were transformed into a myriad of things and classified by species and order.[42]

Master Hu[43] says, "Once heaven and earth came into existence, the Energy is transformed, and it led to the creation of humankind."[44]

---

40. Pangu (盤古) is a Chinese mythical figure. He was the first being in the world and created heaven and earth from chaos.

41. Sino-Vietnamese: 混沌之世天地始分，即有盤古是出 。 According to Olga Dror (*A Study of Religion*, 99n64), the text *Gangjian Hebian* 1:1a claims that Hỗn độn (primordial chaos) is another name for Pangu.

42. Sino-Vietnamese: 太極生兩儀，兩儀生四象，四象變化而次類繁矣 。

43. This possibly refers to Hu Zhitang (胡致堂), or Hu Yin (胡寅), 1098–1156, a neo-Confucian of the Song dynasty.

44. Sino-Vietnamese: 既有天地則氣化而人生焉 。

The Western Scholar says: Since Pangu was truly a human, who had a body and soul like us, it is correct to say that heaven and earth begat his body. It is incorrect, however, to say that heaven and earth begat his soul because heaven and earth possess neither intelligence nor perception. Since they do not think or live, how could they beget humans who think, live, and possess the quality of being the most spiritual among the myriad of things? For this reason, Pangu had to be created by the one great Lord who also created heaven and earth. That Lord is infinitely {p. 11} intelligent and powerful; he created the body and soul, and fused the soul with the body. That is how Pangu came into being.

Furthermore, I was told that Pangu emerged when heaven and earth began to separate. But I have not heard anything about any other human being. If no woman existed at that time, where did Pangu find a wife to continue his lineage? When he came into being, a woman would have had to be born with him so that the two could unite and beget children.

The Eastern Scholar says: It is an oversight that our tradition does not mention the first woman, who was to be Pangu's wife. What does your Western tradition say about her?

The Western Scholar says: Our tradition speaks of a couple who were the ancestors of all human beings. The man's name was Adam, and the woman's name was Eve. According to our tradition, the Lord of Heaven created Adam after he created heaven and earth. {p. 12} He took a short rib from Adam's body and used it to create a body for Eve. He also created a soul to be united with that body, and Eve came into being. Next, the Lord told them to unite as one body of flesh and bone to beget children, thereby perpetuating the human race. Afterwards, the Lord charged them to rule and make use of everything in this world. This is what our tradition teaches us about the couple who are the ancestors of all human beings.

Article 3

On the Sovereign on High

The Western Scholar says: In the Four Books and Five Classics,[45] Confucian scholars teach people to "worship the Sovereign on High and serve the Sovereign on High." So, I ask you: Who is the Sovereign on High [*thượng đế*]?[46]

The Eastern Scholar says: The Sovereign on High is called Heaven by Confucian scholars. However, Heaven refers not to the azure sky that we see above us but to the power of heaven that resides in the sky that we cannot see. The *Classic of Changes* says: "*Qian* represents what is great: originating, penetrating, advantageous [correct and firm]."[47] Master Cheng teaches:

> *Qian* means heaven.
> Oh, heaven!
> When spoken as an absolute, it is called *Dao*.
> When differentiated, it is called by different names:
> {p. 13} In terms of its visible form, it is called the sky.
> In terms of ruling, it is called the lord.
> In terms of active power, it is called the spiritual force.[48]
> In terms of marvels, it is called the gods.
> In terms of nature, it is called *Qian*.
> Therefore, *Qian* is the beginning of all things.[49]

---

45. The Four Books refers to the *Great Learning* (Daxue 大學), the *Doctrine of the Mean* (Zhongyong 中庸), the *Analects of Confucius* (Lunyu 論語), and the *Book of Mencius* (Mengzi 孟子). The Five Classics refers to the *Classic of Odes* (Shijing 詩經), the *Classic of Documents* (Shujing 書經), the *Classic of Changes* (Yijing 易經), the *Record of Rites* (Liji 禮記), and the *Annals of Spring and Autumn* (Chunqiu 春秋). These books make up the Confucian canon for Chinese and Vietnamese scholars to study for their civil-service examinations.

46. The Sino-Vietnamese term *thượng đế* (*shangdi* 上帝) has been rendered variously as High God, Lord on High, Supreme Emperor, Supreme Ruler, and Sovereign on High. In this translation, it is translated as "Sovereign" to avoid confusion with the other term "emperor" (*di* 帝) used for human Chinese rulers. *Di* or *Shangdi* was the high god of the Chinese during the Shang period. It was gradually replaced by Heaven (*tian* 天), originally the sky god of the Zhou people, who conquered the land of the Shang in the sixteenth century BCE. *Shangdi* and *Tian* are used interchangeably in Neo-Confucianism.

47. *Qian* (乾) is the first trigram in the *Classic of Changes*. The first line of the Qian trigram reads, 乾元亨利貞。The text erroneously omits the last word.

48. Literally "demons and gods" (*guishen* 鬼神). For a Neo-Confucian understanding of *guishen*, see a discussion by Dror in *A Study of Religion*, 101–2n82.

49. Sino-Vietnamese: 乾天也，夫天專言之則道也，分而言之則以形體謂之天，以主宰謂之帝，以功德謂之鬼神，以妙用謂之神，以性情謂之乾，乾者萬物之始。The

This is how Master Cheng [Yi] explains the *Qian* trigram. He makes distinctions between the various aspects of the nature of *Qian*, which means Heaven. Master Zhu [Xi] says: "What is the Heart-mind[50] of heaven and earth? What is the Principle of heaven and earth? The Principle is the rational principle; the Heart-mind is the ruler."[51] Consider the saying from the *Tứ Phủ*:[52] "The Heart-mind is the ruler." Consider also the saying from *Nature and Principle*: "The character heart-mind [心] is called sovereign; the sovereign is the ruler of heaven."[53] Thus, the Sovereign on High is Heaven, and Heaven is the Sovereign on High. Since the heart-mind of heaven is the ruler of heaven and the Sovereign on High is also the ruler of heaven, the heart-mind and the Sovereign are both rulers; both are seen as one. {p. 14}

The Western Scholar says: If that is the case, then the Confucian scholars' "Sovereign on High" is identical to heaven, not differentiated from heaven. That is why people often say, "Heaven sees; Heaven punishes." Now, once a year, when the mandarins gather for the "Oath-Taking" ceremony [Hội Minh],[54] the highest official declares: "I bow to the Supreme Emperor, August Heaven, and to the Empress, August Earth" [*Hoàng thiên thượng đế, Hoàng địa kỳ*]. The other officials declare: "We bow to August Heaven and to the Spirit of the Earth" [*Hoàng thiên, Hậu thổ*]. The soldiers declare: "We bow to heaven and earth." They all do this because the Sovereign on High and August Heaven are both identified with heaven (the sky); they are one with heaven.[55] Now I ask you: "Where did the Sovereign on High come from? From himself or from another?"

The Eastern Scholar says: The Sovereign on High came into being on his own. He does not owe his existence to any other being because he is one with Heaven;

Chinese text is followed by a Vietnamese translation by the author. To avoid repetition, I have omitted the author's translation here.

50. The Sino-Vietnamese word *tâm* (心) in Chinese philosophy has a connotation of both heart and mind; thus, I use the compound heart-mind to translate it.

51. Sino-Vietnamese: 問天地之心, 天地之理, 理是道理, 心是主宰。

52. I am uncertain of the meaning; it may be the name of an obscure book.

53. Sino-Vietnamese: 心字似帝, 帝者, 天之主宰也。Cf. *Hội Đồng Tứ Giáo* (1867 Nôm ed.)₂ 8b.

54. See the discussion in Book 1, Article 8.

55. Here the Western Scholar understands the concept of heaven in terms of the physical sky or the natural world. The concept of heaven in Chinese philosophy is more complex; it can mean god, the originator of life and morality, or a cosmic force.

Book 1: The Errors of Confucianism   175

he emerged spontaneously from nothingness. Although it is written that the Supreme Ultimate produced the Two Modes, in reality, the Supreme Ultimate is not a being that created heaven from the outside. It was already residing in heaven when it created it. {p. 15}

The Western Scholar argues further: I believe that the Sovereign on High did not self-generate but originated from another being. As I argued in Article 1, the Supreme Ultimate and heaven (the sky) owe their existence to another being. It follows that if the Sovereign on High is one with heaven, he must also come from another being. Consequently, whoever created heaven also created the Sovereign on High, who is one with heaven. It is, therefore, incorrect for the Confucian scholar to equate the Sovereign on High with heaven because heaven cannot have the same dignity as its lord.

The Western Scholar asks: I have another question: "Does the Sovereign on High possess the intelligence to know what he is doing?"

The Eastern Scholar says: The Sovereign on High possesses not only intelligence but a supreme mind that knows and understands the important work he does. People therefore often pray to Heaven to guide and judge their hearts because they believe that the Sovereign on High has a mind and is all-knowing.

The Western Scholar comments: If the Sovereign on High is the Supreme Mind, then heaven can enlighten people because the Sovereign on High is one with heaven as well as the heart-mind of heaven. If the Sovereign on High is a living and intelligent being, he also brought heaven to life, just as he did the human soul, which lives within and animates the body.

However, {p. 16} I have not seen any sign that heaven is alive. All living things have a physical form. At birth they are small. Then, by eating, they grow in size. Consider the grass and trees, animals and birds, and humans—all are like that. But the azure heaven does not change in size, nor does it grow smaller or larger. It does not eat, it does not produce another heaven, and it does not decline and die. Therefore, heaven is not a living form. For that reason, there cannot be a Sovereign who is identical to heaven and at the same time a living being. In addition, if the Sovereign on High is identical to heaven, then he must follow the movements of heaven—back and forth, never stopping. According to the *Great Learning*, heaven moves back and forth, never stopping: "The heaven circles around nonstop; whatever goes forth will return."[56] It would be absurd to apply this to the Sovereign on High. Therefore, it is difficult and irrational to believe in and accept the Confucian scholars' notion of the Sovereign on High.

For these reasons, there cannot be a Sovereign on High who is identical to heaven, but instead a Sovereign on High who exists outside of and apart from heaven. He is the spiritual one, {p. 17} "the most honored among the gods," infinitely all-knowing, infinitely all-powerful. He created and rules over heaven, earth, humans, and things. Our religion calls him "the true Lord of heaven and earth" and not the "Sovereign on High." We do not want others to think that we see heaven as the Sovereign on High as postulated in your teaching. Therefore, you should join me in believing in the supreme and most noble King, who fashioned heaven, earth, humans, and all things and call him "the true Lord of heaven and earth." Furthermore, instead of saying, "Revere the Sovereign on High and fear the Sovereign on High," join me in saying, "Revere the Lord of Heaven and fear the Lord of Heaven." When the ancient kings worshipped the Sovereign on High, they probably did not intend to worship him as the One identical to heaven; rather, they most likely meant to worship the One who is different from heaven, the One who fashioned heaven and earth. We will discuss this further in Article 6.

---

56. Sino-Vietnamese: 天運循環, 無往不復。 Cf. *Hội Đồng Tứ Giáo*, 9a.

Article 4

On the Origin of the Right Way

The Western Scholar says: The Confucian books teach that there is a great way that everyone must believe, love, study, and practice throughout life. Confucius {**p. 18**} says, "Have sincere faith and love learning; pursue the good way until death."[57] The sages call it "the way of virtue and reason." *Doctrine of Nature* (*Tính Giáo*)[58] teaches that this way resides within all people, just as Master Zhu [Xi] says, "human nature is not a thing; it is only a principle within us."[59] Master Dong [Zhongshu] writes: "As 'the way' [*đạo*] is practiced in the world, there is no difference between past or present."[60] So, I ask you: "Where does that correct doctrine, that natural teaching within the human heart, come from? Who bestows humans with the ability to know right from wrong? How do all people—past and present—have the same nature?

The Eastern Scholar replies: Master Dong [Zhongshu] says, "The ultimate origin of 'the way' is heaven."[61] Furthermore, *Great Learning* explains that, "because Heaven gives birth to people, it must give them the innate virtues of humaneness, righteousness, propriety, wisdom, and trustworthiness."[62] Therefore, Heaven is the source of virtue and moral principles, and it bestows them on humans.

The Western Scholar argues: Since Confucian scholars often believe that heaven and earth are the origins of all things, they teach that the source of the moral principles is heaven and that heaven integrates the way into the human heart. They also say that "the way comes from heaven and earth." However, as I argued earlier, {**p. 19**} heaven is not the origin of all things. First came the noblest Being who fashioned heaven and earth; that Being is the source of all things. Moreover,

---

57. Sino-Vietnamese: 督信好學, 取死善道。

58. This book has not been identified.

59. Sino-Vietnamese: 性非有物, 只是一箇道理, 之在於我者耳。 Cf. *Hội Đồng Tứ Giáo*, 17a.

60. Sino-Vietnamese: 夫道在天下, 無古今之殊。 Cf. *Hội Đồng Tứ Giáo*, 17a.

61. Sino-Vietnamese: 道之大原出於天。 Cf. *Hội Đồng Tứ Giáo*, 17a.

62. Sino-Vietnamese: 蓋自天降生民, 則既莫不與之, 以仁義禮智信之性矣。 Cf. *Hội Đồng Tứ Giáo*, 17a.

I have argued that heaven could not create the human soul because it possesses neither intelligence nor perception. Since heaven does not think or create life, it follows that it cannot beget a human soul, which thinks, lives, and possesses the quality of being "the most spiritual among all things."

Therefore, there must exist a great, infinitely all-knowing and all-powerful Lord, who created humans in both body and soul. He endowed the human soul with the capacity to learn the Five Virtues, which are the moral principles within a person. For that reason, we must not call that way the "way of heaven" or the "mandate of heaven," as Confucian scholars often do. Rather, we must call it the way of the Lord of Heaven. Moreover, we should consider that there is not one but several discrete ways: The first is the way of heaven, the second the way of the earth, and the third the way of humanity. The way of heaven has a heavenly nature that continuously causes heaven to move back and forth, lights up the world, and brings about the four seasons. The way of the earth has an earthly nature that constantly produces grass and trees, the five types of grain, the five types of metal, and the five types of precious stones.[63] The way of humanity is the nature of {p. 20} the Five Virtues, which teach people to do good and avoid evil. Master Hu Wufeng[64] writes:

> The energies of yin and yang make up the visible forms.
> The heavenly way comes from these.
> The qualities of firmness and softness make up the elements.
> The earthly way comes from these.
> Humaneness and righteousness make up the virtues.
> The human way comes from these.[65]

Therefore, the way of humanity comes from the human heart and not from heaven. The way of humanity comes from the great Being who created heaven, earth, and humans. It is he who shows the way to the human heart. There exists such a Being who created the ways of heaven, earth, and humanity, and who endows them with different natures.

---

63. The five types of "grain" are hemp, millet, rice, corn, and bean. The five types of metal are gold, silver, copper, lead or tin, and iron. There is no agreement on the five types of precious stones; however, if following the color of the five elements (as in the case of the five metals), they are yellow stone, white stone, red stone, blue or azure stone, and black stone.

64. Hu Wufeng (胡五峰) or Hu Hong (胡宏), 1105–1061 CE, was a Neo-Confucian philosopher of the Song dynasty.

65. Sino-Vietnamese: 陰陽成象, 而天道著矣。剛柔成質, 而地道著矣。仁義成德, 而人道著矣。

The Eastern Scholar says: I agree that the way of humanity within people does not come from the moving sky. However, in heaven there is the Sovereign on High, who is the Principle of heaven and the Heart-mind of heaven. From this Heart-mind of heaven the moral norms are infused into the human heart.

The Western Scholar replies: If the Sovereign on High, who is the Heart-mind of heaven, is identical to heaven, and if he is also the same as heaven, then he must depend on a heaven that possesses neither intelligence nor perception. Therefore, he does not think or live, as I argued in the previous article. {p. 21} Moreover, the way within the human heart cannot possibly come from the Sovereign on High, the Heart-mind of heaven. On the contrary, the way of humanity can come only from the great Lord, the Supreme Being who created heaven and earth.

The Eastern Scholar asks: Is Confucianism the true way that comes from the great Lord, who created heaven and earth?

The Western Scholar replies: Confucianism has many qualities that belong to the true way of the Lord of heaven and earth. It transmits to the human heart the Five Virtues that everyone must keep among the Five Relations. It teaches people to "cultivate themselves, regulate their families, and govern their nation-states until there is peace in the world."[66] Those ideas belong to the way of the Lord of heaven and earth, the way that is instilled in the human heart.

However, because Confucianism has many flawed teachings intermingled with the correct teachings, it cannot be the true way of the Lord of heaven and earth, nor was it given to the human heart. Consider how Confucian scholars teach people to worship heaven and earth {p. 22} and all creatures but fail [to mention] the great Lord who created heaven, earth, and all things. These scholars teach people to "serve the Sovereign on High and to fear the Sovereign on High," but they identify the Sovereign with heaven and do not differentiate him from heaven. They also teach people to worship the deceased as if these people have the power to protect and bestow favor on their descendants. Thus, Confucianism both conforms to and contradicts the true way of the Lord of Heaven, which resides in the human heart.

---

66. Sino-Vietnamese: 修身齊家治國至於平天下 。 This idea was taken from the *Great Learning*, where self-cultivation is the heart of Confucian formation.

Article 5

On the Great Flood

The Western Scholar says: I have heard in the history book that "in the time of Emperor Yao,[67] the waters swelled up to the sky." Now let me ask the Eastern Scholar: How long did the great flood last?

The Eastern Scholar says: From beginning to end, the great flood lasted twenty years. In the sixty-first year of his reign, Emperor Yao assigned Minister Gun, the task of saving the land of the Nine Regions[68] from this flood. After nine years of trying to control it, Minister Gun failed [and was executed]. Two years later, Emperor Shun[69] ordered Gun's son whose name was Yu[70] {p. 23} to continue the task of flood control. Yu worked hard for another nine years and was finally able to save the Nine Regions from flooding in the eightieth year of Emperor Yao's reign.[71] Master Zhu [Xi] recounts this story in *Outline of History*:[72] "In the year *giáp-thìn*,[73] the sixtieth year of Yao's reign, there was a great flood. The Four Great Ministers appointed Gun minister of public works. By the end of the year *nhâm-tí*, the sixty-ninth year, Gun was not able to control the flood. Yu was sent to control the flood and the land in the year *ất-mẹo*, the seventy-second year. In

---

67. Emperor Yao (堯) is one of the sage-kings of ancient China.

68. "Nine Regions" (*jiuzhou* 九州) is a general name for ancient China. The name refers to the land around the Yellow River that had been partitioned by King Yu the Great into nine prefectures. The reference is taken from the chapter "Tribute of Yu" (Yugong 禹貢) of the *Classic of Documents*.

69. Emperor Shun (舜) was the sage-king who succeeded Emperor Yao.

70. King Yu the Great (大禹) was the founder of the Xia dynasty. King Yu, considered a hero in ancient China, spent thirteen years on flood prevention. His success in controlling the floodwaters won the respect of the people as well as the trust of his lord, Emperor Shun. On his death, Shun passed the leadership to Yu.

71. According to legend, the Yellow River erupted into a huge flood during the time of Emperor Yao. Yu's father, Gun (鯀), was put in charge of flood control by Emperor Yao but failed to alleviate [mitigate] the problem after nine years. He was executed by Yao's successor, Emperor Shun. Yu then took over his father's task and led the people in building canals and levees. After many more years of toil, the flooding problems were solved under Yu's command. In recognition of his accomplishment, Shun established Yu as the founder of the Xia dynasty. The main source of the story of Yu and the Great Flood comes from the *Classic of Documents*.

72. This probably refers to Zhu Xi's *Outline of the Comprehensive Mirror* (Tongjian Gangmu 通鑒網目).

73. The Chinese and the Vietnamese divide time in sixty-year cycles, assigning a name for each year. Each name consists of one "heavenly stem": Giáp, Ất, Bính, Đinh, Mậu, Kỷ, Canh, Tân, Nhâm, Quí; and one "earthly branch": Tí, Sửu, Dần, Mão/Mẹo, Thìn, Tị, Ngọ, Mùi, Thân, Dậu, Tuất, Hợi.

the year *quí-hợi*, the eightieth year, Yu succeeded. Since then, the people of the Nine Regions have prospered [...]"[74]

The Western Scholar says: I would like to examine this story. During such a long and great flood, when the waters had swelled up above the mountains and up to heaven, how did the people survive? There was no place to live and no land to cultivate. During that time, who had the power and ability to build dikes, dig trenches, and drain the water so that there would be dry land? If the great flood covered the earth, no one could have done anything to survive. Everyone would have {p. 24} drowned.

A great flood did indeed occur in ancient times, and it covered the whole earth. People everywhere died in that flood, except for a man named Noah and seven members of his family, who survived on a boat. The great flood did not occur at the time of Emperor Yao, however. It happened a century before, during the time of Noah. But because Emperor Yao told his people that the whole world had once been submerged in a great flood, later generations accepted his story and mistakenly believed that the great flood had occurred during his time. Therefore, it should be said that "in the time of Noah, the waters swelled up to the sky."

There are reasons for saying that the great flood did not occur during Yao's time. According to an account in the *Classic of Documents*, the great flood had been controlled before Yu was even born. How then can you say that Yu was the one who controlled it? What is more, consider the claim that Emperor Shun assigned the task to Yu in the seventy-second year of Yao's reign. From that time, Emperor Yao still ruled for another twenty-ninth years, {p. 25} before Emperor Shun assumed the throne. Shun ruled for another fifty years. Then, Yu the Great ruled for twenty-seven years. If you count the years from the time Yu took over the task of controlling the flood (that is, in the seventy-second year of Yao's reign) until the time of his death, you get 106 years in total. Yu only lived to be one hundred years old. So how can he be the one who saved the Nine Regions from the flood if there were 106 years between the seventy-second year of Yao's reign and Yu's death?

The Eastern Scholar says: Your account is based upon an incorrect report in the *Comprehensive Mirror*[75] that states that "King Yu the Great ruled for twenty-seven

---

74. Sino-Vietnamese: 甲辰六十有一載，洪水為患。思四岳舉鯀為司空。壬子六十有九載，鯀治水績用弗成。乙卯七十有二載，使禹平水土。癸亥八十載，禹治水成功，人丁九洲貢賦，秉玄圭 [...] 謹告成 [功]。 The sentence is incomplete because the last phrase in the manuscript is indecipherable.

75. This probably refers to Sima Guang's *Comprehensive Mirror to Aid in Government* (Zizhi Tongjian 資治通鑑), a critical history written in the Song dynasty, which became a model for other historical narratives.

years." We should accept, instead, Master Zhu's account in the *Outline of History*, which says that "Yu the Great ruled for eight years" only.

The Western Scholar replies: Here is why he is thought to have ruled for only eight years. According to the *Outline of History*, Yu the Great was born before the flood and accepted the task of subduing it when he was not yet fourteen years old. Before he was born, Emperor Shun had ruled for fifty years. After Yu succeeded in controlling the flood, Emperor Yao ruled for twenty-nine years. Thirteen years remain in the total one hundred years of Yu's life. Regardless of how you keep counting, the important task of controlling the flood {p. 26} was far beyond the ability of a child who was not yet fourteen. Because Confucian scholars mistakenly believed that Yu had saved the people from the great flood during the reign of Emperor Yao, they also mistakenly claimed that "in the time of King Yao, the waters swelled up to the sky." The great flood, however, had already occurred before the time of Emperor Yao. But because Yao passed on the story of the ancient flood, later generations mistakenly believed that the great flood happened during his rule.

The Eastern Scholar asks: What was the great flood at the time of Noah like?

The Western Scholar says: When Noah was six hundred years old, the Lord of Heaven made it rain for forty consecutive days. All the rivers and lakes flooded, and all the underground water sources burst forth. For one year, an abundance of water covered the earth, rising fifteen meters above the mountains. At that time, humankind, as well as animals, birds, and reptiles everywhere, drowned. Only eight people, who had been in a boat, were saved from death. The Lord of Heaven chose them to {p. 27} continue the human race: Noah, his wife, their three sons, and their sons' wives. After five months, the Lord of Heaven allowed the waters to slowly recede, causing dry land to emerge at the end of the year. He then told Noah and his sons to leave the boat and move to land, bringing with them the animals, birds, and reptiles that they had kept [housed] during the months of the flood. The people who were born after the flood are the descendants of Noah's three sons. That is the story of the great flood according to our religion.

The Eastern Scholar says: Your story sounds reasonable. It corresponds with Confucius's account of the great flood in the *Classic of Documents*. The book recounts Emperor Yao's words to his officers: "Immense is the flood rising in wide partition. Raging water has submerged the mountains and covered the hilltops.

How vast is the overflow rushing to the sky!"[76] Yao's report suggests that the great flood had caused terrible damage. The water covered the mountains, rose above the mountains, and reached the sky.

The Western Scholar continues: One hundred years after the great flood, the descendants of Noah migrated {p. 28} a great distance and in many directions. Some must have come to the East and settled in the Nine Regions. Because of this, we have come to know the history of the Nine Regions (China) and the world.

The Eastern Scholar asks: So who was the first person to come to the East and found the Nine Regions?

The Western Scholar replies: I think Emperor Yao and some other people arrived in the East. Yao became the first king here because the era of Yao corresponds to the time when Noah's descendants scattered in all directions.

The Eastern Scholar says: What you say also corresponds to what Confucius recorded in the *Classic of Documents*. He wrote only about the affairs of the kings from the time of Emperor Yao onward—not about those of the kings before him.

The Eastern Scholar asks again: How many years have passed between the time of the great flood and the present? And how many years were there been before the flood {p. 29} starting from the creation of heaven and earth?

The Western Scholar replies: There were 1,656 years between the creation of heaven and earth and the great flood, and 4,100 years have passed since the time of the great flood and the present year—the year *nhâm-thân*, or the thirteenth year of Cảnh Hưng's reign [1752].[77] There is another method of counting, however, that apportions more years between the creation and the great flood, and between the great flood and the present time. But since I am more certain about the first method of counting, let us follow my account.

---

76. Sino-Vietnamese: 湯湯洪水方割, 蕩蕩懷山襄陵, 浩浩滔天。From "Canon of Yao" (yaodian 堯典) in the *Classic of Documents*.

77. The year is 1752, since King Lê Cảnh Hưng started his reign in the year of 1739. This is important information, for it gives the internal dating of the manuscript.

Article 6

On Sacrifices to Heaven, Earth, and the Six Spirits of Nature

The Western Scholar says: Confucian scholars teach people to make offerings to heaven, earth, mountains, and rivers. Consequently, offerings are made at the beginning of the year to the Sovereign on High, and then to the earth. Court officials are also ordered to make offerings to the "Six Spirits of Nature" [*lục tông*][78] and to [the spirits of] mountains and rivers. I ask you: Where do these rites come from?

The Eastern Scholar says: Past and present kings have followed the procedures laid out by Confucius in the *Book of Rites*. The chapter "Utensils of Rites"[79] says: "The ancient kings were concerned that the rites were not understood by all below them. Therefore, they offered sacrifices to the Sovereign [on High] in the open space called *giao* [郊][80] in order to establish a place of heaven. They offered sacrifices at the altar of the earth called *xã* [社][81] {**p. 30**} inside the capital, where they recorded the gifts of the earth."[82] Furthermore, the *Classic of Documents* says:

> Emperor Shun makes four types of offerings. The first is a special sacrifice called *loại* [類] that is offered to the Sovereign on High. The second is called *yên* [禋], which is offered to the Six Spirits of Nature. The third is called *vọng* [望], which is offered to the spirits of the mountains and the rivers. The last is called *biến* [遍], which is offered to a host of spirits. These are the four types of sacrifices performed for different orders of gods, each with its own altar. Therefore it is written that the sacrifices offered to the Six Spirits of Nature are sacrifices to the spirits of seasons,

---

78. The meaning of *Lục Tông* (liuzong 六宗) is obscure. From the author's explanation following the *Classic of Documents*, it seems to refer to the spirits of natural phenomena and objects, such as the seasons, heat and cold, the heavenly bodies (sun, moon, and stars), and flood and drought.

79. The text mistakenly ascribes this quotation to "Utensils of Rites" (liqi 禮器). The correct chapter should be "Conveyance of Rites" (liyun 禮運) of the *Record of Rites*.

80. The Sino-Vietnamese term *Giao* (jiao郊) refers to an open space outside the city where sacrifices to heaven are performed.

81. The Sino-Vietnamese term *Xã* (she 社) refers to a lot inside the city-state where sacrifices to the earth are performed.

82. Sino-Vietnamese: 故先王患禮之不達於[天]下也, 故祭帝於郊, 所以定天位也; 祀社於國, 所以列地利也。From "Conveyance of Rites" (liyun 禮運) in *Record of Rites*, sect. 4.

cold and heat, the sun, the moon, the stars, and floods and drought, as well as to a host of other spirits, including the spirits of hills and valleys.[83]

The first king of kings, the Yellow Emperor,[84] performed sacrifices to the Sovereign on High and to the gods. The historical record[85] says: "The [Yellow] emperor enacted laws that established a special palace. He came up with a practice of worshipping and venerating the Sovereign on High and then of the numerous spirits. He proclaimed the appropriate procedure from there."[86]

The Western Scholar comments: It is not appropriate to worship the sun, the moon, the stars, [the spirits of] the seasons, heat and cold, rain and wind, mountains and rivers, and others like them. Because [these natural phenomena] possess no intelligence, they neither think nor have the power to make things happen; they only carry out whatever tasks their master, the Lord of heaven and earth, {p. 31} assigns to them. Thus, they do not know the human heart and are unaware of the worship and trust directed toward them.

The Eastern Scholar says: When Confucian scholars offer sacrifices to the sun, the moon, the stars, floods and drought, mountains and rivers, and others like them, they are actually making offerings to the invisible gods residing within these creations, not to their external forms. Any creation that possesses a mind and power to perform its activities can be called a god. Consequently, the gods who reside within these creations must have the consciousness to understand the affairs of their hosts as well as receive the worship that humans offer them.

The Western Scholar replies: It is not possible for a god to reside within such an [inanimated] creation to have an awareness of that creation's affairs. For a creation does not possess a mind and power outside of its nature; these faculties

---

83. Sino-Vietnamese: 舜肆類於上帝, 禋於六宗, 望於山川, 遍於群神, 四類也, 類禋望階祭, 各意社祀為祇。故曰: 類祭六宗者, 謂祭時也, 祭寒暑也, 祭日也, 祭月也, 祭星也, 祭水旱也, 群神謂丘陵墳衍。 From "Canon of Shun" (Shundian 舜典) in *Classic of Documents*.

84. The Yellow Emperor (Huangdi 黃帝) is a legendary Chinese sovereign and folk hero who is considered in Chinese mythology to be the ancestor of all Han Chinese. He was one of the legendary Five Emperors (the others being Zhuanxu, Ku, Yao, and Shun) mentioned in *Records of the Grand Historian* (Shiji 史記).

85. In Vietnamese, "Sử ký" can refer to several different history books. The source of the quotation has not yet been located.

86. Sino-Vietnamese: 帝作宮室之制, 遂作合恭祀上帝接萬靈, 佈正教焉。

wholly depend on the creation. If a god possesses the intelligence and power and is at the same time one with the [inanimated] creation, then he has no awareness; he is no different from an inanimate object. If there is a conscious god acting within the creation, then that creation is an animated being, for if the creation possesses a mind, it is an animated being. *Nature and Principle* states that "matters of perception belong to the mind," and "perception is a quality of the mind." For this reason, if all creatures of heaven and earth were animated beings, Confucian scholars {**p. 32**} would teach that every creation is an animated being and not that there is an intelligent god residing in the creation who is aware that he is worshipped. Not only that those creations of heaven and earth that the Confucians worship do not possess consciousness, but there exist no such gods in this heaven and earth. You say the Sovereign of High is the god of heaven, and the Queen of the Earth is the god of the earth. But they have the same nature with and are not different from heaven and earth. Therefore, the Sovereign on High must be governed by heaven and the Spirit of the Earth be subjected to the earth. Both heaven and earth are the greatest creations, but they possess no mind, no soul, no will, no power to make things happen; they are not living beings. Other people have claimed that the Supreme Ultimate begat the Two Modes, which are heaven and earth; it also begat the Sovereign on High which is one with the heaven and Spirit of Earth which is one with the earth. But as I have argued in the previous Article 1, if the Supreme Ultimate is also a type of energy [*khí*] that has no soul and no mind, which is not a living being, then how could it beget the Sovereign on High and the Queen of the Earth, which are supposed to be living beings?

Therefore, we must not offer sacrifices to heaven and earth or to the [inanimate] creatures of heaven and earth. Instead, we should offer sacrifices solely to the "true Lord of heaven and earth"—the highest Being who created and rules over heaven and earth, humans and things. {**p. 33**} He makes the movements of the sky and instructs the sun, moon, and stars to give us light. He delivers good weather, rain, and wind for the changing seasons. He causes the earth to produce, at the right time, every kind of plant as well as the five types of grains, the five types of metal, and the five types of stone. He gives life to all kinds of animals, birds, and fish for us to use.

The Eastern Scholar asks: If we must not offer sacrifices to the Sovereign on High, to the Queen of the Earth, or to the aforementioned entities, why, in ancient times, did the sage-king Shun offer sacrifices to the Sovereign on High, to the Six Spirits of Nature, and to the mountains and rivers? Moreover, why did ancient kings perform sacrifices during the *giao* and *xã* ceremonies as described by Confucius in the *Classic of Documents* and *Record of Rites*?

The Western Scholar replies: I am not sure whether those accounts are accurate for the following reasons. Ancient kings, especially the sage-kings Yao and Shun, probably did not offer sacrifices to the Sovereign on High, Queen of the Earth, or the Six Spirits of Nature, as described in the *Classic of Documents* and *Record of Rites*. Those sage-kings were known in the Confucian tradition as people who possessed great wisdom and virtue. Hence, their knowledge was vast and their righteousness abundant. They lived in ancient times when everyone in the world still worshipped the one {p. 34} great Lord who created heaven and earth, humans, and things. Consequently, we must consider that sage-kings rightly worshipped the one true Lord of heaven and earth and called him "the Sovereign on High." They told their people to worship that one Sovereign only.

In later periods, people chased after worldly things. Gradually, their minds became clouded, preventing them from remembering and recognizing the Lord who had created heaven and earth and all things, the Lord who was the most esteemed and most honored of the gods. Since the Lord is invisible, they came to view the visible sky as the Sovereign on High and the creatures in heaven and on earth as objects of worship. After a few generations, the kings and people began to worship in the same way. By the time of Confucius, it was widely believed that Emperor Shun, in ancient times, had not only offered sacrifices to the Sovereign on High but also to the Six Spirits of Nature and to the mountains and rivers. Hence, when Confucius collected and edited the six classics,[87] he included the sacrificial ceremonies of *giao* and *xã*, and the sacrifices to heaven and earth, which were told in other books.

Therefore, we must not take these established rites as genuine or worship the Sovereign on High in the same way as heaven and the {p. 35} creatures of heaven and earth. We must not think that the ancient kings established those rites for the people, for this would not be fitting of sage-kings who ruled people by virtue. Rather, we should think that these kings worshipped the one true Lord of heaven and earth, who is the Sovereign on High and different from the heavens.

[The Spirit of Earth]

The Western Scholar says: When people bury the dead, they often offer sacrifices to the Spirit of the Earth [Hậu Thổ]. What is this rite all about?

The Eastern Scholar says: People perform the rite because the book *Correct Practices of Family Rituals* [*Gia Lễ Chính Hành*] tells them to do so. Ritual offerings to the four seasons, to the five emperors, and to the five spirits originated

---

87. The six classics include the Five Classics and the lost *Classic of Music* (Yuejing 樂經).

during the Qin dynasty. One of the five spirits is named "Minister of the Land". With regard to the rites of the four seasons, the *Record of Rites* says: "In the middle of the year, sacrifices are offered to its divine ruler, the Yellow Emperor, and to his attending spirit, the Minister of the Land."[88] This spirit was Goulong, who held the post {p. 36} of Minister of the Land in ancient times. When King Xuanzong [712–756 CE] re-established the rites for his reign during the Tang dynasty, he took the title "Minister of the Land" to be the actual name of a spirit. During the Song dynasty, when the Duke of Wen[89] wrote the book of rituals, he did not distinguish between the rites performed by kings and the rituals performed by the common people. He took the earlier Tang practice of worshipping the "Minister of Land" and included it in his ritual book. Since that time, when there is a burial, people include a sacrifice to the Minister of the Land and offer up a prayer to him. Later on, during the reign of Song Xiaozong [r. 1163–1189], Master Zhu Wengong,[90] in his *Correct Practices of Family Rituals*, changed the name "Minister of the Land" [Hậu Thổ] to "Spirit of the Earth" [Địa thổ chi thần]. He taught people to offer sacrifices to this spirit on the right side of the tomb, saying: "My parents are buried here. Please guard them well."[91] That is the history of the rite to the Spirit of the Earth. Originally, the rite was dedicated {p. 37} to the Minister of the Land; later, it became the rite to the Spirit of the Earth.

The Western Scholar comments: The rite to the Spirit of Earth is contrary not only to the holy way of the Lord of Heaven, which teaches one to worship only the Lord of Heaven, but also to Confucian rituals. Even if there are sacrifices to the Spirit of the Earth, the officials and the common people should not be allowed to do so, because of the pairing of ceremonies of the Earth with that of Heaven. Only the king, who offers sacrifices to Heaven, may offer sacrifices to the Earth. Since the rest of the people are not allowed to offer sacrifices to Heaven, why should they be allowed to offer sacrifices to the Earth? It is written in the ritual book: "If ritual vessels were found in the households of common people, that would be usurping the sacrifice to Heaven that is reserved only for the king, the special kind of sacrifice offered to the Sovereign on High."[92]

---

88. Sino-Vietnamese: 中舉其帝黃帝，其神后土神。 From "Monthly Proceedings" (Yueling 月令) in *Record of Rites*.

89. This probably refers to the Song historian Sima Guang (司馬光), 1019–1086 CE, whose posthumous title is [Sima] Wengong (司馬溫公).

90. Chu Văn Công (Zhu Wengong 朱文公) is the posthumous name of Zhu Xi.

91. Apparently this prayer was to deter tomb robbers.

92. Sino-Vietnamese: 士庶之家有祀於僭祭天類于上帝。

during the Qin dynasty. One of the five spirits is named "Minister of the Land". With regard to the rites of the four seasons, the *Record of Rites* says: "In the middle of the year, sacrifices are offered to its divine ruler, the Yellow Emperor, and to his attending spirit, the Minister of the Land."[88] This spirit was Goulong, who held the post {p. 36} of Minister of the Land in ancient times. When King Xuanzong [712–756 CE] re-established the rites for his reign during the Tang dynasty, he took the title "Minister of the Land" to be the actual name of a spirit. During the Song dynasty, when the Duke of Wen[89] wrote the book of rituals, he did not distinguish between the rites performed by kings and the rituals performed by the common people. He took the earlier Tang practice of worshipping the "Minister of Land" and included it in his ritual book. Since that time, when there is a burial, people include a sacrifice to the Minister of the Land and offer up a prayer to him. Later on, during the reign of Song Xiaozong [r. 1163–1189], Master Zhu Wengong,[90] in his *Correct Practices of Family Rituals*, changed the name "Minister of the Land" [Hậu Thổ] to "Spirit of the Earth" [Địa thổ chi thần]. He taught people to offer sacrifices to this spirit on the right side of the tomb, saying: "My parents are buried here. Please guard them well."[91] That is the history of the rite to the Spirit of the Earth. Originally, the rite was dedicated {p. 37} to the Minister of the Land; later, it became the rite to the Spirit of the Earth.

The Western Scholar comments: The rite to the Spirit of Earth is contrary not only to the holy way of the Lord of Heaven, which teaches one to worship only the Lord of Heaven, but also to Confucian rituals. Even if there are sacrifices to the Spirit of the Earth, the officials and the common people should not be allowed to do so, because of the pairing of ceremonies of the Earth with that of Heaven. Only the king, who offers sacrifices to Heaven, may offer sacrifices to the Earth. Since the rest of the people are not allowed to offer sacrifices to Heaven, why should they be allowed to offer sacrifices to the Earth? It is written in the ritual book: "If ritual vessels were found in the households of common people, that would be usurping the sacrifice to Heaven that is reserved only for the king, the special kind of sacrifice offered to the Sovereign on High."[92]

---

88. Sino-Vietnamese: 中舉其帝黃帝，其神后土神。 From "Monthly Proceedings" (Yueling 月令) in *Record of Rites*.

89. This probably refers to the Song historian Sima Guang (司馬光), 1019–1086 CE, whose posthumous title is [Sima] Wengong (司馬溫公).

90. Chu Văn Công (Zhu Wengong 朱文公) is the posthumous name of Zhu Xi.

91. Apparently this prayer was to deter tomb robbers.

92. Sino-Vietnamese: 士庶之家有祀於僭祭天類于上帝。

Article 7

On Sacrifices to the Five Emperors and the Five Spirits

The Western Scholar says: You have mentioned that the rites of the four seasons originated during the Qin dynasty as sacrifices to the Five Emperors[93] and the Five Spirits. Can you explain these rites?[94]

The Eastern Scholar says: These rites come from the chapter "Monthly Proceedings" in the *Record of Rites*. The text was written by Lü Buwei,[95] the [adopted] father of Qin Shihuang,[96] to teach the king how to offer seasonal sacrifices to the Five Emperors and the Five Spirits. These [entities] belong to the four directions and center and correspond to the five elements: {p. 38} earth, fire, wood, metal, and water.[97] The five rulers and their attending officials had done great things for their people. That is why the kings of subsequent generations have been offering them sacrifices to commemorate their merit. These rites are as follows:

The three months of spring—the first, second, and third months of the lunar calendar—correspond to the wood element and to the east. King Taihao[98] grows stronger with the power of the wood element, whose governor is Goumang.[99] Therefore, spring offerings are made to Taihao, the "ruler of the green star," and to Goumang, the "governing spirit of the wood element." Goumang was one of King Shaohao's sons.

The three months of summer—the fourth, fifth, and sixth months—correspond to the fire element and to the south. King Yandi[100] grows stronger

---

93. The Five Emperors refers to five mythical kings of the Xia dynasty: Fuxi (伏羲), Shennong (神農), Huang Di (黃帝), Shaohao (少皞), and Zhuanxu (顓頊).

94. See also *Opusculum*, Chapter 2, Article 2.

95. Lü Buwei (呂不韋), ca. 290–231 BCE, was the chancellor of the state of Qin, whose adopted son, Ying Zheng, became the future emperor of unified China.

96. Qin Shihuang (秦始皇) was the king of the state of Qin from 246 to 221 BCE and the first emperor of China from 221 to 210 BCE.

97. Chinese cosmology is patterned after a system of Five Elements, in which each natural element is assigned a direction and a color. In addition to the four directions (east, west, north, south), the "center" is also considered a "direction."

98. Taihao (大皞) is the honorific name of Fuxi, the first mythical king of China.

99. Goumang (句芒) is the wood deity and assistant to Fuxi.

100. Yandi (炎帝) is the honorific name of Shennong, the god-king of agriculture.

with the power of the fire element, whose governor is Zhurong.[101] Therefore, summer offerings are made to Yandi, the "ruler of the red star," and to Zhurong, the "governing spirit of the fire element." Zhurong was a descendant of King Zhuanxu.

The end of the sixth month is the middle of the four seasons. It corresponds to the earth element, which is at the center of the four directions {p. 39} and the four seasons. The Yellow Emperor[102] grows stronger with the power of the earth element, whose governor is Goulong.[103] Therefore, middle-of-the-year offerings are made to the Yellow Emperor, the "ruler of the yellow star," and to Goulong, the "governing spirit of the earth element." After his death, Goulong was honored as the Spirit of the Earth.

The three months of autumn—the seventh, eighth, and ninth months—correspond to the metal element and to the west. King Shaohao[104] grows stronger with the power of the metal element, whose governor is Rushou.[105] Therefore, autumn offerings are made to Shaohao, the "ruler of the white star," and to Rushou, the "governing spirit of the metal element." Rushou was the mentor of King Shaohao's sons.

The three months of winter—the tenth, eleventh, and twelfth months—correspond to the water element and to the north. King Zhuanxu[106] grows stronger with the power of the water element, whose governor is Xuanming.[107] Therefore, winter offerings are made to Zhuanxu, the "ruler of the black star," and to Xuanming, the "governing spirit of the water element." Xuanming was one of King Shaohao's sons.

{p. 40} Sacrifices to the spirits of the seasons are performed in the open space outside the city, where the king goes to welcome the seasons. These sacrifices mark the beginning of spring, summer, autumn, and winter. This is how the rites have been carried out since the time of the Three Dynasties [of Xia, Shang, and Zhou].

---

101. Zhurong (祝融) is the god of fire and of the south.

102. Huang Di (黃帝), or the Yellow Emperor, is considered the founder of Chinese civilization.

103. Goulong (句龍) was the Minister of Land under Huangdi and a soil deity.

104. Shaohao (少皞), ca. 2600 BCE, is traditionally considered to be the successor of the Yellow Emperor and the father of Emperor Zhuanxu.

105. Rushou (蓐收) was an official of King Shaohao.

106. Zhuanxu (顓頊), also known as Gao Yang (高陽), was the last of the mythical kings of the Xia dynasty.

107. Xuanming (玄冥) was the official of King Shaohao.

[The Five Household Spirits]

The "Monthly Proceedings" also refers to the sacrifices to the Five Guardian Spirits. Offerings are made to the Door spirit in the spring, to the Hearth spirit in the summer, to the Gate spirit in the autumn, to the Road spirit in the winter, and to the Central Flow spirit in the middle of the year.

The Door Spirit [Hộ thần] is the guardian of house doors. He is the yang energy that resides within doors in springtime. As the yang energy flows out, he brings life to everything. Therefore, one sacrifices to the Door spirit in the spring. The spleen is his primary sacrificial food, and his altar is set up inside to the west of the door.

The Hearth Spirit [Táo thần] is the guardian of the kitchen. Fire energy grows stronger in summer and displaces yin energy because fire burns everything. Therefore, one sacrifices to the Hearth spirit in the summer. The lungs are his primary sacrificial food, and his altar is set up near the hearth.

The Gate Spirit [Môn thần] is the guardian of the outer gate. He takes on the lesser yin energy during the autumn and gathers up its energy. Therefore, one offers sacrifices to the Gate spirit in the autumn. The liver is his primary sacrificial food, and his altar {p. 41} is set up to the left of the gate.

The Road Spirit [Hành thần], also called the spirit of water, is the guardian of roads. In the winter, as yin energy moves back and forth, water energy is abundant, thus giving rise to the cold. Consequently, one performs sacrifices at the roadside to bring back the yang energy. Therefore, one offers sacrifices to the Road spirit in the winter. The kidney is his primary sacrificial food, and his altar is set up outside the temple gate.

The Central Flow Spirit [Trung Lưu thần] is the guardian of the house. He is also called the Land spirit, for he guards the land. One offers sacrifices to the Central Flow spirit at the end of the summer, in the middle of the four seasons. The heart is his primary sacrificial food, and his altar is set up at the center of the house. This is how the rites have been carried out since the time of the Three Dynasties.

The sacrifices described in the chapter "Monthly Proceedings" can be summarized as follows: {p. 42}

- Spring: Its divine ruler is Taihao. Its attending spirit is Goumang. Its guardian spirit is the Door Spirit.
- Summer: Its divine ruler is Yandi. Its attending spirit is Zhurong. Its guardian spirit is the Hearth Spirit.
- Middle of the year: Its divine ruler is Huangdi. Its attending spirit is Goulong or the Spirit of the Earth. Its guardian spirit is the Central Flow Spirit.

- Autumn: Its divine ruler is Shaohao. Its attending spirit is Rushou. Its guardian spirit is the Gate Spirit.
- Winter: Its divine ruler is Zhuanxu. Its attending spirit is Xuanming. Its guardian spirit is the Road Spirit.

The Western Scholar says: Sacrifices to the Five Emperors the Five Spirits first began in the Qin dynasty. Because these rites did not exist during Three Dynasties—Xia, Shang, and Zhou—Confucius did not include them in the *Record of Rites*.[108] When the Qin rulers wanted to express thanks to the ancient five rulers and the five officials, {p. 43} who cared for their people, the Qin decided to establish rituals to honor them during the four seasons. The sage-kings Yu, Tang, Wen, and Wu, who use the way [*dạo*] to govern their people, obviously knew the right protocols and rituals, but they did not establish these rites; only the Qin did. Moreover, what is the reason for establishing rites for venerating the five rulers mentioned above, when there is no rite that venerates Yao and Shun, whom the Confucian scholars called sage-emperors? Are these emperors not considered to have significantly more merit and virtue than Shaohao and Zhuanxu?

And why are there rituals about welcoming the four seasons? If there is no ceremony to welcome the seasons, will they not come just the same? What kind of intelligence do the four seasons possess? Do they even know that they are being ceremonially welcomed? And what about the sacrificial offerings made to the five guardian spirits of the Door, Gate, Hearth, House, and Road? No king before the Qin rulers had ever mentioned these guardian spirits. If such guardian spirits exist, then there must be countless guardian spirits. For if every house and every road require a guardian spirit, the number of guardian spirits must be equal to the number of houses and roads, {p. 44} just as there are as many village gods as there are villages. With reference to the veneration of the Five Emperors and Five Spirits who govern the five elements, we must look at the reasons behind the common custom of worshipping the dead, which I discuss in Article 14.

Therefore, we must worship and offer sacrifices only to the true Lord of heaven and earth, who is infinitely knowing, who is infinitely powerful, who governs the heaven and earth and everything in it, who makes the seasons change, who takes charge of all affairs in heaven and earth, and who cares for human beings in every way.

---

108. Apparently the Western Scholar makes an error here. The chapter "Monthly Proceedings" (Yueling 月令) is indeed part of the *Record of Rites*.

[Agricultural Rite]

The Eastern Scholar says: There is a special rite for offering sacrifices to Yandi, also known as Divine Farmer (Shennong) who is commonly known as the god of agriculture. In autumn, the ceremonial [procession] that leads down to the field [to plant the rice] is called "Hạ Điền." The ceremonial [procession] that leads back from the field [when the planting is finished or during harvesting] is called "Thượng Điền." During these times, every village offers sacrifices to the Divine Farmer to commemorate his agricultural teachings, as it is written, "By cutting wood to make the blade, and by bending wood to make the plough, the Divine Farmer (Shennong) taught people the necessary skills for growing the five types of grains. Thus, agriculture was developed."[109] During this sacrificial ceremony, there is a recitation of praise to the Divine Farmer, and petitions are made for a successful harvest, {p. 45} prosperity, and peace. I do not know its origin, but this is a common ritual in every village in this country (Annam) as well as in neighboring countries.[110]

The Western Scholar says: To remember and praise the merit of the Divine Farmer for teaching people how to farm is fitting. However, for the reasons that I have discussed and will discuss again in Article 14, it is not appropriate, simply for the sake of honoring him, to consider him a holy being with the power to help people cultivate and to bless them with good harvests and other good things. There is only one Lord of Heaven who endows people with all kinds of skills, giving them the five kinds of grains in the field, possessions in the home, and peace in the village. For that reason, do not put your trust in the Divine Farmer and offer sacrifices to him.

---

109. Sino-Vietnamese: 斲木為耜, 揉木為耒, 始教民藝五穀, 而農事興矣。 I have not been able to locate the source for this quotation.

110. In the pre-modern era, Korea, Japan, and Vietnam belonged to the Sinic world and shared an affinity for Chinese customs and writings.

Article 8

On the Oath-Taking Ceremony and the Chief's Banner Celebration

The Western Scholar says: In this country, there are two solemn ceremonies every year: the Hội Minh ceremony[111] and the Kỳ Đạo celebration.[112] I ask you: What happens during these two ceremonies? {p. 46}

[Oath-Taking Ceremony]

The Eastern Scholar says: The Hội Minh ceremony is celebrated during the last month of the year, when civil and military officials gather to take an oath of loyalty to their king and lord.[113] The ceremony takes place in a spacious square, which has a main gate and two side gates. There is a main altar in the front for sacrifices to heaven and earth. On the left, there are raised platforms [đàn] for venerating the nine recently deceased kings [vua], and on the right, there are raised platforms for venerating the nine recently deceased lords [chúa]. The left side also has high altars for venerating spirits of the highest rank as well as the spirits of the mountains and rivers. At the center, there are three incense tables, where civil and military officials take their oaths. On the lower level, there are twenty-eight small tables along both sides, where soldiers take their oaths.[114] On the day of this solemn ceremony, three chief officials go to the main altar, take a golden knife belonging to the Lord [Trịnh], kill a chicken with it, and drain its blood into a bowl of rice wine. Afterwards, they burn a written copy of the oath, mix the ashes with the blood and liquor, pour the liquid into six cups, and place the cups on the three incense tables. They also prepare many cups of rice wine

---

111. "Hội Minh," spelled "Hội Miêng" in the text, is a ceremony during which subjects take an oath of loyalty to their rulers. This ceremony was first recorded in the year 1028, the first year under the reign of Lý Thái Tông, after his brothers rose up against him in a fight for the throne. See *Toàn Thư*, bản kỷ, 2:14b–15a (translation 1:262). Cf. *Opusculum*, Chapter 2, Article 5.

112. "Kỳ Đạo," spelled "Cờ Đạo" in the text (literally "flag of the chief"), is a memorial service to honor deceased national heroes. Cf. *Opusculum*, Chapter 2, Article 4.

113. At this time, there were two rulers in Tonkin: *vua* (king) who had no real. power, and *chúa* (viceroy or lord), who actually governed the country. From 1600 to 1785, the lordship of Tonkin was in the hands of the Trịnh family.

114. See the diagram of the placement of the altar according to Adriano di Santa Thecla in *A Study of Religion*, 131.

mixed with the blood of a buffalo. [These are placed] on smaller tables for the soldiers taking their oaths.

Once the preparation has been completed, {p. 47} the Prefect of Rites[115] offers sacrifices at altars dedicated to heaven and earth, deceased kings and lords, and other spirits. After the offerings, the mandarin and military officers kneel in front of the three incense tables, recite the oath, and drink the rice wine mixed with chicken blood. The soldiers do the same before their tables. The highest official pledges: "I bow to the Supreme Emperor August Heaven [Hoàng thiên Thượng đế] and to the Empress August Earth [Hoàng Địa kỳ]." The other officials pledge: "We bow to the King of Heaven [Hoàng thiên] and the Queen of Earth [Hậu thổ]." The soldiers pledge: "We bow to Heaven and Earth." Then all recite the following formula: "I come from the such and such prefecture, district, and village. I am [name], and I was born in a such and such year. I swear my complete loyalty to King [name] and to Lord [name].[116] If I do not remain loyal after drinking from this cup of wine and blood, may the Supreme Emperor August Heaven and the Empress August Earth (or the King of Heaven and the Queen of Earth, or Heaven and Earth) and all the spirits strike me down and kill me."

This is how the Hội Minh ceremony is celebrated in Kẻ Chợ (Hanoi). In other prefectures, the head of that prefecture and his officials also take an oath of loyalty.

The Western Scholar comments: It is truly fitting that both the high- and low-ranking officials take an oath of loyalty to wholeheartedly serve their rulers, {p. 48} but is it not absurd to make people seal their oaths by drinking wine with the blood of a chicken or buffalo? Moreover, why should one need to offer sacrifices to heaven and earth, deceased rulers, and other spirits? One only needs to offer sacrifices to the true Lord of heaven and earth, who has the power to rule over everything in heaven and on earth, who keeps people from having wayward hearts, and who helps rulers govern their people justly and peacefully.

[Veneration of the Chief's Banner]

The Eastern Scholar says: Now I must tell you, Western Scholar, about the Kỳ Đạo celebration, which you asked me about earlier. During the second month of

---

115. In a solemn ceremony, either the king himself or an appointed prefect acts as high priest, for in the Confucian tradition, there is no "ordained priest" but rather a ritual specialist.

116. In the text, the author inserts the Latin word *nomen* (name) here.

the year, we choose a spacious place at the river bank in Kẻ Chợ to erect four or five altars on high platforms and thirty-six small altars. The first altar is dedicated to the Supreme Emperor August Heaven and to the Empress August Earth. The second altar is dedicated to Kinh Dương Vương and Lạc Long Quân.[117] The third is dedicated to former kings. The fourth, to the left of the gate to the altar area, is dedicated to the Five Emperors and Five Generals. The fifth and remaining altars are dedicated to a great spirit, either to [the spirit of] Mount Tản Viên,[118] Đổng Thiên Vương,[119] Lý Ông Trọng,[120] Không Lộ,[121] or Giác Hải,[122] among others. {p. 49}.

The ceremony is called the "Veneration of the Chief's Banner" because *kỳ đạo* is a large flag used by a general. On the day of the ceremony, the Lord [Trịnh] goes to his nearby palace to watch. Military officials bring their troops and line up there. Then the Prefect of Rites goes to each altar and offers the sacrifice to heaven and earth, to former kings and lords, to the Five Emperors, to the Five Generals, and to other spirits. He thanks them for their blessings and also requests protection for the king and the lord. He also asks for peace and prosperity for all people. After the offerings are made, mortars [*ống báu long*] are fired, and the chief's large flag is waved near the lord's palace. Then the banner-carrying soldiers wave their flags and fire their pipe cannons [*ống lệnh*]. The ordinary soldiers fire their muskets three times, raise and lower their swords and spears. These actions are meant to drive away the spirits of the rebels who revolted against past kings and lords as well as ensure the tranquility of the country. After the ceremony, the officials and their soldiers gather to greet the lord and compete in sports and games. This is how the Kỳ Đạo ceremony is celebrated in Kẻ Chợ. In other prefectures, the head of the prefecture celebrates the ceremony on the same day.

---

117. Kinh Dương Vương and his son Lạc Long Quân are the mythical founders of Vietnam. According to Vietnamese folklore, Kinh Dương Vương was a third-generation descendant of Shennong, the god of agriculture. His son Lạc Long Quân vanquished demons, civilized the people, and protected them from intruders. The stories of King Dương Vương and Lạc Long Quân are mentioned in *Toàn Thư*, ngoại kỷ, 1:1b–2a.

118. Mount Tản Viên is considered the most sacred mountain in Tonkin.

119. King Dóng, or the Heavenly King of Phù Đổng (see *Errors*, Book 1, Article 10), is a legendary national hero of Vietnam.

120. King Trèm, or Chèm (see *Errors*, Book 1, Article 10), is another national hero of Vietnam.

121. A prominent monk who lived during the reigns of Lý Nhân Tông (r. 1072–1127) and Lý Thần Tông (r. 1128–1138).

122. Another prominent monk who was a contemporary and confrère of Không Lộ. Both Dương Không Lộ and Nguyễn Giác Hải are mentioned in the *Lĩnh Nam Chích Quái*.

{p. 50}

The Western Scholar comments: Heaven and earth, kings and lords of the past, and spirits do not bring peace and security to this country. Rather, it is the Lord of Heaven, creator of heaven and earth and ruler of everything, who gives peace and security to all. Therefore, you must offer sacrifices only to the Lord of Heaven. Do not continue to offer sacrifices to heaven and earth and to the others. Moreover, why do you need to wave flags, fire cannons and muskets, and wave weapons around to drive away the spirits of the rebels? The dead cannot affect us in this life, and we cannot affect them. There is only one Lord of Heaven who sends his angels to punish the people who sin against him. The Lord of Heaven also allows demons to torment sinners. That is why we must fear the power of the Lord of Heaven, who is able to punish people. And yet, we must trust in the mercy of the Lord of Heaven, who is infinitely compassionate.

{p. 51}

Article 9

On Thành Hoàng and Other Spirits

[The Cult of Thành Hoàng]

The Western Scholar says: I have noticed that every village in this country has a cult of Thành Hoàng or the Village God. So I ask you: Which spirit is named Thành Hoàng? And how do they worship him?[123]

The Eastern Scholar replies: Thành Hoàng is the guardian spirit of a village and protects that village. Each village chooses a spirit as its village god, who is the spirit of a deceased person who has shown great merit in that region. Sometimes, it is the spirit of a tiger, a horse, or a dog that has attacked people, or a spirit that has displayed marvelous power. If the villagers can afford it, they build a temple and dedicate it to that spirit. If they cannot afford a temple, they dedicate a place in the village temple to set up an altar for that spirit. Spirits {p. 52} who have been given honorary offices by the king have their own temples. Their names, followed by the characters *Đại Vương*, meaning "great prince," are written on their spirit tablets [in their temples].[124] However, people usually call Thành Hoàng "king."

The national custom stipulates that sacrifices to Thành Hoàng be performed three or four times a year for different purposes. At the beginning of the year, there is a ceremony of Supplication for Tranquility [Kỳ An]. In the tenth month of the year, an offering is made for new crops, and in the eleventh month of the year, there is a ceremony of Supplication for Happiness [Kỳ Phúc]. If there is a drought, there is a ceremony for Bringing Rain [Đảo Vũ]; if there is a plague, there is a ceremony for Dispelling Misfortune [Tống Ách]. During these ceremonies, the whole village offers food for the feast, contributes money for a sacrificial pig, and then gathers to celebrate the sacrifice. In addition, in the first month, the third month, or another month, they solemnly venerate the deity by singing for several days in his honor. Each day after offering sacrifices, they sing songs day and night and play games {p. 53} like wrestling, stick-fighting, or cricket.[125] However,

---

123. See also the description in *Opusculum*, Chapter 2, Article 6 .

124. *Thần vị* (shenwei 神位) is a wooden tablet on which the name and the title of the deceased person are inscribed.

125. In Vietnamese they are called *đánh vật, đánh thó, đánh cầu*.

during the mourning period for the king [*vua*] or lord [*chúa*], all forms of entertainment are prohibited.

[Testing the Spirits]

The Western Scholar asks: You have mentioned that some village gods have been given honorary offices by the king. So I ask you: How does the monarch bestow an honorific office on that spirit?[126]

The Eastern Scholar replies: The monarch nominates spirits to three ranks of dignitary status: the spirits of the supreme rank,[127] the spirits of the middle rank,[128] and the spirits of the lower rank.[129] Before a spirit advances to one of these three ranks, however, it must undergo a test to determine whether he deserves the honor. When the villagers petition a spirit to become their village god, they bring a buffalo to the official and write the name of the spirit on the animal's head. The official commands the spirit to strike the designated buffalo dead if the spirit accepts the rank. If the buffalo is stricken dead before everyone present, the spirit receives the royal certification necessary for becoming a *thần* (deity) and is registered in the official record of spirits. This ceremony is called "establishing the ranks {**p. 54**} and elevating the spirits" [*tạo khoa bạt thần*]. After the ceremony, the villagers carry the royal certification back to the communal hall in a solemn procession that also draws a crowd from neighboring villages. Then, each following year, the head of the prefecture [*ông Phủ*], the head of the district [*ông Huyện*], and the head schoolmaster [*ông Giáo*] offer sacrifices to the spirits of the middle and lower ranks at their respective temples. In the case of the spirits of the supreme rank, a royal official from Kẻ Chợ is summoned to offer the sacrifices.

---

126. On this topic of ranking and certifying spirits, see also the description in *Opusculum*, Chapter 2, Article 7.

127. *Thượng đẳng thần* (spirits of the supreme rank) are spirits whose histories and actions are famous, whose names are clearly known, and who hold the rank of *thượng đẳng thần* from previous, successive dynasties.

128. *Trung đẳng thần* (spirits of the middle rank) are spirits who have been worshipped in the villages but whose deeds are not well known. Phan Kế Bính, *Việt Nam Phong Tục*, 79–80.

129. *Hạ đẳng thần* (spirits of the lower rank) are spirits who are less known and often worshipped in groups. Phan Kế Bính, *Việt Nam Phong Tục*, 80.

The Western Scholar comments: It is fitting to venerate and trust in a guardian deity as the protector of a village. However, one must choose a spirit who truly has the merit and virtues befitting veneration. One must not choose a false spirit who has no merit or power. One must choose a being among those in heaven—beings favored by the Lord of Heaven—because they are worthy of our total trust and reverence. The followers of our religion often choose a holy man or woman—the "patron saint" of their village—to protect the people who live in the area. {p. 55} But the spirits that are worshipped in this country are rebels against the Lord of Heaven. Since they are being punished in hell, they do not have the power to help us and are not worthy of our veneration. There may very well be spirits who exhibit marvelous power, like the ones who strike buffaloes dead in order to achieve a higher ranking. It is, however, the power of the devil, who deceives people into believing in him. Therefore, do not believe in or worship the spirits of the three ranks who, in fact, are demons.[130]

---

130. This reflects the exclusivist attitude of the Western (Christian) scholar who sees other spirits and deities as evil spirits.

Article 10

On King Dóng, King Trèm, King Bạch Mã
[and Princess Liễu Hạnh]

The Western Scholar asks: Who are the most famous deities among the spirits of the supreme rank?

The Eastern Scholar replies: The most famous among those deities are King Dóng, King Trèm, King Bạch Mã, and Princess Liễu Hạnh.[131]

[King Dóng]

King Dóng is also known as [Phù] Đổng Thiên Vương [the Heavenly King of Phù Đổng village].[132] During the reign of King Hùng the Sixth, there was a rich man in Phù Đổng (also known as Dóng) village in the Tiên Du district[133] who had a three-year-old son. The boy ate and grew, but did not speak a single word. At that time, Annam was under attack by powerful enemies. King Hùng sent {**p. 56**} an envoy to announce to the whole kingdom that whoever could fight off the invaders would be rewarded with a high position. When the boy heard the announcement, he suddenly began to speak. He asked his mother to call in the royal envoy. The boy told the official, "Give me a horse and a sword, and the king will not have to worry about his enemies." The envoy returned and reported the matter to King Hùng, who agreed to the boy's request. The boy mounted the horse, brandished his sword, and led the army to victory. Legend has it that the boy from Dóng village rode to Mount Sóc afterward and ascended to heaven. King Hùng built a temple in Phù Đổng in his honor. There are also shrines dedicated to the hero at Thanh Nhàn, on Mount Sóc, and on the location where he left his horse. King Lý Thái Tổ [r. 1010–1028] conferred upon him the title "Soaring-to-Heaven Divine King" (Xung Thiên Thần Vương) at his main temple in Phù Đổng village [hence the name King Dóng]

[King Trèm or Lý Ông Trọng]

King Trèm, or Lý Ông Trọng,[134] lived during the reign of An Dương Vương [r.?–207 BCE].[135] At that time there was a young man by the name of Lý

---

131. See also the description in *Opusculum*, Chapter 2, Article 8.

132. King Dóng, also known in Vietnamese as "ông Dóng" or "thánh Dóng," is a national hero and an immortal.

133. Dror (*A Study of Religion*, 140) identifies the district as Vũ Ninh.

134. Lý Ông Trọng is the posthumous name of Lý Thân, a legendary warrior of the third century, who served the Chinese Emperor Qin Shihuang. His story is told in *Việt Điện U Linh Tập*.

135. An Dương Vương is the title of Thục Phán, who was the ruler of the ancient kingdom of Âu Lạc, which comprised much of today's North Vietnam, Southern Guangxi, and Western

Ông Trọng who lived in [Trèm village] of the Thụy Hương commune, in Từ Liêm district of Quốc Oai prefecture of Đoài province. He was twenty-three cubits tall [two *trượng* and three *thước*].[136] One day, while doing forced labor for the village, he was struck by an official. He fled to China, where he was later made commander-in-chief [*tư lệ hiệu úy*] by Emperor Qin Shihuang. {p. 57} Sometime afterward, when the emperor sent Ma Tian to build a long wall to deter the Huns, he also sent Lý Ông Trọng to protect the Lintao region from invasion. Lý Ông Trọng was known for his incredible strength, and the Huns were afraid of him. When he became an old man, he returned to his home and died there. Emperor Qin Shihuang had a bronze statue of Lý Ông Trọng made to commemorate his service and placed it at the Sima gate in the Hanyang region. There was a machine inside the statue that was operated by thirty people and made life-like movements. When the Huns saw the statue, they thought Lý Ông Trọng was still alive and dared not enter China. Later, during the Tang dynasty, when Officer Zhao Chang was assigned to Annam, he often had a dream about Lý Ông Trọng discussing the *Annals of Spring and Autumn* with him. The officer came to Lý Ông Trọng's village and built a temple there to honor him. When Prefect Gao Pian[137] came to Annam to fight against the rebels from Nanzhao,[138] Lý Ông Trọng appeared {p. 58} to him [in a dream] and helped him win the war. As a sign of gratitude, Gao Pian rebuilt Lý Ông Trọng's temple, erected a statue of him for worship, and named him Commander-in-Chief Lý (Lý Hiệu Úy). Because the temple is located in Trèm village, he is called King Trèm.

Guangdong. He was defeated by the Qin general Zhao Tuo (趙佗), and his kingdom was annexed to the kingdom of Nan Yue in 207 BCE.

136. According to *Tự Điển Tiếng Việt* [Dictionary of Vietnamese Language], ed. Hoàng Phê (Hanoi: NXB Khoa Học Xã Hội, 1988), 1093, there are two units of measurement with the name *trượng*: (a) roughly about 10 Chinese yards (4.7 m) and (b) 4 Vietnamese *thước* (1.6 m). A *thước* or *xích* is 40 cm. In either case, Lý Ông Trọng's height was physically impossible (at least 4.4 m).

137. Gao Pian (高駢) was a general who led a campaign against the Nanzhao in 864–865 and restored Chinese control of North Vietnam. He was credited with building the Đại La citadel (Hanoi), and his deeds are described in *Toàn Thư*, ngoại kỷ, 5:12b–16a. Also see Keith W. Taylor, *The Birth of Vietnam* (Berkeley: University of California Press, 1983), 246–54.

138. Nanzhao (南詔) was an ancient kingdom founded by several Tai-Burmese tribes who occupied the area around what is now province of Yunnan, China. The kingdom went into decline in the late ninth century and fell in 902, when a rebel official killed its last emperor and set up the state of Dali. Dali was eventually conquered by the Mongols in 1253 and became part of Yuan China.

[King Bạch Mã]

King Bạch Mã [White Horse] was first Ma Yuan,[139] a general during the reign of Han Guangwu [25–57 CE]. He led an army to this country, then called Jiaozhou,[140] and fought against the Trưng sisters, who had declared themselves rulers. [After defeating them], he erected a bronze pillar and inscribed these words: "If this bronze pillar is broken, Jiaozhou will be destroyed."[141] Then he returned home and died some time later. After his death, the Trưng sisters honored him by building and dedicating a temple to him[142] in the Phúc Lộc district of Sơn Tây province.[143] There is also a temple dedicated to Bạch Mã [White Horse] in Kẻ Chợ today.[144]

Stories about these three deities are found in the *Historical Chronicle of Great Việt* [*Đại Việt Sử Ký*].

{p. 59}

[Princess Liễu Hạnh]

Princess Liễu Hạnh[145] of the Lê family was born in An Thái commune of Thiên Bản district of Nghĩa Hưng County of Sơn Nam prefecture. After reaching adulthood, she traveled to many regions. When she arrived in Nghệ An province, she married and had a son. She subsequently left her husband, returned to An Thái, and became a courtesan (*con chơi bời*).[146] After her death, Liễu Hạnh often appeared in the form of a beautiful girl. The Lord [Trịnh] conferred on her the title Princess Liễu Hạnh, also known as Lady Thắng, and built a temple to

---

139. Ma Yuan (馬援) was a Chinese general who crushed the Vietnamese revolt led against the Han by the two Trưng sisters in 40–44 CE.

140. Jiaozhou (Giao Châu 交州) is the name of North Vietnam given by the Han administration in 203. Prior to this, it was called Jiaozhi (Giao Chỉ 交趾).

141. Sino-Vietnamese: 銅柱折, 交州滅。 In this quotation, 交州 is used in placed of 交趾, which I think is more original.

142. The information given here is historically inaccurate. Since the Trưng sisters died in battle during their fight against Ma Yuan in 43 CE, they could not have erected a temple for him.

143. *Opusculum* records the location as being in Thanh Hóa province. The Phúc Lộc district is more likely to be in Sơn Tây, which is near the place of the Trưng sisters' revolution.

144. Apparently the author of the text confuses Mã Viện with another deity named Bạch Mã (White Horse). Dror has discussed this error in *A Study of Religion*, 42–47.

145. See Dror's discussion in *A Study of Religion*, 47–49.

146. *Con chơi bời* can mean a prostitute. However, St. Thecla reports that she was killed because people find her singing "disgracefully and shamelessly [*impudica*]" (*Opusculum*, 46; Dror,

her. People everywhere worshipped her in their homes, which is why she is also known as the "Lady" of the world. There is a temple dedicated to her at Cửa Tuân in Kênh Sắt of Quỳnh Lưu District of Nghệ An province. Later, when I discuss the sect of sorcery (Daoism), I will recount the complete story of Liễu Hạnh.

The Western Scholar comments: The four spirits of the supreme rank are demons who appeared in human form and performed marvels in order to make people believe in them. Stories about the child-king Dóng and {**p. 60**} his battle and victory over his enemies, as well as stories about King Trèm, who was twenty-three cubits tall (about the height of five or six persons), are myths and not worthy of belief.

Article 11

On the Kitchen God, the Household Guardian, the Land Guardian, and the Guild Founder

The Western Scholar says: I have noticed that people often worship the Kitchen God [Vua Bếp].[147] So I ask you: Who is this Kitchen god, and how did worship of the Kitchen god begin?[148]

The Eastern Scholar replies: It is written in *Correct Practices of Family Rituals* [Gia Lễ Chính Hành] that sacrifices to the Kitchen god are also sacrifices to Zhurong, who was the Minister of Fire[149] at the time of King Zhuanxu. Furthermore, the Kitchen god is often identified associated with Laomi, the person who gives flavors to food. Consequently, Trịnh Huyên explains that the Kitchen god is both Zhurong and Laomi.

[The Legend of the Kitchen God]

There is a nice story that explains the origin of the Kitchen God.

[Once upon a time, there was a couple.][150]
The husband was {**p. 61**} Trọng Cao;
his wife was Thị Nhi.
One day they talked:
"Our house is rich;

A Study of Religion,145). It is also possible that Liễu Hạnh was some form of entertainer, like a Japanese geisha.

147. In Vietnam, Vua Bếp (the Kitchen God) is also known as Táo Quân (灶君, Lord of Hearth) or Táo Thần (灶神, Hearth Spirit). The popular Kitchen God not only watches over the family but is also a moral force in the lives of all family members. A week before the lunar New Year's Eve, he goes up to heaven to report to the Jade Emperor on the family's domestic affairs of the previous year. The family will then be rewarded or punished according to the Kitchen God's report. People make special offerings to him on the twenty-third day of the twelfth month, the date he goes to heaven to make his report.

148. See also *Opusculum*, Book 1, Article 9.

149. It is not clear if the Minister of Fire (*huazheng* 火政) in the ancient China refers to the minister who is in charge of fire-fighting, or in charge of cooking.

150. The story is told in four-word verses. Here the translation approximates the poetic nature of the original.

our wealth is abundant.
Whose good fortune is it?"
They began to quarrel.
The wife said it was hers;
the husband held it was his.
Trọng Cao became angry and struck Thị Nhị.
She left the house
sitting at the crossroads,
crying and tearing out her hair:
"Oh Heaven, Oh Earth,
my husband has rejected me!
I left the house to him.
Whatever our fortune is,
only the future can tell.
Arguing cannot settle the question.
Good fortune is from heaven,
from the previous karmic affinity."
She considered her feelings.
"Alas, Heaven!
Why do you let good people down?"
Heaven shifted again;
her fate was changed.
She ran into a fine man,
one with position and power.
Fate brought them together;
his name was Phạm Lang.
Seeing Nhi on the road,
he talked to her.
Bringing her home,
he made her his wife,
And she shared his fortune.
Meanwhile, Trọng Cao's fortune had ended.
His life became difficult.
Coming to beg at a house,
he did not know
it was his wife's.
As he was begging there,
she recognized him.
Phạm Lang was out hunting,
and had not yet returned.

Only Thị Nhi was home,
busy with her chores.
Her tears flowed,
feeling pity for her former husband. {p. 62}
She cooked a good meal and
served him food and wine.
He ate and drank his fill.
When Phạm Lang returned,
Thị Nhi was still crying.
Afraid that he would see her,
she told Trọng Cao:
"Go hide in the back
if you want to live.
Bury yourself in the haystack.
Do not delay."
Phạm Lang had brought back
game meats from the hunt.
Going to the haystack,
he lit the fire
to roast the meats,
torching Trọng Cao unwittingly.
Thị Nhi was distraught;
she jumped into the burning hay.
The fire consumed her.
Phạm Lang loved his wife.
He was inconsolable.
He jumped into the fire
to die with her.
Thus, all three people died.
Even the maidservant was in distress.
Mourning her master,
She, too, jumped into the fire
and was burned to death.[151]

---

151. Many stories about the origin of the Kitchen God in Chinese and Vietnamese folklores share a similar plot such as the one described in *Errors*. In one Chinese version, Zhang Dan was a wealthy farmer who had a happy family. However, his wife left him when he became attracted to another woman. He lived extravagantly until exhausting his wealth. His concubine abandoned him, and he was left to wander the streets as a homeless beggar. One day in winter, Zhang became weak and fainted while knocking on a door begging for food. The lovely woman who answered the door took him in and nursed him back to health. When he awoke, he found himself in a small kitchen next to a warm hearth. When he looked out of the window,

This is the story of the Kitchen God, whom people believe in and worship. However, according to the chapter "Monthly Proceedings" of the *Record of Rites*, the Kitchen God is called the Hearth Spirit [Táo Thần]. Furthermore, the book outlines the summer sacrifice to the Hearth [spirit], and this spirit is none other than Zhurong. It is written: "The summer's divine ruler is Yandi, his attending spirit is Zhurong, and his guardian spirit is the Hearth spirit."[152] Consequently, whenever there is a feast, people make offerings to the Kitchen God. Newly married {p. 63} women also pray to the Kitchen God to help them cook fine meals. On New Year's Eve, a picture of the Kitchen God is hung next to the hearth.

[Guardian Spirits]

The Western Scholar asks: Who are the Household Guardian [Thổ Công] and the Land Guardian [Thổ Chủ]?[153]

The Eastern Scholar replies: The chapter "Monthly Proceedings" in the *Record of Rites* teaches us that in the middle of the four seasons, a sacrifice is offered to the guardian spirit of the household, who is also called the spirit of the land. Subsequently, people refer to this spirit as the Household Guardian.

The Buddhists circulate this fanciful story about his origin: Once upon a time, there was a ferocious tiger in another kingdom.[154] It killed many people and no one could overcome it. The king issued an edict in his kingdom saying that whoever could subdue the tiger would be made an official. Five brothers from a Li family, the family of Li Rendun and Li Renyu, captured the tiger. As a reward, the king proclaimed them rulers of five parts of his kingdom.[155] The eldest brother ruled as the Green Lord of the East, the second-eldest brother as the White Lord of the West, the third brother as the Red Lord of the South, the

---

he spied his host. To his surprise, it was his former wife. Embarrassed and unable to look her in the face, he jumped into the hearth. She tried to douse him with water, but the fire continued to blaze. In a flash, his ashes went up to the heavens. Upon receiving the report of Zhang's fate, the Jade Emperor declared Zhang the Kitchen God. See E. T. C. Werner, *Dictionary of Chinese Mythology* (Shanghai, 1932; repr., New York: Julian Press, 1961), 520.

152. See *Errors*, Book 1, Article 7.

153. The "Household Guardian" (Thổ Công) is the house god; the "Land Guardian" or "Local Master" (Thổ Chủ) is the guardian spirit of one's land and field.

154. In the text, the author uses "another kingdom" as a reference to China, which is made explicit in the *Opusculum*. Sino-Vietnamese names of these brothers are Lê Nhân Đôn and Lê Nhân Dục.

155. Cf. *Opusculum*, 48.

fourth brother as the Black Lord of the North, and the fifth brother as the Yellow Lord of the Central. Later, these brothers were worshipped collectively as the Household Guardian.

People also worship the Land Guardian.[156] According to an account in the book *Loại Tư*, {p. 64} goblins used to play chess on Mount Thạch Thất in Sơn Tây Prefecture.[157] During the Jin dynasty, there was a poor wood gatherer named Vương Chất. One day, on his way to gather wood, he stopped to watch the goblins playing chess. He was put under a spell and stayed there for a long time until the blade of his ax had been gnawed away by moths and his face had become badly disfigured. When he returned home, none of his relatives recognized him. Upon seeing that no one was welcoming him, he went and built a modest hut on the corner of his land. When he died, he was given the title "eunuch" [*thái giám*][158] and honored as the Land Guardian [Thổ Chủ].

[Guild Founder]

The Western Scholar asks again: Why do craftsmen and merchants often worship the founders [*tiên sư*] of their craft or trade?

The Eastern Scholar replies: People have respect for teachers. Since all crafts and trades have their originators, people venerate them, pay them due respect, and pray to their Guild Founders to assist them in their crafts and trades. The Guild Founders are honored on the seventh day of the first month, the fifth [day] of the fifth month, and the tenth [day] of the tenth month. In addition, whenever there are {p. 65} memorial feasts for their ancestors, offerings are made to the Guild Founders, the Household Guardian, the Land Guardian, and the Kitchen god. I do not know when this custom began.

---

156. The text has "Household Guardian" (Thổ Công); however, the phrase "Land Guardian" (Thổ Chủ) is more suitable in this context.

157. I am uncertain whether this is a Chinese or Vietnamese story; hence, the names are spelled in Sino-Vietnamese rather than pinyin. During the Jin dynasty, North Vietnam was under Chinese rule.

158. According to Dror (*A Study of Religion*, 148nn159, 162), the "blade of the ax" that was "gnawed away by moths" was an euphemism for "phallus;" hence, his posthumous title "eunuch." There is no known Cult of the Eunuch in Vietnam.

[Further Comments]

The Western Scholar pities those who worship the Guild Founders, the Household Guardian, the Land Guardian, the Kitchen god, and other spirits because their minds have been clouded. They do not know of the great Lord of heaven and earth and all creatures, who rules over everything and assists people in their crafts and trades. Instead, they listen to demons who teach them to worship these spirits.[159]

---

159. In the original text, this passage was put in the same paragraph of the Eastern Scholar's explanation, but its context shows a different line of thought.

Article 12

On the Cult of Confucius and the Great Sages

The Western Scholar asks: I have noticed that Confucian scholars often revere and offer sacrifices to Confucius, the First Sage and Master. So I ask you: Who is Confucius, and what merit does he have among the *ru*?[160]

The Eastern Scholar says: Master Kong (Confucius) is from Changping village in the state of Lu;[161] his ancestors were from the state of Song.[162] His father was Shu Lianghe, and his mother was Zheng Zai. Being childless, she went up to Mount Ni Qiu to pray for a child. The following year, in the twenty-first year of the reign of Zhou Lingwang [551 BCE],[163] she gave birth to a son and named him Qiu {p. 66}. Zhongni is his courtesy (literary) name. As he grew up, he became a learned scholar and edited the six classics: *Odes, History, Rites, Music, Changes*, and *Spring and Autumn*. He had three thousand students, of whom seventy-two were sages. He taught them that the way "to learning is through illuminating illustrious virtue, renewing the people, and resting only after attaining the highest good."[164] He taught eight principles as norms for action:

> When things are investigated, knowledge is extended.
> When knowledge is extended, thought becomes sincere.
> When thought becomes sincere, the mind is rectified.
> When the mind is rectified, the person becomes cultivated.
> When a person is cultivated, order is brought to the family.
> When order is brought to the family, the state is well governed.
> When the state is well governed, peace is brought to the world.[165]

---

160. Also see *Opusculum*, Chapter 1, Article 4.

161. Modern-day Shandong.

162. A state southwest of Lu in modern-day Henan.

163. The exact date of Confucius's birth is not universally agreed upon, although 551 BCE is frequently cited by most biographers in accordance with Sima Qian's *Records of the Grand Historian*, Chapter 47.

164. Sino-Vietnamese: 學事明明德, 新民止於至善。 Cf. the *Great Learning*.

165. Sino-Vietnamese: 物格而后知至, 知至而后意誠, 意誠而后心正, 心正而后身修, 身修而后家齊, 家齊而后國治, 國治而后天下平。 From the opening chapter of the *Great Learning*.

Confucius lived for seven-three years and died in the forty-first year of Zhou Jingwang [479 BCE].[166] Because of his achievements, Confucius exercised great influence on scholars, kings, and the people of the East. As a result, from past to present, not only have Confucian scholars revered Confucius, but also rulers and ordinary people alike have praised and worshipped him. Master Liu writes:

> There is no one, from the king to ordinary people, who has not venerated or worshipped Confucius. In the last thousand years or so, no one has surpassed him in honor. How could it be otherwise? He established a doctrine for the proper relationships between rulers and subjects as well as between fathers and sons. He introduced a doctrine of humaneness and righteousness, as well as ceremonies and music. {p. 67 (69)}[167] Even barbarians from the North and South are unable to ignore his teachings. When Han Gaozu [r. 202–195 BCE] passed through the state of Lu [in 195 BCE], he offered solemn sacrifices to honor Confucius.[168] [Han Huidi (r. 195–188 BCE) conferred upon Confucius posthumous honorific title the "Meritoriously Declarable Duke of Ni"][169] [In 739 CE] Tang Xuanzong [r. 685–762] conferred upon Confucius the posthumous honorific title of "Exalted King of Culture." Song Taizu [r. 927–976] issued an edict that a shrine be built; he commissioned for worship an image of the First Sage and Master. The emperor himself wrote words of praise honoring Confucius and his disciple Yan Hui. [In 1008] Song Zhenzong [r. 968–1022] also conferred upon him the title of "Profound Sage, Exalted King of Culture" and commanded that temples be built in all prefecture capitals to honor Confucius. [In 1308] Yuan Wuzong [r. 1308–1311] raised Confucius to the rank of "Ultimate Sage of Great Perfection, Exalted King of Culture".[170]

---

166. Chinese usually begin tracking their age from the moment of conception. Thus, a person who is seventy-three years old may actually be seventy-two or younger.

167. In the manuscript, several pages are out of order; consequently, the pages are numbered incorrectly. Here the correct page number is noted, and the original number is given in parentheses: 67 (instead of 69).

168. This event marks the beginning of the cult of Confucius.

169. This phrase was left out in the manuscript of *Errors* but preserved in *Opusculum*, 11 (Dror, *A Study of Religion*, 107).

170. Sino-Vietnamese: 自天子至於庶人，莫不崇奉歷千餘年未有如孔子之盛者，豈非君臣父子仁義禮樂之教，雖蠻貊之邦不可斯須臾捨乎。漢高祖過魯以太牢祀孔子。[漢后帝追諡孔子為褒成侯宣尼公]。唐玄宗追諡孔子為文宣王。宋太祖詔喪，執祠廡塑繪先聖先師之像，自為讚書於孔顏之座端。宋真宗加諡孔子為玄聖文宣王，又詔州城作孔子廟。元武宗加封孔子為大成至聖文宣王。

[The Cult of Confucius in Annam]

In Annam, King Trần Thái Tông established the National Academy, where he placed statues of Confucius and the Duke of Zhou [and Mencius][171] as well as portraits of the seventy-two sages for the purpose of offering sacrifices to them. Since then, solemn sacrifices are offered to Confucius twice a year: in spring, in the first week of the second month, and in autumn, in the eighth month. This ceremony originated as early as the Tang dynasty because Emperor Xuanzong decreed that sacrifices to the Great Duke be offered, in the same manner as the sacrifices to Confucius, in the capital and all prefectures during the second and eighth months. However, I do not know which king established the cult of Confucius in this country (Annam). In addition, {p. 68 (70)} schoolteachers and successful candidates in the three levels of civil-service examinations were required to come to Confucius's temple, make offerings, perform sacrifices, and pay homage to him.

The Western Scholar asks the Eastern Scholar again: When Confucian scholars give offerings to Confucius, do they offer sacrifices to any other sage?

The Eastern Scholar replies: Confucian scholars not only sacrifice to Confucius but also to his Four Associates and the Ten Philosophers. The Four Associates are Yan Hui, Zeng Shen, Zisi, and Mencius. Both Yan Hui and Zeng Shen were Confucius's disciples. The former was considered a sage [by Confucius himself], though he died prematurely at the age of thirty-one. Zeng Shen [or Zengzi] was the author of the *Great Learning* and the *Analects*. Zisi [or Kong Ji] was Confucius' grandson and compiled the *Doctrine of the Mean*. Mencius's name was Meng Ke. He studied with Zisi, wrote the book *Mencius*, and lived during the reign of Zhou Xianwang [r. 330–321 BCE], approximately 150 years after Confucius. The Ten Philosophers are:

{p. 69 (71)}

[Min Ziqian, Ran Boniu, Zhonggong, Ziwo, Zigong, Ran Qiu, Zilu, Ziyou, Zixia and Zizhang].[172]

---

171. This reference is taken from *Toàn Thư*, bản kỷ, 5:19a (translation, 2:26) but the manuscript omits the name of Mencius.

172. Since the manuscript is blank, I am supplying the missing information here. There are small variations in the names on this list depending on the local temples.

[Description of the Rite to Confucius]

{p. 70 (72)}

The Western Scholar asks again: How do Confucian scholars make offerings and sacrifices to Confucius and these sages?[173]

The Eastern Scholar replies: In Confucius's Temple, the sage's tablet[174] is placed in the center. Tablets with the names of the Four Associates are placed on either side. Tablets with the names of the Ten Philosophers are behind them. There is an incense table in front of Confucius's tablet. When performing the ceremony, the two masters of ceremony stand on either side of the incense table, while several rite officiants stand at the center, facing the table, with their assistants behind them. The night before the sacrifice, the literati gather at the Temple. One of them says aloud: "We earnestly announce to the First Sage that the ceremony will be performed tomorrow morning." He then examines and kills the sacrificial animals—a buffalo, a pig, and a goat—and places their meat on the sacrificial table. The following morning, the main celebrant prays aloud: "Welcome, Sage King" and then makes offerings of food, wine, meat, and a white silk cloth. Next, he reads an offering oration praising Confucius for editing the six classics that comprise the standard educational texts, further exalting him as the "Ultimate Sage of Great Perfection, King of Culture." He also asks Confucius to grant bright minds to the students so that they may fully understand his teachings, preserve them, {p. 71 (73)} and teach them to the next generation so that they too will know his teachings. The oration also praises the Four Correlates and the Ten Philosophers. After the sacrifice, the master of ceremonies calls out: "Drink the blessings!" The officiant drinks the sacrificial wine in order to receive Confucius's blessing. At the end of the ceremony, the master of ceremonies calls out again: "Farewell to the deity!" Then, the rite officiant and all in attendance prostrate themselves four times to thank Confucius and bid him farewell. After that, they feast on the sacrificial food, drink, and take a portion home. This food and drink are considered special. That is what the cult of Confucius is about.

---

173. Also see *Opusculum*, Chapter 1, Article 5.

174. In the past, the Vietnamese often did not use the name "Confucius" but called him the Sage.

The Western Scholar comments: It is fitting that Confucian scholars revere Confucius, who has supreme wisdom and knowledge and who has great merit in teaching the people of the world the appropriate doctrine. However, your offering of food from this world is futile because he no longer needs it. Also, you should not pray to him for a bright mind and success in examinations because he does not have the power to grant this. Only the Lord of Heaven, the One who has the power and authority to govern everything in heaven and on earth, can grant a bright mind, fame, and prosperity to anyone he wishes. Even Confucius himself was granted, {**p. 72 (74)**} by the Lord of Heaven, the gift of being extraordinarily wise and knowledgeable so that he might teach the people of the world.

Article 13

On the Cult of Thái Công and the Mighty Generals

The Western Scholar says: Military officials often offer sacrifices to the mighty generals of former times. So I ask you: Who is this cult for?

The Eastern Scholar replies: In the nineteenth year of the reign of Tang Xuanzong [732 CE], the king ordered a temple built in the capital and in each of the prefectures to honor Thái Công [Great Duke].[175] Zhang Liang and ten great men among the mighty generals of the past were also to be worshipped there. Offerings are sacrificed to them, in the same manner as to Confucius and his disciples, during the first week of the second and eighth months. Consequently, military officials obey this command to perform sacrifices to the Great Duke, Two Associates, Zhang Liang, Sun Wuzi, and twelve other generals in a solemn ceremony on the first week of the second and eighth months. Statues of the Great Duke and the generals are kept in the Temple of the Military [Vũ Miếu].[176]

The Western Scholar asks: What were the achievements of the Great Duke Jiang and Zhang Liang?
{p. 73 (75)}

The Eastern Scholar answers: The Great Duke Jiang is Lü Wang (Jiang Ziya), who lived during the reign of wicked King Zhou of Yin.[177] He left China for the Eastern Sea and lived there for more than eighty years, fishing the waters of the Wei river. When Si Bo, also known as King Wen of Zhou, went hunting in the area, he met Lü Wang, took him home in his carriage, and honored

---

175. This refers to Jiang Ziya (姜子牙) or Lü Wang (呂望), a military advisor who helped King Wen and Wu to overthrow the Shang dynasty. He was conferred the honorific title Great Duke of Qi (齊太公), hence the name Jiang Taigong (姜太公).

176. The Temple of the Military (Vũ Miếu 武廟) in Hanoi was first erected under the Trần dynasty as the counterpart to the Temple of Culture (Văn Miếu 文廟), but it no longer exists. See Dror's discussion in *A Study of Religion*, 128nn64, 66.

177. King Zhou (紂) is the posthumous name of Di Xin (帝莘), also known as Zhou the Cruel. He was the last ruler of the Shang/Yin dynasty (r. 1154–1122 BCE).

him as the Great Duke. Because King Wen learned the Great Duke's art of warfare, his military strategy became known as the Civil Style. Later, his son King Wu also learned the art of warfare from the Great Duke but referred to it as the Military Style. The Great Duke also taught other styles, namely, the Dragon, Tiger, Leopard, and Dog military strategies. These styles are known collectively as the Six Strategies of Warfare.[178] Years later, the Great Duke surrounded King Zhou in a siege so complete that the king, having no place to flee, committed suicide by throwing himself into a fire.[179] Upon this victory, King Wu gained power and ruled over the entire country. In gratitude, King Wu made the Great Duke the ruler of the state of Qi.[180] During the reign of Tang Dezong [r. 779–805],[181] the Great Duke was posthumously conferred the honorific title of "Accomplished King of the Military" [Vũ Thành Vương]. Because the Great Duke had taught both King Wen and King Wu the art of warfare, people study his tactical strategies for becoming capable military generals {p. 74 (76)} who conduct warfare with skillful stratagems and tactics. Whoever knows the Six Strategies will be able to become a general.

Zhang Liang learned the Great Duke's art of warfare and became a military officer in the state of Han.[182] When Qin Ershi[183] conquered Han, Zhang Liang offered his services to the king of Han[184] and helped him fight against the Qin.

---

178. The *Six Strategies* (Lục Thao 六韜) is the title of a Chinese tactical manual attributed to Jiang Ziya. Its methods can be summarized as follows: (1) The *Civil Strategy*: Be benevolent and help others achieve their aspirations for a better world. (2) The *Military Strategy*: Outwit your opponent through diplomacy and manipulation. (3) The *Dragon Strategy*: Explore the subtle and complex aspects of the situation without ceding control to advisors or becoming confused. (4) The *Tiger Strategy*: Guard against laxity and act in accord with ever-changing conditions. (5) The *Leopard Strategy*: Know your strength and direct it against the weakness of your enemy. (6) The *Dog Strategy*: Time a concentrated attack when the moment is right. For the complete text, see Ralph D. Sawyer and Mei-chun Sawyer, *The Seven Ancient Military Classics of China, Including the* Art of War (Boulder, CO: Westview Press, 1993), 19–106.

179. This refers to the battle of Muye (牧野), when King Wu of Zhou and his military advisor Jiang Ziya defeated Zhou's forces, which were said to outnumber them approximately ten to one.

180. Qi (齊) was a small kingdom during the Spring and Autumn era and Warring States period that lasted from 1046 to 221 BCE. Its territory was located in Shandong province.

181. The manuscript misspells his name as Đường "Túc" Tông. Note that "Túc" and "Đức" are close in orthography.

182. Han (韓) was one of the kingdoms of the Warring States period that lasted from 403 to 230 BCE. Its territory corresponds to the present provinces of Shanxi and Henan.

183. Qin Ershi (秦二世) was Qin Shihuang's successor and ruled from 209–206 BCE.

184. King of Han (漢王) was the title given to Liu Bang (劉邦), who revolted against the harsh government of the Qin emperors and founded the Han dynasty. He was posthumously honored as Han Gaozu.

Subsequently, when the king of Han gained power over China, he conferred upon Zhang Liang the honorific title of "Marquis of Liu" (Lưu Hầu).[185] Afterward, because Zhang Liang had witnessed the emperor mistreat and abuse scholars and military officers, he resigned his commission and left the [military and civilian] world to live a monastic life, with the spirits on a mountain, until his death in the sixth year of Han Huidi [188 BCE].[186]

Sun Wuzi was a general of the state of Wu.[187] The Twelve Generals were drawn from many generations. They are shown in the following chart:

The left wing of the outer temple:
- Jia Geliang, Marquis of Wuxiang and Chancellor of Han
- Tian Xiangru, Head of the Qi Military
- Liao Zi, Minister of Wei
- Han Xin, Marquis of Huai Yin of Han
- Guo Ziyi, Grand Officer of Tang
- Liu Ji, Baron of Ming

The main chamber of the inner temple:
- *On the left:* Sun Wuzi, General of Wu
- *On the right:* Zhang Liang, Marquis of Liu of Han

The right wing of the outer temple:
- Prince Hưng Đạo, named Trần Quốc Tuấn, Great Master of the Trần dynasty
- Li Sheng, Pacifying the West Prince of Tang
- Yue Fei, Great Minister and Prince Zheng of Song
- Guan Zhong, Chancellor of Qi
- Wu Ji, Head of Western River of Wei
- Li Jing, Defense Minister of Tang

---

185. Liu (劉) was the family name of the Han emperor. Receiving the emperor's family name is a high honor; it means that the recipient is considered by the emperor to be part of his family.

186. According to this account, Zhang Liang died in 188 BCE, since Han Huidi reigned from 194–188 BCE.

187. Sun Wuzi or Sunzi (孫[武]子) was an eminent general of the state of Wu during the Warring States period. He was the author of the famous treatise *The Art of War*.

{p. 75 (67)}

The Western Scholar comments: Military officers revere and worship generals at the Temple of the Military with the hope that the generals will help them win in battle. However, these generals have no power to do so because the skills, intelligence, and strength that helped them win a battle or found a state do not belong to them. These things are given to them by the power of the great Lord who created all things in heaven and on earth. Moreover, many who worship these generals have lost battles; the generals were not able to help them at all. Therefore, the Great Duke's military cult and the mighty generals are ineffective.

The Western Scholar argues further: The Great Duke and his descendants were rulers of the state of Qi. If he had had real power, he would not have lost his kingdom to the invaders. For instance, when King Yan of Zhao [r. 311–279 BCE] ordered Yue Yi to attack Qi and conquer seventy-two towns, King Min of Qi [r. 300–284 BCE] had to go into hiding.[188] Later, when Qin Shihuang dispatched Wang Bi to attack Qi, the king of Qi surrendered, and the state of Qi collapsed [in 221 BCE]. If {p. 76 (68)} the Great Duke had had power, he would have been able to save his descendants, and they would have ruled Qi forever.[189] Why did he allow them to lose their states? Moreover, Emperor Tang Xuanzong earnestly prayed in front of the Great Duke's Temple to set an example for later generations. Yet when An Lushan[190] rebelled against him, the emperor fled the capital, Chang'an (Xi'an), and went into hiding in the Shu region (Sichuan). The Great Duke did not have the power to save him. It is enough to revere and honor the Great Duke; however, one should not offer him sacrifices or ask for his help. This would be useless and in vain.

---

188. In 285 BCE, King Zhao of Yan (Yan Zhaowang 燕昭王) (r. 311–279) formed an alliance with the states of Zhao, Qin, Han, and Wei for a joint expedition against the powerful state of Qi. Led by General Yue Yi (樂毅), the campaign was successful, and Qi was nearly destroyed within a year. However, with the death of King Zhao and Yue Yi's subsequent expulsion to Zhao, the Qi army managed to recapture their lost cities.

189. In reality, the Great Duke's descendants ruled the state of Qi for more than eight hundred years, a record in ancient times.

190. The rebellion launched by Sogdian general An Lushan (安禄山), 703–757 CE, was one of the longest and most costly civil wars in Chinese history. It lasted from 753 to 765, spanning the reigns of three Tang emperors. It marked the beginning of the decline of the Tang dynasty.

Article 14

On Funeral Rites and the Veneration of Ancestors

The Western Scholar says: I have noticed that people often do their best to arrange the most solemn funerals for their parents and ancestors. So I ask you: How are those conducted?[191]

The Eastern Scholar replies: When children perform rituals honoring their ancestors, they observe two rites: one is a rite laid out in *Family Rituals*;[192] the other is a Buddhist rite. Here, I will only discuss the Confucian rites described in *Family Rituals*. In Book 3, {**p. 77**} Article 8, I will thoroughly discuss the Buddhist rite, and the Western Scholar will completely understand it.

The *Correct Practices of the Family Rituals* states that immediately after a person stops breathing, a family member climbs to the roof of the house, calls out the name of the deceased, and invites them to return home.[193] Then, the body is shrouded and placed in a bed in the middle of the house. Afterward, a piece of fine silk is knotted into the shape of a person and made into a "soul cloth" [*hồn bạch*][194] that is placed in front of the "soul seat" [*linh toạ*].[195] It is believed that the soul of the deceased will come to the soul seat and enjoy the food offered to it. After being clothed, the body is placed in a coffin. Next, an offering called the "daily food offering" [*triêu diện*] is made, which signifies that an offering of food will be given to the deceased in the morning and evening.[196] Then, the ritual utensils [such as incense burners, incense boxes, cups, decanters, etc.][197] are set

---

191. See also *Opusculum*, Chapter 2, Articles 10 and 11.

192. There are many versions of *Family Rituals* in both China and Vietnam. The most popular Vietnamese version since the eighteenth century has been *Thọ Mai Gia Lễ* [Family Rituals by Tho Mai]. The description of the cult of the ancestors here has many details that may be particular to the ritual manual that the author had access to.

193. The Chinese and Vietnamese believe that when the soul exits the body, it loses its way and easily becomes a wandering ghost if it does not return home with its relatives. This practice is called *hú viá* or *triệu hồn* (calling the soul back).

194. *Hồn bạch* (魂帛) is a cloth of fine silk that is placed on the chest of the dying person. After "calling the soul back," it is knotted into the shape of a human being and represents the soul of the deceased. In modern practice, it has been replaced with a picture of the deceased.

195. *Giường Linh toạ* (靈座, soul seat) is a table setting where an oblation is made to the deceased.

196. In the offering *triêu diện*, rice is offered for one hundred days after the death.

197. I could not make sense of the Vietnamese words for the ritual utensils. Other sources list these common utensils for rituals.

out. A ritual chair [*ỷ*] is placed at the center of the soul seat, and on it are placed a robe and a cap with the soul cloth inside. Food offerings to the deceased person to be worshipped are set out in front of the ritual chair. On the left is the "inscribed banner" [*minh tinh*],[198] and on the right are a blanket and pillow. An incense table [*hương án*] sits in front of the soul seat table.

Four days after the death, the "wearing of the mourning garments" ceremony [*thành phục*][199] is conducted. When the body is kept in the house for a long time [so that relatives may gather], {**p. 78**} food offerings must be made twice a day, in the morning and evening, in addition to the midday meal offering. Each month on the first and full moons, food must be offered to the deceased in the morning. This must be done for three months.

On the day of the burial, the soul cloth is first taken to the ancestral hall. Just as a living person must always inform their elders of their upcoming travels, the soul of the deceased person must also go to their ancestors' hall and greet them. Afterward, the soul cloth is carried back to the soul seat. Then, the "moving of the coffin" rite [*chuyển cữu*] is performed before the coffin is carried out of the house. When this is completed, food is offered at the soul seat again. *Family Rituals* also mentions the custom of imitating Cao Công[200] in order to "get a permission [to enter the underworld] through buying a funeral carriage"[201] for the soul of the deceased. This means buying a paper house to ensure a home for the deceased in the underworld. The common people call this *sắc dạc*,[202] or "funeral house" [*nhà táng*]. When purchasing a funeral carriage, the following lament is read:

> Alas! Father (or Mother), I am in pain when I see you in your present form, leaving me behind. Sorrow pierces my heart {**p. 79**} like being attacked by panic. Tears flow down my face like rain. Today, I have purchased a funeral carriage for you. I pray you will be safe and happy with your dwelling, and may blessings be granted to your descendants. We respectfully pray.[203]

---

198. *Minh tinh* (銘旌), also known as *triệu* (旐), is a piece of silk on which the name, title, and office of the deceased person is written.

199. *Lễ thành phục* (成服, also known as *lễ phát tang*) is a ceremony that marks the beginning of the mourning period. This ceremony is performed after the body has been shrouded and placed in the coffin. The surviving relatives start wearing mourning garments at this time.

200. This may refer to a person or an office.

201. The phrases *khảo văn ngô sắc* (asking the permission) and *có mãi liễu xa* (having bought a funeral carriage) are corrupted in the manuscript, so the translation here is approximated.

202. I am uncertain of the Vietnamese spelling.

203. This is my attempt to supply the Chinese characters for this Sino-Vietnamese paragraph: 痛唯父或母容樣厭氣, 子心之愁切如紜, 面精之淚垂若雨, 今買得柳車, 敬為

After this rite, the coffin is placed on a hand-drawn carriage [*đại dư*].[204] Before the procession, offerings are made to the Protector of Travelers [Dư thần], asking him to protect the soul on its journey, keep it safe, and keep it free from fear [of demons]. *Family Rituals* also adds the rite of informing Loa Tổ,[205] the guardian spirit of the road, of the journey. An offering prayer [*chúc văn*][206] is said: "We solemnly announce this funeral procession to the spirits of the roads in the five directions." The five directions are East, West, North, South, and the Center. Prayers are offered to the guardian spirits of the road in order to keep the road safe for the procession and to prevent demons from disturbing the funeral carriage: "We earnestly implore the Five Emperors and the spirits of the road in all five directions to remember the merits of the spirits of the earth who accompany the soul of the recently-deceased [Name], and to allow it a safe journey."[207] If the coffin is being borne by boat, an offering is made to the god of the river. If mourners stop to rest {p. 80} during the procession, a "middle of the journey" offering [*tế trung đồ*] of is made.[208] At a three-way intersection, an offering is made to the spirits guarding the crossroads [*tế tam kỳ lộ*].

Before lowering the coffin into the grave at the burial site, a "name banner" [*minh tinh*] is draped over the casket. When consecrating a grave, an offering must be made to the god of the earth requesting his assistance for a smooth burial. Upon lowering the coffin halfway into the grave, an offering is made on the right side of the grave to the god of the earth. After halfway filling the grave with dirt, another offering is made to the god of the earth.

After the burial, the "marking of the spirit tablet" ceremony [*đề chủ*][209] is performed, and the posthumous name and title of the deceased are carved into a

---

于親, 故願保守安居, 俾慶流後裕, 虔告 。 The translation is a loose paraphrase since I am unsure of certain words.

204. *Đại dư* is a hand-drawn carriage on which the coffin is placed.

205. "Loa Tổ" may be a misspelling of "Đạo Lộ."

206. *Chúc văn* is another name for *tế văn* (祭文, cultic oration), a type of reading that is delivered at funeral and memorial services.

207. Sino-Vietnamese: 敢昭告于五方道路之神五帝,知功使者土地等神今亡[名]正魂 。

208. *Trung đồ* or *đạo trung* (道中) is an oblation that is made in the middle of the journey. It allows the coffin carriers and the procession to rest and take food because the walk to the burial site is often long.

209. *Đề chủ* or *điểm chủ* (點主, marking the tablet) is the ceremonial inscription on the *thần chủ* (神主, spirit tablet). From this point onward, the spirit tablet replaces the soul cloth as the soul's new "home."

wooden tablet. The tablet is then placed on the altar with the soul cloth behind it, and an offering is made. During the offering, a prayer is said asking the soul to leave the soul cloth and return home in the spirit tablet: "We earnestly pray to [Name]. Your body now returns to the earth and your spirit to the household altar. Your spirit tablet has been made. We implore your venerable soul to move from your old to your new dwelling place. This tablet is where you will rest."[210] Then the spirit tablet is carried home, and a special oblation [*tế ngu*][211] is performed for three days: On the first day, the "First Pacification" offering [*sơ ngu*], is made, on the second, the "Second Pacification" [*tái ngu*], and on the third, the "Third Pacification" [*tam* {p. 81} *ngu*]. When making these offerings, the first offering must be given to the paternal and maternal ancestors and then to the recently departed soul. If these offerings are made, everything will be all right. *Family Rites* states: "When its flesh and bones have returned to the earth, the soul has no place to go." This means that although the body is already resting safely under the ground, the soul is left to wander in search of its home. Thus, one must plan to lead the soul of the deceased home by making offerings to it and inviting it to inhabit the spirit tablet. This ritual is called the rite of "pacifying the soul."

When performing the rite of "pacifying the soul," the ritualist first calls out: "Let the spirit descend" [*giáng thân*]. Then, as he calls out "Pour the wine" [*châm tửu*], the eldest son, acting as master of the ceremonies, offers wine libations on the soul table, takes a cup of wine, pours it on the "mat of reeds" (*sa mao*), and then places cups of wine on the soul table. The same procedure is repeated during two more rounds of libations. During the second round or "second offering" [*á hiến lễ*], a person kneels in front of the incense table, recites a prayer, calls out the names of the descendants who made the food offering, and then calls out to the soul asking it to enjoy the food offering: "May you enjoy it!" [*thượng hưởng*]. The third round of libations is the "final offering" [*thang hiến lễ*]. More wine is poured into the cups during the fourth round or "consumption of the food" [*hựu thực*] offering. Next, the ritualist shouts: "Master of ceremonies, please come forward!". {p. 82} The presiding male mourner comes forth and stands to the east of the altar, and together with the other men standing behind him in rows, he faces

---

210. This is my attempt to supply the Chinese characters for this Sino-Vietnamese paragraph: 敢昭告于[名], 形歸復返, 神返室堂, 神主既安, 伏惟尊靈, 捨舊從新, 是憑是依。 This translation is a paraphrase since I am uncertain of certain words.

211. *Ngu* (虞) is the oblation conducted in the first three days after burial. According to Vietnamese belief, the soul must adapt to its new environment, so oblations are made to "pacify" it. These also serve as meals of thanks to the neighbors and relatives who have helped out during the funeral.

west. The presiding female mourner stands to the west side, and together with the other women standing behind her in rows, she faces east. Then the ritualist calls out: "Close the door" [*hạp môn*], and they close the door of the altar. A curtain is lowered if there is no door. Next, the ritualist makes a "coughing sound" [*hi hâm*][212] to signal a time of silence for the soul to enjoy its food and wine offerings in private. After three more coughs, the ritualist returns and reopens the door or curtain. Then he announces: "Serve the tea" [*dâng trà*]. This indicates that the soul will then take tea after eating the meal. When everything is finished, the ritualist calls out: "The offering is completed" [*lễ thành*]. This signals the end of the oblation. Finally, he calls out: "Farewell to the spirit" [*từ thần*], indicating that the soul is ready to depart. At that moment, the eldest son and relatives present weep and prostrate themselves twice, thanking the deceased for having accepted the offering and bidding the soul farewell. After the "pacification" rite, the soul cloth is buried in a clean plot of land.

After the pacification, food offerings are made to the spirit table on special occasions. There is a solemn offering on the seventh, thirtieth, fiftieth, and a hundredth day after the death. In addition, the *hè* oblation is offered on the fourteenth day of the fourth month, on the fifteenth of the fifth month, and on the sixteenth of the sixth month. Over the next two years, {p. 83} the *bôi* oblation is offered on the full moon of the seventh month during the Middle Period festival [*trung nguyên*].[213] On the first anniversary of the death, a "small memorial" feast [*tiểu tường*] is held. On the second anniversary, the "great memorial" feast [*đại tường*] is held. After twenty-seven months, the *đàm* ceremony is performed, marking the end of the mourning period. From then on, the *giỗ* or *đôi ky* memorial feast is held on the anniversary of the death. The descendants must hold an annual memorial feast for five generations of ancestors. After the fifth generation, an ancestor's spirit tablet is removed from the altar, and their memorial feast is no longer required. Such are the teachings of *Family Rituals* with regard to making offerings to ancestors.[214]

---

212. The word *hi hâm* can be a coughing sound (嘻噷), or mean "enjoy the essence [of the food]" (僖歆).

213. Old lunar calendars divide the year into three periods: The first month is the Upper Period (*thượng nguyên*), the seventh month is the Middle Period (*trung nguyên*), and the tenth month is the Lower Period (*hạ nguyên*).

214. In pre-modern Vietnam, this was not only a custom but also a legal requirement. Failure to perform these sacrificial offerings per legal codes was punishable in accordance with the gravity of the offense.

The Western Scholar argues: People make such offerings to their parents and ancestors because they believe that the souls of their ancestors reside in the soul cloth or spirit tablet and enjoy the food offerings. However, it is impossible for a deceased person to return to consume food and wine offerings from their descendants. Food and drink sustain the bodies of the living. But once the souls of the dead leave their bodies, they have no bodies to sustain. The human soul has a spiritual character; it is the most spiritual entity among all creatures. It does not depend on the body to live but has a life of its own. Therefore, when it leaves the body, the soul does not need food or drink as a living person does. Moreover, when the soul is one with the body, it does not need food. {p. 84} Food is needed only to sustain the life of the body. If you believe that the soul needs food to sustain itself, then it must have food twice a day. But if the soul is offered food only once a year during its memorial feast, how can it sustain itself? A dead body no longer needs food. When one offers food to the soul, one insults the soul, for the soul does not eat or drink. Such an act is merely mocking the soul, making it angry and sad. Therefore, those who make offerings to their ancestors are not being filial; they are proving, rather, to be truly unfilial. Food offerings are for the living; the soul does not consume them at all. Alas, those who make such offerings are profoundly ignorant. If the soul actually consumes these offerings, why does the food still remain? Why does it not disappear? Even if the soul consumes only the essence of the offering, why do the offered foods remain tasty and nourishing? This only proves that the soul in no way returns to enjoy the food offerings at all.

The Eastern Scholar comments: There are some Confucian scholars who believe that offering {p. 85} food to deceased parents is pointless. According to a song of Zhou in the *Classic of Odes*: "After one's parents pass away, one can no longer see their faces, no longer hear their voices. Even if one has delicious food and good clothes, one cannot provide them with these things."[215] This is a useless and wasteful practice, for the many offerings are costly, and the soul cannot enjoy them at all. Moreover, *Analects* states: "Sacrifice [to ancestors] as if [they were] present; sacrifice to the spirit as if the spirit were present."[216] Hence, we do this not because we believe the spirit of the dead is present during the sacrifice. We simply act as if it were present there. Therefore, those Confucian scholars who believe the souls of their parents and ancestors reside in the spirit

---

215. Sino-Vietnamese: 若父母之既歿, 容貌之不可以復見, 音響之不可以復聞, 雖有甘旨輕煖, 無所奉之也。 This is also quoted in the *Hội Đồng Tứ Giáo*, 26b.

216. Sino-Vietnamese: 祭如在, 祭神如神在。

tablets and enjoy the offerings do not follow the teachings of Confucius and other great scholars. In the foreword to the *Great Learning*, Zhu Xi chastises those who do not adhere to the classics: "No matter what the book says, I do what I want. So what good is learning?" [217] These are scholars who do not take the teachings of the classics seriously, who ignore them, and who follow their own thinking. If one acts this way, one should not be called a scholar but an ignorant person.

The Western Scholar argues further: During the sacrifice, there is the rite of "serving the wine {p. 86} to the descending spirit" [*giáng thần châm tửu*], that is, pouring wine onto the *sa mao* so that the soul will descend and enjoy the libations. What is the reason for pouring wine onto the *sa mao* for the spirit to descend if the soul is already present in the spirit tablet after the "marking of the tablet" ceremony [*đề chủ*]? Furthermore, if one believes that the soul is already present in the spirit tablet, why must one still perform the "pacification" rite so that the soul will settle and reside there? These practices are contradictory and make no sense.

The Eastern Scholar comments: The rites outlined in *Family Rituals* are not the only practices that make no sense. There are also other absurd practices that contradict Confucian teachings. Although Confucian scholars teach that the use of spirit money is a Buddhist practice, they still use it at funerals. The two customs of making offerings to the guardian spirits of the road and purchasing funeral houses [*nhà táng*] that are later burned are also Buddhist customs. Making offerings on the seventh, thirtieth, fiftieth, and a hundredth days are also Buddhist rituals. The person who wrote the *Family Rituals* is a Confucian scholar, and yet he has incorporated into his manual many Buddhist customs and beliefs that contradict the rationality and the practice of the Confucian way.[218]
{p. 87}

The Western Scholar asks the Eastern Scholar: Do the king, his officials, and the common people have ancestral temples?

---

217. Sino-Vietnamese: 書自書, 我自我, 何益之有。I cannot locate this sentence in the introduction to the *Great Learning*.

218. This comment refers to ritual manuals in Tonkin, not to Zhu Xi's *Family Rituals*, which does not contain these practices.

The Eastern Scholar replies: Only the king and his high- and low-ranking officials have ancestral temples. According to the chapter "Royal Regulations" in the *Record of Rites*:

> The ancestral temple of the Son of Heaven consists of seven shrines: three on the left, three on the right, and one for his great ancestor [that faces south]—in all, seven. The temple of a feudal prince consists of five such shrines: two on the left, two on the right, and one for his great ancestor—in all, five. The temple of a great official consists of three such shrines: one on the left, one on the right, and one for his great ancestor—in all, three. Other officials have only one temple (that is, a temple to their late fathers. He has no temple to his great ancestor).[219]

Zhu Xi comments: "Since the common people are not allowed to build ancestral temples, they offer their sacrifices on the east side of their houses in the main chamber. There they place the spirit tablets of their great-great-grandparents, great-grandparents, grandparents, and parents. They also build three-chamber ancestral halls where they worship five generations[220] of ancestors."

Zhu Xi has made a diagram of a three-chamber ancestral hall in the chapter "Understanding the Rites" in the *Correct Practices of Family Rituals*. The spirit tablet of the great-great-grandfather is placed in the middle chamber on the left. The great-great-grandmother's tablet is on his right. Their tablets are side by side. The tablet of the great-grandfather is placed in the same chamber on the right. {p. 88} The great-grandmother's is placed on his left. Their tablets are side by side. The tablet of the grandfather is placed in the east chamber next to the middle chamber. The grandmother's is on his right. The tablet of the late father is placed in the west chamber, and the late mother's is to his right near the west wall. That is the arrangement of the ancestral hall, where the tablets of five generations of ancestors are worshipped. The tablets of previous generations are removed. This is how the secondary branches of the family and clan worship their ancestors.

---

219. This is a slight alteration from verse 26 of the chapter "Royal Regulations" (王制) of the *Record of Rites*: 天子七廟, [左]三昭 [右]三穆, 與太祖之廟而七。諸侯五廟 [左]二昭 [右]二穆, 與太祖之廟而五。大夫三廟, [左]一昭 [右]一穆, 與太祖之廟而三。士一廟 [即考廟, 士無太祖廟]。

220. The five generations include the speaker. Chinese and Vietnamese familial hierarchy counts a total of nine generations: (1) great-great-grandparents (*cao tổ*); (2) great-grandparents (*tằng tổ*); (3) grandparents (*tổ*); (4) late father (*khảo*) and mother (*tỉ*); (5) the subject (*ngã*); (6) children (*tử*); (7) grandchildren (*tôn*); (8) great-grandchildren (*tằng tôn*); (9) great-great-grandchildren (*huyền tôn*).

In the case of the protoancestor and his main line of descent, their descendants must worship them forever and may not remove their tablets. If a family member earns a title and an official position in the imperial court, he must be worshipped as a protoancestor. The eldest son of the family's main line must care for his tomb and the ancestral hall as well as offer sacrifices to the protoancestor forever. A special plot of land, or the "inheritance field" [*hương hoả*], is set aside and passed from eldest son to eldest son. This land provides the means for them to carry out their filial duties. Similarly, in the royal court, the king divides his land and property among his children so that they have the means to carry out their worship duties.

{p. 89}

The Western Scholar comments: The many reasons given to justify a cult for ancestors are merely words to express the breadth of knowledge. However, these practices do not benefit the ancestors. The Lord of Heaven has sent them, as living souls, to live in a place of reward or punishment from whence they are unable to return. If they are still in purgatory, we ask a priest to offer Masses for them. We gather the relatives to pray that the souls of our ancestors will soon ascend to paradise to enjoy eternal blessings. These ritual practices bring actual benefit to the ancestors. Why would one expend resources on conventional rituals that bring no real benefit to the soul, simply to be extolled for fulfilling filial duties? Such behaviors are foolish and futile. Moreover, using sustenance for the body and offering it up to the soul is an act of contempt. Those practicing such rituals are in fact unfilial and violate the practice of our Holy Way.[221]

The Western Scholar asks again: When descendants make offerings to their ancestors, do they actually believe that their ancestors will grant them wealth and honor?

The Eastern Scholar replies: They do believe this. As a result, they strive to make solemn offerings to their ancestors.

The Western Scholar comments: When their parents were alive, they were able to support their children and provide them with a life of riches and honor.

---

[221]. This passage seems to be directed to the Christian converts who might have wanted to retain traditional customs concerning ancestral worship. Catholic Christians often refer to their religion as the "Holy Way" or "Holy Teaching."

{p. 90} After their parents passed away, they could no longer help the children because they were no longer of this world. If the deceased parents had the power to assist their children in this world, why have the fortunes of some devoted worshippers (of parents and ancestors) turned from riches and honor to hardship and destitution? Why is there no help from the ancestors to keep their descendants as wealthy, honored, and prosperous as before? It is the duty of the living to help the dead, not the duty of the dead to help the living. A descendant's duty to arrange solemn funerals for their ancestors is simply repaying a filial debt to those who gave birth to them. This is a great debt that no one can ever repay sufficiently. If descendants believe that their ancestors will reward their efforts with wealth, honor, and longevity, they are gravely mistaken.

{p. 91}

Article 15

On Geomancy

The Western Scholar says: I have noticed that some people request the assistance of geomancers for finding auspicious plots of land to bury their ancestors. I ask you: Why do people use geomancy, and how is it done?

The Eastern Scholar replies: People ask geomancers to locate auspicious burial plots for their ancestors because they believe that by doing so, they will gain wealth, honor, longevity, good fortune, and be blessed with many children. Geomancy originated with Kan Heng during the Chen dynasty,[222] and Yang Juncong[223] followed suit. Liao Yu, who lived during the Tang dynasty, wrote many books on geomancy. He taught that a plot of land should have the following features: The left side of the plot should have an azure dragon [*thanh long*] and on the right, a white tiger [*bạch hổ*]. In the front, there should be an open space [*minh đường*], and in the back, a small hill [*huyền vũ*]. Prosperity will come to those who bury an ancestor in the center of the plot. The left side of the plot should face east and the right side west. The front should face south with the north at the back. [The explanation is as follows:] The left side of the grave, called the azure dragon of the east, should face east, the direction governed by {p. 92} the wood element and the color green. The right side of the grave, called the white tiger of the west, should face west, the direction governed by the metal element and the color white. The front of the grave, called the vermillion bird of the south, should face south, the direction governed by the fire element and the color red. The back of the grave, called the black tortoise of the north, should face north, the direction governed by the water element and the color black.[224]

---

222. Apparently the author is mistaken here, for the Kham Dư Gia (堪輿家) school of diviners/geomancers was already in existence during the Han dynasty. Is it possible that Kan Heng (Kham Hành) was a person in this tradition? For a history of geomancy in premodern China, consult J. J. M. De Groot, *The Religious System of China* (1882; repr., Taipei: Ch'eng Wen Publishing, 1976), 3:982–1010.

223. Yang Juncong (楊君從) of Jiangxi, who lived during the Tang dynasty, was credited to be the founder of the Form School of Chinese *fengshui*, which involves environment analysis based on the observation of forms without the use of a compass.

224. The azure dragon, white tiger, vermillion bird, and black tortoise are mythical creatures that represent the four directions of Chinese constellations.

The Western Scholar comments: Believers in geomancy regard the form and shape of the grave as a channel for good fortune. How can a grave have any power to provide good fortune to the descendants of the person buried there? How can it ensure wealth, fame, children, and longevity, which are gifts granted to us by the Lord of Heaven? Besides, in ancient times, no one knew anything about geomancy, and yet there were people who led lives of wealth, honor, and leisure. Nevertheless, many people have practiced geomancy since the times of the Chen, Sui, and Tang dynasties.[225] Not only has it been useless to them, but it has brought them bad fortunes as well. I imagine that the inventors of {p. 93} geomancy shared the same fate.

The Eastern Scholar says: You are correct! Kan Yu's[226] descendants fell into ruin, Yang Juncong was executed by the king, and Liao Yu was childless. [Another example is] Gao Pian, who lived during the Tang dynasty and was known for his great skills in geomancy.[227] Emperor Tang Yizong [860–874 CE] appointed him governor of Annam. Wherever he saw an auspicious burial spot that he divined might produce a king, he would destroy it so that his own descendants might rule Annam for a long time. However, when Emperor Tang Xizong [r. 874–888] called him back to China, Gao Pian left his grandnephew Gao Yun behind to rule Annam. Collectively they ruled for thirty years. When King Liang Taizu appointed Liu Yan governor of Annam [in 907],[228] Gao Pian's descendants lost their right of succession. In another example, General Huang Fu was sent to invade Annam during the Ming dynasty in order to capture Hồ Quý Ly and his son.[229] After completing his military mission, Huang Fu, a skillful geomancer, stayed in Annam and traveled throughout the country in search of his own auspicious burial plot. Then King Lê Thái Tổ started a revolution against the Ming occupying forces and drove them home. Once again, the Ming emperor sent General Liao Sheng and General Huang Fu to

---

225. Sixth to tenth century CE.

226. It could be that Kan Yu (Kham Dư) and Kan Heng (Kham Hành) are the same person. Both names are used in this Article.

227. Vietnamese legends about his geomancy skills are told in *Lĩnh Nam Chích Quái*, especially in the stories of Mount Tản Viên and Tô Lịch river.

228. In 907. Cf. *Toàn Thư*, Ngoại kỷ, 5:17b (translation, 1:203).

229. Hồ Quý Ly (r. 1400–1401) and his son Hồ Hán Thương (r. 1401–1407) were founders of the brief Hồ dynasty. They were considered usurpers of the Trần thrones. After offering to help the Trần under false pretenses, Ming Chengzu sent troops to invade Vietnam in 1406 and took both of them prisoner.

recapture Annam. King {p. 94} Lê Thái Tổ slew Liao Sheng, captured Huang Fu, and brought him back to China as a prisoner. Such was the fate of Huang Fu, who was skilled in geomancy. Not only did he fail to become a king of Annam, but he also lost a battle and became a prisoner. Such is the efficacy of geomancy!

{p. 95}

BOOK 2: THE ERRORS OF DAOISM

Preface

THE WAYS OF Laozi (Daoism) and Śākyamuni (Buddhism) are the heterodox, alien [dị đoan][1] teachings of emptiness [hư vô] and quiescence [tịch diệt]. These two ways are contrary to morality and cultural norms in every way. They contain nothing good nor anything consistent with the orthodox way (Confucianism), often plotting and scheming against it and telling lies to deceive the ignorant. They also muddy the minds of many noble persons and cause them to lose sight of the right and virtuous way. In addition, the deceiver often speaks with charisma, as if he were speaking the truth. In the same way, Daoism and Buddhism frequently use crafty words resembling the truth in order to make people believe. So when a gentleman hears something, he must examine it thoroughly; no wise person should believe everything he hears because people can fabricate teachings in hopes of becoming famous. They do not always pay attention to whether these teachings have sound reasoning.

{p. 96} Sometimes we inherit things that have been invented by previous generations. These things later become widespread and develop into customs. The people of later generations then claim that they must accept these old rules and ancient customs as norms. Whoever does not follow these norms passed down by their forebears is accused of being wrong and ignorant. As a result, everyone takes on and practices these customs without fully understanding the falsehoods involved. Therefore, in the following two books, I ask the reader to examine the flaws in the two false heterodox doctrines of Laozi and Śākyamuni. I hope that

---

1. *Dị đoan* (yiduan 異端, alien custom) is often understood in the Christian context as "superstition." In Confucian terminology, it only means a strange or different belief. *Mê tín* (mixin 迷信, false belief) is a Confucian word that is closer to the notion of superstition.

people will come to a better understanding of these creeds, steer clear of their deceitful magic and divination, and reject them once and for all. In this way, you will not fall into the trap and harm yourself in this life and in the next. In Book 2, I will discuss the errors of Daoism and other errors that are ostensibly similar to the beliefs of the true way.

{p. 97}

INDEX OF THE ERRORS OF DAOISM

Article 1:   On the Founding of Daoism by Laozi
Article 2:   On the Spread of Daoism by Zhang Yi and Zhang Jue
Article 3:   On the Healing Work of Sorcerers
Article 4:   On the Twelve Yearly Governing Spirits
Article 5:   On the Nine Stars and the Thunder God
Article 6:   On Auspicious and Inauspicious Times
Article 7:   On Hà Bá, Phạm Nhan, and Liễu Hạnh
Article 8:   On Divination
Article 9:   On Astrology and Forecasting Events
Article 10: On the Five Constellations
Article 11: On Physiognomy and Reading Chicken Feet
Article 12: On Solar and Lunar Eclipses

{p. 98}

Article 1

On the Founding of Daoism by Laozi

The Western Scholar says: In this country of Annam, there are many followers of Daoism. So I ask you: Who founded Daoism?[2]

The Eastern Scholar replies: The founder of Daoism was Laozi, also known by the names Lao Tan, the Immortal Lao, and the Lord Lao.[3] Laozi was born in Huguang province[4] on the fifteenth day of the second moon in the seventh year of the reign of Zhou Lingwang [565 BCE]. He lived for eighty-one years and died at Hangu Pass [in Xieli district] in the thirty-fifth year of the reign of Zhou Jingwang [485 BCE]. According to Zhen Xishan in his commentary on the *Analects*, Laozi was a contemporary of Confucius: "Lao Tan, Yang Zhu,[5] and Mo Di (Mozi)[6] all lived during the same era as Confucius." When Confucius was thirty-four years old, "he went to the court of the Zhou emperor to ask Laozi about rituals."[7]

---

2. See also *Opusculum*, Chapter 3, Article 1.

3. Laozi (老子), literally Old Master, is the title given to a person of whom we know little. In *Records of the Grand Historian* (*Shiji*), Sima Tian identifies Laozi as Lao Tan (老聃) and conflates him with Li Er (李耳), a historical person in the Warring States era: "Laozi was a native of the Quren hamlet in Li village, located in the Ku district of the state of Qu. His given name was Er, his school name was Dan, and his family name was Li." Modern scholars have disputed this account. See Fung Yu-lan, *A History of Chinese Philosophy* (Princeton, NJ: Princeton University Press, 1952), 1:171–72.

4. This is now central China.

5. Yang Zhu (楊朱), 370–319 BCE, was a Chinese philosopher during the Warring States period. Known for his egoistical and sophistical alternative to Confucian thought, Yang Zhu's ideas are preserved in chapter 7 of the *Liezi*. See Fung Yu-lan, *A History of Chinese Philosophy*, 1:133–43.

6. Mozi, whose original name was Mo Di (墨翟), 470–391 BCE, was a Chinese philosopher during the Warring States period. He advocated a doctrine of "inclusive love" (*jian ai* 兼愛), which was in opposition to the Confucian attachment to family and clan structures. For Mozi's philosophy, see Fung Yu-lan, *A History of Chinese Philosophy*, 1:76–105; Wm Theodore de Barry and Irene Bloom, *Sources of Chinese Tradition*, 2nd ed. (New York: Columbia University Press, 1999), 1:64–76.

7. Many sources have recounted this episode, but it is likely that the author is quoting from the *Discourse of the Confucian School* (*Kongzi jiayu*).

Legend has it that Laozi lived in his mother's womb for eighty-one years. One day, his mother went out for a walk. While she was resting at the foot of a prune tree, he bit her left side and was born from there; his mother died as a result. It is also written that Lao Tan rode {**p. 99**} a green buffalo to heaven.

The cult of Laozi began when Emperor Song Zhenzong [r. 997–1022] visited the tomb of Laozi and conferred upon him the title of "Supreme Lord Lao" [Thái Thượng Lão Quân]. This happened in the seventh year, the *giáp-dần* year, of Emperor Song Zhenzong [1004 CE]. Later, when Emperor Song Huizong [r. 1100–1126] came into power, he became a devoted Daoist and called himself the lord of Daoism: "The emperor conferred upon himself the title 'Head of Daoism, Emperor Lord of Daoism.'" Sorcerers offered solemn sacrifices to Laozi every year, praying for good fortune and protection from harm.

The Western Scholar asks the Eastern Scholar: Which of Laozi's teachings do people consider fundamental?

The Eastern Scholar replies: In the *Classic of the Way and Power* [*Daodejing*],[8] Laozi taught:

> The Way gave birth to One;
> One gave birth to two;
> Two gave birth to three;
> And Three gave birth to myriads of things.[9]

That is the great way of voidness and spontaneity [*hư vô tự nhiên chi đại đạo*].[10] In addition, Laozi created the arts of magic, alchemy, sorcery, magic potions for immortality, and methods for invoking spirits and offering sacrifices to the deceased.[11]

---

8. The *Đạo Đức Kinh* (*Daodejing* 道德經), commonly ascribed to Laozi, is the most important text of Daoist philosophy. Most scholars today think that the text is an anonymous work from the Warring States era. Renowned for its poetry, it is has been the most translated Chinese text into English since the nineteenth century. For a recent and readable translation by Irene Bloom (1999), see de Barry and Bloom, *Sources of Chinese Tradition*, 1:77–94.

9. Sino-Vietnamese: 道生一，一生二，二生三，三生萬物。虛無自然之大道。 *Daodejing*, chap. 42. Cf. *Hội Đồng Tứ Giáo*, 4a.

10. See also *Errors*, Book 1, Article 1.

11. Here the author wrongly credits Daoist magic and sorcery of later generations to Laozi.

The Western Scholar reasons: It is wrong to regard "nonbeing" as the way. Since "nonbeing" [*hư vô*] is "emptiness" [*không*], how can it have the power to bring anything {p. 100} into existence? If one regards "being" as the way, this has some use for us. But if one sees "nonbeing" as the way, it is of no use to anyone. Moreover, those who seek magic and alchemy reap no rewards from these practices. They only waste money and encounter misfortune all the same. Eastern Scholar, since you are a learned man with a profound knowledge of history, you should be able to testify to what I have said.

The Eastern Scholar says: When the emperors Qin Shi Huang and Han Wudi [r. 141–87 BCE] were destitute, they sought the help of Daoist deities. But these deities failed to help them. Take, for example, Emperor Qin Shi Huang. While he was crossing the sea to Mount Ming Zhou in search of immortality, he died in a storm at sea. Emperor Han Wudi wasted a lot of effort and resources while following the Daoist sect of Huang-Lao.[12] And even though Emperor Tang Xianzong took Daoist medicine, he ended up succumbing to diabetes and dying a laughingstock. Finally, Emperor Song Huizong, a devoted Daoist, performed pious sacrifices. Yet when he was captured and humiliated by the Jin in the northern desert [in 1125], Daoist deities did not help him.[13] We can therefore call Daoism an "empty {p. 101} doctrine," which contains nothing real or beneficial. So I ask you: Has this method ever actually contributed to the art of ruling? Poor fates await those who follow Daoism.

---

12. This second-century sect was also known as *Taiping dao* (太平道, the way of the great peace), which incorporated Daoist philosophy, popular religious beliefs, and Chinese cosmology. Its main deity was Huang Lao, a combination of the Yellow Emperor (Huangdi) and Laozi.

13. After passing the throne to his son, Emperor Huizong (宋徽宗) (r. 1100–1125) and his family were captured when the Jurchen ransacked the Song capital Kaifeng in 1127. He died a prisoner in Manchuria in 1135.

Article 2

On the Spread of Daoism by Zhang Yi and Zhang Jue

The Western Scholar asks the Eastern Scholar: Who spread Daoism?[14]

The Eastern Scholar replies: Daoism spread quickly because members of the Zhang family studied it and passed it on. The first Zhang to take it on was Zhang Liang, a court official of Han state, who later served during the Han dynasty.[15] He studied and practiced Laozi's magic and later passed it on to his descendants. His grandson, Zhang Yi, learned to fly using Laozi's magic and taught many disciples. When Zhang Yi died at the age of thirty, his disciples created a story to honor him: "Our master has ascended to heaven." According to a Daoist story, Emperor Song Huizong once had a dream in which Zhang Yi helped him fight against the rebels. The emperor thought Zhang Yi had become a god,[16] so he conferred upon him the title of "Jade Emperor, {p. 102} Supreme Lord" [Ngọc Hoàng Thượng Đế].[17] According to history, however, Emperor Huizong did not confer that title upon Zhang Yi but rather ascribed it to heaven.[18]

According to Buddhists, the Jade Emperor was the son of King Guang Yen (Quang Nghiêm) of the Miao Le (Diệu Lạc) kingdom. His wife, Queen Bao Yueguang (Bảo Nguyệt Quang), was barren.[19] One night, she dreamt that the Daoist god Yuanshi [Tianzun][20] brought her a little boy. Upon waking,

---

14. See also *Opusculum*, Book 2, Article 2.

15. On Zhang Liang, see *Errors*, Book 1, Article 13. Han (韓) and Han (漢) are written by two different characters.

16. Literally, "attaining the Dao" (*đắc đạo*).

17. Chinese 玉皇上帝 (Yuhuang Shangdi), commonly known in English as the Jade Emperor. Both Chinese Buddhists and Daoists claim him as their own. Buddhists identify him with the Indian god Indra and call him the Jade Emperor (Yudi 玉帝), jade being a symbol of purity. Daoist tradition, however, associates the Jade Emperor with Zhang Daoling (張道陵), one of eight Daoist immortals, not with Zhang Yi. See Werner, *Dictionary of Chinese Mythology*, 598–601.

18. According to E. T. C. Werner, Emperors Zhenzong (宋真宗) (r. 997–1022) and Huizong (宋徽宗) (r. 1100–1125), of the Song dynasty conferred various titles upon Yuhuang. *Dictionary of Chinese Mythology*, 600.

19. These names does not match any historical figures and place, Chinese or Vietnamese.

20. Yuanshi Tianzun (元始天尊) or Primeval Lord of Heaven, is one of the highest deities of religious Daoism, one of the Three Pure Ones (三清). He is said to govern the highest heaven, and later passed on the task to his assistant the Jade Emperor.

she discovered that she was pregnant. The following year, she gave birth to a son on the ninth day of the first month and named him Ngọc Hoàng [Jade Emperor].[21]

The Western Scholar comments: The manner of the Jade Emperor's birth is clearly fictional. He cannot be the son of King Guang Yen, for there is no kingdom by the name of Miao Le on the world map.[22] Besides, if the Jade Emperor were a descendant of the Zhang family, he could not have become the prince of Miao Le.

The Eastern Scholar continues: Later on, Zhang You,[23] {p. 103} an eighth-generation descendant of Zhang Liang renowned for his magic and charms [continued the spread Daoism]. He taught magic to Zhang Jian, who passed it on to Zhang Lu. Then came Zhang Jue[24] of the Luju district, who lived during the time of Han Lingdi [r. 168–188]. He studied the books of the Huang-Lao sect, wrote his own on magic and charms, taught many followers, and took on the appellation of "Daoist Master of Great Peace" [Thái Bình Đạo Trú]. He practiced magic and sorcery and was able to heal people with good results. He traveled all over the country for ten years, enchanting many; his followers numbered more than thirty-thousand. When the Han emperor tried to stop him, Zhang Jue called on his followers to rebel. They wore yellow bands across their foreheads to distinguish themselves from the Han soldiers, thus earning them the name "Yellow Turbans."[25] The Han army attacked them many times without success. Only later was General Cao Cao[26] able to disband them.

There is another account of Zhang Jue: Zhang Jue once went into the forest in search of medicinal herbs. He met an old man, who called him into a cave and

---

21. See also the legend of the Jade Emperor in Werner, *Dictionary of Chinese Mythology*, 600.

22. This argument is repeated in *Hội Đồng Tứ Giáo*, 13b.

23. Also known as Zhang Daoling.

24. Styling himself as the "Great Teacher," Zhang Jue or Zhang Jiao (張角) was the leader of a second-century Daoist movement called the "way of great peace." According to Zhang Jiao, the deity Huang-lao had given him a sacred book called *Essential Keys to Great Peace* (*Taiping Yaoshu* 太平要術).

25. Together with his brothers, Zhang Bao and Zhang Liang, Zhang Jue started the Yellow Turban military campaign the against the Han dynasty in 184. All three brothers died in battle the next year, but the rebellion continued until it was quashed by Cao Cao in 192.

26. Cao Cao (曹操), 155–220, was a warlord and chancellor during the final years of the Eastern Han dynasty. He was posthumously honored as King Wu of the Wei kingdom.

gave him a book entitled *Magical Keys to Great Peace* [*Thái Bình Yếu Thuật*].[27] Zhang Jue asked the old man his name, and the man replied, "I am {p. 104} the spirit of Mount Nanyang." Then the old man suddenly disappeared. Zhang Jue took the book home. In the first month of the following year, there was a plague, and many people fell ill. Based on a recipe from the book, Zhang Jue made a potion. He wrote the characters "Jade Emperor, Supreme Lord" on a piece of paper, burned it, and mixed the ashes with water. He gave the potion to people to drink and thus cured many. As a result, many more people sought out his powers. He called himself "the Great Virtuous Benevolent Master" [Đại Hiền Lương Sư]. Because Zhang Jue practiced magic and taught it far and wide, Daoist magic spread everywhere. During the Tang dynasty, someone put together the *Anthology of Magical Arts* [Âm Dương Tạp Thư]. The book contained deceptions, sorcery, and false promises, including this superstition of choosing an auspicious time to bury the dead, so one's descendants may attain prosperity. People followed these teachings until the Song and Yuan dynasties.

[Daoism in Annam]

The Western Scholar asks the Eastern Scholar: In this country Annam, when did the practice of Daoist sorcery begin?

The Eastern Scholar replies: A Chinese Daoist named Xu Zongdao boarded a merchant ship and arrived in Annam in the year *nhâm-dần*, the fifth year of the *Dade* [great virtue] era of the Yuan dynasty in China and the tenth year of the Hưng Long reign of King Trần Anh Tông [1302]. {p. 105} He settled on a river bank in Yên Hoa[28] and practiced Daoist magic, rituals, and sacrifices.[29] Daoist sorcery then spread throughout the time of King Minh Tông [r. 1314–1329], King Hiến Tông [r. 1329–1341], and King Dụ Tông [r. 1341–1369]. Followers proliferated for over the next fifty years. In the tenth month of the eleventh year of the Đại Trị reign of King Trần Dụ Tông [1368], the king summoned to the capital Daoist priest Huyền Vân, a native of the Chí Linh district in the Eastern

---

27. This is a deliberate play on the homonyms, for the word *yếu* (要) in book *Essential Keys to Great Peace* (*Thái Bình Yếu Thuật* 太平要術) sounds like *yêu* (妖), so the book is called the *Magical Keys to Great Peace* (*Thái Bình Yêu Thuật* 太平妖術). The book may be a variation of the *Taiping jing* (太平經, Scripture of the Great Peace), an important Daoist scripture.

28. Now the Yên Phụ region in Hanoi.

29. See the account in the *Toàn Thư*, Bản kỷ, 6:17a (translation, 1:92).

prefecture. The king asked him about Daoist sorcery and allowed him to settle in the Huyền Thiên grotto.[30] Daoist sorcery has continued there to this day.

The Western Scholar comments: Daoist sorcerers of past and present have always relied on the magic of Laozi. But if their medicine is so effective and they possess the secret of immortality, why was the medicine not used to prolong their lives and save them from death? Take Zhang Jue and his brother Zhang Liang.[31] Zhang Jue died of an illness while fighting King Han Lingdi. His brother went on to lose the battle. After the king's victory, {**p. 106**} he had Zhang Jue's corpse exhumed and cut up into many pieces. He then mounted his head on a spike and displayed it in the capital.[32] Now if Zhang Jue had the power to heal people, why did he not save himself from death? Why did he allow his body be desecrated in such a manner?

---

30. *Toàn Thư,* Bản kỷ, 7:28a.

31. Here Liang (Lương) is written in a different character (梁) from that of Zhang Liang (良), who served under Han Gaozu.

32. This refers to the rebellion of the Yellow Turbans in 184, led by the followers of the Taiping Daoist sect. Zhang Jue and his brothers, Zhang Liang and Zhang Bao, were their leaders. The rebellion was brutally suppressed, but the Han dynasty was severely weakened and soon came to an end.

Article 3

On the Healing Work of Sorcerers

The Western Scholar asks the Eastern Scholar: What do sorcerers do when they treat sick people?[33]

The Eastern Scholar replies: When sorcerers treat the sick, they first conduct sacrificial rituals to Laozi, to the Jade Emperor, to the Governing Spirit of the year,[34] and to other spirits. They make sacrificial offerings to the ancestors of the sick person. They recite prayers to these spirits and ask them to cast out the malevolent spirits afflicting the sick person. They beat drums, ring bells, and shout loudly to scare the harmful spirits away. From time to time, they make a paper boat with a sail and paddles—like a real one—and place it on a pond or a river. Then, they compel the evil spirits to enter that boat, drive the spirits from the sick person, and prevent them from {p. 107} returning to afflict the patient further. Finally, they give the sick person a potion in which the ashes of a therapeutic charm have been mixed with medicine.[35] When needed, they order the sick person to be carried to another house so that the malevolent spirits or souls of their deceased ancestors will not find and afflict them again. Sometimes, sorcerers order the corpse of a deceased relative to be exhumed and reburied in another spot, the idea being that the spirit will stop tormenting their descendants if they are pleased with their new and better location. Other times, sorcerers advise that corpses be exposed to the heat and rain rather than being reburied. The belief is that the deceased will suffer there and then decide to leave the sick person alone. Still other times, sorcerers will send out an assistant to collect the material soul of the sick person using a wand. It is widely known that: "Men have three spiritual souls [*hồn*] and seven material souls [*viá*]; women have three spiritual souls and nine material souls."[36]

In addition, sorcerers often make protective talismans by writing magic characters on pieces of paper. People wear these talismans on their bodies or hang

---

33. See also *Opusculum*, Book 2, Article 3.

34. See *Opusculum*, Book 2, Article 4.

35. For examples of therapeutic charms, see Henri Doré, *Research into Chinese Superstitions* (Shanghai, 1914; repr., Taipei: Ch'eng-wen, 1966), 2:165–209.

36. Vietnamese believe that the soul of a human person has two components: a spiritual, immortal component called *hồn*, and a material component called *viá* or *phách*.

them on their doors. As a result, elephant trainers in the capital seeks out this type of talisman each year so that they may keep their elephants safely contained in the barn. Moreover, female mediums [bà cốt] also treat the sick {p. 108} and perform strange ritual acts. These most commonly include pretending that the soul of a deceased ancestor has taken possession of their bodies. In this ritual, the possessed sorcerers and mediums order the living to bow to the spirits of their ancestors and offer them food. After eating and drinking their fill, they then tell the living silly stories about the dead and their living relatives.

The Western Scholar comments: Sorcerers and female mediums seek only to benefit themselves by consuming the offerings of food. People are cured by good medicine, not by tricks used to deceive them. How can beating a drum and wailing loudly have any power to cure the sick? The sick person only suffers more, or their condition worsens. Even if sorcerers could cure the sick, it would not be because of their skills. It would be because a demonic power helps them deceive people.

The Eastern Scholar continues: Some sorcerers make voodoo dolls[37] and send them out to harass people. The dolls throw dirt into houses, put sand into cooking pots, burn down {p. 109} houses, or visit other such disasters upon the victim.[38] This evil trade also existed during the time of Han Wudi. Once, while the king was taking a nap, he dreamt that three-hundred wooden men were beating him with a stick. Upon waking, the king, thinking that he had been harmed by demonic spirits, ordered Jiang Chong[39] to arrest the crown prince and whomever else may have performed this black magic. The crown prince sent his troops to stop the king's soldiers from arresting him. When he failed to deter them, he ran away, but the king continued to pursue him. The crown prince committed suicide. Later on, the king erected a temple in a lake to commemorate his son. He called it the Palace of Mourning and waited for the soul of his son to return. Although voodoo has been around for a very long time, no one dares practice the art here in this country, Annam. Kings and lords prohibit it under pain of death.

---

37. The doll is made of straw, paper, or wood and has the name of a person inscribed on it.

38. According to *Opusculum* (65), the motivation behind such an act is to compel the victim "to return to the same magicians for liberation from such incommodities or misfortunes; and the magicians will destroy the previous evil deeds with a different magic" (*A Study of Religion*, 167).

39. I am uncertain of the name here.

There are magicians called "hypnotizers" [*thầy thiếp tính*] who can render a medium unconscious as if they were dead. Upon waking, the medium recounts what they witnessed in the underworld concerning the fate and condition of the deceased. The medium claims that their soul has truly traveled to Hades and seen {p. 110} everything with their own eyes. Such talk is deception from the devil.

Article 4

On the Twelve Yearly Governing Spirits

The Western Scholar says: Sorcerers often worship the Governing Spirits [Hành Khiển].[40] So I ask you: Who are these spirits?

The Eastern Scholar replies: Sorcerers originated the story of the twelve kings who had the power to bring calamity to the people under their rotating governance. Each of the twelve was in charge for a year and then replaced by another the following year. During each appointed reign, the ruling king's heavenly army brought plagues and death to the world. People needed to make offerings to appease them.

According to one tradition, worshipping the twelve governing kings originated with the official Mengzong during the Song dynasty. In the first year of the Dương Đức era of King Lê Gia Tông [1672] in Annam, a mandarin named Trịnh Thiên Xuân and a sorcerer named Trịnh {p. 111} Đạo Kiêm—both natives of the Giang Lục commune in the Gia Phúc district of Hạ Hồng county—listed the twelve governing kings in their book *Hồng Lục Thư*. Their names were published on the calendar as follows:[41]

> The Year of the Rat is under the jurisdiction of King Chu, the governing spirit of the star of Thiên Ôn. His assistant minister is Judge Quý.[42]
> The Year of the Buffalo[43] is under the jurisdiction of King Triệu, the governing spirit of the star of Tam Thập Lục Thương. His assistant minister is Judge Khúc.
> The Year of the Tiger is under the jurisdiction of King Nguy, the governing spirit of the star of Mộc Tinh. His assistant minister is Judge Tĩnh.
> The Year of the Cat[44] is under the jurisdiction of King Trịnh, the governing spirit of the star of Thạch Tinh. His assistant minister is Judge Liễu.

---

40. See also *Opusculum*, Chapter 3, Article 4. In Chinese/Vietnamese folk religion, Hành Khiển (行遣) is a deity who controls the world for one year. Since there are twelve years in the cycle, there are twelve deities who take turns governing human affairs. These are seen as troublesome spirits who often bring about natural disasters, plagues, and calamities. Offerings are therefore made at the end and in the beginning of the year to bid farewell to the old deity and welcome the new.

41. See a similar list from modern author Toan Ánh, *Tín Ngưỡng Việt Nam* [Vietnamese Religious Beliefs] (Saigon, 1966; repr. Hochiminh City: Văn Nghệ, 2000), 1:188.

42. These are the names of stars and constellations according to traditional astronomy. I have not been able to identify the Chinese characters for most of these.

43. This is the Year of the Ox in the Chinese calendar.

44. This is the Year of the Hare in the Chinese calendar.

The Year of the Dragon is under the jurisdiction of King Sở, the governing spirit of the star of Hoả Tinh. His assistant minister is Judge Y.

The Year of the Snake is under the jurisdiction of King Ngô, the governing spirit of the star of Thiên Hao. His assistant minister is Judge Hứa.

The Year of the Horse is under the jurisdiction of King Tần, the governing spirit of the star of Thiên Hoa. His assistant minister is Judge Ngọc.

The Year of the Goat[45] is under the jurisdiction of King Tống, the governing spirit of the star of Ngũ Đạo. His assistant minister is Judge Lâm. {p. 112}

The Year of the Monkey is under the jurisdiction of King Tề, the governing spirit of the star of Ngũ Miêu. His assistant minister is Judge Tống.

The Year of the Rooster is under the jurisdiction of King Lỗ, the governing spirit of the star of Sơn Nhạc. His assistant minister is also Judge Khúc.

The Year of the Dog is under the jurisdiction of King Việt, the governing spirit of the star of Thiên Cẩu. His assistant minister is Judge Việt.

The Year of the Boar is under the jurisdiction of King Lưu, the governing spirit of the star of Ngũ Ôn. His assistant minister is Judge Nguyễn.

These twelve kings were formerly vassal lords appointed by the Zhou emperors. The sorcerers use this chart to make offerings to the appropriate calamity king of the year in order to save people from illness.

The Western Scholar comments: The twelve kings were feudal lords appointed by the Zhou. Since they did not exist before that time, who was the spirit that governed life and death? If these Governing Spirits caused death, how did the people of the Xia and Shang periods survive before the Zhou era? Moreover, if these spirits accepted offerings that protected people from death and disability, {p. 113} why were there so many deaths during the year of the plague? Since the Governing Spirits have no power at all, we should not make offerings to them.

The Eastern Scholar says: According to the *Compendium* [Tống Luận], "after moving the capital to the East, Zhou's descendants became incompetent. As a consequence, their vassal lords seized power."[46] Since the lords of these vassal states were disloyal to the king of Zhou, they did not deserve to become Governing Spirits in heaven. Moreover, if these Governing Spirits made people sick in order to obtain offerings, they were corrupt and unrighteous. Consequently, one must not believe that they have any power.

---

45. This is the Year of the Sheep in the Chinese calendar.

46. Sino-Vietnamese: 周室東遷之後, 王政不行, 諸侯多僭. I have been not able to identify the full title of this work.

Article 5

On the Nine Stars and the Thunder God

The Western Scholar says: When sorcerers treat people, they often make offerings to the stars. So I ask you: Which stars are the sources of troubles?

The Eastern Scholar says: Sorcerers often consult *Hồng Lục Thư*,[47] in which there is a chart of nine stars. The book lists their names and the troubles they bring:[48]

> The La Hầu constellation has nine stars. {p. 114} At *hợi* hour (9:00–11:00 p.m.) on the eighth of each month, the stars descend to the southern part of the sky. A man born during that time—the hour of La Hầu or hour of "trouble in mouth and tongue"—will have diseases of the eyes, throat, and mouth; a woman will have diseases of the blood as well as difficult childbirths.
>
> The Thổ Tú constellation has five stars. At *hợi* hour (9:00–11:00 p.m.) on the ninth of each month, the stars descend to the central part of the sky. Anyone born during that time—the hour of Thổ Tú or hour of the "disastrous star"—will not have peace at home. They will often fall ill, have trouble raising cattle, and encounter disaster when traveling.
>
> The Thủy Diệu constellation has six stars. At *hợi* hour (9:00–11:00 p.m.) on the twenty-first of each month, the stars descend to the northern part of the sky. A man born during that time—the hour of Thủy Diệu or hour of the "auspicious star"—will be prosperous, but a woman will not.
>
> The Thái Bạch constellation has eight stars. At *tuất* hour (7:00–9:00 p.m.) on the fifteenth of each month, the stars descend to the western part of the sky. Anyone born during that time—the hour of Thái Bạch [or hour of "trouble"]—will often meet misfortune and would do best to watch out for trouble.
>
> The Thái Dương constellation has ten stars. At *hợi* hour (9:00–11:00 p.m.) on the twenty-seventh of each month, the stars descend to the eastern part of the sky. A man born during that time—the hour {p. 115} of Thái Dương

---

47. I have not been able to locate this work.
48. See a similar list by Toan Ánh, *Tín Ngưỡng Việt Nam*, 2:214–18.

[or hour of "great yang"], will be intelligent and wealthy, but a woman will be sickly and attract trouble.

The Vân Hán constellation has fifteen stars. At *hợi* hour (9:00–11:00 p.m.) on the twenty-ninth of each month, the stars descend to the southern part of the sky. Anyone born during that time—the hour of Hoả [Đức] or "disastrous star"—will have misfortune, disasters, difficulty in childbirth, and trouble raising cattle. They must guard themselves against troubles.

The Kế Đô constellation has twelve stars. At *tuất* hour (7:00–9:00 p.m.) on the twenty-eighth of each month, the stars descend to the western part of the sky. Anyone born during that time—the hour of Kế Đô or hour of the "inauspicious star"—will attract disaster. If they move away, they will be prosperous; if they stay at home, they will be poor and lowly.

The Thái Âm constellation has seven stars. At *tuất* hour (7:00–9:00 p.m.) on the twenty-sixth of each month, the stars descend to the northern part of the sky. A man born during that time—the hour of Thái Âm or hour of the Chú Dương star—will be prosperous, but a woman will meet misfortune and fall into poverty.

The Mộc Đức constellation has twenty stars. At *tuất* hour (7:00–9:00 p.m.) on the twenty-fifth of each month, the stars descend to the eastern part of the sky. A man born during that time—the hour of Mộc Tinh or hour of Càn Nguyên—will have diseases of the eyes. A woman will have diseases of the blood, and a husband and wife {**p. 116**} will quarrel.

The practice of performing sacrifices to the stars in order to change one's fortune originates from Nghiêm Quân Bình.[49]

The Western Scholar comments: If offering sacrifices to the constellations brings about good fortune and protection from disaster and disease, why do the people who perform sacrifices still have diseases and trouble? Why do the people who did not offer sacrifices remain prosperous and healthy? One should not make sacrifices to the stars.

[On the Thunder God]

The Eastern Scholar says: The school of sorcerers also originated the story of the Thunder God, Chief Messenger Trương, who often takes the form of a hawk. When he is angry, he shouts out thunder and lightning in five directions—east,

---

49. I have not been able to identify this person.

west, north, south, and central—striking people, animals, and trees. People become frightened when they hear his booming voice. For this reason, sorcerers often give people a replica of a thunderbolt so that they may protect themselves against being struck by the Thunder God.

The Western Scholar says: You should not believe this story. Thunder and lightning are caused by the heat that is produced when hot and cold air come into contact with each other. When vapor {**p. 117**} or cold air meets dry or hot air, it makes a sound. When dry air hits cold air, it creates lightning. The sound that lightning makes when it strikes is called thunder. Wherever lightning strikes, it destroys. Anyone who does not believe this can take a piece of hot, burning iron and stick it into cold water. Will he not see that the hot and cold air clash and cause sparks? Will he not hear the noise this makes? Whoever has thought about this will know that thunder and lightning are caused by cold and hot air, not by a Thunder God named Chief Messenger Trương.

The Eastern Scholar says: Western Scholar, what you have just said is also written in *Outline of Pharmacopoeia* [Cương Mục Bản Thảo].[50] The book criticizes the custom of a certain country whose people cast thunderbolts every year, offering them up to the Thunder God so that he might make thunder.

---

50. The pharmacopeia *Bencao Gangmu* (本草綱目) by Li Shizhen (李時)is a manual of Chinese medicine. I have not been able to locate the materials on thunderbolts in this book.

Article 6

On Auspicious and Inauspicious Times

The Western Scholar says: Sorcerers often warn people to watch out for auspicious days and avoid inauspicious days. I ask you: What is this custom all about?

The Eastern Scholar says: Sorcerers create these deceptions to make people fearful. Then they perform rituals to combat a victim's {**p. 118**} misfortune, showing off their power and taking offerings from people for helping them. Sorcerers also claim that there are ill-fated years and preordained times of disaster. There are days of death, days to kill, days on which one is prone to drowning, and certain hours when accidents are likely to happen. Sorcerers tell people to avoid these inauspicious times, appease the spirits, and make sacrifices of atonement.

In ancient times, there were no guidelines regarding lucky or unlucky hours and days. People did not choose favorable times to act or unfavorable times to avoid action. In modern times, the Tang era *Anthology of Magical Arts* [Âm Dương Tạp Thư][51] spreads the lies and deceptions of sorcerers, claiming that by acting on lucky days during lucky hours, one can be prosperous. By avoiding unlucky days and hours, one can avoid mishaps.

Two people from Gia Phúc district, Hạ Hồng county—the mandarin Trịnh Thiên Xuân and the sorcerer Trịnh Đạo Kiêm—wrote up these practices in *Hồng Lục Thư*. Their book appeared in Annam in the first year of the Dương Đức era of King Lê Gia Tông [1672 CE]. The authors also composed and distributed astral charts for sorcerers to follow.

The Western Scholar comments: Why do people need to choose a favorable time to act? Results are good or bad not because of auspicious or inauspicious timing but because people {**p. 119**} do good and avoid evil. If there are lucky or unlucky days, then why do twins, born of the same mother on the same day and time, end up with different fortunes? Why is one wealthy and elegant but the other poor and base? Why does one enjoy longevity but the other a short lifespan? Their fortunes are determined not by timing but by the Lord of Heaven.

---

51. I have not been able to locate this work.

The Eastern Scholar says: Let us reflect further.[52] In ancient times, when King Wu fought King Zhou on *giáp tí* day,[53] King Wu won the battle and killed King Zhou. If that day was so lucky, why did King Zhou lose? And if that day was unlucky, why did King Wu win? King Wu became king because he was virtuous; King Zhou was evil, so he lost his kingdom.[54] Moreover, one should take no heed in one's "day of death" by avoiding going out to work or to conduct business. Life and death are natural phenomena; birth and death occur every day. People die not because of unlucky days but because of other causes. That is why many deaths occur every day. The great Lord in heaven decides how long a person lives; a person will die when his or her date of death arrives.

---

52. This may be a scribal error, for the argument is from the Western Scholar's view.
53. The first day of a sixty-year cycle.
54. See the story of how King Zhou lost the battle in *Errors,* Book 1, Article 13.

{p. 120}

Article 7

On Hà Bá, Phạm Nhan, and Liễu Hạnh

The Western Scholar asks: Since sorcerers and female mediums often act in the names of Hà Bá, Phạm Nhan, and Liễu Hạnh, can you explain the origins of these three spirits?

[The Duke of the River]

The Eastern Scholar answers: Hà Bá is the spirit of the river.[55] During the time of King Wei Lie, in the Warring States era, in the *giáp-tí* year or ninth year of his reign [417 BCE], Duke Ai of Qin wanted to build a citadel along the Long river. The duke offered Hà Bá his daughter's hand in marriage to gain his support. In accordance with Qin custom, the King of Wei made his people offer a bride to the spirit of river. The people of Wei suffered greatly because of this custom.

[Another explanation is that] in the Three Kingdoms era [221–265 CE], there was a man from the Huayin district who was able to lift a large eight-sided rock that revealed a source of drinking water. Later, people called him the Duke of the River (Hà Bá).

The common people believe that Hà Bá is the king of deep water who often goes up the mountain to get stone and lumber.[56] They also believe that girls drown because the king of water wants to take a bride. Sorcerers and mediums originated a story saying that {p. 121 (211)} when people cross a river or a well and later become ill, it is because the Duke of the River has captured their souls; they must make offerings to him to regain them. In addition, when carrying a funeral casket on a boat, one must make offerings to Hà Bá [to ensure safe passage].

---

55. In China, there are specific guarding spirits for different bodies of water: the great seas, rivers, streams, lakes, ponds, and wells. In Vietnam, Hà Bá (河伯) is a name for the spirit of the river who is associated with flooding and drowning. Certain parts of Vietnam today still suffer from annual floods; consequently, temples and shrines dedicated to him are often located in major watercourses in the Mekong Delta (South Vietnam) and Hue (Central Vietnam).

56. This is a myth to explain flood and landslide.

The Western Scholar comments: Hà Bá does not have the power to capture anyone's soul. If one has to get back one's soul from him in order to live, then why do so many people survive illnesses without doing anything except taking medication? And why do people still die despite making offerings to him? If Hà Bá has the power to save people, why did the people of Wei, who worshipped him, lose their country to the Qin? And why did the Qin surrender to the Han despite the fact that they worshipped him? Therefore, do not believe in the power of Hà Bá.

[Phạm Nhan]

The Eastern Scholar says: Phạm Nhan was born in the Ming era.[57] His father Nguyễn Bá Tiên, or Nguyễn Bá Quang, came from the Dihong stream area, in the Minglei district of Yinzhu county in China. His mother was Nguyễn Thị Tri, an Annamese from the Đồng Trật commune in the Đông Triều district of Kinh Chu county. Phạm Nhan's nickname was "hammer boy" (thằng Búa), his formal name was Nguyễn Bá Linh, and he was also known as Phạm Thạch or Phạm Thành. {p. 122 (212)}

During the reign of Trần Anh Tông [r. 1294–1314 CE], he sneaked into the royal harem and committed fornication. The king sent the Great Prince Hưng Đạo whose name was Trần Quốc Tuấn[58] to capture him. The criminal was executed and cut into three pieces. At the moment of disembodiment, a demon entered his body and called himself the Prince Consort Phạm Nhan. Any woman who is possessed by Phạm Nhan can rid herself of him by going to a sorcerer. The sorcerer captures and imprisons Phạm Nhan by using red ink to write an amulet on a piece of yellow paper. He then writes a mandate ordering King [Trần] Anh Tông to send the Great Prince Hưng Đạo to kill the demon.[59]

---

57. This should be during the Yuan dynasty (1257–1368). If Phạm Nhan lived during the reign of Trần Anh Tông (1294–1314) and was executed by Prince Hưng Đạo (d. 1300), he must have lived in the late thirteenth century.

58. Trần Quốc Tuấn, whose title was Prince Hưng Đạo (1228–1300), was a military commander of the Trần dynasty. Considered a national hero after repelling two invasions by the mighty Mongol armies, he has been worshipped by Vietnamese as the divine protector of the nation. There are many temples dedicated to him, and his cult still exists today.

59. The story of Phạm Nhan seems to be based on the account in the appendix concerning the legends associated with Prince Hưng Đạo in the *Việt Điện U Linh Tập*. In this fourteenth-century work, the story is told as follows: "Phạm Nhan's name was Nguyễn Bá Linh. His father was a merchant in Guangdong province, and his mother was from An Bài village in our

Book 2: The Errors of Daoism   255

The Western Scholar comments: Phạm Nhan is a criminal. If the king had him executed, why do sorcerers believe him to have the power to harm people? Besides, sorcerers are commoners. By whose authority can they order King [Trần] Anh Tông to have Prince Hưng Đạo capture a demon for them? Moreover, the king had already had Phạm Nhan executed once before. So why did he have to have it done again? This story is nonsense, not worth listening to.

[Princess Liễu Hạnh]

The Eastern Scholar says: I already mentioned Liễu Hạnh in Article 10 of the first book. However, {p. 123 (213)} I have not told the sorcerer's account of her story:[60] Liễu Hạnh was the daughter of Đế Thích or the Jade Emperor.[61] Her father sent her spirit down to the hill of Vân Cát in Annam, where it wandered until she was born into the Lê family in the An Thái commune in the Thiên Bản district of Nghĩa Hưng county in Sơn Nam prefecture. When she died at the age of thirty-seven, her spirit took on human form again and traveled throughout the country. When she came to the Nghệ An region in the Duyên (or Lục) Quán area, she opened a concession stand. One day, a young scholar stopped by for refreshment. Struck by her beauty, he married her, and they had a son. When the child was three years old, Liễu Hạnh told her husband, "I am the daughter of Indra. The Jade Emperor sent me down to the world to be the daughter of the Lê family, and I took human form. Now it is time

---

country. He earned a doctorate at the Yuan court. Since he had excellent magical skills, he often sneaked into the royal harem and committed fornication. He was caught and sentenced to execution. However, since the Yuan army was planning to attack our country, Bá Linh volunteered to be their guide in exchange for sparing his life. In the battle at Bạch Đằng river, he was captured by Prince Hưng Đạo and was decapitated in his mother's village. His head was thrown into the river. . . . Before being executed, he asked the prince: 'What are you going to give me to eat?' The prince angrily answered: 'You can eat the blood from birth deliveries.' Thus, after his death, Bá Linh's spirit was left to wander the country. Whenever he sees a woman giving birth, he possesses her, and she immediately goes into a coma—no medicine can bring her out of it. Relatives of the ill woman come to the temple of Prince Hưng Đạo to pray. They take an old mat belonging to the temple and quickly cover the patient with it or have her lie on it. Next, they give the patient a potion of water mixed with an offering of incense ashes to revive her. In some cases, just bringing the mat home is enough to facilitate the recovery process. How marvelous is the power of Prince Hưng Đạo!" (my translation).

60. Many legends about Liễu Hạnh have circulated since the eighteenth century. One version may be preserved here in *Errors*. Apparently, Liễu Hạnh's cult was so popular in the eighteenth century that the author of *Errors* found it necessary to cover her twice, in Book 1, Article 1 and here in Book 2, Article 7.

61. It seems like the author conflates Đế Thích and Ngọc Hoàng (Jade Emperor) as the same person.

for me to return home; you must stay here and raise our son." After saying this, she disappeared and went [back] to the An Thái commune. She appeared as a beautiful girl in fine clothing who seduced travelers with magic. Her fame spread throughout the area. The Lord [Trịnh] honored her with the title Princess Liễu Hạnh, also known as Lady Thắng. A temple was built for her {p. 124 (214)} with two finely dressed women standing in attendance at the left and right of her statue. She often appears in the form of a young girl to seduce and hypnotize men, saying: "I am taking your soul. If you want to live, you must worship me." Therefore, people worship her everywhere. In their homes, there is a picture of her seated and flanked by her two attendants.

The Western Scholar comments: Liễu Hạnh is a demon, not a being from heaven. A celestial being is chaste and does not engage in seducing scholars and men as she did. She is surely a goddess of lust, and her temple is a temple of lust. We must practice scholar Hồ Dīnh's advice and burn down temples of lust whenever we pass one.

The Eastern Scholar says: There are many other deities and spirits that sorcerers and mediums rely on and pray to:[62] Mạnh Tông,[63] the One-legged God [Độc Cước],[64] Xưng Số Sát, the Three Honorables [Tam Danh],[65] the Three Leaders [Tam Đầu],[66] the Three Persons [Tam Vị],[67] Tử Dương,[68] the Nine

---

62. Many of the deities and spirits listed here might be particular to the region where this manuscript was written. Some names are generic and obscure, for example, the Three Names or the Three Heads, etc. There is a similar listing of names in *Opusculum*, Chapter 3, Article 5, 172–75.

63. The person who is said to have conceived of the annual worship of the 12 Governing Spirits. See *Errors*, Book 2, Article 4 above.

64. A warrior god from China, the "one-legged" deity is worshipped by mediums and sorcerers. For more information, see *A Study of Religion*, 173n81.

65. According to Dror (*A Study of Religion*, 173–74n83), Xưng, Số, Sắt (or Sưng, Sỏ, Sắt in *Opusculum*) are the names of the Three Honorables (Tam Danh). However, it is also possible that "Tam Danh" is a corruption of "Tam Thanh," the high deities of Daoism.

66. This spirit is not identified, but it is possibly a corruption of Tam Đảo, a mountain in North Vietnam.

67. This spirit is not identified.

68. According to the information given in *Opusculum* (70), Tử Dương was a criminal who lived during the Han dynasty. Since he terrified others with his impiety, he is venerated to prevent him from doing harm.

Tails [Cửu Vĩ],[69] King Dóng,[70] King Càn,[71] King Đinh,[72] King Bạch Hạc,[73] King Mê Hê,[74] Lady Quế,[75] Lady Trì,[76] the Water King (Thủy Tế), and the Water Creature (thủy tộc).[77]

---

69. Dror suggests that this spirit is a water spirit. See *A Study of Religion*, 175–76nn92, 94.

70. The legend of King Dóng was mentioned in *Errors*, Book 1, Article 10.

71. This spirit has not been identified.

72. This refers to King Đinh Tiên Hoàng (r. 968–979), who freed Vietnam from a warlord, united the country, and established the imperial tradition. His main temple is located in the ancient capital Hoa Lư in Ninh Bình province.

73. His story appears in *Việt Điện U Linh Tập*. When the official Lý Thường Minh built a temple in the Bạch Hạc region, he invited powerful spirits to come and be worshipped. Two spirits appeared and competed against each other. The winner was declared the guardian spirit of that region.

74. According to Dror (*A Study of Religion*, 146n151), this may be a reference to Lady Mỵ Ê, the wife of Champa's king Sạ đấu. Upon her capture by the Vietnamese, she committed suicide in a display of loyalty to her husband. Lady Mỵ Ê is honored by Vietnamese, and her story appears in *Việt Điện U Linh Tập*.

75. According to Dror (*A Study of Religion*, 146n151), Lady Quế is one of Princess Liễu Hạnh's attendants.

76. *Opusculum* (71) records this as "Chúa Trì" (Lady of the Pond).

77. The Water King and the Water Creature are generic names for spirits of giant fish or other sea creatures. Fishermen often worship them for protection.

{p. 125 (215)}

Article 8

On Divination

The Western Scholar says: Now let us discuss the practices of sorcerers, such as divination, fortunetelling, astrology, reading chicken feet, and physiognomy. Those who engage in these practices copy the rituals and assist one another. Since people often seek divination and diviners are many, I ask you: How do diviners practice divination?[78]

The Eastern Scholar replies: In ancient times, King Fuxi saw, in the River Meng, a kind of dragon-horse[79] that had markings with a particular pattern. The pattern had eight parts: At the top there were nine dots, at the bottom one, on the left three, on the right seven, on the top left and top right two and four respectively, on the bottom left and bottom right six and eight respectively, and five in the center. Fuxi took the eight directions from this chart drawn on the dragon-horse's back and created the eight trigrams: *qian, kan, gen, zhen, xun, li, kun,* and *dui*. He then expanded them— eight times eight—to 64 hexagrams of 6 lines each, a total of 384 lines.

Later, King Wen [of Zhou] assigned a name and a meaning to each hexagram, and the Duke of Zhou provided explanations for each line. Confucius then added the "Great Appendix" [*Hệ Từ*], {p. 126 (216)} which records the stories of past kings for the purpose of teaching morality to younger generations. At the age of fifty, Confucius studied the *Classic of Changes* and adopted the doctrine of the mean as his guiding moral principle. Consequently, he did not engage in excessive behaviors. Instead, he examined the pros and cons of such behaviors for the purpose of self-correction. People of the past used the *Classic of Changes* as a guide for moral living, doing good, and avoiding evil.

In later eras, diviners took the eight trigrams from the *Classic of Changes* and turned the three lines of each trigram *qian, kan, gen, zhen, xun, li, kun,* and *dui* into a means of divination.[80] Nowadays, they pray to Fuxi, King Wen, the Duke of Zhou, Confucius, the great saints, the great sages, and other spirits for assistance in fortune-telling. Afterward, they examine the correspondences and

---

78. See also *Opusculum*, Chapter 4, Article 1.

79. A mythical beast.

80. Each of the eight trigrams is made up of three lines: solid (yang) or broken (yin).

Book 2: The Errors of Daoism

oppositions among the five elements, metal, wood, water, fire, and earth, to determine whether the event in question would be beneficial or destructive. They then divine by throwing two coins.[81]

When a person consults a diviner, he brings money and a plate of betel leaves that the diviner offers to the spirits. The diviner holds the plate of betel leaves above his head and prays to the spirits of the sages, asking them to help him reveal the fortune. The client also prays to the spirits of the sages in silence: "I ask the sages for a sign—good or bad—{p. 127 (217)} concerning my family affairs, household business, family relationships, and any disturbances in of my ancestors' tombs. Please assist the diviner in telling me my fortune." Then the diviner takes the coins and throws them into a basin three times, saying: "The first line of a trigram ... the second line ... the third line." Each time, he reads the coins to see whether the result is yang (one heads, one tails) or yin (two coins that have landed on the same side). Then, considering the corresponding trigram, he says: "Is it true that in the past few years you have suffered a misfortune, loss of goods, sickness or injury? If you agree with this assessment, I will tell you more." In saying this, he forces the client to agree, for who does not experience some sort of misfortune in a period of three or four years? If the diviner is unable to make a prediction, he says: "This forecast is unfavorable [*bất thuận*]. There is no explanation in the divination book."

If he fails to make a prediction about a particular issue, he will move on to another or offer a suggestion, such as making a proper reburial because the tomb of the client's ancestors has been disturbed. He might also suggest making monetary or other offerings to the spirits because one of the client's ancestors has made a transgression in the underworld. In this way, the client pays the diviner to restore peace to the household; otherwise, lives and wealth will be lost. The diviner also says things like: "If a husband and wife have incompatible astrological signs, they must pretend to divorce {p. 128 (218)} and then remarry so that they can live together peacefully." To those having difficulty raising a healthy child, he says: "Give up the child to another family for adoption; then the child will live." Or to those who suffer misfortunes in their households, he says: "A fierce spirit or a fire spirit is occupying the land; a magician must be hired to make a talisman to control it. Then everything will be fine." Or he says: "The main road or a side street has interrupted the energy [of the house] or there is a disturbance in a particular direction. A stone dog must be buried to guard that direction; then the trouble will be gone." He also says: "There is trouble in the household because of

---

81. The two-coin divination is called *xin [quẻ] âm dương* (asking for the sign of yin or yang) in Vietnamese. If the coins land on the same side, this is yin, which is bad. If one coin lands heads and the other tails, this is yang, which is good.

incompatible astrological signs among family members. This often causes sickness. Lady Liễu Hạnh must be worshipped in the house, a special bamboo [*trúc đài*] must be planted in the yard outside, and incense offerings must be made to heaven in the evening." The fortuneteller listens for a client's accidental disclosures and sees them as opportunities for creating business and making money.

The Western Scholar comments: Because people are ignorant and uncritical, they consult diviners whenever they have to decide something. And diviners often worship guardian spirits in their houses. These spirits are the devil, who is a liar. When a diviner or female medium makes predictions by casting coins, the devil assists them by talking about this or that trouble in order to scare people or give them cause for concern. Then, they do whatever the diviner tells them to do. {**p. 129 (219)**} Evil spirits often possess male and female mediums and tell people strange things that send them into a panic. Since people tend to seek life and avoid death, they will do whatever the diviner tells them. Hence, is divination not an evil practice? After consulting a diviner, one begins to worry. As a proverb goes, "Breath produces vapor; divination produces ghosts." Through divination, one brings home a ghost and invites evil. It is a waste of time and resources. There is no benefit.

The Eastern Scholar says: The history books say that "after the decline of the Shaohao[82] era, people became terrified and began to deceive one another with the stories of gods and demons. Every family practiced mediumship and profaned sacrifices; subsequently, disasters increased."[83] Any generation fond of divination will meet the same fate.

---

82. King Shao Hao is a legendary figure. He was said to be the elder son of Yellow Emperor (Huang Di), who was the mythic sage-king of prehistoric China.

83. Sino-Vietnamese: 少昊時衰，天下之人，相懼以神，相惑以怪，家為巫史，民瀆于祀，災害荐至。

Article 9

On Astrology and Forecasting Events

The Western Scholar says: I have heard that many people engage in the arts of astrology and event-forecasting. So I ask you: What are these practices?

The Eastern Scholar replies: During the Spring and Autumn era, there was a man named Wang Xu,[84] also known as Master Guigu, who practiced the art of astrological divination in the state of Jin. He wrote a book on divination entitled *Four Letters to Discern One's Fate* [Tứ Tự Kinh Tiên Định Số]. A diviner uses a person's date and time of birth {**p. 130 (220)**} to chart that person's horoscope. Consider, for example, a person born in *giáp-tí* year in *ất-sửu* month on *bính-dần* day at *đinh-sửu* hour.[85] These four letters will generate a reading of the person's fate. In this art of divination, there are six readings. The first reading is on personal matters and determines whether a person's life will be good or bad. The second reading focuses on the family and reveals the number and fate of their siblings. The third reading centers on career life and looks at whether a person will have success or failure. The fourth reading examines marriage and predicts whether the person will live in harmony with their spouse. The fifth reading predicts how many children the person will have and looks at their futures. The sixth reading involves a prediction of later life to see whether this person will have longevity. That is the art of astrological divination originating from Master Guigu.

The art of event forecasting goes back to Sun Bin,[86] a disciple of Master Guigu. Sun Bin created the art of event forecasting when he used his fingers to calculate and

---

84. Wang Xu (王詡), better known as Master Guigu (鬼谷子), was a founder of the School of Diplomacy (縱橫家, "School of Vertical and Horizontal") during the Warring States period. He was known for his strategic and diplomatic skills. According to historian Sima Qian, Guiguzi was the teacher of famous diplomats, statesmen, and military strategists, including Su Qin, Zhang Yi, Sun Bin, and Pang Juan. Popular belief ascribes the art of fortune-telling to him.

85. As explained before, the Vietnamese and Chinese share a similar lunar calendar of a sexagenary cycle. Each year, month, day, and hour are assigned a name that is a pairing of one of the ten heavenly stems with one of the twelve earthly branches. The cycle begins with *giáp-tí* and ends with *quý-hợi*.

86. Sun Bin (孫臏) was a military strategist who lived during the Warring States period. He was tutored in military strategy by the hermit Guiguzi. While serving in the state of Wei, he was accused of treason. His sentence was having his face tattooed and his kneecaps removed, which rendered him handicapped for life. Sun later escaped from Wei and rose to prominence

determine whether an action was favorable or not. In this system, the twelfth month is called *thân hậu tí*, the eleventh *đại cát sửu*, the tenth *công tào dần*, the ninth *thái xung mẹo*, the eighth *thiên trác thìn*, the seventh {p. 131 (221)} *thái ất tị*, the sixth *thắng quang ngọ*, the fifth *tiểu cát mùi*, the fourth *truyền tống thân*, the third *tòng khôi dậu*, the second *a khôi tuất*, and the first *đăng minh họi*. Based on these months, one can calculate the good and bad events that are in store for a person.

Both Sun Bin and Pang Juan[87] were disciples of Master Guigu, and both served in the Wei court. Since Pang Juan was jealous of Sun Bin's superior skills, he plotted against Sun Bin and cut off his left leg. After the incident, a Qi envoy rescued Sun Bin and brought him to Qi. King Wei of Qi made him his military advisor. When going into battle, Sun Bin would stay in the carriage and calculate conditions favorable for victory. Later, when Qi attacked Wei, Pang Juan lost the battle and committed suicide.

Those who foretell marital relationships compare the man and woman's year, month, day, and hour of birth to predict when the couple should marry or whether they will be able to sustain a lifelong relationship. The art of predicting [a good] marriage originates with a Song official named Li Chunfeng.[88] The king of Song was suddenly attacked by his enemies, and his troops were unable to arrive in time to save him. So Li Chunfeng devised a scheme to help the king by giving him his daughter's hand in marriage and putting together a book of divinations as a wedding gift. In the book, he named the eight words—the year, month, day, and hour—that were auspicious times to go into {p. 132 (222)} battle. Using the eight letters (as a code to attack) was a military tactic. In later generations, however, many things were added to this book to misinform people.

---

in the state of Qi by serving as a military strategist and commander. He is the author of a tactical manual that bears his name: *Sun Bin's Art of War*.

87. Pang Juan (龐涓) was a military general of the state of Wei during the Warring States period. A classmate of Sun Bin, he was jealous of the latter's talents and secretly plotted against him while the two were serving under King Hui of Wei (known in the book *Mencius* as Liang Huiwang). Accused of treason, Sun Bin nearly lost his life and was forced to escape from Wei. The two became sworn enemies when Sun Bin learned of Pang Juan's betrayal. At the battle of Maling between Wei and Qi (432 BCE), Pang Juan was ambushed by Sun Bin's army and killed in battle.

88. The author might be confusing this person with a famous Sui-Tang mathematician and astronomer named Li Chunfeng (李淳風, 602–670) who worked at the Imperial Astronomy Bureau and was responsible for instituting calendar reform (which adds intercalary months to the lunar calendar). Li is the author of a number of treatises on mathematics and numerology. Because of his reputation as a skillful astrologer, a few works on divination and esoteric practices were later credited to him.

The Western Scholar says: If it is possible to use the art of divination to predict favorable conditions for taking action and avoiding disaster, no one would have to endure hardship. If Guigu was skilled enough in the art of divination to write about it, why was he unable to predict that one of his disciples would lose his leg? Why did he not warn him? If Sun Bin was such a master in the art of event-forecasting, why did he not know that Pang Juan was going cut off his leg? Why did he not avoid him? And if Guigu had taught his two disciples the art of warfare, why did he not know that they would later use it to fight each other to the death? Therefore, books on divination and the art of event-forecasting are useless and do not predict anything.

The Eastern Scholar further comments: In the time of Tang Taizong, an official named Lü Cai[89] criticized the book *The Fate of Fortune* [Lộc Mệnh]. He said to the emperor: "People who were born at the same time should share the same fortune, yet their wealth and status are different—one person is rich, and the other is poor. Consider twins delivered from the same womb but with different life spans. One lives, and the other dies [in infancy]. Their fates are not the same. Obviously, the claims made in the book *The Fate of Fortune* are not true."{p. 133 (223)}. People respected Lü Cai for his words of reason.

---

89. Lü Cai (呂才) was a Chinese musician during the reign of Tang Taizong (r. 626–649). Lü was also good at alchemy, astronomy, mathematics, history, and geography. I cannot confirm his view on fortunetelling as described in the text here.

Article 10

On the Five Constellations

The Western Scholar says: There are people who look to the Five Constellations to predict the future. So I ask you: What are the Five Constellations that these people are basing their predictions on?

The Eastern Scholar replies: The manual of warfare recounts the following story: During the Han dynasty, there was a certain person named Zhang Liang[90] who came to Xiali. One night, a deity gave him a book to teach him the art of warfare. Zhang Liang used the book to help the Han king conquer the country. When he died, the book was not passed on to anyone but was put in a pillow and buried with him. Later, in the time of the Jin dynasty, five people dug up Zhang Liang, took the book, and passed it on. After several generations, the book became known as the *Secret Book Inside the Pillow* [*Chẩm Trung Bí Thư*][91] and was used by the military to predict the outcomes of battles.

{p. 134 (224)} The Five Constellations are mapped out as follows:

> The Tuệ constellation in the east is governed by the wood element. When it moves in the spring or summer, the enemy soldiers will win. When it moves in the autumn or winter, Lord Trịnh's soldiers will win. When the stars move to the western quadrant, the enemy will attack. When they move to the eastern[92] quadrant, there will be drought. When they move to the northern quadrant, there will be flooding.[93]
>
> The Huỳnh Hoặc constellation in the south is governed by the fire element. When it moves in the spring, the enemy soldiers will retreat. When it moves in the summer, autumn, or winter, the enemy soldiers

---

90. The same Zhang Liang mentioned in *Errors*, Book 1, Article 13.

91. I am not able to identify this book.

92. Perhaps this should this be "southern." A possible scribal mistake.

93. At this time, the Trịnh were trying to suppress various rebellions throughout Tonkin. Famine, plagues, natural disasters, and peasant uprisings were constant occurrences in Tonkin between 1730 and 1770. Apparently, this text is describing an application to contemporary problems.

will win. When the stars go to the center of the sky,[94] there will be plagues and a bad harvest. When they go to the western quadrant, there will be drought. When they move to the northern quadrant, there will be flooding.

The Bắc Thần constellation in the north is governed by the water element. When it moves in the autumn or winter, the enemy soldiers will win. When it moves in the spring, they will retreat. When it moves in the summer, the lord's soldiers will triumph. When the stars go to the eastern quadrant, there will be victory without a fight. {p. 135 (225)} When they move to the center, there will be peace. When they go to the southern quadrant, there will be drought and an enemy attack. When they go to the northern quadrant, there will be flooding.

The Thái Bạch constellation in the west is governed by the metal element. When it moves in the spring or summer, the enemy soldiers will win, and when it moves in the autumn, the lord's soldiers will win. When it moves in the winter, the enemy soldiers will retreat. When the stars go to the eastern quadrant, the enemy will attack; when they go to the center, there will be a bad harvest and famine. When they move to the southern quadrant, there will be drought, and when they move to the northern quadrant, flooding.

The Điền Trấn constellation in the center is governed by the earth element. When it moves in the spring, the enemy soldiers will win; when it moves in the summer or winter, they will lose. When it moves in the autumn, there will be victory without a fight. When the stars go to the southern quadrant, there will be drought. When they go to the western quadrant, there will be an enemy attack. When they go to the northern quadrant, there will be flooding, and when they go to the eastern quadrant, famine. {p. 136 (226)}

The Western Scholar comments: The Five Constellations and the stars are not writings in the sky that describe the human affairs of this world. How then can a person who follows the constellations know which side will win or lose in battle? Winning or losing a battle depends on the military skills of generals and the strength of an army, not on the power of any star. There is a great Lord in heaven who governs everything in heaven and on earth and who allows this side to win

---

94. This means straight up from where one stands, central to all four directions.

and that side to lose. If he allows someone to see the future, that person will know which side will win a battle. Because of their belief in the stars, many people have consulted the *Secret Book Inside the Pillow* to predict the outcome of a battles. But they later discovered that what the book says is not true: The side they predict will win will actually end up losing. Therefore, do not believe in the power of the Five Constellations.

Article 11

On Physiognomy and Reading Chicken Feet

The Western Scholar says: Since there are those who divine by reading facial features and chicken feet, I ask you, Eastern Scholar: What are these practices all about? {p. 137 (227)}

[Physiognomy]

The Eastern Scholar says: Physiognomists look at facial and physical features to predict a person's fortune. Those who wish to be rich and famous ask for a physiognomist's reading, and they believe that what is said is true.

The Western Scholar comments: Those who read the facial and physical features of a person can only see the exterior. How can they see the interior of a person? Riches and honor do not come from a person's body but from their mind and the help of others. Again, do good and evil arise from facial features? Good and evil come from within a person. It is better to change one's heart than to have a facial reading. It is better to correct the errors of one's ways than to have a physical reading. What one must examine and read is a good or evil way of life if one wishes to avoid trouble and to reap the benefits that bring true blessings in this life and the next.

[Reading Chicken Feet]

The Eastern Scholar says: Readers of chicken feet take a chicken and first offer it to heaven and earth. Then he kills it and cooks it in water. Afterward, he cuts off its two feet and puts them into a basin of cold water. Then he takes them out and examines {p. 138 (228)} how they look—whether the toes are straight or crooked. If they are all straight or all crooked, nothing can be discerned. If the middle toe bends toward the left or right toe, it is a bad sign, and one must not take action. If other toes bend toward the middle toe, this is a good sign, and one should take action. The middle toe is considered the "heaven and earth" toe, which points to a good sign. Those who are about to begin a task or embark on a journey often read chicken feet before doing so.

The Western Scholar comments: If chicken toes have the power to guide people, why does one read the feet of a dead chicken and those of a live one? Why is the middle toe of a chicken called the "heaven and earth" toe when the chicken is dead but not when it is alive? Moreover, how is it that heaven and earth use such base means for sending signs regarding important human affairs? There are those who see auspicious signs in chicken feet, but when they take action, the results turn out badly. Therefore, do not believe in divination based on reading chicken feet.[95]

---

95. Apparently, this form of divination was popular in the seventeenth and eighteenth centuries. Alexandre de Rhodes mentioned it in his *Histoire du Royaume de Tunquin,* part 1, chap. 24.

{p. 139 (229)}

Article 12

On Solar and Lunar Eclipses

The Western Scholar says: In this country, there is a ritual for rescuing the sun and the moon when they lose their light. So I ask you: What is the ritual about?

The Eastern Scholar replies: People believe that the sun and moon consume each other[96] on the day of a solar eclipse or on the night of a lunar eclipse. Therefore, on that day or night, everyone—from officials to the commoners—goes outside, sets up an altar, offers incense, beats drums, rings bells and other instruments, and shouts, "Please leave each other alone!" They do so in order to drive the sun and moon away from each other so that they won't eat each other—similar to driving off wild animals so that they don't prey on chickens and pigs. Lord [Trịnh] and his officials perform this ritual in the capital (Kẻ Chợ). On the local level, prefecture officials, county officials, and district officials also perform this ritual in their own areas.

The Western Scholar comments: The sun and the moon lose their light for the following reasons: Solar eclipses {p. 140 (230)} occur on the thirtieth day or the first day of the month when the two heavenly bodies meet each other during their regular cycles. The sun is on top, and the moon is at the bottom. This blocks the sun and causes darkness during the day. When the sun moves forward, sunlight can be seen again. Lunar eclipses occur on the fifteenth or sixteenth of the month when the sun and the moon line up during their regular cycles. The earth's shadow blocks the sunlight on the moon, resulting in darkness at night. When the earth's shadow moves forward, the sun's light that shines on the moon can be seen again. This is what really happens during solar and lunar eclipses, not the sun and moon eating each other as people say.

The Eastern Scholar comments: Our books give the same explanation that you, Western Scholar, give. Master Hu Zhitang writes: "Solar eclipses happen on a regular basis," which means that solar eclipses always occur at a particular time.

---

96. In Vietnamese, the words for solar eclipse and lunar eclipse literally mean "the sun is eaten" (*nhật thực*) and "the moon is eaten" (*nguyệt thực*).

{p. 141 (231)}

BOOK 3: THE ERRORS OF BUDDHISM

Preface

THE TWO HETERODOX ways of Śākyamuni and Laozi often use clever words that sound true. Buddhism especially often speaks in that way. It exalts Śākyamuni greatly, claiming he created heaven, earth, humans, and things and that he possesses power over heaven and earth to grant wealth, fame, and longevity to people. Moreover, Buddhism frequently uses inspiring words to exhort people to practice virtue: words such as "quiescence" [*tịch diệt*], "compassion" [*từ bi*], "purity of mind" [*thanh tịnh*], "merit" [*công đức*], and other similar words. For this reason, people who do not exercise a critical mind take Buddhist teachings to be true and right, and as a result, they have come to believe in Buddhism. Many scholars of the Confucian tradition have also fallen into this wicked way. In this Third Book, we will examine the errors, false doctrines, magic, and divination practices of Buddhism and strive to teach people how to recognize these deceptions and avoid the tricks {p. 142 (232)} that Buddhism uses to mislead people. No one should listen to the crafty words that only ostensibly describe the virtuous way. In fact, they are all empty, useless, and wicked words that bring people harm. Let the learned person who has been tricked into Buddhism understand the arguments discussed in this book. May he leave the false way that he has been blindly following and quickly return to the genuine way of virtue—the true way and principles—that everyone must follow in order to attain true blessings in this life and in the next.

{p. 143 (233)}

INDEX OF THE ERRORS OF BUDDHISM

Article 1:   On the Origin of Buddhism
Article 2:   On the Spread of Buddhism to China
Article 3:   On the Confucian Evaluation of Buddhism
Article 4:   On the Buddhist Story of Creation in Nine Eons
Article 5:   On the Real Meaning of the Nine Eons
Article 6:   On the Meaning of the Words *Không* [Emptiness] and *Phật* [Buddha]
Article 7:   On the Precepts against Killing and Teachings on Reincarnation
Article 8:   On the "Protection for the Journey" Prayer
Article 9:   On the Burning of Paper Mausoleums and Joss Paper
Article 10: On Hell
Article 11: On Quan Âm (Avalokiteśvara) and the Wandering Souls
Article 12: On the Custom of Erecting the *Nêu* Pole and the Sprinkling of Lime Powder on New Year's Eve

{p. 144 (234)}

Article 1

On the Origin of Buddhism

The Western Scholar says: Many people in this country worship the Buddha. They use many resources to build temples as well as perform ceremonies and feasts. Also, many people have become monks who reside in temples and live in the service of the Buddha. So I ask you: Who is the Buddha?

The Eastern Scholar replies: The Buddha is a native of the Tianzhu kingdom (North India) in the West [of China]. He was born on the eighth day of the fourth month in the *giáp-dần* year during the reign of Zhou Zhaowang [r. 1052–1002 BCE]—not during the twenty-fourth year but during the twenty-sixth year of his reign [1027 BCE].[1] His father was King Śuddhodana, and his mother was Lady Māyādevī. According to the account of the seventh *kalpa* [eon] in the book *Lamp of the Mind* [Tâm Đăng],[2] "Śākyamuni Buddha was the son of Lady Māyādevī and King Śuddhodana. He was born on the fifth watch on the eighth day of the fourth month in the *giáp-dần* year."[3]

[Zhu Xi's] *Outline of History* [Cương Mục] recounts: On the eighth day of the fourth month in the year *giáp-dần* during the reign of Zhou Zhaowang, Lady Māyādevī, the wife of a western regional king, went out to the garden of Lumbini. When she stopped to rest at a pipa tree, she immediately gave birth to Śākyamuni, whose given name was Siddhartha. who was the original Buddha. The Tianzhu kingdom is also known as Yindu and Shendu[4] [in Chinese].

---

1. The traditional birthday of the Buddha in Chinese sources does not correspond to that of the Pali texts. This may be an attempt by Chinese Buddhist apologists to "prove" the antiquity of Buddhism, in contrast to Daoism and Confucianism. Modern research places the time of the Buddha between the seventh and fifth centuries before Christ, though there is no universal agreement on the exact years. (The years 624–544 BCE, 563–483 BCE, and 448–368 BCE have been suggested.) Nevertheless, the eighth of the fourth lunar month is still celebrated across East Asia as the Buddha's birthday.

2. A book compiled in Vietnam, which was one of the main sources on Buddhism for the author and Adriano di Santa Thecla. For a discussion of this obscure work, see Dror, *A Study of Religion*, 51–54.

3. Sino-Vietnamese: 釋迦牟尼佛生摩耶夫人為母，與淨飯王為父，[至]甲寅年四月初八日五更而出世。*Tâm Đăng* [Lamp of the Mind], Institute of Sino-Vietnamese Studies (ms. A 2481), 3a.

4. India has various names in Chinese sources. The most common was Thiên Trúc or the land of a Thousand Bamboos (tianzhu 天竺). Other forms are Ấn Độ (Yindu 印度), Thân Độc

Book 3: The Errors of Buddhism

In the West, there are many big countries. In the East there {p. 145 (235)} is China, or "the land of nine regions." The king of Tianzhu was required to pay a tribute to King Lý Hồ[5] but failed to do so for many years. When King Lý Hồ planned to invade Tianzhu, Śuddhodana wanted to send an envoy to appease him, but no one dared go. When the crown prince Siddhārtha volunteered, the king happily dispatched him with many fine tribute gifts. When King Lý Hồ saw the many precious tributes, he was pleased and abandoned his plan to attack Tianzhu. Moreover, he gave the crown prince his daughter Yaśodharā's hand in marriage, as well as a noblewoman and concubine named Như La.[6] When Siddhārtha returned to his country, his father wanted to pass on the throne to him, so he moved him into the east side of the palace. As Siddhārtha enjoyed his wealth and fame, he thought to himself, "Even if I became a king, people will only honor me when I am alive. When I die, no one will remember me." He thought that by leaving his home to become an ascetic he would earn the respect of people for generations. Therefore, at the age of thirty, he left everything behind—his parents, wives, children, and throne. He went up to the mountain, became an ascetic, and founded Buddhism.

According to *Lamp of the Mind*, Śākyamuni "renounced the throne, adopted an ascetical life, and became the Buddha at Vulture Peak."[7] "The *Sutra in Forty-Two Sections* [Tứ Thập Nhị Chương kinh][8] {p. 146 (236)} also mentions: "When the Buddha left home, he first came upon the Himalayas, where he led a religious life."[9] The *Lamp of the Mind* states: "On the eighth day of the [twelfth] month in the *quý-mùi* year, Śākyamuni became the Buddha."[10] There were thirty years between the *giáp-dần* year [when he was born] and the *quý-mùi* year [when he was enlightened]. After Śākyamuni founded Buddhism on the mountain, his

---

(Shendu 身毒), and Thân Đậu (Shendou 腎豆)—all variant transcriptions of "Indus" (the ancient name of the region).

5. I have not been able to identify this person or the source of this story. Neither appears in any standard Buddhist account.

6. I cannot decipher the original Sanskrit. "Như La" could be a corruption of another title for the Buddha "Như Lai" (Tagagatha), or the name of his son "La Hầu La" (Rahula).

7. Sino-Vietnamese: [釋迦]不統王位修行成佛靈鷲山也。 *Tâm Đăng*, 3a. This mountain outside of the ancient city Rajgir is one of the holiest sites of Buddhism.

8. It was perhaps one of the earliest *sūtra* (scriptures) translated into Chinese. According to the Chinese tradition, the *Sutra of Forty-Two Sections* (四十二章經) was translated by Kaśyapa-matanga and Dharmaraksa in Luoyang around 67 CE. For an English translation, see Robert H. Shaft, "The Scripture in Forty-Two Sections," in *Religions of China in Practice*, ed. Donald S. Lopez (Princeton, NJ: Princeton University Press, 1996), 360–71.

9. This sentence is not found in the standard text of *Sutra of Forty-Two Sections*. Perhaps it is from the preface of a version of the sutra circulating in Tonkin at the time.

10. Sino-Vietnamese: 貴未年[十]二月初八日釋迦成佛。 This sentence is not found in my copy of *Tâm Đăng* (ms 2481). Vietnamese often celebrate the day of Śākyamuni Buddha's

teachings were collected into a book called the *Sutra of Forty-Two Sections*. The *Nirvana Sutra* [Nát Bàn kinh][11] recorded the words of Śākyamuni to his disciples: "O monks! When I die, if you love my teachings and treasure them as jewels, you yourselves will become masters."

The Buddha taught some of his forty-two maxims to his monks. The first maxim states: "A person who leaves his family to join a *sangha* (Buddhist community) and who devotes himself wholeheartedly to the practice of the true *dharma* (Buddhist teaching)[12] is called a '*śramana*'[13] (ascetic)."[14] [Another maxim states:] "He who shaves his head and face to become a *śramana* and receive the *dharma* must abandon all worldly wealth and possessions. He must beg, seeking only what is necessary."[15] {**p. 147 (237)**} The Buddhist monks obeyed his teachings. Thus, Śākyamuni lived on the mountain with his many disciples and practiced Buddhism until the age of seventy-nine, when he passed away and was buried in Kuśinarā (Kuśinagara) in the Western region.[16] According to *Lamp of the Mind*, "at sunset on the fifteenth of the second month in the *nhâm-thân* year, the Buddha entered into nirvana."[17]

---

enlightenment on the eighth day of the twelfth, not the second, lunar month. It is possible that the author of *Errors* mistakenly left out the Chinese character "ten", reducing twelve to two.

11. This is a major Mahayana scripture that deals with the final months of the Buddha's life. Its full title is *Mahāparinirvana Sūtra*, but to avoid confusion with a similar Pali text, it is most often referred to as the *Mahāyanā Nirvana Sūtra*.

12. *Dharma* is a Sanskrit word meaning "law" or "method." For Buddhists, it means the "teaching of the Buddha."

13. *Śramana* is a pre-Buddhist word that was used to denote a group of mendicant monks who opposed brahmanic rituals and focused instead on the cultivation of self.

14. Sino-Vietnamese: 辭親出家, 識心達本, 解無為法, 名曰沙門。 *Sutra of Forty-Two Sections*, Section 1. Note that the version used in this manuscript is slightly different from the common version.

15. Sino-Vietnamese: 剃除鬚髮, 而為沙門, 受道法家, 去世資財, 乞求取足。 *Sutra of Forty-Two Sections*, Section 4.

16. The text says that the Buddha was buried at "Tiểu-tây-tường-tích-lang-kiều." According to Buddhist tradition, the Buddha passed on to nirvana in the ancient city of Kuśinarā or Kuśinagara. He was then cremated, and his relics were venerated in different stupas all over South Asia.

17. Sino-Vietnamese: 壬申年二月十五日酉時佛入涅槃。 Cf. *Tâm Đăng*, 20a.

Article 2

On the Spread of Buddhism to China

The Western Scholar asks the Eastern Scholar: Buddhism was founded by Śākyamuni in the West of China. How did Buddhism come to the East?

The Eastern Scholar replies: Buddhism existed in India for more than a thousand years but did not come to China until the reign of Han Mingdi [58–75 CE]. The *History of Eastern Han*[18] records the event as follows:

> In the *ất-sửu* year, the eighth year of the Yongping [everlasting peace] era [64 CE], the king heard that there was a deity in the West named Buddha. Therefore, he sent envoys to Tianzhu [India] to inquire about the religion and return with its scriptures and monks. [The monks of this religion, also called *śramana,* were considered to be otherworldly.][19] That is how his sect appeared and how {p. 148 (238)} his images were created in China.[20]

> The commentator Fan Shiyong[21] reports that "during the Yongping era [58–75 CE], the king sent envoys to Tianzhu (India) to obtain the *Sutra of Forty-Two Sections*. He stored it at the stone palace Lantai, and he erected statues of Buddha at the Qingliang tower and Xianjie mausoleum."

[The preface of] *Sutra of Forty-Two Sections* mentions:

> During the Yongping (eternal peace) era, because [Emperor] Han Mingdi had had a dream about a golden figure [of a man], he knew that the way of the Buddha was coming to the east.[22] Consequently, he sent Cai Yin

---

18. This may be another name of the *Hou Hanshu* (後漢書, Book of the Later Han), which recorded the events of the Han dynasty from Han Guangwu [r. 25–57 CE] onward.

19. This phrase seems to be an addition to the text; it is not found in Santa Thecla's version of the quotation. See Dror, *A Study of Religion,* 187.

20. Sino-Vietnamese: 永平乙丑八年初, 帝聞西域有神, 其名曰佛人, 使之天竺求其道, 得其書及沙門以來 [精於其道者, 號曰沙門] 於是中國始得其術, 圖其形像。The author also supplied his own Vietnamese translation, which I do not repeat here.

21. The author of the *General Discussion* (Tổng Luận), a book on history in the Ming dynasty. It is quoted by the author of this text and also by Adriano di Santa Thecla.

22. Han Mingdi's legendary dream was used by many Chinese sources to date the beginning of Chinese Buddhism. The earliest versions do not mention the name of the monks, which

and Qin Jing to the west to meet two Indian monks, Kaśyapa-matanga and Dharmaraksa. They used a white horse to carry the Sanskrit sutras—written on leaves—to the capital Luoyang. Then [the monks] translated these sutras from Sanskrit into Chinese and published them so that all could have access to their teachings.[23] {p. 149 (239)}

The Western Scholar asks: Since the Tianzhu kingdom (India) in the West was a great distance from China, how did Emperor Han Mingdi know that the Buddha lived there?

The Eastern Scholar replies: During the reign of Han Wudi [r. 140–87 BCE], China developed trading and diplomatic relationships with many kingdoms in this western region [Tianzhu], so there were already routes to that region. Ban Gu, who wrote *History of the Han Dynasty*, recorded:

> In the *bính-dần* year, the second year of the Yuanding [original stability] era [115 BCE], [the Han envoy] Zhang Qian went on a diplomatic mission to the kingdom of Bactria and opened communications between the western region and China. In the *kỷ-mão* year, the third year of the [Taichu] reign [102 BCE], after [the diplomatic mission to] the kingdom of Fernaga, Han envoys who came to the western region were able to hold office there.[24]

From that time on, the Han court knew about the affairs of India and other kingdoms in the western region. Therefore, it is not surprising that Han Mingdi had heard about a deity from the western region named Buddha.
p. {150 (240)}

---

led scholars to believe that this sutra was not compiled until the fourth or fifth centuries. See Kenneth Ch'en, *Buddhism in China: A Historical Survey* (Princeton, NJ: Princeton, University Press, 1964), 29–36; Tsukamoṭo Zenryu, *A History of Early Chinese Buddhism from Its Introduction to the Death of Hui-yüan*, trans. Leon Hurvitz (Tokyo: Koshanda, 1985), 1:41–50.

23. Sino-Vietnamese: 漢永平年間, 明帝因夢金像, 乃知佛道相備東下, 遣蔡愔秦景使西國, 晤[迦葉]摩騰竺法[蘭]二梵僧, 白馬馱是葉梵文, 解之洛都, 譯梵成漢, **首出此經**, 備基闡訓。The author also supplied his own Vietnamese translation, which I do not repeat here.

24. Sino-Vietnamese: 丙寅元鼎二年, 張騫使烏孫, 於是西域始通於漢矣。己卯[太初]年**自大宛**之後, 漢使入西域益得職。The author also supplied his own Vietnamese translation, which I do not repeat here.

The Western Scholar asks again: How have people responded to Buddhism since Han Mingdi brought Buddhism to China?

The Eastern Scholar replies: When Han Mingdi first brought Buddhism to China, there were many high officials who wanted to please the emperor by worshipping the Buddha, including the emperor's brother Chu Wangying. The author of *History of the Han Dynasty* comments: "Among the royal household and the nobles, Chu Wangying is the most fond of this religion."[25] Since members of the royal household and the nobles worshipped the Buddha, the common people followed suit; Buddhist temples and shrines sprang up everywhere. Then, during the reign of Han Lingdi [r. 168–189 CE], the emperor built a temple inside the royal palace to worship the Buddha.[26]

From the time of the Wei and Jin dynasties, the worship of Buddha proliferated. The number of Buddhist and Daoist monks and nuns increased daily. [During the Three Kingdom era] Wei Wendi [r. 220–226 CE] often went to Buddhist temples to hear *dharma* talks, and he adopted a vegetarian lifestyle. Then, during the period of the Northern and Southern kingdoms [420–589 CE], the dowager empress of Northern Wei built the Yongning temple and a stupa that was nine-hundred cubits high.[27] Monks were assigned to a thousand temples. Buddhism was at its height during the period of the Northern Wei dynasty [386–534 CE]. [In the South] King Liang Wudi [r. 502–549 CE] was even more devoted to Buddhism. In the first year of Datong [great flow] era [527 CE], he went to the Tongtai temple, shed his royal robes, donned a monk's robes, and recited the {p. 151 (241)} Nirvana sutra for the people. He sold himself into service at the temple three times, and his subordinates were forced to pay a ransom each time in order to get him back. In the first year of the Dadong [great convergence] era [535 CE], he went to the Tongtai temple again to preach the *Three Mental Faculties Sutra* [Tam Tuệ Kinh]. On that night, a fire came down from heaven and burned the stupa to the ground. King Liang Wudi commented, "The conflagration was caused by an evil spirit." Then he rebuilt a twelve-story stupa.

Then, in the Tang dynasty, Emperor Gaozu [r. 618–626 CE] did not like the fact that Buddhist and Taoist monks were not involved in civil service. He

---

25. Sino-Vietnamese: 而王公貴人,獨楚王英最先好之 。

26. According to Dror (*A Study of Religion*, 189), Santa Thecla attributes this information to Fan Shiyong.

27. Literally, ninety *trượng*. A *trượng* is ten *thước*, roughly about ten cubits (four to five meters). Since there was no standard of measurement, the length varied from place to place.

granted the request of official Fu Yi[28] that Buddhism be suppressed. Emperor Gaozu therefore issued an imperial edict and had Buddhist and Taoist monks and nuns cast from their temples, resulting in one hundred thousand Buddhist monks and nuns becoming laicized. However, his son Emperor Taizong [r. 627–649 CE] went back to build stupas to venerate the Buddha. His grandson Gaozong [r. 650–683 CE] often visited Buddhist temples to offer incense. During the reign of Xianzong [806–820 CE], a relic of Buddha's finger was taken to China to be worshipped in Buddhist temples. [It is on record that] a royal envoy carried the relic to the capital for veneration in the first month of the *kỷ-hợi* year, the fourteenth[29] year of his reign [819 CE]. In the second month, the relic was taken to other temples.

After the Tang dynasty, there were the Five Periods of the Later Liang, Later Tang, Later Jin, Later Han, and Later Zhou houses. Then came the Song, Yuan, {p. 152 (242)} Ming, and Qing dynasties. In those Chinese dynasties, some emperors favored Buddhism, and other emperors detested it. However, no one strived to suppress Buddhism completely; that is why Buddhism spread everywhere.

[Buddhism in Annam]

The Western Scholar asks the Eastern Scholar: Which king of Annam propagated Buddhism, as we know it today, throughout the land?

The Eastern Scholar replies: In our country Annam, before the Lý dynasty, the mother of King Lý Thái Tổ, whose surname was Phạm, visited the Đồng Tiêu temple on Mount Tiêu in the Tiêu Sơn ward in the An Phong district. After her visit, she conceived and gave birth to a son on the twenty-second day of the second month in the *giáp-tuất* year, the fifth year of Thái bình [great peace] era of the Đinh dynasty [974 CE]. When the boy was three years old,

---

28. Fu Yi (傅奕) (555–639) was a Daoist scholar and grand astrologer (*Taishiling*, the officer in charge of creating the calendar) under Emperor Tang Gaozu. As one of the most determined adversaries of Buddhism, he presented a petition to the emperor in 621 insisting that the religion be banned. He cited Buddhism's tenets of celibacy and withdrawal from civil duties—including subjection to civil authority—as threats to Chinese social stability.

29. The manuscript has "fourth year." However, this would be the year *đinh-hợi*—not *kỷ-hợi* as given in the text. The scribe probably left out the word "thập" (十 ten) by mistake. See also the same quotation in *Errors*, Book 3, Article 3.

he was adopted by Lý Độ Văn[30] and given the name [Lý] Công Uẩn. When he grew up, he served in the court of King Lê Thái Tổ (Lê Đại Hành) [r. 981–1006], and later in the court of King Lê Trung Tông [r. 1005]. King Lê Trung Tông was murdered by his brother [Lê] Ngọa Triều [r. 1005–1009]. When King Ngọa Triều died, court officials elected Lý Công Uẩn king.[31] He changed the dynastic name to Lý and moved the capital to the Đại La citadel, which is the present capital. Inside the capital, he built the Hưng Thiên royal temple; outside the capital, he built the Thắng Nghiêm temple and other regional temples. {p. 153} He gave money to temples everywhere for casting bells and carving statues of the Buddha; he also selected and ordained one thousand monks in the capital.[32]

His grandson, King Thánh Tông [r. 1054–1072 CE], built the Báo Thiên stupa that was twelve stories and three hundred cubits high.[33] King Lý Nhân Tông [r. 1072–1127 CE] built a stupa at the Lâm Sơn temple and traveled all over to build Buddhist temples and stupas.[34] The Lý kings have been the most devoted to Buddhism in [the history of] Annam. Lý Huệ Tông [r. 1210–1224 CE], who had no son, chose his daughter, later Queen Lý Chiêu Hoàng [r. 1224–1225 CE], to succeed him and left the throne to become a Buddhist monk. He was later killed by Trần Thủ Độ.[35] Queen Chiêu Hoàng's passing the throne to her husband, a man from the Trần family, marked the end of the Lý family's dynastic rule.

More Buddhist temples were built during the Trần dynasty. Whenever there was a disaster or plague, a temple was built for people to worship. King Trần Anh Tông [r. 1293–1314 CE] published the Buddhist books *Phật Giáo Pháp Sự, Đạo Trường Tân Văn, Công Văn Cách Thức*[36] and also issued guidelines on how temples should be built in the villages. From that time on, Buddhist followers multiplied. People scrambled to express their devotion: They prayed for children,

---

30. According to the *Toàn Thư*, Bản kỷ, 2:1a, the person name's was Lý Khánh Vân.

31. *Toàn Thư*, Bản kỷ, 1:31a–2:1a (translation, 1:244–49).

32. *Toàn Thư*, Bản kỷ, 2:3b (translation, 1: 250).

33. This stupa, called Đại Thắng Tự Thiên or Bảo Thắng Tự Thiên, was built in 1057. See *Toàn Thư*, Bản kỷ, 3:1b–2a (translation, 1:287).

34. Completed in 1094. See *Toàn Thư*, bản kỷ, 3:11b, 12b (translation, 1:298–99).

35. The name is misspelled as Trần Thúc Đại in the manuscript. See *Toàn Thư*, Bản kỷ, 4:31b–34b (translation, 1:362–64).

36. In 1290, the king had these books printed and distributed in the country. See *Toàn Thư*, Bản kỷ, 6:8a (translation, 2:82). I am uncertain whether *Phật Giáo Pháp Sự Đạo Trường Tân Văn* is one book or two.

honors, and offices; they made reparations for ancestors' transgressions, they recited sutras and did penance. Monks and nuns crowded the temples {p. 154 (244)} but were ignorant of the overall doctrine. They only knew how to recite the mantra *nam mô* and pray for blessings. They strived to solicit donations and produced meritorious works to entice people. Everything I have told you can be found in the *History of the Great Viet*.

Article 3

On the Confucian Evaluation of Buddhism

The Western Scholar asks the Eastern Scholar: What value do Confucian scholars place on Buddhism?

The Eastern Scholar replies: Generally speaking, Confucian scholars belittle and vilify Buddhism. They say first and foremost: "Buddhism teaches a strange doctrine," or "[The Buddha] is of barbarian descent; he did not acknowledge the moral duties between ruler and subject or the relationship between father and son."[37] They call Buddhism "the heterodox teachings of emptiness [*hư vô*] and quiescence [*tịch diệt*]."[38] They say that "[Buddhism] is not the holy way, but the wicked way—an evil in the world." They reproach Han Mingdi for bringing Buddhism to China: "Alas! The sins of Mingdi are known to heaven." You, Western Scholar, should read the comments of great scholars to understand the Confucian attitude toward Buddhism.

[The first account is] Fu Yi's petition at the time of Tang Gaozu: In the *bính-tuất* year, the ninth year of his majesty's reign [621 CE], the grand astrologer Fu Yi presented a petition requesting that Buddhism be banned:

> The Buddha lived in the West, a land far away, where he preached his strange doctrine. {p. 155 (245)} When his barbarian scriptures were translated into Chinese, people were steered toward libertine and erroneous lifestyles that caused them to become disloyal to their rulers and unfilial to their parents. Buddhists, with their shaved heads, showed no reverence to kings or parents. They led idle and unproductive lives and evaded paying their taxes. They deceived people citing the doctrine of the three hells and the six ways of reincarnation, which caused people to try to earn merit in a false way. They caused harm to the true way. Oh, what a shame!
>
> Prior to Buddhism's arrival during the Han dynasty, kings were enlightened, subjects were dutiful, and dynasties lasted for long periods of time. But since the time that people began worshipping this alien deity, Western barbarians have invaded China, kings have become

---

37. These lines are from Han Yu's famous petition against Buddhism, as we will read later.

38. This sentence is from the preface of Zhu Xi's commentary on the *Great Learning*, as we will read later.

weak and subjects toadies. Thus, governance has deteriorated, and dynasties have been shortened. The histories of Liang Wudi and Qi Xiang are clear examples of such outcomes. Nowadays, the number of monks and nuns in the empire exceeds a hundred thousand. I hereby petition His Majesty to pair them off so that they will produce male and female offspring. It takes ten years for these children to grow up and twelve years to educate them; we will have {p. 156 (246)} enough soldiers then.[39]

Since the emperor also disliked the monks and priests, who—as affirmed by Fu Yi—dodged public service and refused to obey imperial laws and orders, the emperor issued an edict ordering the officials in charge to expel the monks, nuns, and priests from monasteries across the country.

Next, Han Yu,[40] an official under Emperor Tang Xianzong, spoke out to the emperor [against Buddhism]. According to the story, in the first month of the *kỷ-hợi* year, the fourteenth year of his majesty's reign [819], a royal envoy took a relic of the Buddha to the capital for veneration. In the second {p. 157 (247)} month, the relic was taken to other temples. Han Yu made a petition saying:

Buddhism is only a worship system of barbarians. From the time of the Yellow Emperor to the time of emperors Yu, Tang, Wen, and Wu, everyone enjoyed longevity, and every household was at peace. At that time, Buddhism had not yet appeared. Buddhism was first brought to China at the time of Han Mingdi. From that time on, chaos and rebellions occurred frequently; dynasties became unstable. From the time of the Song, Qi, Liang, Chen, and Northern Wei [dynasties], each dynasty became more deeply devoted to Buddhism than the one before, and yet their reigns were short. Only Liang Wudi had a long reign, forty-eight

---

39. Sino-Vietnamese: 佛在西域言妖路遠，漢譯胡書恣其託假，[故]使不忠不孝削髮而揖君親，遊手遊食易服以逃租稅。偽啟三塗謬張六道。遂使愚迷妄求功德。其為害政良可悲夫。自漢已前初無佛法，君明臣良祚長年久。自立胡神羌戎亂華，主庸臣佞政虐祚短，梁武齊襄足為明鏡。今天下僧尼數盈十萬，請令匹配產育男女，十年長養一紀教訓可以足兵。The author also supplied his own Vietnamese translation, which I do not repeat here. Note that in these passages the author of *Errors* presented only excerpts and paraphrases of the petition. For a complete Chinese text and an English translation, see J. J. M. De Groot, *Sectarianism and Religious Persecution in China* (1903; repr., New York: Barnes and Noble, 1972), 1:36–42. For a discussion on Fu Yi's petition, see Arthur Wright, *Studies in Chinese Buddhism* (New Haven, CT: Yale University Press, 1990), 112–23.

40. Han Yu (韓愈, 768–824) was a high official in the Tang dynasty. A Confucian reformer, he opposed the advancement of Daoism and Buddhism at court. In 819, he petitioned the emperor Tang Xianzong, bidding him not to venerate the relic of the Buddha's finger bone.

years altogether. The emperor was devoted to Buddhism—three times he sold himself into servanthood at a Buddhist temple. Later, he was nevertheless oppressed by Hou Jing {**p. 158 (248)**} and died of starvation in Tai city. His country had been lost. He worshipped the Buddha in hopes of receiving blessings, and yet what he got was misfortune. Thus, one can see that the Buddha was not worthy of being believed in. The Buddha was of barbarian origin; he did not acknowledge the righteous duties between ruler and subject or the relationship between father and son.... Therefore, I [Han Yu] petition Your Majesty to relinquish the bones [of the Buddha] to the official in charge so that he can destroy them by fire and water, cut off the error at the root, dispel the confusion of the people, and thus prevent the false beliefs of future generations.[41]

In the time of Emperor Song Xiaozong [r. 1163–1189 CE], Master Zhu [Xi] wrote in the preface to his commentary on the *Great Learning*:[42]

The heterodox teachings of [Daoist] emptiness and [Buddhist] quiescence[43] are loftier than the great learning, yet they are not true teachings. They seek to devise ways of trickery for achieving fame and fortune. This leads to the unfortunate consequence that the noble person is unable to hear the basic teachings of the great learning and that the petty man is unable to reap the benefits of the rewards of a good rule. As a result, they have both become blind and trapped; trickery becomes an incurable disease. Therefore, during the Five Periods [following the Tang dynasty], this decline resulted in extreme corruption and chaos.[44]

---

41. Sino-Vietnamese: 以為佛者夷狄之一法耳。自黃帝以至禹湯文武, 皆享壽考, 百姓安樂, 當是時, 未有佛也。漢明帝時, 始有佛法。其後亂亡相繼, 運祚不長。宋齊梁陳元魏已下, 事佛漸謹 年代尤促。唯梁武帝在位四十八年, 前後三[度] 捨身為寺家奴。[其後] 竟為侯[景] 所逼, 餓死臺城, 國亦尋滅。事佛求福, 乃更得禍。由此觀之, 佛不足信亦可知矣[...]夫佛本夷狄之人, 不知君臣之義, 父子之恩。乞以此骨付[之]有司, 投諸水火, 永絕根本, 斷天下之疑, 絕後代之惑。 The author also supplied his own Vietnamese translation, which I do not repeat here. Again, this is only an excerpt. For the full text, see De Groot, *Sectarianism and Religious Persecution in China*, 1:54ff.

42. This is known as *Great Learning: Chapters and Verses* (Daxue Zhangju 大學章句).

43. This is the source of the phrase "*dị đoan hư vô tịch diệt chi giáo*" (the heterodox teachings of emptiness and quiescence) that is often repeated in this text.

44. Sino-Vietnamese: 異端虛無寂滅之教, 其高過於大學而無實, 其磋權謀術數, 一切以就功名之說。使其君子不幸而不得聞大道之要, 　其小人不幸而不得蒙至治之澤, 晦盲否塞, 反覆沈痼, 以及五季之衰而壞亂極矣 。 The author also supplied his own Vietnamese translation, which I do not repeat here.

During the Song dynasty, Master Cheng, Master Qiu of Mount Qiong, Master Jin of Mount Ren, Master Chen of Xin'an, and many other Confucian scholars all belittled and vilified Buddhism. In the time of Ming Taizu [r. 1368–1398 CE], the official Fan Shiyong, author of *General Discussion*, also criticized {**p. 160 (250)**} Buddhism as being contrary to reason [*phi lý*].

[The Vietnamese Confucian View of Buddhism]

During the Hồng Thuận reign of king Lê Tương Dực [r. 1509–1516 CE], the official Vũ Quỳnh wrote an essay in *History of the Great Viet*:

> Generally speaking, the downfall of the Lý and Trần dynasties resulted from a breakdown of the social structure.[45] The true cause of their decline was their embracing of heterodoxy. They took money from the royal treasury to make Buddha statues, copper from the royal storehouse to cast temple bells, and paper from the royal office to write Buddhist sutras. The Lý and Trần kings worshipped Buddha diligently, and yet when Lý's descendants were killed by the wicked and ferocious Trần Thủ Đạc (Độ),[46] the Buddha was unable to save them. The entire Trần clan was devoted to Buddhism: From their kings came abbots, from the royal harem came nuns, and from the noble houses came monks. And yet when the Trần's descendants were killed by the deceitful Hồ Quý Ly {**p. 161 (251)**}, the Buddha was unable to save them. Therefore, how does the worship of Buddha benefit anyone at all?[47]

The Western Scholar comments: Confucian scholars belittled and vilified Buddhism only after the Tang dynasty. Before the Tang period, however, none of the Confucian scholars were critical of Buddhism. Therefore, it seems that before the Tang period, Confucian scholars were probably fond of that religion; they worshipped the Buddha like any other deity because Confucianism also teaches spirit worship.

---

45. Literally, "the disorder of [three] bonds and [five] constant virtues." This refers to the practice of endogamy among the Lý and Trần nobility.

46. Scribal error: The name should be "Trần Thủ Độ."

47. Sino-Vietnamese: 大抵李陳之亡，雖由綱常之紊亂，亦由異端之蠱惑。發庫錢而造佛像，發庫銅而鑄洪鐘，發庫紙而寫佛經。李陳之事佛謹矣。然殺李氏之子孫者，纔出於陳守度之凶險，而佛不能救。以天子而為大士，以妃嬪而為丘尼，以王主而為眾僧，陳家之事佛篤矣，然弒陳氏之宗室者，皆出於胡犛之奸甚，而佛不能渡。則

The Western Scholar asks again: Why were Confucian scholars, who worked to belittle and vilify Buddhism, not able to eradicate it? On the contrary, it attracts more and more followers each day. From the highest to the lowest levels [of society], many have followed Buddhism. Even learned Confucians and teachers of Confucianism worship the Buddha like everyone else!
{p. 162 (152)}

The Eastern Scholar replies: Because commoners are uneducated and cannot think critically, and because Confucian scholars are mesmerized by Buddhism, people from the highest to the lowest echelons [of society] have fallen victim to the deception and seduction of Buddhism and its heterodox teachings.

The Western Scholar says: However, many Confucian scholars have belittled and vilified Buddhism; they can neither destroy it nor prevent people from following it. The reason for this is that Buddhism and Confucianism are very much alike in terms of rituals and worship. Both accept the notion of mortals becoming gods and the worship of them. Confucian scholars can only admonish Buddhists against worshipping the Buddha if they do not worship deified mortals themselves. If they too worship spirits who are deified mortals, how can they tell Buddhists to refrain from worshipping their deities? Confucians must first worship the great Lord who created heaven, earth, and everything, and follow his commandments. Only then can they admonish Buddhists to abandon their ways. Buddhism is contrary to the orthodox way—the way that everyone must believe in and follow, the way that teaches everyone to worship and love {p. 163 (253)} only the true Lord of heaven and earth. Since Confucian scholars do not hold such a belief, they can neither persuade people to abandon Buddhism or weaken it in this country.

奉佛之事,果何補哉。 The author also supplied his own Vietnamese translation, which I do not repeat here. The author of *Errors* mistakenly ascribes this passage to Vũ Quỳnh. Its author was Lê Tung, who wrote a summary essay entitled "Việt Giám Thông Khảo Tổng Luận" in 1514 as a preface for *Toàn Thư*; (translation, 1:125).

Article 4

On the Buddhist Story of Creation in Nine Eons

The Western Scholar says: I have heard about the Buddhist story of creation in nine eons.[48] Thus I ask you: What is the story of the nine eons all about?[49]

The Eastern Scholar says: The story about the creation in nine eons is difficult to follow. However, I will tell you about it as it recounted in Buddhist books.[50]

This is what they say about the first eon: Before anything existed, a drop of dew appeared from emptiness.[51] This is Buddha nature [Phật tính]. It divided into three parts: The first was green and formed the heavens. The second part, yellow, formed the earth, and the third part, white, formed human beings. These parts then came together as one and became what is known as the Primordial Source (Nguyên thỉ). The three parts of the single dewdrop concentrated into something resembling a stone egg. The egg broke into four pieces. The first piece became the heavens, the second {p. 164 (254)} became the earth, the third became the father, and the fourth became the mother. The Primordial Source flowed in four directions to create heaven and earth. The Buddha, together with Tỳ lô,[52] emerged from the Primordial Source before heaven and earth. Then the Primordial Source formed another source called Mục Mũi.[53] This was made up of clear and turbid essences and lacked an

---

48. Literally "kiếp" or "kiếp ba", from the Sanskrit *kalpa*, a word meaning eon.

49. See also *Opusculum*, Chapter 5, Article 3.

50. Although this creation account purports to be Buddhist, its content is not really Buddhist, except for a brief reference to the birth of Śākyamuni Buddha in the seventh eon. The rest of the account is a mixture of Chinese mythology and Taoist sources. According to Santa Thecla, the sources of this account are the books *Esoteric Branches* (Bí Chi) and *Lamp of the Mind* (Tâm Đăng). The story given in *Errors* is incoherent because it leaves out too many details. For a fuller account, see Dror, *A Study of Religion*, 191–202.

51. According to Dror, this should be understood as "a drop pregnant with emptiness." *A Study of Religion*, 192n64.

52. *Lô* or *Tỉ Lô* is defined in Rhodes's *Dictionarium Annamiticum Lustanium et Latinum* (Rome, 1651), as "the second stage of human life when the embryo was formed; this stage is referred to by idolators as the second stage of human life, or as they say, *kiếp* (eon)" (417, my translation). Dror suggests that Tỉ Lô is short for Tỉ Lô Giá Na or Vairocana, the Buddha Supreme and Eternal. This cosmic Buddha is venerated in Mahayana Buddhism as an eternal being, the source and originator of all things. *A Study of Religion*, 192–93n59.

53. Mục Mũi, also spelled as Mộc Mỗ or Mục Mỗi, is defined in Alexandre de Rhodes's catechism as "the created body when the rational soul is first infused as spoken by some idolatrous

Book 3: The Errors of Buddhism

intelligent nature. At that time, the sky had not closed, and the earth had not yet taken form. A great power from the void energy created the Buddha and formed heaven, earth, and human beings. All things thus came out of emptiness from *Qian* (heaven). *Qian* was formed by this single energy called Buddha nature. And so it is said: "Conditioned by one energy, Buddha nature was transformed into heaven and earth."[54]

This is what they say about the second eon: There was once a couple named Tu Là of Heaven[55] and Ma Ha of Earth.[56] He made ten pillars out of his ten bones, and she fashioned nine beams from the nine sections of her intestines. In this manner, the two of them created heaven and earth: "Ma Ha of Earth uses her body to support heaven. *Qian* and *Kun* (heaven and earth),[57] [day and night, water and fire,][58] the Three Powers,[59] the Four Forms,[60] the sun and {**p. 165 (255)**} the moon, and the Eight Trigrams all spring from these two people."[61]

This is what they say about the third eon: There suddenly appeared the Five Ministers.[62] The first, called the Green Minister of Great Change [*thái dịch*], was 150 cubits[63] tall. The second, the Red Minister of Great Beginning [*thái sơ*], was 130 cubits tall. The third, the White Minister of Great Origin [*thái thuỷ*],[64] was 110 cubits tall. The fourth, the Black Minister of the Great Element [*thái tố*], was 150 cubits tall. The fifth, the Yellow Minister of Great Polarity [*thái cực*],

---

sect." (*Catechismus*, Second day, in Phan, *Mission and Catechesis*, 255). Jean Louis Tabert's *Dictionarium Annamitico-Latinum* has a similar definition: "*organizatum corpus cum primum anima infunditur*." (Serampore,1838), 318.

54. Sino-Vietnamese: 緣得一氣佛性變成天地也 。 Cf. *Tâm Đăng*, iv.

55. Tu Là might be Asura, a celestial titan of the Indo-Buddhist tradition.

56. Ma Ha is phonetic rendering of a Sanskrit term meaning "greatness."

57. Being the first two hexagrams, they are often used together to denote the combination of yang and yin, or heaven and earth.

58. The four word has been omitted in this text, but it is present in *Tâm Đăng* (2a) and quoted in *Opusculum*, 90 (Dror, *A Study of Religion*,193).

59. Tam Tài (*san cai* 三才): the three powers of heaven, earth, and human beings.

60. Tứ Tượng (*si xiang* 四象): the subdivision of yin and yang into greater and lesser yin and greater and lesser yang.

61. Sino-Vietnamese: 用身資助天地, 造為乾坤[子午水火]三才四象日月八卦, 此二人 。 Cf. *Tâm Đăng*, 1b–2a.

62. In *Opusculum* (91), these are five brothers.

63. Or "15 *trượng*." A *trượng* is ten *thước*, roughly about ten cubits (four to six meters). Since there was no standard of measurement, the length varied from place to place.

64. The manuscript has "Đại Thuỷ." The characters for Thái (太) and Đại (大) are often mixed up.

was 100 cubits tall.[65] [And so it is said that] these five ministers transformed the five colors [to make heaven and earth].[66] It is also said: "There were thirty six layers of heaven and thirty layers of earth, and everything evolved from them."[67]

This is what they say about the fourth eon: Suddenly there was a primordial man named Pangu,[68] who had a human body and a dragon's head. He was fifty cubits tall. At that time, the clear and the turbid energies had not yet separated and were still mixed in chaos. Pangu brought heaven and earth into balance by extracting the clear energy to make heaven and the turbid energy to make the earth. Everything came out of his body. Opening his eyes, he made the day; closing them, he made the night. His left eye became the sun, his right eye the moon. At the time of creation, there was darkness; light did not yet exist. Each day, the heavens rose by one *trượng* (ten cubits), and the earth grew one layer thicker each day. Since Pangu was tall and lived for a thousand years, the heavens were pushed even higher, and the earth was made even thicker to create space [for the world].
{p. 166 (256)}

This is what they say about the fifth eon: During this time, there were three leaders: Heavenly August, Earthly August, and Human August.[69] Heavenly August was three hundred cubits tall and had twelve heads and twelve siblings. Earthly August was one hundred fifty cubits tall and had eleven heads and eleven siblings. Human August was one hundred cubits tall and had nine heads and nine siblings. It is also said that "Heavenly August created the twelve earthly branches and the ten heavenly stems.[70] Earthly August separated the days and nights, and Human August formed the mountains and streams."[71]

This is what they say about the sixth eon: During this time, the sky was not yet complete. A woman named Nüwa[72] used five cubits of stone to mend it. She

---

65. These five names are cosmological terms used in Daoism.

66. Sino-Vietnamese: 五相变為五色 [同造天地也] 。 The last five words were omitted in *Errors*. Adriano's *Opusculum* (91) gives the full quotation. Cf. *Tâm Đăng*, 2a.

67. Sino-Vietnamese: 其天有三十六層, 其地有三十層, 而变化也。Cf. *Tâm Đăng*, 2a.

68. See also *Errors*, Book 1, Article 2 about Pangu.

69. This is an oblique reference to the three major clans, or the Three August Ones (*Tam Hoàng*), who ruled China in antiquity.

70. The twelve earthly branches are: *tí, sửu, dần, mão, thìn, tị, ngo, mùi, thân, dậu, tuất, hợi*. The ten heavenly stems are: *giáp, ất, bính, đinh, mậu, kỉ, canh, tân, nhâm, quý*.

71. Sino-Vietnamese: 天皇為十二支又為十干, 地皇分晝夜, 人皇相山川其相一也。 I cannot locate this reference in my copy of *Tâm Đăng* (ms. A 2481).

72. Nữ Oa (Nüwa 女媧), the mythical sister or wife of Fuxi; she allegedly was involved with the creation of the sky.

formed the shape of heaven to last forever so that it would never have to stretch again. There were also three other people during this time—Ma Ha, Đại Ngộ Chân Trí, and Ban Nhược[73]—who took five hundred catties[74] of gold and five hundred catties of copper to form the sun and five hundred catties of silver to form the moon. Inside the sun there was a three-legged heron. Inside the moon there was a rabbit and the palace of the Queen Mother [of the West][75]—the mother of the immortals. They also say that the Five Emperors were born during this age. They were Yuanshi Tianzun,[76] Xuhuang Dadao,[77] the Jade Emperor,[78] {p. 167 (257)} Taishang Laojun,[79] and Guyun Tianshi.[80]

This is what they say about the seventh eon: The Buddha once resided in the realm of Song Lâm. On the fifteenth day of the seventh month of the *quý-sửu* year, the Tathāgata[81] [Buddha] left heaven and descended to the earth. After meeting Yama[82] in the southern region of the world, he was guided into the womb of Lady Māyādevī. Conceived by her, he became the son of Śuddhodana. He was born at the *dần* hour [3:00–5:00 a.m.] on the fifth watch of the eighth day of the fourth month in the *giáp-dần* year. Immediately after his birth, the Tathāgata took seven steps in each of the four directions, and lotus flowers sprung up in his footprints. He pointed his left hand to the heavens and his

---

73. According to Dror, the names are slightly different: Ma Ha Đại Ngộ (Great Awakening), Chân Trí (Genuine Mind), and Ban Nhược (*Prajna*, Wisdom). See Dror, *A Study of Religion*, 198nn100–101.

74. Literally, a *cân*, which is about six hundred grams.

75. Vương Mẫu or Tây Vương Mẫu (Xi Wangmu 西王母), often translated as "Queen Mother of the West," is a goddess who is associated with immortality.

76. Nguyên Thỉ Thiên Tôn (Yuanshi tianzun 元始天尊) (Celestial King of the Primordial Beginning) is one of the three supreme gods of Daoism.

77. Not much is known about the deity Hư Hoàng Đại Đạo (Xuhuang daidao 虛皇大道) (Great Way of the King of Emptiness).

78. In Chinese mythology, Ngọc Hoàng Thượng Đế (Yuhuang shangdi 玉皇上帝) (Jade Emperor, Supreme Lord) is the highest and most popular god of the celestial court.

79. Thái Thượng Lão Quân (Taishang laojun 太上老君) (Great Supreme Lord Lao) is the title conferred upon Laozi by Emperor Song Renzong (宋仁宗), r. 1022–1063. Laozi was turned into a Daoist god in the Song dynasty. He is discussed in *Errors*, Book 2, Article 1.

80. Cù Vân Thiên Sư (Quyun tianshi 瞿雲天師) (Cù Vân the Celestial Master). Olga Dror suggests that Vân (雲) might be a substitute for Đàm (曇) in the word Cù Đàm (瞿曇), which is a transliteration of the Buddha's family name, Gautama. *A Study of Religion*, 197n98.

81. Tathāgata or Như Lai (如來) means "one who had come and had gone [to nirvana]." This is one of the epithets the Buddha applied to himself and other buddhas.

82. Yama or Diêm Vương (Yanwang 閻王) is the god of the dead in the Buddhist pantheon, appropriated from earlier Brahmanic tradition.

right hand at the earth.[83] A tree of immortality sprang forth from the heavens, and his mother, Lady Māyādevī, took its leaves and mixed them with water to wash herself and her baby. Another account says: At noon[84] on the eighth day of the fourth month in the *giáp-dần* year, while Lady Māyādevī was in labor, nine dragons spouted water to bathe her. She gave birth to the prince, and his father named him Siddhārtha.

This is what they say about the eighth eon: Out of nature came a buddha named Đại Ngộ Chân Trí who helped sentient beings. When Śākyamuni Buddha left Heaven and moved to Vulture Peak [Linh Thứu], the black mountain, his disciples, {**p. 168 (258)**} the monks Chân Trí and Ban Nhược, caught three carp that were eating grain. They brought them to Śākyamuni Buddha, who taught people that [. . .].[85] During that time, there were three ministers who governed the realms of heaven, earth, and humans. The first was Thổ Công, who governed the world of heaven, the second was Thổ [. . .],[86] who governed the world of the earth; and the third was Kiên Lao,[87] who governed the world of humans.

This is what they say about ninth eon: Without a cause came a father and a mother; without a cause emerged yin and yang energies. When the two energies met, the father [yang] looked down and saw the mother [yin]; she looked up and saw him. [From this union] came [Tỳ] Lô, who is also called Ban Nhược [*prajna*]. He was born out of the empty nature [*tính không*] from above.[88]

---

83. For this legend and other legends about the Buddha's birth, see Patricia Karetzky, *The Life of the Buddha: Ancient Scriptural and Pictorial Traditions* (Lanham, MD: University Press of America, 1992), 9–31.

84. Apparently there are two accounts of the birth of Buddha here because the times of birth are different. In the first account, he was born in the early morning; in the second account, at noon.

85. The story ends abruptly in the manuscript. Adriano (*Opusculum*, 93–94) tells the complete story as follows: "Śākyamuni had compassion for people who were without the means to sustain a long life. Because of this, his three servants were turned into three kinds of fish, three rivers, and five species of fruit, birds, and animals. Đại Ngộ Chân Trí and Ban Nhược, who led solitary lives near a stream called Bàn Cổ, saw three carp eating crops and shaking down grain. Chân Trí caught them and brought them to Śākyamuni, who just happened to be there. Śākyamuni ordered King Shennong to cultivate the fields and plant rice to feed these fish. He also ordered the king to gather the crops and winnow the grain to feed the people, and then pass on to future generations the art of cultivating fields, gathering the harvest, and winnowing grain for their sustenance." This account is taken from the first chapter of *Lamp of the Mind*.

86. The manuscript is missing a word here.

87. I have not been able to identify this figure.

88. This is a very obscure passage. According to Adriano (*Opusculum*, 93), the source of this story is from *Esoteric Branches* (Bí Chi), which he recounts: "a man and a women, or a father and a mother, met each other, or discovered each other. The man looked down at the woman, and the woman looked up at the man, and so vacuum from above moved below, and was called Tỳ Lô, and its name was Ban Nhược, and a certain percussive musical instrument came into being." Dror, *A Study of Religion*, 199.

Article 5

On the Real Meaning of the Nine Eons

The Western Scholar says: Everything you, Eastern Scholar, have told me about the Buddhist account of the nine eons is lies and errors. Their words are crafty and obscure, and their content is completely hollow and meaningless. Why do people believe in such a strange and odd account circulated by the Buddhists? Anyone who uses his mind to analyze this will not be able to accept the story and will ridicule it. {p. 169 (259)} First, how can we possibly believe the Buddhist teaching that "Śākyamuni created heaven, earth, human beings and everything"? Śākyamuni was not born until the seventh or eighth eon,[89] and heaven, earth, and everything else had already been created in previous eons. So how could he have created heaven, earth, and everything? Moreover, why were heaven and earth created but not completed in the first eon? Why did Tu Là of Heaven and Ma Ha of Earth have to make pillars and beams to support the heavens in the second eon? The story also says that the Five Ministers also created heaven and earth, but it happened in the third eon. And in the fifth eon, Pangu separated the heavens from the earth; every day the heavens were raised and the earth was pressed down. And in the sixth age, Nügua took five pieces of stone to mend the sky; then two or three people cast the sun and the moon [out of precious metals]. Who would listen to such strange tales? Or is it possible that Buddhism says one thing and means another?

The Eastern Scholar says: You are right. The Buddhist stories about the nine eons do indeed differ, for there are two teachings in Buddhism: one is external, and the other is internal.[90] These two groups teach the same doctrines, but with

---

89. Adriano di Santa Thecla reports that according to *Lamp of the Mind*, Śākyamuni was born in the seventh age, and according to *Esoteric Branches*, he was born in in the eighth.

90. This possibly refers to Mật tông (密宗), the esoteric form of Buddhism that was popular in Vietnam along with the Zen and Pure Land sects. Adriano di Santa Thecla offers another explanation: "[The doctrine which Śākyamuni] as a teacher passed on to his disciples is two-fold: one part of it is external, another is internal. . . . If, in the external doctrine, many things appear interwoven in stories and fables, in the internal doctrine they have their real appearance. Śākyamuni passed along the external doctrine and made it known to everybody; the internal doctrine, however, he shared with one, or in any case with a few, well-tested and faithful students, and strictly ordered them to keep it in secret." (Dror, *A study of Religion*, 191).

different meanings. Priests[91] have been trying to keep the Buddhist book *Secret Transmission* {p. 170 (260)} away from the public to prevent people from learning the true meaning of Buddhist teachings. These priests tell each other to keep this book secret: "Keep the secret. Keep the secret that one must not reveal or pass on—even for a thousand measures of gold." Therefore, everything in the accounts of the nine eons that I described earlier is true. First of all, you must realize that everything in the nine stories relates to the act of intercourse that gave birth to humans. The Buddhist account speaks of three people: a father, a mother, and a child. Buddhists also refer to the bodily parts of these three people.

Therefore, the [true] meaning of the first eon relates to the time when Śākyamuni was conceived in his mother's womb. Before conception, there is no mother or father. Once a child is conceived, then there is a father, mother, and child. [These three are] represented by heaven, earth, and human beings: Heaven is the father, earth is the mother, and man is the child. Hence, [they say] that when Śākyamuni was conceived in his mother's womb, he created heaven, earth, and man. This means that from that time on, there was his father, his mother, and himself. The unintelligent and {p. 171 (261)} frightened Mục Mũi refers to Śākyamuni when he was still in his mother's womb.

The second eon actually refers to the time of his birth, after nine months and ten days in his mother's womb. At that time, Śākyamuni's parents actually became his father and mother [in the conventional sense].

The third eon actually refers to the growth of the five organs inside Śākyamuni's body. The five organs are the liver, heart, lungs, kidney, and spleen—represented by the [ministers'] five colors: green, red, white, black, and yellow.

The fourth eon actually refers to [the development of] Śākyamuni in the womb. A five-month-old fetus is symbolized by the five-*trượng* (fifty cubits) body, and the turbidity refers to the still undeveloped parts of the body.

The fifth eon actually refers to the fact that when Śākyamuni was born, his father was thirty years and twelve months old, so the Heavenly King was thirty *trượng* tall and had twelve heads. His mother was fifteen years and eleven months old, so the Earthly King was fifteen *trượng* tall and had eleven heads. Śākyamuni was in his mother's womb for nine months and ten days, so the Human King was ten *trượng* tall and had nine heads.[92]

---

91. Literally, *đạo sĩ* (道士) means "religious scholar." However, *đạo sĩ* is also a compound noun denoting a Daoist priest or monk. This use of the word in the Buddhist context might mean that the alleged "Buddhist" writings were of Daoist origin.

92. The explanation does not quite fit here in the case of Śākyamuni. Technically, it should be "nine *trượng* tall and ten heads" to correspond with the nine months and ten days of gestation.

The sixth eon means that after Śākyamuni's mother had conceived him in her womb, she used the five elements of her five internal organs to nourish him. When she gave birth to him, she became his mother forever {**p. 172 (262)**}. From that time forth, her status as his mother cannot be disputed.

The actual meaning of the seventh eon refers to the nine-month gestation period when Śākyamuni was in his mother's womb. Other stories are fanciful tales meant to make people respect Śākyamuni and honor him as one who came from heaven.

The actual meaning of the eighth eon refers to the fact that Śākyamuni lived from his mother's blood just like anyone else. The story of how he taught his disciples to save the fish, however, belongs to the Buddhist precept of nonkilling. The three ministers who govern the heavenly, earthly and human realms refer to only three people—the father, mother, and child.

The true meaning of the ninth eon refers to the intercourse between the father and the mother for the purpose of procreation. These are the actual meanings of the nine eons that the Buddhists formulated.

Article 6

On the Meaning of the Words Không [Emptiness] and Phật [Buddha]

The Western Scholar says: Many Buddhists believe *không* [emptiness][93] to be their fundamental teaching as well as the basis of all things. They often use this word [in their teaching]. So I ask you: What do {**p. 173 (263)**} Buddhists mean by the word *không*?

[*Không* (Emptiness) Explained]

The Eastern Scholar says: Many Buddhists deem *không* to be their basic teaching as well as the origin of all things. The ideogram *không* (空) consists of two words: the word *huyệt* (穴) on the top and the word *công* (工) on the bottom. The word *huyệt* refers to the mother, and the word *công* refers to the father. The two unite to beget children. Therefore, Buddhism teaches that all things are born out of *không*. For this reason, stone pillars are often erected in the courtyard in front of Buddhist temples, temple doors are shaped like the character *huyệt*, and the pillars are shaped like the character *công*. Together, they form the character *không*. This character represents the gate through which the Buddha comes: "A painting of the Buddha comes out of a locked gate."[94] Moreover, Buddhists often add the word *không* to the four existing energies in the human body—wind, fire, water, earth—calling them the Five Fires [*ngũ hoả*]. They give them the expression: "*Phật đà vô nam da*" [Homage to the Buddha].[95] [Each word in the expression refers to its respective element.] The word *Phật* symbolizes fire; *đà*, wind; *vô*, water; *nam*, earth; and *da*, emptiness. These five elements are applied to father, mother, and child.

Furthermore, Buddhism often {**p. 174 (264)**} says, "Life is empty (*không*). Death is also empty." Śākyamuni has taught: "Life comes; at death, it is gone. Then [at

---

93. Emptiness or *Không* (空) is the Sino-Vietnamese translation of the Sanskrit word *śunyatā*. It is the basic concept of Mahayana Buddhism in which all existence is unreal, illusory, or impermanent. In this doctrine, all things are compounds of unstable elements and possess no self-essence. Alternative translations include vacuity, emptiness, nonexistence, immateriality, unreality, etc.

94. This translation is approximate since I am unsure of the last two characters in the phrase.

95. The correct word order should be "Nam mô Phật đà da," which corresponds to the Sanskrit phrase "Namo buddhaya" (Homage to the Buddha).

rebirth], life comes again." The book *Secret Transmission* [Bí Truyền][96] explains this phrase as follows:

> When life enters from emptiness, it descends into the "outer hollow" [*ngoại không*].[97] The outer hollow is the top of the head. From this natural void, the seed of life descends to the two feet. When it goes back up, it rises like a cloud to the "outer hollow of the heavenly sea" [*thiên hải ngoại không*] and then departs from the top of the head. That is why they say: "At death, it is gone; then [at birth], life comes again."[98]

When people are conceived in their mother's womb, life first comes through the fontanel on the top of the head. From there, it gradually drifts downward through the body all the way to the two feet. When people die, life first leaves the two feet and then gradually travels all the way up through the body until it reaches the fontanel at the top of the head or the "outer hollow of the heavenly sea." The Buddhist phrase "Life is empty; death is also empty"[99] stems from this phenomenon. It means that life enters the body through the "hollow space"—or fontanel—at birth and exits through it at death. This cycle of coming and going is called the "returning cycle" [*luân hồi*].[100] Everything I have told you is the true meaning of the word *không*, which many Buddhists regard as the essence of everything when they remark: "Life is empty; death is also empty." Therefore, the made-up Buddhist teachings that "out of emptiness comes {p. 175 (265)} everything, and death is a return to emptiness" and "there is transmigration or rebirth in another realm after death" are lies that deceive and mislead people by using words that sound good and seem virtuous.

---

96. Adriano refers to this book as *Bí Chi* (Esoteric Branches), a book purported to be the secret teachings of the Buddha handed down from generation to generation. I have not yet found this book.

97. This refers to the fontanel as explained in the text.

98. Sino-Vietnamese: 生來者自空降外空而來, 外空者頂頭上也, 虛無自然, 子從於兩足而來, 還雲升到於天海外空是頂上而出, 故曰 死去又生來。

99. The common understanding of this phrase refers to the interdependence between life and death, representing the transitional stages in human life. Here, the author tries to give a physiological explanation of life and death: life is the descent of some nonmaterial energy or the soul to the body through the fontanel. When death comes, the energy leaves the body.

100. *Luân hồi* (lunhui 輪迴) is the Buddhist concept of the transmigration of life, moving up and down the six realms of existence: gods (*deva*), titans (*asura*), humans, animals, hungry

[The Various Meanings of "Buddha"]

The Western Scholar asks the Eastern Scholar: What is the meaning of the word *Phật* [Buddha]?

The Eastern Scholar replies: Buddhists associate things relating to the human body with things in heaven and on earth and make them analogous with one another. Therefore, they combine the characters *nhân* (人) and *thiên* (天) to create the word *Phật*. "*Phật* (伏) is made up of human and heavenly beings."[101] They also say: "*Phật* comes from human beings, and human beings come from heaven and earth."

Buddhists often compare the five internal organs to the five agents, the five elements,[102] the five seasons, and the five directions. Since there are only four directions, four seasons, four energies, and four elements, they often add an extra word to these sets to make them five: "Space" or "hollow" (*không*) is added to the four elements. "Ending of the season" (*quý*) is added to the four seasons, and "center" (*trung ương*) is added to the four directions. This was done, in order to correlate the five elements, the five seasons, and the five directions with the five organs: the heart, liver, spleen, lungs, and kidney.

Another explanation of the word *Phật* (伏) is that it was formed by combining the character for "human" (*nhân* 亻 or 人) with the character for "two" (*nhị* 二), meaning a man and a woman bringing a child to life. {p. 176 (266)}

[On Other Buddhist Concepts]

The Western Scholar says: [I have heard the phrase] "A buddha is the heart-mind (*tâm* 心); the heart-mind is a buddha." So, I ask you, Eastern Scholar: What does this phrase mean?

---

ghosts (*preta*), and hell-beings. Here, the text gives a physical explanation of *luân hồi* as the coming and returning of life based on a literal reading: *luân* (輪, the wheel) and *hồi* (迴, return).

101. This character for *Phật* (伏), which is different from the more common character 佛, also appears in some *Nôm* texts. Adriano also describes this particular explanation of the word *Phật* in Sino-Vietnamese characters as the "human and *deva*" being; *Opusculum*, 84 (Dror, *A Study of Religion*, 86). Perhaps it is taken from one of the epithets applied to the Buddha as the "teacher of men and *devas*" (*nhân thiên sư* 人天師).

102. The five Buddhist elements (*ngũ đại* 五大) (earth, water, fire, wind, space) are slightly different from the traditional Chinese five agents (*ngũ hành* 五行), also called the five elements (wood, fire, earth, metal, water).

The Eastern Scholar replies: Buddhists regard both "emptiness" (*không* 空) and "heart-mind" (*tâm* 心) as their basic doctrines. For this reason, the *Sutra of Forty-Two Sections* teaches: "Take 'emptiness' as the way; take 'heart-mind' as the way."[103] Buddhists often take "heart-mind" as the way because the heart occupies the most important place among the five internal organs. Since the character for the heart has four dots, Buddhists often draw four dots to symbolize the image of the Buddha. Because of this practice, they often say, "Buddha resides within one's heart-mind" and "Buddha is the heart-mind; the heart-mind is a buddha." This is the real meaning of the teaching of Buddhism, which I have touched upon. If you, Western Scholar, want to learn more about it, you should read the book *Secret Transmission*. Furthermore, you can read works by the scholar Lê Ích Mục, who is knowledgeable in Buddhism and who can explain everything about it. He lived in a Buddhist temple during the rule of the Trịnh lords. I have heard that in your religion there is also a three-volume book called *Doctrine of Superstitions* [*Dị Đoan Chi Giáo*][104] that discusses the issues presented in *Secret Transmission*. If you do not have this book, look for it and read it to gain full knowledge of the errors of Buddhism.

If we follow the true meaning {**p. 177 (267)**} of Buddhist teachings as Buddhists explain them, we must bear in mind that the Buddha is no different from or more worthy than any other human being. According to Buddhist teachings, all people are buddhas since everybody possesses a heart-mind as well as other characteristics that the Buddha possessed. In spite of the fact that Śākyamuni called himself the Buddha and wanted people to worship him and everything in his body, everyone possesses the same things in their bodies as he did. They are therefore equal to him. Although Buddhist disciples often tell tales and relate mysteries about the Buddha, everyone also has in their bodies all the characteristics that Buddhists talk about. Hence, everyone is equal to the Buddha and Buddhist disciples.

The Western Scholar asks the Eastern Scholar again: Was the book *Secret Transmission* passed down from Śākyamuni?

---

103. Sino-Vietnamese: 以空為道, 以心為道。 This quotation cannot be found in the *Sutra of Forty-Two Sections*.

104. According to Adriano (*Opusculum*, vii; Dror, *A Study of Religion*, 84), this book (now lost) was written by Hilario di Gesù (Hilario Costa), the apostolic vicar of East Tonkin (r. 1737–1754).

The Eastern Scholar replies: The book that was passed down by Śākyamuni is called the *Sutra of Forty-Two Sections*.[105] It was brought back by the Han envoy who went to Tianzhu [India] to acquire Buddhist scriptures for Emperor Han Mingdi. I discussed this in the second article of this book. *Secret Transmission* was fabricated by priests of later generations who added many of their own doctrines to the teachings of Śākyamuni—things that the Buddha had never taught his disciples. {p. 178 (268)} For example, in the story of the nine eons, the book mentions Pangu, the Three Augusts, the Five Emperors,[106] the Three Powers, and the Eight Trigrams. These figures belong to the Confucian teachings of the East (China), which are different from the teachings of the West (India).

Moreover, *Secret Transmission* speaks of the Three Religions of the East and compares their origins. The book asserts that "the three ways of Confucianism, Daoism, and Buddhism were born at the same time and out of the same energy source. Confucianism is the way of Confucius, Daoism is the way of Laozi, and Buddhism is the way of Śākyamuni. Confucian scholars call these the three powers."[107] Laozi and Confucius were born five hundred years after Śākyamuni,[108] since the latter was born during the reign of Zhou Zhaowang [r. 1052–1001 BCE] and the other two during the reign of Zhou Lingwang [r. 571–544 BCE]. For this reason, it was not possible for Śākyamuni to mention these two figures [in this book]—people who were not born until many generations later. Therefore, the author of *Secret Transmission* must be someone who lived after Laozi and Confucius. After Emperor Han Mingdi imported Buddhism into China, the person who wrote the book *Secret Transmission* must have borrowed Confucian teachings and included them in his book in an effort to placate Confucian scholars and encourage them to live in harmony with Buddhism. At one time, Buddhism was a foreign teaching, but now it

---

105. Some modern scholars have questioned the Indian origin of this work. Robert Shaft suggests that this work may be a Central Asian or Chinese composition imitating the style of the *Dhammapada*. See "The Scripture in Forty-Two Sections," 260.

106. *Tam Hoàng Ngũ Đế* (sanhuang wudi 三皇五帝) are the mythical and sage-kings of ancient China. The Five Emperors refers to Taihao (Fuxi), Yandi (Shennong), Huangdi, Shaohao, and Chuan Xu. The first three of the Five Emperors are sometimes called the Three Augusts. The last two are identified with Yao (Nghiêu 堯) and Shun (Thuấn 舜). See also *Errors*, Book 1, Article 7.

107. Sino-Vietnamese: 儒道釋三教所謂同一氣生：儒者孔子道也。道者老聃道也。釋者釋迦道也。儒之所謂三才。The idea that the Three Religions came from the same source (三教同原) was common during the Ming dynasty in China and in eighteenth-century Vietnam.

108. Apparently, Chinese Buddhists pushed back Śākyamuni's birthday by five hundred years, making him older than Laozi and Confucius and proving that their religion was older and therefore superior.

has become part of the native culture and transformed itself into a native religion. For this reason, Buddhists honor Confucius {**p. 179 (269)**} as one of the buddhas; hence, the Buddhist calendar in *Lamp of the Mind* also records Confucius's birthday: "The fourth day of the fifth month is the birthday of the Sage of Great Perfection, King of the Literati." The book also includes a list of Confucius's ancestors because Buddhists desire harmonious relationships with Confucian scholars.

Article 7

On the Precepts Against Killing and Teachings on Reincarnation

The Western Scholar asks: Buddhism forbids killing and teaches reincarnation.[109] So I ask you: What are these teachings about?

The Eastern Scholar replies: In the *Sutra of Forty-Two Sections*, it is forbidden to kill a sentient being, such as chickens, pigs, cattle, wild birds, animals, fish, sea creatures, snakes, reptiles, bees, and insects. It is also taught that anyone who kills a creature will come back in the next life as the same creature and eventually be killed by another person. Furthermore, anyone who does not kill will die only once and will never have to be reborn into the cycle of birth and death,[110] or at least, he will earn enough merit to be reborn as a human being and not as an animal. Ban Gu, the author of *History of the Han Dynasty*, made the following derogatory comment about Buddhism:

> Generally speaking, [Buddhism] takes the concept of voidness and nothingness [*hư vô*] as its basic teaching; it values compassion and {p. 180 (270)} not killing. [It teaches that] after death, the human spirit does not perish but receives another bodily form. In this world, every act of good or evil has a consequence. Hence, the best thing to do is to cultivate one's mind to become a buddha.[111] [*Vietnamese translation follows.*][112]

This is the great commandment of Buddhism.

---

109. It is common to translate *luân hồi* (輪迴) as "reincarnation" or "rebirth." However, the strict Buddhist interpretation of the word is "transmigration." After each life, one is born again into one of the six realms of life and death. This does not necessarily mean that a person will come back as another human being, as in certain Hindu teachings.

110. Hindus and Buddhists believe that the cycle of birth and death, called *saṃsāra*, is a never-ending process based on one's own karma. The only way to end this cycle is to seek liberation (Sanskrit: *mokṣa*) through Hindu or Buddhist practices.

111. Sino-Vietnamese: 其自大抵, 以虛無為宗, 貴慈悲不殺, 以為人死, 精神不滅, 隨復受形, 生時所行善惡, 皆有報應, 故所貴所修練精神, 以至為佛。

112. In the Vietnamese translation, the author of *Errors* paraphrases the Chinese text as follows: "Buddhists view emptiness as their basic teaching; they teach kindness toward others and compassion toward animals. When a person dies, their soul does not die but comes back in another bodily form. If a person has acted kindly and did not kill when they were alive, that person will be human again. But if that person did evil or killed, they will come back as an animal. Therefore, whoever focuses on observing the precepts and cultivating themselves will become a buddha."

The Western Scholar comments: The Buddhist teaching and claim that people are reborn as another human or animal after death is quite contrary to reason. Consider this: If a person's ancestors or parents die and are reborn into another household, and if [by chance] they come to work as servants in a descendant's home, then whenever the master curses and beats these servants, is he not abusing his ancestors or parents? Again, if a person's grandmother or mother dies and is reborn in another household, and if a descendant later [by chance] takes this person as a wife {p. 181 (271)} or concubine without knowing that she was his grandmother or mother, is this not a case of incest?

Furthermore, if a person's ancestors often kill animals for food, die, and then become animals themselves, whenever the descendants kill these animals for the sacrificial feast, are they not killing their own ancestors? Besides, after the ages of the Three Dynasties, each household was asked to raise [at least] five chickens and two pigs in order to have enough meat to feed the elderly as well as make sacrifices of oxen and goats during memorial feasts.[113] For more than 1,300 years—from the time of the great flood to the time of Śākyamuni—everyone, including the Buddha's ancestors, did not abstain from meat. If people are really reborn as animals because they have killed another creature, why are there more and more people and not more and more animals?[114]

The Eastern Scholar comments: Your argument against reincarnation is indeed correct. I will add more arguments. If the ancestors and parents have already been reborn into another household, what is the point of celebrating memorial feasts or performing atonement ceremonies? If their parents have been reborn as another person, the children should worship that person instead. Likewise, if a parent comes back as an animal, their children should worship that animal instead. Furthermore, before the Buddha (Śākyamuni)'s renunciation at the age of thirty, he often hunted birds and animals for food. {p. 182 (272)} After he died, should he not have been reborn [by the law of karma] as a bird or as an animal and then killed by other people? Besides, Buddhist monks force the horse to carry them, the mule to carry their possessions, and the ox to cultivate their fields. These animals are mistreated until death. Afterward, they make the animals' horns into wind instruments for the nuns to blow every month and every year and use their skins to make drums for ritualists to beat day and night [during

---

113. A solemn feast requires a sacrifice of three animals: an ox or buffalo, a goat or sheep, and a pig.

114. See also similar arguments in *Hội Đồng Tứ Giáo*, 15a–15b.

their ceremonies]. They kill cats to make pens out their fur so that they can copy the sutra; they rob chickens of their eggs so that they can paint images of the Buddha. Moreover, they teach novices to burn their elderly monks to prepare for self-immolation. Thus, Buddhist monks show little or no compassion and violate the precepts against killing animals and people. Therefore, whoever considers the arguments I have presented will know that the precept of not killing and the teaching on transmigration are truly irrational, false, and hollow teachings that Buddhism has fabricated. On the other hand, I explained the true meaning of rebirth [*luân hồi*], as taught by their inner teaching, in the section above.

The Western Scholar says: The holy way of the Lord of Heaven also has a teaching about a "rebirth" [*luân hồi*].[115] However, the meaning is different from what has been described here. At the end of time, the Lord of Heaven will resurrect the dead in their bodies. Good people will live again in their glorious bodies, go to paradise, and enjoy eternal blessings. The wicked will live again in their ugly bodies, and they will descend to hell to suffer eternal damnation. That is the {**p. 183** (**273**)} true rebirth that will happen to everyone in the future. We must believe in this kind of rebirth.

---

115. Interestingly, the Christian scholar here uses the same Buddhist word *luân hồi* to describe the resurrection of the body.

Article 8

On the "Protection for the Journey" Prayer

The Western Scholar says: Buddhist monks often recite the "Protection for the Journey" prayer [*kinh bảo đàng*].[116] So, I ask you: What is that prayer all about?

The Eastern Scholar replies: First when a person is about to die, a Buddhist monk recites the "Protection for the Journey" prayer [to guide the soul in the netherworld]. He calls out to the soul: "Buddha's nature! Oh, Buddha's nature! Do not come out through the eyes, ears, nose, mouth, or lower orifices; otherwise, there will be trouble. Come out through the fontanel." Buddhism calls the fontanel the "gate of heaven" [*thiên môn*]. The book *Secret Transmission* states: "The head represents heaven. At death, if the soul exits through the 'outer hollow of the heavenly sea' (the fontanel), it will rise to heaven. If it exits through the eyes, ears, nose, mouth, or lower orifices, it will not become immortal." After death, the monk tells the soul of the deceased to identify itself as the "child of the Buddha" [*phật tử*] when it travels in around the netherworld. The soul should trust the Buddha to lead it away from hell. If it follows the Buddha's guidance, it will be led to the Buddha's land; otherwise, it will end up in the three hells and suffer hunger and thirst for eternity. If the soul erroneously follows the evil path, its descendants will suffer a great deal, and it will need saints and bodhisattvas to save it. Therefore, Buddhist teachers tell a person that the proper thing to do is to submit to the Buddha. One can reap the benefits of calling on him in a time of need. The Buddhist monk recites the sutras to pray for the deceased {**p. 184 (274)**} and to protect his or her soul along the journey.

The monk tells the soul that once in the netherworld, it must first cross the Âm Không Bridge on the way to Thanh Bình. Then, the soul goes to Hoàng Tuyền Mountain, where it will come across a well and a tall coconut tree. Thousands and thousands of people are wandering about in that area. There, the soul will encounter General Gió Xá Tắc Lộ, who guards the place. Upon meeting him, the soul must show him its permit to enter.

---

116. *Bảo Đàng* (保唐) literally means protection along "the path from the gate of a temple to the main hall".

After passing the checkpoint, the soul proceeds to the Tự Nhiên ferry station on the Ái Hà river, where General Tô Giang is in charge. Upon meeting him, the soul must once again show its documentation to go through. The soul may see a copper boat with silver paddles. But it must not get on this boat because it is the wrong one. When the soul sees a golden boat with golden paddles, it must try to get on this boat. The soul should ask: "Is it Trương Chiên, the ferryman? Will you take me to the other side?" The ferryman will ask back: "Who is it that knows my name?" Then the soul must show its permit again. Upon seeing this documentation, the ferryman will take the soul on his boat to the other side of the river. Upon disembarking, the soul travels straight ahead for about a mile. When arriving at a sand dune called Tràng Sa, the soul will see a crossroads. There is a bridge there, Âm Không,[117] that is made of copper pillars and iron boards. {p. 185 (275)} The soul should stop and rest there. If hungry, the soul can take out the food that was prepared for it and eat.

After resting a bit, the soul continues on its journey. Never travel on the eastern road, for the east is guarded by the large dog Phi Liêm. Never travel on the southern road, for the south is guarded by the spirit Hoả Lô, who can set people on fire. Never travel on the northern road, for the north leads to the three hells. The soul should[118] travel on the southwestern road, for the southwest has a silver road, which is the religious path. Travelling on the silver road, the soul no longer needs to go in a circle, carry a torch [to light its way], or make a bridge [to cross water].

The soul continues for about a mile to the base of a mountain that displays the three words "Phổ Đà Sơn" [Mount Pokatala].[119] There are nine types of gem-like lotus flowers there. Saints and bodhisattvas recite the name of Amitābha Buddha[120] in this place. The soul bows to them and says, "My name is such and such. I was born in the other world, and now after death, I have arrived in this realm. I was ignorant and did not know the dharma. Fortunately, I met an enlightened master, took refuge in the Three Jewels, and recited the sutras devoutly. After death, I received a certificate of passage thanks to my Buddhist merit." Then, the soul kneels, folds his hands, and begins to confess his true nature. {p. 186 (276)} Then

---

117. The manuscript has "Âm Huyệt." This could be an error. It should be "Âm Không," since the characters *không* (空) and *huyệt* (穴) are often confused, as described in *Errors*, Book 3, Article 6. Also, in *Hội Đồng Tứ Giáo* (31b), this is called Âm Không Bridge.

118. The text has "should not." This is a scribal error, for it is contrary to the general sense.

119. The residence of Avalokiteśvara bodhisattva.

120. This is a rough translation.

Amitābha Buddha and the bodhisattvas Avalokiteśvara and Mahāsthāmaprāpta appear and greet the soul, which recites: "Homage to the Western Bliss Paradise, where there are countless realms[121] and where there are numerous monks[122] of the same name and the same title: 'great compassionate accompaniers.' Homage to Amitābha Buddha." Then he recites the following religious poem:

> Living, you are responsible for your good or evil actions.
> Dying, you are relieved of your *karma*.
> O soul, remember to chant the name of Buddha.
> Even if you fall into hell, you will be released.[123]

After reciting the "Protection for the Journey" prayer, the Buddhist monk draws a nine-dragon amulet with a stick and then tears down the repentance residence to set the soul free. He takes a golden stick and composes a letter with it, thus issuing the soul's permit for travel in the netherworld. The soul will carry this permit on its sleeve. A man carries it on the left, and a woman on the right.[124]

The Western Scholar says: Why does the Buddhist monk ask the soul to exit the body through the fontanel rather than through the lower orifices? When the soul leaves the body, it exits only through the fontanel, for it is through the fontanel that the soul first enters the body. Life descends from the head to the toes, and in death it reverses direction, ascending from the toes to the head. That is why the Buddha taught, "Life is empty; death is also empty." However, the soul is a spirit different from the body; it does not require a gate to enter or exit the body. It comes in and out of the body in a mysterious way that we do not comprehend.

What you have said about going to the Buddha's land {**p. 187 (277)**} is hard to accept. Only those who are uneducated and do not think critically would believe in such nonsense. The land of the Buddha is the kingdom Tianzhu [India], which countless travelers from the west have passed through. They do not encounter the Âm Không Bridge, Mount Hoàng Tuyền, the well, or the coconut tree. They do not cross the Ái Hà river with the help of ferryman Tự Nhiên. They do not come to a crossroads or to a bridge called Âm Không made of copper beams and

---

121. Literally, three thousand of sixty thousand of one hundred thousand (*tam thiên lục vạn ức*) realms.

122. Literally, 10 of 19,500 (*nhất thập nhất vạn cửu thiên ngũ bách*) monks.

123. *Hội Đồng Tứ Giáo* (31b) cites the same poem.

124. This description of the "Protection for the Journey" is the most difficult section to translate, for the text includes many obscure words that cannot be verified.

iron spans. Moreover, the kingdom of Tianzhu is a barbaric country, where dark-skinned people and savages live. That country is not as civilized as Annam. So for what reason should the Annamese soul seek to go to the Buddha's land?

Besides, the soul of a blessed person already has a happy place to live, and the soul of a wicked person has already been condemned to hell. A Buddhist monk or ceremonialist [*cao công*][125] can in no way change the reward and punishment of the afterlife by reciting the prayer of "Protection for the Journey" to the Buddha's land. With regard to the religious poem:

> One does not have to do good or avoid evil.
> For at death, all crimes are forgiven.
> Ask the soul to recite the Buddha's name.
> Even if it falls into hell, it will be released.[126]

The poem teaches that it does not matter whether one does good or evil. One only needs to diligently recite the Buddha's name for protection; then one does not have to worry about being condemned to hell. If this is true, then why does Buddhism teach monks to practice religious precepts, refrain from eating meat, recite the sutra, and give alms? {**p. 188 (278)**} Buddhism is full of empty and false words that one should not listen to.

The Eastern Scholar says: When the Buddhist monk finishes reciting the "Protection for the Journey" prayer, he offers sacrifices to the guardian spirits of the three roads [*tam kỳ lộ*], who are Ban Niên Đại Thuê Thần, Đoạn Huyên Nhất Thần, and Tuy Hàn Tướng Quân, or Danh Lan, Danh Lực, and Danh Lai.[127] He also makes offerings of silver and gold as well as meat and wine to the four guardians, the meritorious monks, and the evil spirits. After performing the sacrifices, he sends the evil spirits back to where they belong in order to prevent them from harming the soul of the deceased. He does this by striking the coffin with a knife three times to ward off the Wood Spirit (*mộc thần*):

> With the first strike, I chop away the disasters from heaven so the soul can reap the benefits.

---

125. I am uncertain of the exact meaning, but in this context, it refers to someone who is involved in funeral practices.

126. Here the Western Scholar paraphrases and reinterprets the religious poem shared by the Eastern Scholar in the previous section.

127. These names are obscure.

With the second strike, I chop away the disasters from earth so the soul can enter the heaven.

With the third strike, I chop away the disasters caused by the Wood Spirit,[128] dispersing all misfortune so the soul can go to the Land of Bliss [tịnh thổ][129] and the deceased's family may have long-lasting luck.[130]

Then all respond: "Long live the soul."[131]

During the ceremony of "controlling the spirit" [am phù hạ quan] before putting the body in the coffin, one takes three coins and enough rice to fill the deceased's mouth.[132] The first coin and a portion of the rice are put into the left side of the mouth, the second coin and rice into the right, and the third coin and rice into the middle (on the tongue). If this is done, the soul will never be hungry. Then, one makes the "soul cloth" [hồn bạch], writes the "name banner" [minh tinh], and writes the "soul banner" [linh phưởn]. This is where animate and inanimate souls[133] reside. After shrouding, {p. 189 (279)} the body is transferred to the coffin. Then one performs the rite of "Calling Back the Soul" [triệu hồn], saying: "May the spirits help bring the deceased's soul to its glorious destiny. If the soul gets stuck wandering the Three Realms [tam giới][134] or gets lost on the roads, bridges, four directions, or scenic areas, please lead it back [to the right path]."

---

128. People believed that every tree had a spirit. When a tree was cut down to make a coffin, its spirit remained in the wood, so it was important to expel the spirit of the wood as well.

129. The Land of Bliss (淨土), or *Sukhavati* in Sanskrit, is the Western Paradise of Pure Land Buddhism. It is also known as the Buddha's Land (佛國).

130. This is known as the *Lễ Phạt Mộc* (Ceremony of Striking the Coffin). People believed that evil spirits hid in the coffin. Thus, before placing the body into the coffin, the ceremonialist had to "strike" the coffin three times in order to drive away and stop evil spirits from bothering the deceased and the living. He uses a knife to do so while saying a mantra to expel the evil spirits.

131. Sino-Vietnamese: 第一斬斬天殃,亡者得吉昌。第二斬斬地殃,亡者得生天。第三斬斬木殃,凶眾去他方,亡者超淨土,家眷壽延長。各唱: 千秋萬萬歲。

132. This is known as *Lễ Phạn Hàm* (Ceremony of Putting Rice into the Mouth). People put three coins and a handful of rice into the mouth of the deceased. They believed that the rice was food for the journey in the netherworld and that the three coins were for paying the toll. Rich people could substitute three pieces of gold for the coins and nine pearls for the rice.

133. Literally, "the three *hồn* and the seven *phách*." Chinese and Vietnamese believe that the human soul has two main components: *Hồn* is the animate or spiritual soul (which has three subtypes), and *phách* (or *vía*) is the inanimate or material soul (which has seven subtypes). At death, spiritual souls go to heaven, and material souls go down the earth.

134. Buddhist cosmology divides the many worlds into three types: the realms of sensuous desire, form, and pure spirit.

The Western Scholar comments: The rites that Buddhist monks perform at funerals are empty and false. The act of putting coins and rice into the mouth of a deceased person to save them from starvation or to help them attain eternal life is the greatest of deceptions. An intelligent person must reject this practice, for the soul is a spirit. When it leaves the body, it no longer needs bodily nourishment. Furthermore, how can three coins and a handful of rice provide eternal nourishment for the soul? In addition, how can a monk call a wandering soul back to his or her home? Once the soul leaves the body, it will enter paradise if it has merit; if it has sinned, it will go to hell. What kind of power does a Buddhist monk have over a soul to recall it? Such talk is only a boasting that deceives people into believing in his power.

The Eastern Scholar says: In addition, Buddhists have taken on the custom of wearing mourning garments as specified in the Confucian *Family Rituals*. When a Buddhist monk or a ritualist comes to distribute the mourning garments on the fourth day after the deceased has passed away, he takes a round plate and a bowl of water. He then takes a pair of scissors and cuts off the hair of children mourning parents or of a wife mourning a husband. {p. 190 (280)} Before the hair-cutting ceremony, he reads a funeral oration in verses:

> From Mount Côn Lôn comes the iron core
> To make the famous Mô (Mạc) Da knife.
> Cutting away my hair
> To repay the hardship of parents [in raising children].
> Hard work is the way of filial piety
> So that more blessings can be acquired.
> May their souls enter the Buddha's land.
> So that their descendants may enjoy prosperity and fame.[135]

First, the monk cuts some hair on the back of the head, then some hair on the front, leveling it to the eyes. The Confucian ritual, in contrast, does not permit cutting the hair; on the contrary, it teaches that one should let the hair grow long. Therefore, whoever follows the Confucian ritual does not have their hair cut by monks, but instead, mourners wear the prescribed garments for specific types of mourning, for example, the fatherly mourning garments

---

135. Sino-Vietnamese: 崑崙出鐵石, 莫耶名剪刀, 割披肴餘血, 報父母劬勞, 持勤孝子道, 福德等彌高, 靈者超佛國, 子孫富貴豪。The text is in five-word verses, so this translation is approximate.

[*trảm thôi*],[136] or motherly mourning garment [*tề thôi*],[137] and other types of mourning garments according to the degree of relationships.[138] The persons in mourning do not cut off their hair like Buddhists but wear proper mourning garments. Those unfamiliar with the Confucian family ritual see other people cutting off their hair and follow suit. Haircutting is a heterodox custom originating from Buddhism.

The Western Scholar comments: The practice of cutting one's hair originates with Śākyamuni. When he became the founder of Buddhism, he told his disciples, the *bhiksus*, to shave off one's hair and beard when they become novice monks [*śramanas*]. At that point, Buddhist monks [*bhiksus*] began to obey the teachings of the Buddha. When they became *śramanas*, they shaved their heads. As a result, these monks instituted the funeral custom of requiring people to cut their hair. Buddhists who shave their heads are truly barbarians. That custom {p. 191 (281)} is the custom of savages. Hence, an Annamese with good manners should not follow that barbaric custom.

---

136. *Trảm thôi* (斬衰) is a funeral garment that a son wears to mourn his late father.

137. *Tề thôi* or *Tư Thôi* (齊衰) is a funeral garment that a son wears to mourn his late mother. In some cases, a son without a father can wear *trảm thôi* to mourn his mother.

138. Literally, *Mộ phục* (墓服, garment for one-year mourning); *Đại công* (大功, garment for nine-month mourning); *Tiểu công* (小功, garment for five-month mourning); and *Ti ma* (緦麻, garment for three-month mourning).

Article 9

On the Burning of Paper Mausoleums and Joss Paper

The Western Scholar says: When rich people give their parents a proper funeral, they often have a large, decorated paper mausoleum made, which they burn after the burial. In the seventh month, they have a ceremony for the soul after which sacrificial animals made of paper are also burned. Furthermore, each time a sacrifice is offered, paper money and paper bars of gold and silver are burned. So, I ask you: What is the meaning of this custom?

The Eastern Scholar replies: Because people believe that burning joss paper produces actual tools and materials for their deceased parents and ancestors to use in the netherworld, they follow the custom of burning funeral effigies and paper money.

In the book *Family Rituals*, Master Zhu Xi quotes Master Zhao: "Paper money originates from the [time of the] chief historian Yin to Wang Yu."[139] Master Zhu Xi himself also used paper money in funeral sacrifices. [Another story says that] in the Later Tang period, a man named Cai Lun had a shop where joss paper items were made. Since he wanted his business to thrive, he discussed a scheme with his wife one day. He would pretend to die for three days, and his wife would cry and mourn {**p. 192 (282)**} after efforts to revive him had failed. Then she would burn the joss paper—ingots of gold and money—while praying: "I burn these monetary offerings for my husband so that he may live again." She followed the plan, and he came back to life again. Seeing this, people started believing in the power of burning joss paper. Whenever a person became ill, the family purchased joss paper and burned it for their recovery. From that time on, the custom of burning joss paper has been observed.

In Annam, since the time of the Lý and Trần dynasties, devout Buddhists regularly go to Đông Hồ village to purchase joss paper. In the seventh month [during the ceremony of Ulambana], joss paper items are also burned at ceremonies where people pray for the dead and wandering souls.

The burning of paper mausoleums originates from a book written by Duke Gao,[140] who lived during the Ming dynasty. He tells the following story in his book: One night, Shu Di was relaxing in his courtyard. Looking up at

---

139. Wang Yu (王璵), who lived during the Tang dynasty, is credited with the use of paper money for imperial sacrifices.

140. This may refer to a real person or be a generic name for a ritualist here. The name could mean "Eunuch Gao," for eunuchs were powerful during the late Ming dynasty.

the moon, he saw the fairy Heng E[141] [the daughter of the Jade Emperor] and fell in love with her. Heng E conceived, and nine months and ten days later, she gave birth to a son and named him Chang Cheng. When Chang Cheng grew up, he asked about his father. Heng E told him that his father was a mortal named Shu Di. Chang Cheng rode the White Rooster to the world of mortals and brought his father back to heaven. When the Jade Emperor came to meet his son-in-law, he gave him a bowl of water, a peach, and a small knife. Shu Di did not use the knife but instead bit off the peach and ate it [without slicing it]. {p. 193 (283)} The Jade Emperor considered him rude and sent him back to the earth. Upon returning, Shu Di saw that his palace was in ruins, except for a single pillar of copper. Feeling angry, he bashed his head against the pillar and died. After he died, his soul was transformed into a water hen or coot. His body, however, was laid naked and uncovered on the ground. Chang Cheng came down from heaven, covered his father's body with leaves, and commissioned a decorated mausoleum ten thousand cubits high for his father. But before he could use it to house his father's body, a violent storm came and blew the mausoleum out to sea. The Admiral Wu Gang seized the mausoleum and kept it. Chang Cheng acquired some money and asked the Great Supreme Lord Lao to go and reclaim it. In a written contract, Wu Gang agreed to return the mausoleum to Chang Cheng for housing his father's remains. Since then, whoever wants a mausoleum to house their relative's remains must first pray to Duke Gao to get it from Wu Gang and then buy [a paper version] and burn it so that the deceased will have a house in the netherworld.

The Western Scholar says: Those who burn paper mausoleums and joss paper only waste money and effort, for the dead in the netherworld are spirits. They do not have bodies like when they were alive; hence, they have no need of material things. If burning paper items can turn them into real tools and materials for the deceased to use, one would first have to make a paper doll of the deceased and burn that too. The deceased needs a body in order to enjoy using money and other materials as the living do.

{p. 194 (284)}

---

141. Heng E (姮娥), also known as Chang E (嫦娥), is a fairy who resides in the moon. Originally, she was a mortal, wife of the archer Hou Yi (后羿), who lived during the legendary reign of Emperor Yao. Legend has it that she stole an immortal potion from her husband and drank it. Her body became light like the air, and she flew to the moon.

The Eastern Scholar comments:[142] I do not think that the mortal Shu Di's love for the moon fairy, Heng E, could possibly have caused her to conceive and bear a son. And if Chang Cheng was the grandson of the Jade Emperor, then he would have had the spiritual powers to prevent the storm from carrying his father's mausoleum to the high seas. He would not have had to exchange it for gold when the mausoleum was captured by Wu Gang. Furthermore, no one can live on the moon, for the sky moves around like a wheel with no moment of rest. How can anyone live under such conditions? Heng E was the wife of Hou Yi[143]—the one who shot down the extra suns during the reign of Emperor Yao. She did not have the power to live on the moon. Shu Di was a mortal named Wang Di Du Yu who lived during the Ming dynasty, not a contemporary of Heng E. The history book mentions that in the mountain of Shu there was a humane king named Wang Di Du Yu, who was the brightest and kindest person. Therefore, do not purchase paper mausoleum because of the story of Duke Gao.

---

142. The comment seems to come from the Western Scholar rather than the Eastern Scholar.

143. Hou Yi (后羿), or the Divine Archer, was a heroic figure in Chinese mythology. According to legend, ten suns appeared in the sky in ancient times. The heat scorched the earth; no crops could grow, and people suffered. Since Hou Yi was a skillful archer, he took on the task of shooting down nine suns, leaving only one to light the earth.

Article 10

On Hell

The Western Scholar says: According to Buddhist teachings, a person who dies with bad karma[144] will be punished in hell.[145] So I ask you: What is hell all about?

The Eastern Scholar says: First, Buddhism teaches that there are "earthly prisons," also known as Hades, which are governed by the ten lords {**p. 195 (205)**} or the Netherworld Kings of Ten Palaces[146]—the first being King Yama.[147] There are also five generals who guard the five gates of these prisons: the White King, the Black King, the Red King, the Green King, and the Yellow King. Buddhists also had a story about those who live in hell and how they are able to continue to use materials from this world, which their children send to them. Therefore, descendants must burn paper goods of money, gold, and clothing. This transforms these things into real money, gold, and clothing for their ancestors to use in the netherworld. The descendants also burn these items to make offerings to the prison chiefs in order to lighten their ancestors' sentences.[148] Furthermore, Buddhism teaches people to perform ceremonies of atonement to redeem their ancestors from bad karma and guarantee their release from prison.

The Western Scholar asks the Eastern Scholar to explain: What is the rite of "breaking the prison" [*phá ngục*][149]?

---

144. Literally, "crime" (*tội*). Bad karma is the Buddhist equivalent of the Christian concept of sin. But there is a crucial difference: Sin is a theological concept—an offense against God by not keeping the divine laws, or a state of being alienated from God. In Buddhism, people accrue good or bad karma as a consequence of their actions, independent of divine judgment. Vietnamese use the word "crime" to denote sin and/or "bad karma."

145. Literally, the "earthly prison" or *địa ngục* (地獄) is a place of punishment in the netherworld. The ancient Vietnamese had no concept of hell, which was introduced with the arrival of Buddhism. The popular term that describes the realm of death is *âm phủ* (陰府), or "abode of the dead." It is analogous to the Greek concept of Hades and contrasts with the realm of the living—the *dương gian* (陽間). In this work, the author equates the "earthly prison" with the "abode of the dead," although they are not the same.

146. Traditional Chinese hell is divided into ten palaces, each of which is governed by a god or a buddha. For a detailed description of the Ten Netherworld Kings (*thập điện minh vương*), see Doré, *Research into Chinese Superstitions*, 7:250–302.

147. *Yama*, or *Diêm Vương* (閻王), is an Indian king of the dead who was incorporated into the pantheon of Mahayana Buddhism.

148. This custom is still popular among the North Vietnamese today.

149. See also *Opusculum*, 105–7 (Dror, *A Study of Religion*, 213–15).

The Eastern Scholar says: During the three years of mourning, Buddhists often perform the ceremony of atonement by inviting monks to their homes. After days of abstaining from meat, reciting the sutras, and making offerings to atone for the bad karma of the patron's ancestors, the monks perform the rites of "breaking the prison" on the last day. On that day, four [bamboo] poles are put in the house and arranged into a square. Then the paper is used to cover the structure like a box. Four gates are drawn on four sides, with one gate in the middle of the top to resemble a prison cell. Then the chief monk puts on {p. 196 (286)} his ceremonial cap and robe and solemnly offers sacrifices to the Netherworld Kings of the Ten Palaces and to the ten lords who govern the realm of the dead. He also offers sacrifices to Ksitigarbha [*ngục tàng vương*][150] and to the five kings who guard the five doors: The Green King guards the eastern door; the White King, the western door; the Red King, the southern door; the Black King, the northern door; and the Yellow King, the central [or top] door. Before offering their sacrifices, the monks walk three times around the mock prison in procession, chanting sutras and sprinkling holy water as they walk. After offering the sacrifices, the chief monk tosses two coins to solicit an affirmative sign that their offerings and prayers have been accepted by the spirits. Then he takes a walking stick and beats open the paper gates. This releases the deceased's soul from prison. This is how the rite of "breaking the prison" is performed according to the book *Hoàng Đô Lĩnh*.[151] The arrangement of the prison walls is shown as follows:

	South Red King	
East Green King	Center Yellow King	West White King
	North Black King	

---

150. Ksitigarbha, known in Chinese as the "King of the Earth Treasure" (Dizang Wang), is a buddha of the netherworld. For the Chinese interpretation of this buddha, see Doré, *Research into Chinese Superstitions*, 7:235–49.

151. I am uncertain of the title. Adriano di Santa Thecla refers to this as *Hoàng Đô Vĩnh*. Dror proposes that it is the first three words of the phrase "Hoàng Đô Vĩnh Cố" (Let the fortune of the emperor be eternal and firm). These words were often found on the title pages of texts written during the time of the Lê dynasty. See *A Study of Religion*, 207n159.

{p. 197 (287)}

The Western Scholar comments: Buddhists often make up solemn ceremonies to entice people into believing in Buddhism. However, if we think critically about it, many Buddhist teachings and rituals are nonsense, deceptive, and useless. If a Buddhist monk has the power to break open a prison and rescue the soul inside, who gives him his power to this? If it is Śākyamuni who gives him that power, why does the *Sutra of Forty-Two Sections* say absolutely nothing about it? This rite only originated during the time of Liang Wudi, who instituted the ceremonies for atonement: "Liang Wudi established the ceremonies for the dead." Furthermore, atonement ceremonies and the rite of "breaking the prison" are actually contrary to Buddhist teachings, for the Buddha taught: "Life is empty; death is also empty. Everything is empty." If the dead return to emptiness, what point is there in redeeming the deceased's bad karma and breaking open the prison door? When the dead return to emptiness, everything should cease to exist. Hence, the custom of burning paper money, gold, and clothing for the dead to use in the netherworld is nonsense and misleading.[152] Another reason that the custom is misrepresentative is that people in hell no longer {p. 198 (288)} have a need for the material things of this world. The living need these things because they have bodies. The dead are spirits without bodies; thus, they have no use for material things.

The Eastern Scholar says: In your religion, there is a rite similar to the Buddhist rite of breaking open the prison. The Buddhist monk can use this fact to defend his practice against your criticisms.

The Western Scholar says: It is impossible for the Buddhist monk to use it against me! In my religion, there is a rite to save the dead from purgatory. This is performed when someone sinned and repented while they were alive but did not complete the penance before they died. After death, he or she still needs to complete the penance in purgatory. The merciful Lord of Heaven has allowed the living to pray and perform a rite (Catholic Mass) to atone for the souls in purgatory. On the other hand, if a person commits a mortal sin while he or she was alive and did not repent, the person's soul is condemned to hell for eternal punishment. In this case, we are not able to save his or her soul and therefore do not pray or perform a rite (Mass) for that person. This is the teaching of the holy way of the Lord of Heaven on atonement for the dead.

---

152. Strictly speaking, the custom of burning joss paper and paper items is not a Buddhist one but belongs to folk practice.

The Eastern Scholar says: What you have said sounds right, and I agree with your reasoning. Now I will explain {**p. 199 (289)**} to you all the Buddhist teachings on hell. Buddhist monks have devised prayers for the living to redeem the dead. Ten days are set aside each month for this. Each day is dedicated to a particular buddha, who has the power to help the individual, who vows to abstain from meat, and who promises to pray to the Buddha of that particular day. The prayer is a mantra starting with two words "*nam mô*" [Sanskrit: *namo*] followed by the name of a buddha prescribed for that day. Since the person must recite this mantra a thousand times, he or she often uses a rosary-like one-hundred-bead ring to keep track of the counting—ten counts are equal to a thousand times. The book *Lamp of the Mind* provides this calendar. For example, on the first day, one chants: "*Namo* [homage to] *Dīpankara Buddha*."[153] If one recites this chanting a thousand times, one will not lose his way to bliss[154] at death. On the full moon one chants, "*Namo Amitābha Buddha*,"[155] and on the thirtieth day "*Namo Śākyamuni Buddha*,"[156] and so on.[157]

The Western Scholar asks the Eastern Scholar again: What is the meaning of the two words "nam mô" that Buddhists recite?

The Eastern Scholar says: Buddhists ascribe multiple meanings to these two words, which is why they often emphasize these two words in their prayers. The

---

153. Dīpankara is known in Chinese as the "Light Bearer Buddha" (Dengran fo 燈燃佛) or the "Fixed Light Buddha" (Dingguang fo 定光佛). He is the first of the twenty-four mythical buddhas who appeared before Gautama. For the Chinese understanding of this buddha, see Doré, *Research into Chinese Supersitions*, 6:89–102.

154. The translation of this phrase is approximate.

155. Amitābha or A Di Đà (阿彌佗) is the buddha who governs the Western Paradise. He is revered by the Pure Land sect, which is considered the largest Buddhist sect in China, Japan, and Vietnam.

156. Śākyamuni or Thích Ca Mâu Ni (釋迦牟尼) is the historical Buddha, whose name was Siddhārtha Gautama.

157. Adriano di Santa Thecla gives a fuller calendar of the buddhas and bodhisattvas to whom one prays each a month: On the first, one prays to Dīpankara (Định Quang Vương); on the eighth, to Bhaisajyaguru (Dược Sư); on the fourteenth, to the thousand buddhas of the present eon (Hiền Kiếp Thiên); on the fifteenth, to Amitābha (A Di Đà); on the eighteenth, to Ksitigarbha (Địa Tạng Vương); on the twenty-third, to Mahāsthāma-prāpta (Đại Thế Chí); on the twenty-fourth, to Avalokiteśvara (Quán Thế Âm); on the twenty-eighth, to Lochana (Lô Xá Na); on the twenty-ninth, to Bhaichadyaradja and Bhaichadjyaradjasamudgata (Dược Vương, Dược Thượng); and on the thirtieth, to Śākyamuni (Thích Ca Mâu Ni). *Opusculum*, 97; Dror, *A Study of Religion*, 204–5 and nn. 143–50.

book *Lamp of the Mind* explains these two words as follows: "*nam* means 'the heaven covers'; *mô* means 'the earth supports.'*[158]* *Nam* is the father; *mô* is the mother. *Nam* is water; *mô* is fire. *Nam* is the heart-mind; *mô* is nature. *Nam* is fatherhood; *mô* is motherhood. *Nam* is the *Kan* trigram; *mô* is {**p. 200 (290)**} the *Li* trigram. *Nam* refers to *yin*; *mô* refers to *yang*. *Nam* is the *Qian* trigram; *mô* is the *Kun* trigram. *Nam* is the sun; *mô* is the moon. *Nam* is the substance; *mô* is the action. *Nam is* the form-body; *mô* is the dharma-body. Thus, *nam* and *mô* refer to the ins and out of everyday life.[159]

---

158. Apparently the Vietnamese proverb "Heaven covers; the earth supports" (*thiên phù địa tải*) is made to fit the yin-yang concept of *nam mô*. Here *nam* refers to heaven, and *mô* refers to the earth.

159. Sino-Vietnamese: 南為天覆, 無為地載。南為父, 無為母。南為水, 無為火。南為心, 無為性。南為性父, 無為性母。南為坎, 無為離。南陰無陽, 南乾無坤。南為日, 無為月。南為体, 無為用。南為色身, 無為法身。故日內外南無。*Tâm Đăng*, 9a.

Article 11

On Quan Âm (Avalokiteśvara) and the Wandering Souls

The Western Scholar says: People often worship a buddha named Quan Âm and rely on this buddha to help them. So I ask you, Eastern Scholar: Who is this Buddha Quan Âm (Avalokiteśvara)?[160]

The Eastern Scholar replies: In Buddhism, there are many "bodhisattva" buddhas, or "the ones who have the power to save people from evils."[161] The most beloved among these bodhisattvas is Quan Âm because she has more power to save people than any other buddha.[162] Buddhist tradition tells her story as follows:

Quan Âm, the daughter of King Miaozhuang, was born Princess Miaoshan—also known as Mẫu Thiện in Vietnamese. Quan Âm guarded her virginity and did not want to marry. Her father got angry and sent her away. Quan Âm went to the Xiangshan district in Guangdong province and took refuge in a small temple on Mount Xiang. She remained there with the nuns and did not return home. [After repeated attempts to call her back had failed], the king sent people to burn down the temple. All of the nuns burned to death, except Quan Âm, who had held on to a weeping willow branch and was unharmed by the fire. She then told people: "I have already achieved my enlightenment and now have great miraculous power."[163] {p. 201 (291)} She

---

160. Quan Âm is the Vietnamese version of Avalokiteśvara, the bodhisattva of compassion. She was known as Guanyin in China, Kannon in Japan, and Kwon-um in Korea. In Vietnam, she is often called "Lady Buddha" (*Phật bà*).

161. In Mahayana Buddhism, bodhisattvas are enlightened beings who defer their entrance into nirvana in order to help the sentient beings of this world reach nirvana as well. These enlightened beings are said to have powers to save people from evils and aid them on their quest of enlightenment. No doubt, the most popular of all bodhisattvas in Vietnam is Quan Âm, who personifies the virtue of compassion.

162. The cult of Quan Âm in Vietnam is apparently a mixture of the native tradition of goddess worship and the cult of Guanyin in China. Chapter 25 of the *Lotus Sutra*, which discusses Avalokiteśvara's promise that those who believe in her will be saved from harm, is the basis for the cult of Guanyin in China. There are volumes of literature about Guanyin. The most comprehensive discussion is Chun-Fang Yü, *Kuan Yin: The Chinese Transformation of Avalokiteśvara* (New York: Columbia University Press, 2001).

163. The story of Quan Âm here is based on the Legend of Miaoshan, which has been circulating in China since the twelfth century. For a thorough discussion of the different versions

is also referred to as the "one who has a thousand eyes and a thousand arms" [*thiên thủ thiên nhỡn*] or Lady Buddha, who often appears on the South China Sea. Buddhists have chosen the twenty-fourth day of each month to recite her name a thousand times to save themselves from falling into hell. *Lamp of the Mind* states: "Those who earnestly pray to the bodhisattva a thousand times will not go to hell to be punished." This is the reason why many people worship Quan Âm in their homes.

The Western Scholar comments: If Quan Âm truly has great power to perform miracles, why was she unable to save the nuns from being burned to death by her father? Since she was unable to protect her nuns from harm, how can she save anyone else? Those who worship Quan Âm believe she has the power to save them from harm, but when they are victims of fire disasters, theft, robbery, and illness, we do not see anyone appearing to save them. Furthermore, a normal human being has two eyes, two ears, and four limbs. No human person ever has three or four eyes, let alone a face with ten eyes and a body with a thousand arms. This is very odd for a human being. And if this is not a human being, then it must be a demon. Buddhist books often contain untrue stories, which are criticized in the book *General Discussion*: "In general, these stories contain ghosts and demons as well as false doctrines of malice. They are used to deceive people."[164]

The Eastern Scholar says: Quan Âm is truly a demon, not a human being. There is no mention {p. 202 (292)} of a king named of Miao Zhuang in the history of China. The Buddhist book tells this strange tale, and people make pictures and statues of this king. Consequently, the demon appears in the form of a lady Buddha for people to worship. In reality, she is a demon.

---

of this legend, see Glen Dudbridge, *The Legend of Miao-shan* (1978; repr., Oxford: Oxford University Press, 2004). Apparently the story somehow found its way into Vietnam very early and has fostered the cult of the "Third Princess" in the renowned Perfume Pagoda in the province of Ha Tay, North Vietnam. Most Vietnamese trace the legend of Quan Âm to this story of the "Third Princess" and to another indigenous story entitled "Quan Âm Thị Kính." In this story, the heroine went through an extraordinary hardship because her compassionate character was misunderstood during life. Only after her death is her true identity as a bodhisattva revealed.

164. Sino-Vietnamese: 況復有鬼怪人妖, 邪說暴行, 以惑世誣民者乎。

[Concerning Lost Souls]

The Western Scholar says: I have seen people care for wandering souls by cooking rice porridge on the first and the fifteenth days of the month and then sprinkling it on leaves for the souls to consume.[165] So I ask you: What is this practice about?

The Eastern Scholar says: People say that wandering souls are abandoned souls who have no descendants to make offerings for them, so they turn to begging from the living. They also say that these wandering souls have such thin necks and spindly legs that they cannot walk firmly on the ground and must, therefore, live on tree branches [like birds]. Since they cannot eat rice [or solid food], people cook rice porridge for them and sprinkle the soup over leaves so that they can eat. Buddhists tell this tale: Once upon a time, there was a woman named Hành Mãn who was destined to die at the age of thirty. She sold food and drink to passersby near a bridge. One day, three messengers called the Wandering Souls came down from heaven to take her soul. Knowing this, she treated them to a fine feast, allowing them to eat and drink their fill. After the feast, the three messengers told Hành Mãn, "Your life has already expired; however, since you treated us so well, we will change the record to have you live for three thousand years."[166]

The Western Scholar says: The wandering souls are destitute spirits. The reason people make offerings of rice porridge and sprinkle it over leaves for them to eat {p. 203 (293)} is not because they are caring for them but because they are afraid that these wandering souls will steal the food offered to their ancestors. They make such offerings to ward them off. As for the story of the three wandering souls—messengers from heaven and enforcers of the record of one's life—that they have the power to change people's lifespans and make them live longer is truly a flat-out lie. Who has the power to change the time of death determined by heaven? Therefore, the story of the three Wandering Souls, who changed the record so that Hành Mãn could live to three thousand years, is fictitious.

---

165. See also the discussion in *Opusculum*, 98–99 (Dror, *A Study of Religion*, 206).

166. In Chinese characters, thirty (三十) differs from three thousand (三千) by one small stroke.

Article 12

On the Custom of Erecting the Nêu Pole and the Sprinkling of Lime Powder on New Year's Eve

The Western Scholar says: In this country, everyone—from high officials to commoners—follows the custom of erecting a *Nêu* pole and sprinkling lime powder for protection.[167] What is this custom about?

The Eastern Scholar says: Buddhists tell the following story: Once upon a time, a demon and the Buddha were competing with each another to see who was superior in magic. First, the demon closed a small bird in his hand and posed a riddle to the Buddha: "Is this bird alive or dead?" If the Buddha said "alive," the demon would kill it [before opening his hand]. If he said "dead," the demon would release it alive. The Buddha could not answer the riddle, so he ran toward the door and straddled the threshold. He asked: "Am I coming in or going out?" If the demon said "out," he would walk in; if the demon said {p. 204 (294)} "in," he would walk out. The demon could not answer him, so he got angry and threw the bird at the Buddha's head. As a consequence, a statuette of a bird is often mounted on the top of a monk's walking stick.

Next, they competed in sea diving to see who could stay underwater longer. The demon dived first but could not hold his breath for long. Then the Buddha dived. He stayed under the water for so long that snails had attached themselves to his head. That is why we see "snails" on the head of Buddha's statue[168] in Buddhist temples. Then, the two competed in other games, and the Buddha won every time. Finally, the Buddha and the demon competed for territory. While the demon was still at sea, the Buddha quickly ran to land. Wherever he went, he erected a *Nêu* pole [to claim his territory] and made bows and arrows with lime powder to shoot at the demon. As a result, whenever the demon sees a *Nêu* pole and lime-powdered bows and arrows, he does not dare cross the territory that the Buddha has claimed. Buddhists write these stories to show the power of the Buddha over the demon.

Once a year, people erect a *Nêu* pole. On the last day of the year (the thirtieth of the twelfth month), they cut down bamboo to make the pole. Then, they tie

---

167. See also *Opusculum*, 103 (Dror, *A Study of Religion*, 211–12).

168. Vietnamese statues of the Buddha often portray him with curly locks resembling an assembly of snails (*ốc*). This is the origin of the name "Bụt ốc" (snails on the Buddha's head).

stacks of gold-paper money to the top of the pole and place the pole in the front yard. They also sprinkle lime powder at the gate and around the house to mark the Buddha's territory and ward off the demon. The *Nêu* pole is displayed until the seventh day of the New Year when it is taken down. This custom is repeated every year, as described in Buddhist sources.

{p. 205 (295)}

The Western Scholar comments: Buddhist books are written by devils who make up legends to praise the Buddha and entice people to believe in him. Whoever believes these stories will fall for the devil's tricks. If they say the demon cannot enter the Buddha's territory, how it possible that households with a the *Nêu* pole and sprinkled lime powder continue to suffer from illnesses caused by evil spirits? As a result, they have to call in a sorcerer to make amulets and perform ceremonies to drive the demons away. If a person puts up a *Nêu* pole to mark the Buddha's territory and arms himself with a bow and arrows, but the demon is still able to enter his house to cause illness, then the Buddha does not really have the power to protect him. If the demon does not dare enter the territories claimed by the Buddha, then why do Buddhist books say, "It is the same spirit known by different names. At home, we call it the 'Household Guardian' [Thổ công], in the fields the 'Soil Deity' [Thổ kỳ], in the river the 'Dragon King' [Long vương], and in the Buddhist temple the 'Dragon God' [Long thần]"? This spirit is the devil. If the demon can enter a Buddhist temple, he is present everywhere, so the *Nêu* pole and the lime-powdered weapons are totally ineffective.

APPENDIX A

Adriano di Santa Thecla's Opusculum

The *Opusculum de sectis apud Sinenses et Tunkinenses* (hereafter abbreviated as *Opusculum*) is a 19 by 25 cm manuscript, preserved as the AMEP Volume 667. The manuscript is made up of 121 pages, eight of which are introductions numbered with roman numerals. It also has a two-page table of contents. There are blank pages at the end of the chapters on Confucianism, Daoism, and Fortune-tellers, and after the second chapter on Buddhism, reducing the actual text to 109 pages. The treatise was written in Latin with the insertion of passages in Sino-Vietnamese and vernacular Vietnamese written in Roman script. It also included several diagrams describing the layout of the places in which the ceremony to Confucius, the Hội Minh ceremony, and the Buddhist rite of "breaking the prison" (*phá ngục*) occur.

The book was a treatise on the religions of the Chinese and Tonkinese based on the observations of Adriano di Santa Thecla with additional information from the Dominican missionary Francisco Gil de Federich (1702–1745)[1] and others, including the literati. Adriano wrote this treatise to explain the religions of the Chinese and Tonkinese to European readers. He included a description of all the Three Religions, as well as the development of Christianity in China and in Tonkin. Unfortunately, he never completed the work due to many interruptions—which he described as wars and other matters. As Adriano admitted, the treatise was an opportunity to expand on other missionaries' writings about the religions of Tonkin. In the preface to *Opusculum*, he wrote,

> The possibility of writing this treatise was provided by the *Index Historicus* of the Tonkin mission, which [the] illustrious Father Ilario [Hilario] di Gesù, bishop of Corycus, and vicar apostolic of East Tonkin, compiled for use by his brothers

---

1. Gil de Federich was a Spanish Dominican who came to Tonkin in 1735. Two years later he was imprisoned as a result of religious persecution and was decapitated in 1745. He seemed to be well versed in the Vietnamese language and customs and had opportunities to discuss the Christian faith with an "uncle of the Lord." For his biography, see Marillier, *Nos pères dans la foi*, 2:116–17.

living in this mission, in which he discussed these three sects [Tam Giáo] following the information that previous missionaries passed on in books transcribed from Chinese and Annamite script. It seemed necessary to me to re-examine and to make a new investigation of the sects and to consult the Chinese books, literati, and experts. When it was done, I discovered many contradictions and followed the most trustworthy of the suggested versions, to which I added others.[2]

While the work was still in its early stage, Adriano di Santa Thecla sent his manuscript to Gil de Federich to examine, correct, and add further information. He also made an inquiry about special ceremonies (for example, the Kỳ Đạo ceremony) among the court ministers and literati. In composing his work on the religions of Tonkin, Adriano acknowledges incorporating materials from Hilario's *Dị Đoan Chi Giáo* and *Đại Học Chi Đạo*. *Opusculum* was highly valued among missionaries. An early version had already been sent back to Europe with an introduction by Bishop Louis Néez, the vicar apostolic of West Tonkin. In a letter to the directors of the MEP in Paris dated December 15, 1749, Néez wrote,

> I have our students write [= make a copy] of the Chronology of China and Tonkin and an abridged chronology of the history of the religion, which was composed by the Reverend Father Adriano di Santa Thecla, an Italian Augustinian, missionary of the Propaganda in Tonkin. It is a new book, at least concerning Tonkin, and perhaps concerning China. Since this Father sent this work to Rome, I guessed that I would do you a favor by sending a copy to your library. I wish it had been written better and more precisely. I corrected there quite a number of mistakes. Maybe there are still many more others than these. Please be so kind as to excuse an old man who is alone and overloaded with his affairs.[3]

As a survey of religion, the *Opusculum* is a systematic treatment of the Chinese and Vietnamese religions. It is divided into six chapters discussing (1) the sect of the literati (Confucianism), (2) the cult of spirits, (3) the sect of magicians (Daoism), (4) fortune tellers and diviners, (5) the sect of the Buddha, (6) and the Christian religion among the Chinese and Vietnamese. The treatise is mainly a description of Chinese and Vietnamese religions. Unlike the author of *Errors*, Adriano di Santa Thecla refrained from giving his opinions on what he observed, except when he discussed the merit of sacrifices.[4]

The Complex Relationship Between Errors *and* Opusculum

A comparison of the table of contents between the two works exhibits a striking parallel in the topics discussed:

---

2. *Opusculum*, vi (Dror, *A Study of Religion*, 83).

3. Néez to the seminary directors at Paris, December 15, 1749 (AMEP, vol. 687, folio 691). Also see Marillier, *Nos pères dans la foi*, 2:126.

4. See *Opusculum*, Chapter 1, Article 11 (Dror, *A Study of Religion*, 153–57).

Tam Giáo Chư Vọng [Errors of the Three Religions]	Opusculum de sectis apud Sinenses et Tunkineses
Preface	On the Sects of the Chinese and Annamites
Book 1: The Errors of Confucianism	*Chapter 1: On the Sect of the Literati*
Art. 1: On How the Supreme Ultimate Created Heaven and Earth	Art. 1: On Confucius, the Founder of This Sect
Art. 2: On the Origin of Pangu	Art. 2: On the Studies, Books, and Doctrine of this Sect
Art. 3: On the Sovereign on High	Art. 3: On the Religion of this Sect
Art. 4: On the Origin of the Right Way	Art. 4: On the Cult of the Famous Confucius
Art. 5: On the Great Flood	Art. 5: On the Solemn Sacrifice to Confucius
Art. 6: On Sacrifices to Heaven, Earth, and the Six Spirits of Nature	*Chapter 2: On the Spirits and their Cult*
	Art. 1: On the Spirits of Heaven and Earth
Art. 7: On Sacrifices to the Five Emperors and the Five Spirits	Art. 2: On the Kings Called Thánh [Saints], and Especially on Those to Whom Sacrifices Are Made Four Times a Year
Art. 8: On the Oath-Taking Ceremony and the Chief's Banner Celebration	
	Art. 3: On the Spirits Whom the Military Worship
Art. 9: On Thành Hoàng [the Village God] and Other Spirits	Art. 4: On the Ceremony of Tế Kỳ Đạo
Art. 10: On King Dóng, King Trèm, King Bạch Mã [and Princess Liễu Hạnh]	Art. 5: On the Ceremony Hội Minh, or on Taking the Oath of Loyalty
	Art. 6: On the Tutelary Genies Called Thành Hoàng
Art. 11: On the Kitchen God, the Household Guardian, the Land Guardian, and the Guild Founder	Art. 7: On the Ceremony Tạo Khoa Bạt Thần, That Is, on the Probation and Ranking of Spirit
Art. 12: On the Cult of Confucius and the Great Sages	Art. 8: On Vua Daóng and Vua Trèm and Several Others
Art. 13: On the Cult of Thái Công and the Mighty Generals	Art. 9: On Tiên Sư, Thổ Công, Vua Bếp, and Others, Who Have a Cult Among Ordinary People
Art. 14: On Funeral Rites and the Veneration of Ancestors	
Art. 15: On Geomancy	Art. 10: On the Spirits of the Deceased
	Art. 11: Important Remarks on Sacrifices
	Art. 12: On Sacrifice to Living Vua and Chúa

Tam Giáo Chư Vọng [Errors of the Three Religions]	Opusculum de sectis apud Sinenes et Tunkineses
Book 2: The Errors of Daoism	Chapter 3: On the Sect of Magicians
Art. 1: On the Founding of Daoism by Laozi	Art. 1: On Lão Tử [Laozi], the Founder of This Sect
Art. 2: On the Spread of Daoism by Zhang Yi and Zhang Jue	Art. 2: On the Growth of This Sect
	Art. 3: On the Magic of This Sect
Art. 3: On the Healing Work of the Sorcerers	Art. 4: On the Religion of This Sect
Art. 4: On the Twelve Yearly Governing Spirits	Art. 5: On Ngọc Hoàng [the Jade Emperor], Who Are Worshipped
Art. 5: On the Nine Stars and the Thunder God	Chapter 4: On Fortune-Tellers and Diviners
Art. 6: On Auspicious and Inauspicious Times	Art. 1: On the Fortune-Tellers Thầy Bói and Thầy Khoa
	(manuscript ends here)
Art. 7: On Hà Bá, Phạm Nhan, and Liễu Hạnh	Art. 2: On Thầy Xem Số [Astrologist], Xem Tướng [Physiologist], Xem Giò [Reader of Chicken Feet], Thầy Địa Lý [Geomancer] (*omitted*)
Art. 8: On Divination	
Art. 9: On Astrology and Forecasting Events	Art. 3: On Other Diviners (*omitted*)
Art. 10: On the Five Constellations	
Art. 11: On Physiognomy and Reading Chicken Feet	
Art. 12: On Solar and Lunar Eclipses	
Book 3: The Errors of Buddhism	Chapter 5: On the Sect of Worshippers of Phật [Buddha] or Fo
Art. 1: On the Origin of Buddhism	
Art. 2: On the Spread of Buddhism to China	Art. 1: On Thích Ca, the Founder of This Sect Among Indians
Art. 3: On the Confucian Evaluation of Buddhism	Art. 2: On the Spread of This Sect in China
	Art. 3: On the Doctrine of This Sect
Art. 4: On the Buddhist Story of Creation in Nine Eons	Art. 4: On the Main Idols Worshipped in This Sect
Art. 5: On the Real Meaning of the Nine Eons	Art. 5: On the Temple and People Devoted to the Cult of Phật
	Art. 6: On the Ceremonies in Honor of Phật

Tam Giáo Chư Vọng [Errors of the Three Religions]	Opusculum de sectis apud Sinenes et Tunkineses
Art. 6: On the Meaning of the Words *Không* [Emptiness] and *Phật* [Buddha]	*Chapter 6: On the Christian Religion among the Chinese and the Annamites*
	Art. 1: On the Christian Religion in China
Art. 7: On the Precepts Against Killing and Teachings on Reincarnation	Art. 2: On the Persecution of the Christian Faith in China
	(manuscript ends here)
Art. 8: On the "Protection for the Journey" Prayer	Art. 3: On the Christian Religion Among the Annamites (*omitted*)
Art. 9: On the Burning of Paper Mausoleums and Joss Paper	Art. 4: On the Persecution of the Christian Faith in Tonkin (*omitted*)
Art. 10: On Hell	
Art. 11: On Quan Âm (Avalokiteśvara) and the Wandering Souls	
Art. 12: On the Custom of Erecting the *Nêu* Pole and the Sprinkling of Lime Powder on the New Year's Eve	

A closer examination of the materials presented in the two works reveals that both share sufficient material in common to suggest they arose from the same literary source. The question of our interest naturally is: which depends on which? Three logical solutions can be suggested for the intertextual dependency between the two:

Either (1) *Errors* is a Vietnamese adaptation of *Opusculum*,
or (2) *Opusculum* an expansion of *Errors*,
or else, (3) both works depend on a previous, though now lost, common source.

On the surface, it seems that if we set the dating of *Errors* based on internal evidence to 1752 (see my discussion in chapter 2), then the manuscript was written two years later than *Opusculum*, which has the explicit date of 1750. If this were the case, then *Errors* may be a Vietnamese adaptation of *Opusculum*.

However, I have strong reasons to doubt that it was the case, for several reasons.

First, Adriano di Santa Thecla admitted that he relied on previous works, notably those of Hilario di Gesù, who composed some writings on the three sects in Vietnamese for the use of his confrères in the mission. In addition, he was constantly revising the text as more information was made available to him. The author of *Errors*, on the other hand, did not indicate that he relied on any previous written work on the three religions for his composition.

Second, the arrangement of the topics in *Opusculum* is more logical, moving from the general to the particular, and from the most compatible to the least compatible with Christianity, as the author understood it. He divided the materials on Confucianism (which were treated as one in *Errors*) into two chapters to reflect the difference between Confucianism and the native cult of spirits. He also did the same with material on Daoism, splitting it into two chapters, dealing with what would properly count as Daoist, and what seemingly were the practices of the popular religions. By doing so, Adriano di Santa Thecla acknowledged the existence of a separate category of religion from the traditional triple division of Vietnamese religions. If *Errors* was an adaptation of *Opusculum*, it would be difficult to explain why its author had abandoned this approach.

Third, the style of writing is quite different between the two works, even when they treat the same material. While the *Opusculum* is a series of essay-like articles, *Errors* is written in the style of a dialogue using simple sentences. The latter is imbedded with quotations from Chinese and Vietnamese sources. Some of these quotations also appear in *Opusculum* together with Adriano di Santa Thecla's translation. However, the Sino-Vietnamese materials in *Opusculum* were mostly short sentences. The longer quotations that appear in *Errors* were either left out or paraphrased in *Opusculum*. This shows that the author of *Opusculum* was familiar with both Sino-Vietnamese, but not fluent enough to translate long quotations from Chinese sources into Latin. In the *Opusculum* we find that there are a number of misspellings of the Sino-Vietnamese.

Furthermore, judging from the handwriting, the text is not written at a consistent pace and size. The *Opusculum* manuscript exhibits evidence of having been written by two scribes. Someone who was familiar with Latin out the main text and left ample space for the insertion of Vietnamese and Sino-Vietnamese by a second scribe. This is not the case with *Errors*. Another particular feature is that the style of *quốc-ngữ* in *Opusculum* was closer to the orthography of late eighteenth- or early nineteenth-century writing, rather than the mid-eighteenth-century style of *quốc-ngữ* of *Errors* and related materials like the 1758 *Phép Giảng Đạo Thật* (which I have discussed in chapter 5 above).[5]

Given the above observations, we must raise the question of whether the Latin *Opusculum* could be an adaptation of the Vietnamese *Errors*, rather than the other way around.

In determining the dependency of one text upon another, certain criteria worked out by biblical scholars during the debate between the primacy of Mark or Matthew in

---

5. Dror (*A Study of Religion*, 31–32) notes that this text of the *Opusculum* is a copy, not the original written by Adriano di Santa Thecla himself, since the handwriting was different than that of Adriano's letter, such as AMEP, vol. 689, folio 55.

the Synoptic Gospels could be useful. By the middle of the nineteenth century, biblical scholars had long noted the similarity between the two Gospels. They questioned whether Mark was a reduction of Matthew (Griesbach's theory), or Matthew was an expansion of Mark (as in the two-source theory). The majority of biblical scholars today accept the primacy of Mark for several reasons. First, a later text would most likely improve upon an earlier text, refine its style of writing, and rearrange its materials in a more coherent scheme; if we have two texts of which one is coarse (Mark) and the other is embellished (Matthew), it is more likely that the unrefined one is the earlier text. Second, a later text would expand, rather than contract, the particulars of the original text, especially as regards unfamiliar concepts or customs (e.g., Matthew gives details on Jesus's temptations in the desert). Third, the later text would keep all the relevant materials from the original and would not omit any important information. Thus, there is nothing important in Mark that is not included in Matthew. Finally, a later text would "explain away" embarrassments or mistakes in the original text, rather than the other way around (e.g., Matthew's explanation of why Jesus needed to be baptized at all).

Applying these criteria to the comparison of *Errors* and *Opusculum*, we see a similar situation. Of all the material in common between the two works, the tendency of *Errors* is to be brief and *Opusculum* expansive. For example, in the sacrifices to Confucius, the ceremonies of Kỳ Đạo and Hội Minh, the ranking of the spirit, and the Buddhist ritual of "breaking the prison," *Opusculum* gives a much longer description than *Errors*, including the configuration of the place of the ceremony. The tendency toward expansion rather contraction can also be seen in *Opusculum* treatment of Vietnamese spirits. In addition to presenting the material on King Dóng and King Trèm (an almost word-for-word translation of the accounts in *Errors*), it also includes an account of the spirit Sơn Tinh of Mount Tản Viên. Since Sơn Tinh was one of the major spirits of Vietnam, it is unlikely that the author of *Errors* omitted it, if he was adapting from *Opusculum*. The conflation of the Bạch Mã spirit with the Chinese general Ma Yuan appears in both texts.[6] It is more likely that the author of *Opusculum* copied this mistake from *Errors*, rather than the author of *Errors*, who seemed to be more familiar with the Vietnamese history and language, repeats the mistakes in *Opusculum*. In short, there is more persuasive evidence that *Errors* does not use *Opusculum* as its source. It is more likely that the author of *Opusculum* relied on *Errors*, or at least an earlier version of it, rather than the other way around.

We then must consider the third option, that is, both were contemporary works and dependent on a previous lost manuscript (most likely the *Dị Đoan Chi Giáo* written by Hilario di Gesù). The author of *Errors* was writing to a Vietnamese audience as a didactic instrument of faith, so he presented the information that necessary for his audience to understand the danger of wrong worship. Adriano di Santa Thecla's

---

6. See a discussion on this conflation by Dror, *A Study of Religion*, 42–47.

concern was to explain to his missionary confrères aboirut the religious beliefs and customs of the both the Chinese and Vietnamese people. The different goals might explain why the two works were different in their presentations of the Three Religions. There are materials in *Errors* that *Opusculum* does not cover and vice versa. But since they still share a common thread, it is highly possible that their authors drew from a common source, which was available to them during the process of writing and editing. Taken together, these two works can help supplement each other's shortcomings, and give the audience a more comprehensive view of the religious practice of eighteenth-century Vietnam.

APPENDIX B

Glossary of Sino-Vietnamese Terms Used in the Translation

Term	Character	Translation
Á hiến lễ	亞獻禮	second offering
Bạch hổ	白虎	white tiger
Bát quái	八卦	eight Trigrams
Càn	乾	Heaven, first trigram
Châm tửu	斟酒	pour the wine
Chuyển cữu	轉柩	Moving of the coffin
Cương Mục (book)	綱目	*Outline of History*
Cửu Châu	九州	Nine Regions, China
Dị đoan	異端	alien custom/doctrine, heterodoxy
Dịch Kinh (book)	易經	*Classic/Book of Changes*
Dư thần	輿神	Protector of Travelers
Đại Học (book)	大學	*Great Learning*
Đại tường	大祥	great memorial feast
Đại Vương	大王	great prince
Đạo (concept)	道	*Dao*, Way, path
Đạo (philosophy)	道	Daoism
Đảo Vũ	禱雨	bringing rain
Đàn	壇	sacrificial platform
Địa thổ chi thần	地土之神	Spirit of the Earth
Gia Ngữ (book)	家語	*Discourse of the [Confucian] School*

Term	Character	Translation
Gia Lễ (book)	家禮	*Family Rituals*
Gia Lễ Chính Hành	家禮正行	*Correct Practices of Family Rituals*
Giáo	教	teaching, doctrine, religion
Hành khiển	行遣	Governing Spirit of the Year
Hạ đẳng thần	下等神	spirits of the lower rank
Hành thần	行神	Road Spirit
Hậu thổ	后土	Queen/Spirit of the Earth
Hoàng địa kỳ	皇地祺	Empress August Earth
Hoàng thiên	皇天	August Heaven
Hoàng thiên Thượng đế	皇天	Supreme Emperor August Heaven
Hội Minh	會盟	oath-Taking
Hồn bạch	魂帛	soul cloth
Hỗn độn	混沌	primordial chaos
Hư	虛	void, hollow, empty, unreal, vacant
Hư không	虛空	void, hollow, empty
Hương hoả	香火	inheritance field
Hư vô	虛無	empty, nonexistent, false, unreal
Hư vô tịch diệt	虛無寂滅	vacant and quiet
Hương án	香案	incense table
Huyền vũ	玄武	mysterious martial
Khí	氣	energy, material force
Khôn	坤	earth, second trigram
Không	空	emptiness, hollow, void (in space)
Kỳ An	祈安	Supplication for Tranquility
Kỳ Đạo	旗導	chief's banner
Kỳ Phúc	祈福	Supplication for Happiness
Lão giáo	老教	Daoism
Lễ (virtue)	禮	propriety

Glossary of Sino-Vietnamese Terminology in the Text

Term	Character	Translation
Lễ (ceremony)	禮	rites, rituals
Lễ Khí (book chapter)	禮器	Utensils of Rites
Lễ Vận (book chapter)	禮運	Conveyance of Rites
Lễ Ký (book)	禮記	*Record/Book of Rites*
Linh toạ	靈座	Soul seat
Lục thao (book)	六韜	*Six Strategies* (of military tactics)
lục tông	六宗	Six Spirits of Nature
Lưỡng nghi	兩儀	Two Modes/Dynamics, yin and yang
Lý	理	Principle, reason
Minh đường	明堂	Open space
Minh tinh	銘旌	name banner
Môn thần	門神	Gate Spirit
Nhân (virtue)	仁	humaneness, benevolence
Nho	儒	*ru*, literati, Confucian
Nho giáo	儒教	Confucianism
Nghĩa	義	eighteousness
Ngọc hoàng	玉皇	Jade Emperor
Ngu (rite)	虞	pacifying the soul, reposing the soul
Ngũ đế	五帝	Five Emperors
Ngũ đức	五德	Five Virtues
Ngũ hành	五行	Five Elements/Agents
Ngũ kinh	五經	Five Classics
Ngũ luân	五倫	Five Relations
Ngũ phương	五方	Five Directions
Ngũ tạng	五臟	Five Organs/Viscera
Ngũ thường	五常	Five Norms/Constant Virtues/Morals
Phật	佛	Buddha
Phật giáo	佛教	Buddhism

Term	Character	Translation
Quân tử	君子	noble persons, gentlemen
Quỷ	鬼	demon
Quỷ thần	鬼神	spiritual beings
Sa môn	沙門	*Śramana*, buddhist ascetic
Sơ ngu	初虞	first Pacification offering
Sử ký (book)	史記	*History*
Tái ngu	再虞	second Pacification
Tam cương	三綱	Three Bonds
Tam giáo	三教	Three Religions, Triple Religion
Tam tài	三才	Three Powers (heaven, earth, humans)
Tâm	心	heart, mind, heart-mind
Tam ngu	三虞	third Pacification
Tâm Đăng (book)	心燈	*Lamp of the Mind*
Táo quân	灶君	Kitchen God, Lord of Hearth
Táo thần	灶神	Hearth Spirit
Tế	祭	sacrifice
Tế Kỳ Đạo	祭旗導	Veneration of the Chief's Banner
Tế văn	祭文	Cultic oration
Thái cực	太極	Supreme/Great Ultimate
Thái công	太公	Great Duke
Thái giám	太監	eunuch
Thành hoàng	城皇	Village God, Guardian Deity
Thanh long	青龍	azure dragon
Thành phục	成服	mourning garments
Thần	神	spirit, deity, god
Thần vị	神位	spirit tablet
Thập triết	十哲	Ten Philosophers/Sages
Thi Kinh (book)	詩經	*Classic/Book of Odes*

Glossary of Sino-Vietnamese Terminology in the Text

Term	Character	Translation
Thiên	天	Heaven, sky
Thiên chủ	天主	Lord of Heaven (God)
Thiên địa	天地	heaven and earth
Thiên hạ	天下	the empire, the world
Thổ công	土公	Household Guardian
Thổ chủ	土主	Land Guardian
Thư Kinh (book)	書經	*Classic/Book of Documents*
Thượng đẳng thần	上等神	spirits of the supreme rank
Thượng đế	上帝	Sovereign-on-High, Supreme Ruler
Tịch diệt	寂滅	quiescence of passion; nihilation
Tiên sư	先師	Primary Teacher, Guild Founder
Tiên vương	先王	Ancient/deceased rulers
Tiểu tường	小祥	small memorial feast
Tín (virtue)	信	sincerity, trustworthiness
Tính Giáo	性教	*Doctrine of Nature*
Tính Lý (book)	性理大全	*Nature and Principle, Metaphysics*
Tịnh thổ	淨土	Land of bliss, Pure Land
Tống Ách	送厄	Dispelling Misfortune
Trí	智	wisdom, knowledge, prudence
Triêu điện	朝奠	daily food offering
Trung đẳng thần	中等	Spirits of the middle rank
Trung Dung (book)	中庸	*Doctrine of the Mean*
Trung Lưu thần	中流神	Central Flow Spirit
Trung nguyên	中原節	Middle Period festival
Trượng	丈	10 cubits
Tứ Thập Nhị Chương Kinh (book)	四十二章經	*Sutra of Forty-Two Sections*
Tứ thư	四書	Four Books
Tứ phối	四配	Four Associates/Correlates

Term	Character	Translation
Tứ tượng	四象	Four Forms/Images
Tự nhiên	自然	nature, spontaneity
Vạn vật	萬物	myriad of things
Văn Miếu	文廟	Temple of Literature/Culture
Vật	物	matter, substance, creature, thing
Vô	無	nonbeing, without, negation
Vô cực	無極	limitlessness, ultimate nonbeing
Vũ Miếu	武廟	Temple of the Military

Bibliography

PRIMARY SOURCES
Unpublished Sources

Archives of Mission Etrangères de Paris (AMEP)
- Vol. 667. Adriano di St. Thecla, *Opusculum de Sectis apud Sinenses et Tunkinenses* (1750).
- Vols. 687, 688, 689, and 690. Letters from Tonkin.
- Vol. 1060. *Dictionarium Annamitico-Latinum* (1774).
- Vol. 1089. *Tam Giáo Chư Vọng* [Errors of the Three Religions] (1752).
- Vol. 1095. *Thánh Giáo Yếu Lý Quốc Ngữ* [Essential Teachings of the Holy Religion (Christianity) in Vietnamese] (1774).
- Vol. 1183. *Phép Giảng Đạo Thật* [True Religion Explained] (1758).

Institute of Hán Nôm Studies (Viện Hán Nôm)

- *Tâm Đăng* [Lamp of the Mind]. Ms. A 2481.

Sino-Vietnamese and Vietnamese Sources

Bento Thiện. "History of Annam." 1659. Translated by George Dutton. In *Sources of Vietnamese Tradition*, edited by George Dutton, Jaynes S. Werner, and John K. Whitmore, 223–26. New York: Columbia University Press, 2012.
Chơn Đạo Dẫn Giải [True Religion Explained]. 3rd ed. Quinhon: Imprimerie de Quinhon, 1923.
Đại Việt Sử Ký Toàn Thư 大越史記全書 [Complete Chronicle of the Great Việt]. 1697 ed. Translated from Sino-Vietnamese by Ngô Đức Thọ (Vol 1), Hoàng Văn Lâu (Vols 2 & 3). 1992. Reprint, Hànội: NXB Khoa Học Xã Hội, 2004.

Gendreau [Đông], Pierre-Marie. *Thư Chung về việc Dối Trá Địa phận Tây Đàng Ngoài* [Common Letter regarding False and Superstitious Things in Diocese of West Tonkin]. 2nd ed. Kẻ Sở, 1924.

Hội Đồng Tứ Giáo 會同四教 [Conference of the Four Religions]. 1867 *Nôm* ed. Edited and translated Vietnamese by Trần Kim-Vinh and Nguyễn Huy-Hùng. Houston, TX: NXB Dũng Lạc, 2002.

Hồ Sĩ Tân. *Thọ Mai Gia Lễ* 壽梅家禮 [Family Rituals of Tho Mai]. Translated in Vietnamese by an anonymous translator. Hanoi: NXB Hanoi, 2009.

Khâm Định Việt Sử Thông Giám Cương Mục 欽定越史通鑑綱目 [Imperially Ordered Mirror and Commentary on the History of the Viet]. 1884 ed. Translated in Vietnamese by Hoa Bằng, Phạm Trọng Điền, and Trần Văn Giáp. 1957. Reprint, 2 vols, Hanoi: NXB Giáo Dục, 2007.

Lê Triều Hội Điển 黎朝會典 [Collective Regulations of the Lê Dynasty]. Translated by Trần thị Kim Anh in Nguyễn Ngọc Nhuận, ed. *Một Số Điển Chế và Văn Bản Pháp Luật Việt Nam: từ thế kỷ XV đến XVIII* [An Anthology of Ancient Vietnamese Regulations and Legal Codes: from the fifteenth to the eighteenth century]. 2 vols. Hanoi: NXB Khoa Học Xã Hội, 2009. Vol. 2, 12–218.

Lý Tế Xuyên. *Việt Điện U Linh Tập* 越甸幽靈集 [Departed Spirits of the Viet Realm]. Translated by Lê Hữu Mục. Saigon: Khai Trí, 1960.

Majorica, Girolamo. *Thiên Chúa Thánh Giáo Khải Mông* 天主聖教開蒙 [Introduction to the Holy Religion of the Lord of Heaven]. 1630s. N.p.: 2003.

Phan Huy Chú. *Lịch Triều Hiến Chương Loại Chí* 歷朝憲章類誌 [Categorized Records of the Institutions of Succesive Dynasties]. Translated by Trần Huy Hân, Cao Huy Giu, Nguyễn Thế Đạt, Nguyễn Trọng Hân. 1960. Reprint, 2 vols. Hanoi: NXB Giáo Dục, 2006.

Quốc Triều Chiếu Lệnh Thiện Chính [A Collection of Imperial Decree and Regulations: 1619–1705]. Translated by Deloustal Raymond in "La justice dans l'ancien Annam. Traduction et commentaire du Code des Lê." *BEFEO* 13, no. 5 (1913), 1–59.

Phạm Đình Hổ, "Ritual for Venerating Heaven." 1790s. Translated by George Dutton and Matthew Cochran. In *Sources of Vietnamese Tradition*, edited by George Dutton, Jaynes S. Werner, and John K. Whitmore, 186–88. New York: Columbia University Press, 2012.

Rhodes, Alexandre de. *Phép Giảng Tám Ngày / Cathechismus in octo dies divisus*. 1651. Facsimile edition, introduced by Nguyễn Khắc Xuyên. Hochiminh City: Tủ Sách Đại Kết, 1993.

Trần Thế Pháp. *Lĩnh Nam Chích Quái* 嶺南摭怪 [Strange Tales from the South of the Passes]. Translated by Lê Hữu Mục. Saigon: Khai Trí, 1960.

Other Primary Texts

100 Roman Documents Concerning the Chinese Rites Controversy (1645–1941). Translated by Donald St. Sure and edited by Ray R. Noll. San Francisco: The Ricci Institute for Chinese-Western Cultural History, University of San Francisco, 1992.

Adriano di Santa Thecla. *Opusculum de sectis apud Sinenses et Tunkinenses / A Small Treatise on the Sects among the Chinese and Tonkinese*. Annotated, translated and introduced by Olgar Dror, as *A Study of Religion in China and North Vietnam in the Eighteenth Century*. Ithaca, NY: Cornell University Press / SEAP, 2002.

Baldinotti, Giuliano. "La relation sur le Tonkin du P. Baldinotti." 1626. Italian text and French translation by Mario Cardi. *BEFEO* 3 (1903): 71–78.

Baron, Samuel. *A Description of the Kingdom of Tonqueen*. London, 1685. Reprinted in *Views of Seventeenth-Century Vietnam: Cristoforo Borri on Cochinchina and Samuel Baron on Tonkin*, edited by Olgar Dror and K. W. Taylor, 187–283. Ithaca, NY: Cornell University Press / SEAP, 2006.

Borri, Christoforo. *Relatione della nuova missione delli P.P. della Compagnia de Giesu*. Rome, 1631. Translated anonymously as *An Account of Cochin-china in Two Parts*. 1732. Reprinted in *Views of Seventeenth-Century Vietnam: Cristoforo Borri on Cochinchina and Samuel Baron on Tonkin*, edited by Olgar Dror and K. W. Taylor, 89–185. Ithaca, NY: Cornell University Press / SEAP, 2006.

Chan, Wing-tsit. *A Source Book of Chinese Philosophy*. Princeton, NJ: Princeton University Press, 1963.

Chu Hsi. *Chu Hsi's Family Rituals: A Twelfth-Century Chinese Manual for the Performance of Cappings, Weddings, Funerals, and Ancestral Rites*. Translated by Patricia Buckley Ebrey. Princeton, NJ: Princeton University Press, 1991.

Costello, Joseph, trans. and intro. *The Letters and Instructions of Francis Xavier*. St. Louis: The Institute of Jesuit Sources, 1992.

Dampier, William. "Mr Dampier's Voyages, Vol II, Part I: His Voyage from Achin in Sumatra, to Tunquin, and Other Places in the East Indies." In *A Collection of Voyages in Four Volumes*. London: James and John Knapton, 1729.

De Bary, Wm Theodore, and Irene Bloom, eds. *Sources of Chinese Traditions*. 2nd ed. Vol. 1. New York: Columbia University Press, 1999.

De Marini, Giovani Filippo. *Delle Missioni del Padri della Compagnia di Gesu nella Provincia del Giappone, e particolarmente di quella di Tunkino*. 1663. Translated in French by Simon de Riencourt as *Relation nouvelle et curieuse des Royaumes de Tunquin et de Lao*. Paris, 1666.

D'Elia, Pasquale, ed. *Fonti Ricciane: documenti originali concernenti Matteo Ricci e la storia delle prime relazioni tra l'Europa e la Cina* (1579–1615), 3 vols. Rome: La Liberia dello Stato, 1942–49.

La Paz, Juan de. *Diversas cartas del estado de la Iglesia de Tunquin donde era vicarisimo*. N.p., 1718.

———. *Opusculum in quo ducenta et septuagina quarttuor quaesita a RR. PP. Missionaris Regini Tunkini proposita totidemque Responsiones ad ipsa continentur, experditae per Adm R. P. Fr Joannem de Paz*. Manila, 1680.

———. *Respuesta à 274 questiones de los Missioneros de Tunquin*. N.p., 1687.

Hertz, Solange. *Rhodes of Vietnam: The Travels and Missions of Father Alexander de Rhodes in China and Other Kingdoms of the Orient*. Westminster, MD: Newman Press, 1966.

Hội Đồng Tứ Giáo. 1867 nôm ed. Translated and annotated by Anh Q. Tran in "*Hội Đồng Tứ Giáo/Conference of the Four Religions*: A Christian Encounter of the Three Religions in the Eighteenth-Century Vietnam," 40–123. STL thesis, Jesuit School of Theology at Berkeley, 2006.

I Ching. Trans. Richard Wilhelm and Cary Baynes. Princeton, NJ: Princeton University Press, 1967.

Launay, Adrien. *Histoire de la mission de la Cochinchine: Documents historiques*. Vol. 1, *1658–1728*. Paris, 1923. Vol. 2, *1728–1771*. Paris, 1924. Vol. 3, *1771–1823*. Paris, 1925.

———. *Histoire de la mission du Tonkin 1658–1717—Documents historiques*. Paris, 1927.

Legge, James. *The Chinese Classics*. 7 vols. London: Trubner, 1861–1872.

Marillier, André. *Nos pères dans la foi: notes sur le clergé catholique du Tonkin de 1666 à 1765*. 3 vols. Paris: Églises d'Asie, 1992–1995.

Rhodes, Alexandre de. *Cathechismus pro iis, qui volunt suscipere Baptismum in Octo dies divisus*. Rome, 1651. Translated by Peter C. Phan in *Mission and Catechesis*, 211–315. Maryknoll: Orbis, 1998.

———. *Dictionarium Annamiticum-Lusitanum et Latinum*. Rome, 1651.

———. *Divers voyages et missions du P. Alexandre de Rhodes en la Chine, & autres royaumes de l'Orient*. Paris, 1653.

———. *Histoire du royaume de Tunquin, et des grands progrez que la prédication de l'Evangile y a faits en la conversion des infidelles. Depuis l'année 1627, jusques à l'année 1646*. Lyon, 1651.

Ricci, Matteo. *Tianzhu Shiyi* [The True Meaning of the Lord of Heaven]. Translated with introduction and notes by Douglas Lancashire and Peter Hu Kuo-chen, SJ. St. Louis: The Institute of Jesuit Sources, 1985.

Scalia, Pietro, ed. *Epistolario III°: Lettere di P. Ilario Costa di Gesù*. Rome: Edizione Presenza Agostiniana, 2000.

Taberd, Jean Louis. *Dictionarium Annamitico-Latinum*. Serampore, 1838.

Tavernier, Jean-Baptist. "Relation du Royaume de Tunquin." In *Recueil de plusieurs relations et traitez singuliers et curieux de J. B. Tavernier, chevalier, baron d'Aubonne*. Paris, 1679. Translated as "A New and Singular Relation of the Kingdom of Tunquin (1639–45)". In *A Collection of Several Relations and Treatises Singular and Curious*. London, 1680.

Tissanier, Joseph. *Relation du voyage du P. Joseph Tissanier de la Compagnie de Jésus. Depuis la France, jusqu' au Royaume de Tunquin. Avec ce qui s'est passé de plus mémorable dans cette Mission, durant les années 1658, 1659, & 1660* (Paris, 1663). Reprinted in *Mission de la Cochinchine et du Tonkin*, edited by Fortuné de Montézon and Edmond Estève, 65–102. Paris: C. Douniol, 1868.

SECONDARY SOURCES
Vietnamese Language

Bùi Đức Sinh. *Lịch Sử Giáo Hội Công Giáo Việt Nam* [History of the Vietnamese Catholic Church]. Saigon: Chân Lý, 1972.

———. *Dòng Đa Minh trên Đất Việt* [Dominicans in Vietnam]. Saigon: Chân Lý, 1972.

Cao Thế Dung. *Việt Nam Công Giáo Sử Tân Biên* [A New History of Vietnamese Catholicism]. Gretna: Dân Chúa, 2002.

Chan Ching-ho and Isabelle Landry-Deron, eds. *Mục Lục Thư Tịch Hán Nôm Tàng Trữ tại Hội Thừa Sai Ba-Lê* [Catalogue of works in Chinese and *Nôm* scripts preserved in the archive of the Society of Paris Foreign Mission]. Paris, Église d'Asie, 2004.

Đào Duy Anh. *Việt Nam Văn Hoá Sử Cương* [An Outline History of Vietnamese Culture]. Hue, 1938.

Đinh Khắc Thuân. *Giáo Dục và Khoa Cử Nho Học thời Lê ở Việt Nam qua Tài Liệu Hán Nôm* [Confucian Education and Examination during the Lê Dynasty in Vietnam in Hán-Nôm Sources]. Hanoi: NXB Khoa Học Xã Hội, 2009.

Đỗ Quang Chính. *Dòng Tên trong Xã Hội Đại Việt (1615–1773)* [The Jesuit Presence in Vietnamese Society: 1615–1773]. Hochiminh City: Antôn & Đuốc Sáng, 2007.

———. *Hòa Mình vào Xã Hội Việt Nam* [Christian Immersion into Vietnamese Society]. Hochiminh City: Antôn & Đuốc-Sáng, 2007.

———. *Lịch Sử Chữ Quốc Ngữ: 1620–1659* [History of the *Quốc-ngữ* Script: 1620–1659]. Saigon: Ra Khơi, 1972. Reprint, Hochiminh City: Antôn & Đuốc Sáng, 2007.

Đỗ Trinh Huệ. *Văn Hoá, Tôn Giáo, Tín Ngưỡng Việt Nam dưới Nhãn Quan Học Giả L. Cadière* [Views from the scholar L. Cadière on Vietnamese culture, religion and belief]. Huế: NXB Thuận Hoá, 2006.

Đoàn Thiện Thuật. *Chữ Quốc Ngữ Thế Kỷ XVIII* [*Quốc-ngữ* of the Eighteenth Century]. Hanoi: NXB Giáo Dục, 2008.

Episcopal Conference of Vietnam. *Giáo Hội Công Giáo Việt Nam: Niên Giám 2016* [Annals of the Vietnamese Catholic Church 2016]. Hanoi: NXB Tôn giáo, 2016.

Hoàng Phê, ed. *Tự Điển Tiếng Việt* [Dictionary of Vietnamese Language]. Hanoi: NXB Khoa Học Xã Hội, 1988.

Huỳnh Văn Tòng. *Báo Chí Việt Nam: Từ Khởi Thuỷ Đến 1945* [History of Vietnamese journalism, from the beginning to 1945]. Hochiminh City: NXB TP HCM, 2000.

Ngô Đức Thịnh. *Đạo Mẫu Việt Nam* [Goddess Worship in Vietnam]. 2 vols. Hanoi: NXB Tôn Giáo, 2009.

Nguyễn Duy Hinh. *Người Việt Nam với Đạo Giáo* [Vietnamese and Daoism]. Hanoi: NXB Khoa Học Xã Hội, 2003.

Nguyễn Hồng. *Lịch Sử Truyền Giáo Việt Nam, Q. 1: Các Thừa Sai Dòng Tên, 1615–1665* [History of Missions in Vietnam, Vol. 1: Jesuit Activities, 1615–1665]. Saigon: Hiện Tại, 1959. Reprint, Hanoi: NXB Tôn Giáo, 2009.

Nguyễn Kim Sơn. "Về Nho Học và Nho Giáo Việt Nam Thế Kỷ XVIII—Đầu Thế Kỷ XIX" [Confucian Studies and Vietnamese Confucianism in the Eighteenth and Early Nineteenth Centuries]. In *Một Số Vấn Đề về Nho Giáo Việt Nam* [Issues on Vietnamese Confucianism], edited by Phan Đại Doãn, 49–96. Hanoi: NXB Chính Trị Quốc Gia, 1998.

Nguyễn Lang [Thich Nhat Hanh]. *Việt Nam Phật Giáo Sử Luận* [History of Vietnamese Buddhism]. 2 vols. 1974, 1978. Reprint (2 vols. in one), Hanoi: NXB Văn Học, 2000.

Nguyễn Minh Ngọc, Nguyễn Mạnh Cường, Nguyễn Duy Hinh. *Bồ Tát Quán Thế Âm Trong Các Chùa Vùng Đồng Bằng Sông Hồng* [Quan Âm in the Buddhist Temples of the Red River Delta]. Hanoi: NXB Khoa Học Xã Hội, 2004.

Nguyễn Quang Hưng, *Công Giáo Việt Nam Thời Kỳ Triều Nguyễn (1802–1883)* [Vietnamese Catholicism during the Nguyen (1802–1883)]. Hanoi: NXB Tôn Giáo, 2007.

Nguyễn Tường Bách. *Từ Điển Phật Học* [Dictionary of Buddhism]. Hue: NXB Thuận Hoá, 1999.

Nguyễn Vinh Phúc and Nguyễn Duy Hinh. *Các Thành Hoàng & Tín Ngưỡng Thăng Long—Hà Nội* [The Guardian Spirits and Their Cults in Hanoi]. Hanoi: NXB Lao Động, 2009.

Phan Kế Bính. *Việt Nam Phong Tục* [Customs of Vietnam]. Hanoi, 1915. Reprint, Saigon: Khai Trí, 1973.

Tạ Chí Đại Trường. *Thần, Người và Đất Việt* [Deities, People, and Vietnamese Land]. Westminster: Văn Nghệ, 1989.

Toan Ánh. *Tín Ngưỡng Việt Nam* [Vietnamese Religious Beliefs]. Saigon, 1966. Reprint, Hochiminh City: Văn Nghệ, 2000.

Trần Trọng Kim. *Việt Nam Sử Lược* [A Brief History of Vietnam]. 1921. Reprint, Hochiminh City: NXB TP Hồ Chí Minh, 2000.

Trần Văn Kiệm. *Giúp Đọc Nôm và Hán Việt* [A Vietnamese Dictionary in Ancient and Modern Scripts]. N.p., 1998.

Trịnh Khắc Mạnh and Chu Tuyết Lan. *Thư Mục Nho Giáo Việt Nam* [A Bibliography on Confucianism in Vietnam]. Hanoi: NXB Khoa Học Xã Hội, 2006.

Trịnh Thị Dung. *Hình Tượng Bồ Tát Quan Âm Trong Phật Giáo Việt Nam* [Image of Avalokitesvara in Vietnamese Buddhism]. Hanoi: NXB Tôn Giáo, 2012.

Trương Bá Cần. *Lịch Sử Phát Triển Công Giáo ở Việt Nam* [History of the Development of the Catholic Church in Vietnam]. 2 vols. Hanoi: NXB Tôn Giáo, 2008.

Viện Nghiên Cứu Hán Nôm. *Nho Giáo ở Việt Nam: Kỷ Yếu Hội Thảo Quốc Tế* [Confucianism in Vietnam: International Conference Proceeding]. Hanoi: NXB Khoa Học Xã Hội, 2006.

Viện Nghiên Cứu Hán Nôm. *Nghiên Cứu Tư Tưởng Nho Gia Việt Nam Từ Hướng Tiếp Cận Liên Ngành* [Confucian Thought in Vietnam: Studies From an Interdisciplinary Perspective]. Hanoi: NXB Thế Giới, 2008.

Vũ Ngọc Khánh and Phạm Minh Thảo. *Linh Thần Việt Nam* [Gods and Spirits in Vietnam]. Hanoi: NXB Văn Hoá Thông Tin, 2002.

Western Languages

Alberts, Tara. *Conflict and Conversion: Catholicism in Southeast Asia, 1500–1700*. Oxford: Oxford University Press, 2013.

Barbagallo, Ignazio and Gabriele M. Raimondo. *Gli Agostiniani Scalzi nel Vietnam e nella Cina*. Rome: Edizioni Presenza Agostiniana, 1997.

Becker, Adam H., and Annette Yoshiko Reed, eds. *The Ways that Never Parted: Jews and Christians in Late Antiquity and the Early Middle Ages*. Minneapolis: Fortress, 2007.

Becker, Carl. *Breaking the Circle: Death and the Afterlife in Buddhism*. Carbondale: Southern Illinois University Press, 1993.

Bevans, Stephan B. *Models of Contextual Theology*. Rev. ed. Maryknoll: Orbis, 2002.

Birdwhistell, Anne. *Transition to Neo-Confucianism: Shao Yung on Knowledge and Symbols of Reality*. Stanford, CA: Stanford University Press, 1989.

Birrell, Anne. *Chinese Mythology: An Introduction*. Baltimore: Johns Hopkins Press, 1993.

Blofeld, John. *Bodhisattva of Compassion: The Mystical Tradition of Kuan Yin*. 1988. Reprint, Boulder, CO: Shambala, 2009.

———. *The Sutra of 42 Sections and Two Other Scriptures of the Mahayana School*. London: The Buddhist Society, 1977.

Bonifacy, A. *Les Débuts du Christianisme en Annam: Des origines au commencement du 18e siècle*. Hanoi: Imprimerie Tonkinoise, 1930.

Borayin, Daniel. *Border Lines: The Partition of Judaeo-Christianity*. Philadelphia: University of Pennsylvania Press, 2006.

Boucher, Sandy. *Discovering Kwan Yin, Buddhist Goddess of Compassion*. Boston: Beacon Press, 1999.

Brockey, Liam Matthew. *The Jesuit Mission to China, 1579–1724*. Cambridge: Belknap Press, 2007.

Bryce, Mary Charles. "Evolution of Catechesis from the Catholic Reformation to the Present." In *A Faithful Church: Issues in the History of Catechesis*, edited by John H. Westerhoff III and O. C. Edwards, 204–35. Wilton: Morehouse-Barlow, 1981.

Cadière, Leopold. *Croyances et pratiques religieuses des Viêtnamiens*. 2nd ed. 3 vols. 1944–1956. Reprint, Paris: École Française d'Extrême-Orient, 1992.

Cao Huy-Thuan. *Les missionnaires et la politique coloniale française au Viêtnam 1857–1914*. Paris, 1969. Reprint, New Haven, CT: Yale Southeast Asian Studies, 1990.

Ch'en, Kenneth. *Buddhism in China: A Historical Survey*. Princeton, NJ: Princeton University Press, 1964.

Chadwick, Henry. *Heresy and Orthodoxy in the Early Church*. Brookfield: Variorum, 1991.

Chan, Wing-tsit, ed. *Chu Hsi and Neo-Confucianism*. Honolulu: University of Hawai'i Press, 1986.

Chan, Wing-tsit. *Chu Hsi: Life and Thought*. Hongkong: Chinese University Press, 1987.

———. *Chu Hsi: New Studies*. Honolulu: University of Hawai'i Press, 1989.
Chang, Carsun. *The Development of Neo-Confucian Thought*. 2 vols. New York: Bookman Associates, 1957–1962.
Chappoulie, Henri. *Aux origines d'une Église: Rome et les missions d'Indochine au XVIIe siècle*. Paris: Bloud et Gay, 1943–1948.
Chapuis, Oscar. *A History of Vietnam: From Hong Bang to Tu Duc*. Westport: Greenwood Press, 1995.
Ching, Julia. *Chinese Religions*. Maryknoll: Orbis, 1993.
———. *The Religious Thought of Chu Hsi*. Oxford: Oxford University Press, 2000.
Cleary, J. C. "Buddhism and Popular Religion in Medieval Vietnam." *Journal of American Religion* 59, no. 1 (Spring 1991): 93–118.
Collani, Claudia von. "Charles Maigrot's Role in the Chinese Rites Controversy." In *The Chinese Rites Controversy: Its History and Meaning*, edited by David Mungello, 149–83. Nettetal: Steyler Verlag, 1994.
Conzelmann, Hans. "Christians and Jews from the Beginning of Christianity until the Time of Origen." In *Gentiles/Jews/Christians: Polemics and Apologetics in the Greco-Roman Era*, 235–342. Minneapolis: Fortress, 1992.
Cornille, Catherine. *The Im-possibility of Interreligious Dialogue*. New York: Crossroad Press, 2008.
Costa, Horacio de la. *The Jesuits in the Philippines: 1581–1768*. Cambridge, MA: Harvard University Press, 1967.
Coulet, Georges. *Culte et religions de l'Indochine Annamite*. Saigon: Ardin, 1929.
Criveller, Gianni. *Preaching Christ in Late Ming China. The Jesuit Presentation of Christ from Matteo Ricci to Giulio Aleni*. Taipei: Ricci Institute for Chinese Studies, 1997.
Cummins, J. S. *A Question of Rites: Friar Domingo Navarette and the Jesuits in China*. Brookfield: Ashgate, 1993.
———. "Two Missionary Methods in China: Mendicants and Jesuits." *Archivo ibero-americano* 38 (1978): 33–108.
D'Costa, Gavin. *Christianity and World Religions: Disputed Questions in Theology of Religions*. West Sussex, UK: Wiley-Blackwell, 2009.
———. *Christian Uniqueness Reconsidered: The Myth of a Pluralistic Theology of Religion*. Maryknoll: Orbis, 2005.
D'Elia, Pascual, ed. *Fonti Ricciani*. 3 vols. Rome: 1949–1955.
De Groot, J. J. M. *The Religious System of China*. 6 vols. 1882. Reprint, Taipei: Ch'eng Wen Publishing, 1976.
———. *Sectarianism and Religious Persecution in China*. 2 vols. 1903. Reprint, New York: Barnes and Noble, 1972.
Dehergne, Joseph. *Répertoire des jésuites de Chine de 1552 à 1800*. Rome: Institutum Historicum Societatis Iesu, 1973.
Do, Thien. *Vietnamese Supernaturalism: Views from the Southern Region*. New York: Routledge Curzon, 2003.

Doré, Henri. *Research into Chinese Superstitions*. 13 vols. Shanghai, 1914. Reprint, Taipei: Ch'eng-wen Publishing, 1966.

Dror, Olga. *Cult, Culture, and Authority: Princess Liễu Hạnh in Vietnamese History*. Honolulu: University of Hawai'i Press, 2007.

Dror, Olga, and K.W. Taylor, eds. *Views of Seventeenth-Century Vietnam: Christoforo Borri on Cochinchina and Samuel Baron on Tonkin*. Ithaca, NY: Cornell University Press / SEAP, 2006.

Dudbridge, Glen. *The Legend of Miaoshan*. 1978. Reprint, Oxford: Oxford University Press, 2004.

Dulles, Avery. *A History of Apologetics*. Philadelphia: Westminter, 1971.

Dumoutier, Gustave. *Le Rituel funéraires des Annamites*. Hanoi: F. H. Schneider, 1907.

———. *Annamese Religions*. Translated by Thompson. New Haven, CT: Human Relations Area Files, 1955. Originally published as *Les Cultes Annamites. Un Extrait de la Revue Indochinoise*. Hanoi: F. H. Schneider, 1907.

Dunn, James D. G. *The Partings of the Ways between Christianity and Judaism and Their Significance for the Character of Christianity*. London: SCM, 1991.

———, ed. *Jews and Christians: The Parting of the Ways A.D. 70–135*. Tübingen: Mohr, 1992.

Dunne, George. *Generation of Giants: The Story of the Jesuits in China in the Last Decades of the Ming Dynasty*. Notre Dame: Notre Dame University Press, 1962.

Duong Ngoc Dung. "An Exploration of Vietnamese Confucian Spirituality: The Idea of the Unity of the Three Teachings." In *Confucian Spirituality*, edited by Tu Weiming and Mary Evelyn Tucker, 2:300–301. New York: Crossroad Press, 2004.

Dupuis, Jacques. *Toward a Christian Theology of Religious Pluralism*. Maryknoll: Orbis, 1997.

Durand, Maurice. *Technique et pantheon des mediums viêtnamiens*. 1955. Reprint, Paris: École Française d'Extrême-Orient, 1992.

Dutton, George. *The Tây Sơn Uprising: Society and Rebellion in Eighteenth-Century Vietnam*. Honolulu: University of Hawai'i Press, 2006.

Dutton, George, Jaynes S. Werner, and John K. Whitmore. *Sources of Vietnamese Tradition*. New York: Columbia University Press, 2012.

Ebrey, Patricia B. *Chu Hsi's Family Rituals: A Twelfth-Century Chinese Manual for the Performance of Cappings, Weddings, Funerals, and Ancestral Rites*. Princeton, NJ: Princeton University Press, 1991.

———. *Confucianism and Family Rituals in Imperial China: A Social History of Writing about Rites*. Princeton, NJ: Princeton University Press, 1991.

Edgar, William and K. Scott Oliphint. *Christian Apologetics Past and Present: A Primary Source Reader*. Wheaton: Crossway Books, 2009.

Edwards, Mark, Martin Goodman, Simon Price and Chris Rowland, eds. *Apologetics in the Roman Empire: Pagans, Jews, Christians*. Oxford: Oxford University Press, 1999.

Elman, Benjamin A., John B. Duncan, and Herman Ooms, eds. *Rethinking Confucianism: Past and Present in China, Japan, Korea, and Vietnam*. Los Angeles: University of California Asian Pacific Monograph Series, 2002.

Endres, Kristen. *Performing the Divine: Medium, Market, and Modernity in Urban Vietnam*. Copenhagen: Nordic Institute of Asian Studies, 2011.

Eno, Robert. *The Confucian Creation of Heaven*. Buffalo: State University of New York Press, 1990.

———. "Deities and Ancestors in Early Oracle Inscriptions." In *Religions of China in Practice*, edited by Donald Lopez Jr., 41–51. Princeton, NJ: Princeton University Press, 1996.

Farrer-Halls, Gil. *The Feminine Face of Buddhism*. Wheaton: Quest, 2002.

Fjelstad, Karen, and Nguyen Thi Hien. *Possessed by the Spirits: Mediumship in Contemporary Vietnamese Communities*. Ithaca, NY: Cornell University Press / SEAP, 2006.

Forest, Alain. *Les missionaires Français au Tonkin et au Siam XVIIe–XVIIIe siècles: Analyse comparée d'un relative succès et d'un total échec*. 3 vols. Paris: L'Harmattan, 1998.

Fredericks, James. *Faith among Faiths: Christian Theology and Non-Christian Religions*. New York: Paulist Press, 1999.

Fung, Yu-lan. *A History of Chinese Philosophy*. 2 vols. Translated by Derek Bodde. Princeton, NJ: Princeton University Press, 1952.

Gallagher, Louis J. *China in the Sixteenth Century: The Journals of Matteo Ricci: 1583–1610*. New York: Random House, 1953.

Gallagher, Michael Paul. *Clashing Symbols: An Introduction to Faith and Culture*. London: Dartman, Longmann & Todd, 1997.

Giran, Paul. *Magie & religion annamites; introduction à une philosophie de la civilisation du peuple d'Annam* (Paris: A. Challamel, 1912).

Gispert, Marcos. *Historia de las Misiones Dominicanas en el Tungkin*. Avila, 1928.

Goodrich, Anne Swan. *The Chinese Hells: The Peking Temple of Eighteen Hells and Chinese Conceptions of Hell*. St. Augustine: Monumenta Serica, 1981.

Graham, Angus C. *The Book of Lieh-tzu*. London: John Murray, 1960.

———. *Two Chinese Philosophers: Ch'eng Ming-tao and Ch'eng Yi-ch'uan*. London: Lund Humphries, 1958.

Grant, Robert. *Gods and the One God*. Philadelphia: Westminster Press, 1986.

———. *Greek Apologists of the Second Century*. Philadelphia: Westminster Press, 1988.

Hardy, Andrew, Maurro Cucarzi, and Patrizia Zolese, eds. *Champa and the Archaelogy of My Son (Vietnam)*. Singapore: National University of Singapore Press, 2000.

Hauguard, William. "The Continental Reformation of the Sixteenth Century." In *A Faithful Church: Issues in the History of Catechesis*, edited by John H. Westerhoff III and O. C. Edwards, 109–73. Wilton: Morehouse-Barlow, 1981.

Hà Văn Tấn. *Buddhist Temples in Vietnam*. Rev. ed. Hanoi: Thế Giới Publishers, 2008.

Hendrische, Barbara. *The Scripture on Great Peace: The Taiping jing and the Beginnings of Daoism*. Berkeley: University of California Press, 2006.

Hick, John, and Paul Knitter, eds. *The Myth of Christian Uniqueness: Toward a Pluralistic Theology of Religions*. Maryknoll: Orbis, 1987.

Hsia, R. Po-chia. *A Jesuit in the Forbidden City: Matteo Ricci, 1552–1610*. New York: Oxford, 2010.

Inagaki, Hisao. *The Three Pure Land Sutras: A Study and Translation from Chinese*. Berkeley: Numata Center for Buddhist Translation and Research, 1995.

Jamieson, Neil L. *Understanding Vietnam*. Berkeley: University of California Press, 1993.

Johnson, Luke Timothy. *Among the Gentiles: Greco-Roman Religion and Christianity*. New Haven, CT: Yale University Press, 2009.

Kahlos, Maijastina. *Debate and Dialogue: Christian and Pagan Cultures c. 360–430*. Burlington, VT: Ashgate, 2007.

Karkkainen, Veli-Matti, ed. *An Introduction to the Theology of Religions*. Downers Grove: InterVarsity, 2003.

Kasoff, Ira E. *The Thought of Chang Tsai, 1020–1077*. Cambridge: Cambridge University Press, 1984.

Keenan, John P. *How Master Mou Removes Our Doubts: A Reader-Response Study and Translation of the Mou-Tzu Li-Huo Lun*. Albany: State University of New York, 1994.

Kelly, Liam C. *Beyond the Bronze Pillars: Envoy Poetry and the Sino-Vietnamese Relationship*. Honolulu: University of Hawai'i Press, 2005.

———. "Confucianism in Vietnam: A State of the Field Essay." *Journal of Vietnamese Studies* 1, nos. 1–2 (2006): 314–70.

Kloetzli, Randy. *Buddhist Cosmology: From Single World System to Pure Land*. Delhi: Motilal Banarsidass, 1983.

Knitter, Paul. *Introducing Theologies of Religions*. Maryknoll: Orbis, 2004.

———. *No Other Name? A Critical Survey of Christian Attitudes toward the World Religions*. Maryknoll: Orbis, 1985.

———, ed. *The Myth of Religious Superiority: A Multifaith Exploration*. Maryknoll Orbis, 2005.

Kung, Hans, and Julia Ching. *Christianity and Chinese Religions*. New York: Doubleday, 1989.

Lach, Donald F., and Edwin J. Van Kley. *Asia in the Making of Europe*. Vol 3, book 3, *A Century of Advance: Southeast Asia*. Chicago: University of Chicago Press, 1993.

Launay, Adrien. *Histoire génerale de la Sociéte des missions étrangères*. Paris: 1894.

———. *Les missionaires français au Tonkin*. Paris, 1900.

Laven, Mary. *Mission to China: Matteo Ricci and the Jesuit Encounter with the East*. London: Faber & Faber, 2011.

Li Zhicao. "Preface to *Tianzhu Shiyi*" in *Tianxue Chuhan*. 1629. Translated by David Mungello, in *Sources of Chinese Tradition*, vol. 2, *From 1600 to the Twentieth Century*, compiled by Wm Theodore de Bary and Richard Lufrano, 145–46. New York: Columbia University Press, 2000,

Li, Tana. *Nguyễn Cochinchina: Southern Vietnam in the Seventeenth and Eighteenth Centuries*. Ithaca, NY: Cornell University Press / SEAP, 1998.

Lieberman, Victor. *Strange Parallels: Southeast Asia in Global Context, c. 800–1830*. Vol. 1, *Integration on the Mainland*. Cambridge: Cambridge University Press, 2003.

Lieu, Judith M. *Christian Identity in the Jewish and Graeco-Roman World*. Oxford: Oxford University Press, 2004.

———. *Neither Jew nor Greek? Constructing Early Christianity*. Edinburgh: T&T Clark, 2002.

Liu, Shu-Hsien. *Understanding Confucian Philosophy: Classical and Sung-Ming*. Westport: Greenwood Press, 1998.

Lopez Jr., Donald, ed. *Religions of China in Practice*. Princeton, NJ: Princeton University Press, 1996.

Majumdar, R. C. *Champa: History and Culture of an Indian Colonial Kingdom in the Far East 2nd–16th Century AD*. 1927. Reprint, Delhi: Gian Publishing House, 1985.

MacMullen, Ramsay, and Eugene N. Lane, eds. *Paganism and Christianity, 100–425 C.E.: A Source Book*. Minneapolis: Fortress, 1992.

Marka, Mary Lelia. *The Hsiao Ching*. New York: St. John University Press, 1961.

Marthaler, Berard L. *The Catechism Yesterday and Today: The Evolution of a Genre*. Collegeville, MD: Liturgical Press, 1995.

Maspero, Henri. *Taoism and Chinese Religions*. Translated by Frank A. Kierman. Amherst: University of Massachussets, 1981. Originally published as *Le Taoïsme et les religions chinois* (Paris, 1950).

Maybon, Charles B. *Histoire moderne du pays d'Annam, 1592–1820*. Paris: Plon Nourrit, 1919.

———. *Les marchands européens en Cochinchine et au Tonkin, 1600–1775*. Hanoi: Revue Indochinoise, 1916.

———. "Une factorerie anglaise au Tonkin au XVIIe siècle (1672–1697)." *BEFEO* 10 (1910): 169–204.

McLeod, Mark W., and Nguyen Thi Dieu. *Culture and Customs of Vietnam*. Westport: Greenwood Press, 2001.

McLeod, Mark W. *The Vietnamese Response to French Intervention, 1862–1874*. New York: Greenwood Publishing, 1991.

Menegon, Eugenio. "Jesuits, Franciscans, and Dominicans in Fujian: The Anti-Christian Incidents of 1637–1638." In *Scholar from The West*, edited by Tizziana Lippielo and Roman Malek, 219–62. Nettetal: Steyler Verlag, 1997.

Metzler, Joseph. "Propaganda Fide Congregation." In *A Dictionary of Asian Christianity*, edited by Scott Sunquist, 677. Grand Rapids, MI: Eerdmans, 2001.

Minamiki, George. *The Chinese Rites Controversy from Its Beginnings to Modern Times.* Chicago: Loyola Press, 1985.

Mitchell, Donald W. *Buddhism.* New York: Oxford University Press, 2002.

Mitchell, Leonard L. "The Development of Catechesis in the Third and Fourth Centuries: From Hippolytus to Augustine." In *A Faithful Church: Issues in the History of Catechesis*, edited by John H. Westerhoff III and O. C. Edwards, 49–78. Wilton: Morehouse-Barlow, 1981.

Mungello, D. E., ed. *The Chinese Rites Controversy: Its History and Meaning.* Monumenta Serica Monograph Series 30. Nettetal: Steyler Verlag, 1994.

Norton, Barley. *Songs for the Spirits: Music and Mediums in Modern Vietnam.* Chicago: University of Illinois Press, 2009.

Nguyen, Cuong Tu. *Zen in Medieval Vietnam: A Study and Translation of the Thiền Uyển Tập Anh.* Honolulu: Kuroda Institute, University of Hawai'i Press, 1997.

Nguyen Huy-Lai, Joseph. *La tradition religieuse, spirituelle et sociale au Viêtnam: Sa confrontation avec le christianism.* Paris: Beauchense, 1981.

Nguyễn Nghị, ed. *Catholic Churches in Vietnam: Architecture—History.* Hochiminh City: City General Publishing House, 2004.

Nguyen Ngoc Huy. "The Confucian Incursion into Vietnam." In *Confucianism and the Family*, edited by Walter H. Slote and George A. De Vos, 91–136. Albany: State University of New York Press, 1998.

Nguyen Ngoc Huy, Ta Van Tai, and Tran Van Liem. *The Lê Code: Law in Traditional Vietnam.* Athens: Ohio University Press, 1987.

Nguyễn Tài Thư. *Buddhism in Vietnam.* Hanoi: Thế Giới Publishers, 1993.

Nguyen Van Huy and Laurel Kendall, eds. *Vietnam: Journeys of Body, Mind, and Spirit.* Berkeley: University of California Press, 2003.

Nguyen Van Huyen. "Contribution a l'étude d'un génie tutélaire annamite Li-phucman." *BEFEO* 38 (1938): 1–110.

———. *La civilization annamite.* Hanoi: Impremerie d'Extrême-orient, 1944.

———. *Le Culte des Immortels en Annam.* Hanoi: Impremerie d'Extrême-orient, 1944.

Nguyen Van Khoan. "Essai sur le '*Dinh*' et le culte du genie tutélaire des villages au Tonkin." *BEFEO* 30 (1930): 107–39.

O'Harrow, Stephen. "Men of Hu, Men of Han, Men of Hundred Man: The Biography of Si Nhiep and the Conceptualization of Early Vietnamese Society." *BEFEO* 75 (1986): 249–66.

O'Neill, Charles and Joaquin Dominguez. *Diccionario Historico de la Compañia de Jesus.* Rome: Institutum Historicum Societatis Iesu, 2001.

Palmer, Martin and Jay Ramsay, with Man-Ho Kwok *Kuan Yin Myths and Prophecies of the Chinese Goddess of Compassion.* Charlottesville: Hampton Roads Publishing, 2009.

Panikkar, Raimon. *The Intra-Religious Dialogue.* New York: Paulist, 1999.

Patricia Karetzky. *The Life of the Buddha: Ancient Scriptural and Pictorial Traditions.* Lanham, MD: University Press of America, 1992.

Paul Giran. *Magie & religion annamites; introduction à une philosophie de la civilisation du peuple d'Annam.* Paris: A. Challamel, 1912.

Pfister, Louis. *Notices biographiques et bibliographiques sur les jesuites de l'ancienne mission de Chine: 1552–1773.* 2 vols. Shanghai, 1932.

Phạm Quỳnh Phương. *Hero and Deity: Tran Hung Dao and the Resurgence of Popular Religion in Vietnam.* Bangkok: Mekong Press, 2009.

Phan, Peter C., ed. *The Asian Synod: Text and Commentary.* Maryknoll: Orbis, 2002.

Phan, Peter C. *Being Religious Interreligiously: Asian Perspectives on Interfaith Dialogue.* Maryknoll: Orbis, 2004.

———. *In Our Own Tongues: Perspectives from Asia on Mission and Inculturation.* Maryknoll: Orbis, 2003.

———. *Mission and Catechesis: Alexandre de Rhodes and Inculturation in Seventeenth-Century Vietnam.* Maryknoll: Orbis, 1998.

Phan, Phat-Huon. *Việt Nam Giáo Sử.* 2 vols. Saigon, 1961. Translated by the author as *History of the Catholic Church in Vietnam, 1533–1933.* Longbeach: Cuu The Tung Thu, 2000.

Plopper, Clifford. *Chinese Religion Seen Through the Proverb.* Shanghai, 1935. Reprint, New York: Paragon Book Reprint, 1969.

Race, Alan. *Christians and Religious Pluralism: Patterns in the Christian Theology of Religions.* Maryknoll: Orbis, 1983.

Rambo, A. Terry. *Searching for Vietnam: Selected Writings on Vietnamese Culture and Society.* Kyoto: Kyoto University Press, 2005.

Ramsay, Jacob. *Mandarins and Martyrs: The Church and the Nguyen Dynasty in Early Nineteenth-Century Vietnam.* Stanford, CA: Stanford University Press, 2008.

Roland, Jacques. *Les Missionnaires portugais et les débuts de l'Église catholique au Viêtnam.* 2 vols. Reichstett: Định Hướng Tùng Thư, 2004.

Rosso, Antonio. *Apostolic Legations to China in the Eighteenth Century.* South Pasadena: Perkins, 1948.

Ruether, Rosemary Radford. *Faith and Fratricide: Theological Roots of Anti-Semitism.* New York: Seabury Press, 1974.

Ruiz-de-Medina, Juan, and Felipe Gomez. "Vietnam." In *Diccionario Historico de la Compañia de Jesus (DHCJ)*, edited by Charles O'Neill and Joaquin Dominguez, 4:3953–69. Rome: Institutum Historicum Societatis Iesu, 2001.

Rule, Paul. *K'ung Tzu or Confucius? The Jesuit Interpretation of Confucianism.* Sydney: Allen and Unwin, 1986.

———. "Towards a History of the Chinese Rites Controversy." In *The Chinese Rites Controversy: Its History and Meaning*, edited by David Mungello, 249–66. Nettetal: Steyler Verlag, 1994.

Sadakata, Akira. *Buddhist Cosmology: Philosophy and Origin*. Translated by Gaynor Sekimori. Tokyo: Kosei Publishing Co, 1997.

Sawyer, Ralph D., and Mei-chun Sawyer. *The Seven Ancient Military Classics of China, Including the* Art of War. Boulder, CO: Westview Press, 1993.

Schneiders, Sandra M. *The Revelatory Text: Interpreting the New Testament as Sacred Scripture*. Milwaukee: Liturgical Press, 1999.

Schreiter, Robert. *Constructing Local Theologies*. Maryknoll: Orbis, 1985.

Schurhammer, Georg. *Francis Xavier: His Life and Times*. Vol. 4, *Japan and China 1549–1552*. Rome: The Jesuit Historical Institute, 1982.

Schutte, Josef Franz. *Valignano's Mission Principles for Japan 1573–1582*. Translated by John J. Coyne. 2 vols. St. Louis: The Institute of Jesuit Sources, 1980–1985.

Schwartz, Benjamin. *The World of Thought in Ancient China*. Cambridge, MA: Harvard University Press, 1985.

Scott, Janet Lee. *For Gods, Ghost and Ancestors: The Chinese Tradition of Paper Offerings*. Seattle: University of Washington Press, 2007.

Shaft, Robert H. "The Scripture in Forty-Two Sections." In *Religions of China in Practice*, edited by Donald S. Lopez, 360–71. Princeton, NJ: Princeton University Press, 1996.

Shih, Joseph. *Le Père Ruggieri et le problème de l'évangélisation en Chine*. Rome: Pontificia Universitas Gregoriana, 1964.

Shorter, Aylward. *Toward a Theology of Inculturation*. Maryknoll: Orbis, 1988.

Shortland, John R. *The Persecutions of Annam: A History of Christianity in CochinChina and Tonking*. London: Burns and Oates, 1875.

Simon, Peter, and Ida Simon-Baroudh. "Les Génies des Quatre Palais." In *L'Homme* 10, no. 4 (1970): 81–101.

Sloyan, Gerald S. "Religious Education: From Early Christianity to Medieval Times." In *Shaping the Christian Message*, edited by Gerald S. Sloyan, 3–45. New York: Macmillan Publishing, 1958.

Schmidt-Leukel, Perry, ed. *Buddhism, Christianity and the Question of Creation*. Burlington, VT: Ashgate, 2006.

Schineller, Peter. *A Handbook of Inculturation*. New York: Paulist Press, 1990.

Spence, Jonathan. *The Memory Place of Matteo Ricci*. New York: Penguin, 1985.

Standaert, Nicholas. *The Fascinating God*. Rome: Editrice Pontificia Universistà Gregroriana, 1995.

———, ed. *Handbook of Christianity in China*. Vol 1, *To 1800*. Leiden: Brill, 2001.

———. "Responses & Reflections," in *Christianity and Cultures: Japan and China in Comparison 1543–1644*, ed. Antoni M. Üçerler, 61–64. Rome: Institutum Historicum Societatis Iesu, 2009.

Standaert, Nicholas, and Adrian Dudink, eds. *Chinese Christian Texts from the Roman Archives of the Society of Jesus*. 12 vols. Rome: Procura Generaliza della Compagnia Di Gesù, 2002.

Sullivan, Francis. *Salvation Outside the Church: Tracing the History of the Catholic Response.* New York: Paulist Press, 1992.
Sunquist, Scott W., David Wu Chu Sing, and John Chew Hiang Chea, eds. *A Dictionary of Asian Christianity.* Grand Rapids, MI: Eerdmans, 2002.
Ta Van Tai. *The Vietnamese Tradition of Human Rights.* Berkeley: University of California, Institute of East Asian Studies, 1988.
Taylor, Keith W. "Authority and Legitimacy in 11th century Vietnam." In *Southeast Asia in the 9th to 14th Centuries,* edited by David C Marr and A. C. Milner, 139–76. Singapore: Institute of Southeast Asian Studies, 1986.
———. *The Birth of Vietnam.* Berkeley: University of California Press, 1983.
———. *A History of the Vietnamese.* Cambridge: Cambridge University Press, 2013.
———. "Nguyen Hoang and the Beginning of Vietnam's Southward Expansion." In *Southeast Asia in the Early Modern Era: Trade, Power and Belief,* edited by Anthony Reid, 42–65. Ithaca, NY: Cornell University Press, 1993.
———. "Vietnamese Confucian Narratives." In *Rethinking Confucianism: Past and Present in China, Japan, Korea, and Vietnam,* edited by John B. Duncan and Herman Ooms, 337–69. Los Angeles: University of California Press, 2002.
Taylor, Keith W., and John K. Whitmore, eds. *Essays into Vietnamese Pasts.* Ithaca, NY: Cornell University Press / SEAP, 1995
Taylor, Philip. *Goddess on the Rise: Pilgrimage and Popular Religion in Vietnam.* Honolulu: University of Hawai'i Press, 2004.
Teiser, Stephen F. *The Ghost Festival in Medieval China.* Princeton, NJ: Princeton University Press, 1988.
———. *Scripture on the Ten Kings and the Making of Purgatory in Medieval Chinese Buddhism.* Honolulu: University of Hawai'i Press, 1994.
Thich Nhat Hanh. *Master Tang Hoi: First Zen Teacher in Vietnam and China.* Berkeley: Parallax Press, 2001.
Thompson, Laurence G. *Chinese Religion: An Introduction.* 5th ed. San Francisco: Wadsworth Publishing, 1996.
Tran Ham Tan. "Étude sur le Văn-miêu de Hanoi (Temple de la Littérature)," *BEFEO* 45, no. 1 (1951): 89–118.
Tran Quoc Vuong. "The Legend of Ông Dóng." In *Essays into Vietnamese Past,* edited by Keith Taylor and John Whitmore, 13–41. Ithaca, NY: Cornell University Press / SEAP, 1995.
Tran, Van Doan. "Confucianism: Vietnam." In *Encyclopedia of Chinese Philosophy,* edited by Antonion S. Cua, 173–74. New York: Routedge, 2003.
Tran Van Giap. "Le Bouddhisme en Annam des origins au XIIIe siècle." *Bulletin de l'École française d'Extrême-Orient* 32 (1932): 191–268.
Tran Van Toan. "L'antropologie religieuse au Viêtnam du XVIIIe siècle: Essais de synthèse par les Augustins déchaussés." In *Anthropologie et missiologie: XIXe–XX siècles: Entre connivance et rivalité,* edited by Olivier Servais and Gerald van't Spijker, 303–22. Paris: Karthala, 2004.

———. "Le regard des missionaries catholiques sur le bouddhisme au Vietnam du XVIIe au XIXe siècle." In *L'altérité religieuse, un défi pour la mission chrétienne*, edited by Françoise Jacquin and Jean-François Zorn, 59–86. Paris: Karthala, 2001.

Tran, Anh Q. "*Hội Đồng Tứ Giáo/Conference of the Four Religions*: A Christian Encounter of the Three Religions in the Eighteenth-Century Vietnam." STL thesis, Jesuit School of Theology at Berkeley, 2006.

———. "Inculturation, Mission, and Dialogue in Vietnam: The 'Conference of Representatives of Four Religions,'" in *Beyond Conversion and Syncretism: Indigenous Encounters with Missionary Christianity, 1800–2000*, edited by D. Lindenfeld and M. Richardson, 167–94. New York: Berghahn Books, 2012.

Tran, Nhung Tuyet, and Anthony Reid, eds. *Việt Nam: Borderless Histories*. Madison: University of Wisconsin Press, 2004.

Unger, Ann Helen, and Walter Unger. *Pagodas, Gods, and Spirits of Vietnam*. London: Thames and Hudson, 1997.

Villarroel, Fidel. "The Chinese Rites Controversy: Dominican Viewpoint." *Philippiniana Sacra* 28 (1993): 5–61.

Vu Khanh Tuong. "Les Missions Jesuites avant les Missions Étrangères au Vietnam: 1615–1665." Master's Thesis, Institut Catholique de Paris, 1956.

Watson, James, and Evelyn Rawski, eds. *Death Ritual in Late Imperial and Modern China*. Berkeley: University of California Press, 1988.

Werner, E. T. C. *Dictionary of Chinese Mythology*. Shanghai, 1932. Reprint, New York: Julian Press, 1961.

Westerhoff III, John H., and O. C. Edwards, eds. *A Faithful Church: Issues in the History of Catechesis*. Wilton, CT: Morehouse-Barlow, 1981.

Whitmore, John K. "Chiao-chih and Neo-Confucianism: The Ming Attempt to Transform Vietnam." *Ming Studies* 4 (1977): 51–91.

———. "From Classical Scholarship to Confucian Belief in Vietnam." *Vietnam Forum* 9 (1987): 49–65.

———. "Literati Culture and Integration in Dai Viet, c. 1430–1840." In *Beyond Binary Histories: Reimagining Eurasia to c. 1830*, edited by Victor Lieberman, 221–43. Ann Arbor: University of Michigan Press, 1997.

———. *Vietnam, Ho Quy Ly, and the Ming (1371–1421)*. The Lac Viet Series, 2. New Haven, CT: Yale South East Asia Studies, 1985.

Wieger, Leon. "Notes sur la première catéchèse écrite en chinois 1582–1584." *AHSI* 1 (1932): 72–84.

Wiest, Jean-Paul. "Learning from the Missionary Past." In *The Catholic Church in Modern China: Perspectives*, edited by Edmond Tang and Jean-Paul Wiest, 181–98. Maryknoll: Orbis, 1991.

Wilken, Robert Louis. *The Christians as the Romans Saw Them*. 1984. Reprint, New Haven, CT: Yale University Press, 2003.

Wilkinson, Endymion. *Chinese History: A Manual*. Cambridge, MA: Harvard University Asia Center, 1998.

Willis Jr., John. "From Manila to Fuan." In *The Chinese Rites Controversy*, edited by D. G. Mungello, 111–28. Nettetal: Steyler Verlag, 1994.

Wilson, Stephen G. *Related Strangers: Jews and Christians, 70–170 CE*. Minneapolis: Fortress, 1995.

Wilson, Thomas A. *Genealogy of the Way: The Construction and Uses of the Confucian Tradition in Late Imperial China*. Stanford, CA: Stanford University Press, 1995.

———, ed. *On Sacred Grounds: Culture, Society, Politics, and the Formation of the Cult of Confucius*. Cambridge, MA: Harvard University Press, 2002.

Wolters, O. W. "Historians and Emperors in Vietnam and China: Comments Arising Out of Le Van Huu's History, Presented to the Tran Court in 1272." In *Perceptions of the Past in South East Asia*, edited by Anthony Reid and David Marr, 73–78. Singapore: Heineman Educational Books, 1979.

———. *Two Essays on Đại Việt in the Fourteenth Century*. New Haven, CT: Yale Southeast Asia Studies, 1988.

Wong, Eva *Lieh-tzu: A Taoist Guide to Practical Living*. Boston: Shambala, 1995.

Woodside, Alexander. "Classical Primordialism and Historical Agendas of Vietnamese Confucianism." In *Rethinking Confucianism: Past and Present in China, Japan, Korea, and Vietnam*, edited by John B. Duncan and Herman Ooms, 126–28. Los Angeles: University of California Press, 2002.

———. *Vietnam and the Chinese Model: A Comparative Study of Vietnamese and Chinese Government in the First Half of the Nineteenth Century*. 1971. Reprint, Cambridge, MA: Harvard University, 1988.

Wright, Arthur. *Buddhism in Chinese History*. Stanford, CA: Stanford University Press, 1959.

———. *Studies in Chinese Buddhism*. New Haven, CT: Yale University Press, 1990.

Yao, Xinzhong. *An Introduction to Confucianism*. Cambridge: Cambridge University Press, 2000.

Young, Stephen B. "The Orthodox Chinese Confucian Social Paradigm versus Vietnamese Individualism." In *Confucianism and the Family*, edited by Walter H. Slote and George A. DeVos, 137–61. Albany: State University of New York Press, 1998.

Yü, Chun-Fang. *Kuan Yin: The Chinese Transformation of Avalokiteshvara*. New York: Columbia University Press, 2001.

Zenryu, Tsukamoro. *A History of Early Chinese Buddhism from Its Introduction to the Death of Hui-yüan*. 2 vols. Translated by Leon Hurvitz. Tokyo: Koshanda, 1985.

Zhang, Dainian. *Key Concepts in Chinese Philosophy*. Translated and edited by Edmund Ryden. New Haven, CT: Yale University Press, 2002.

Zurcher, Erik. *The Buddhist Conquest of China: The Spread and Adaptation of Buddhism in Early Medieval China*. 1959. Reprint, Leiden: Brill, 2007.

Index

Adriano di Santa Thecla, xiii, xiv, 29, 30, 70, 71, 103, 152, 157, 323–24, 327–29
Amida. *See* Amitābha Buddha
Amitābha Buddha (A Di Đà), 9, 113, 125–26, 304–5, 316, 316n155
An Lushan (An Lộc Sơn), 219
Analects (Lunyu, Luận Ngữ), 63, 65n48, 173n45, 213, 225, 236
ancestor worship, 3, 14, 78–79
   and Buddhism, 124–25 (*see also* Ritual: Rite of Breaking the Prison)
   Christian interpretation, 32, 44, 126–29, 225–29
   as filial duty, 31–32, 111
   practice of, 114–22 (*see also* ritual: funeral and memorial)
   traditional interpretation, 109–13
   and Vietnamese Catholics, 129–32 (*see also* China: Rites Controversy)
Andrew Tri, 25n16
Annals of Spring and Autumn (Chunqiujing, Xuân Thu Kinh), 65n48, 173n45, 202
Annam, 1n3, 21–23, 161, 201, 231–32, 306. *See also* Đại Việt; Catholic mission of, 26–28, 32, 44 (*see also* Augustinians; Dominicans; Jesuits; MEP)
Anthology of Magical Arts (Âm Dương Tạp Thư), 241, 251
Antoine Trần Văn Toàn, xiv

Arjona, Juan de, 28
astrology, 139, 142, 251–52, 261–66
August Earth, 82–83, 174, 195–96
August Heaven, 77–78, 82–83, 174, 195–96
Augustinians, xiii, 24, 28–30, 70–71, 324
Avalokiteśvara (Quan Âm), 9, 103, 105–6, 271, 318n160, 318–19, 327

Bắc Đẩu, 12
Baldinotti, Giuliano, xii, 91
Bamboo Grove (Trúc Lâm) school, 9
Ban Gu (Ban Cố), 276, 300
Bao Yueguang (Bảo Nguyệt Quang), 105, 239
Baron, Samuel, xii, 15–17, 84, 91, 98, 157
Beijing, 40–42, 55
Bellarmine, Robert, 59
Benedict XIV, 42
Book of Hồng Lục (Hồng Lục Thư), 65, 246, 248, 251
Bottaro, Tommaso a Sestri, 29
Brahma (Phạm Thiên), 10n35
British, the, 24n9
Buddha, 106, 137, 141–42, 150, 275, 281, 289–90, 294, 305
   land of, 113, 125–26, 305, 307n129, 308 (*see also* Buddhism: Pure Land)
   life of, 272–74
   meaning of, 296–97
   teaching of, 300, 309, 315
   worship of, 277–78, 282–85

Buddha nature, 286–87, 303, 306
Buddhism, 15–16, 150
  in China, 275–78
  concept of afterlife, 123–26, 313 (*see also* Transmigration of soul)
  Confucian evaluation, 133–34, 284
  esoteric teaching, 286–99
  funeral rites, 303–9
  Pure Land, 125
  in Vietnam, 7–10, 278–80
  Zen, 8–10, 14

Cadière, Léopold, 2, 14, 77, 155
Cai Lun (Thái Luân), 310
Cambodia, 27
Cảnh Hưng, 70, 183
Cao Bằng, 23
Cao Cao (Tào Tháo), 240
Castaneda, Jacinto, xi
Catechism
  of Majorica, 59
  of Rhodes, 58–61, 66–67, 69, 82, 84, 141n21, 152, 157
  of Ricci, 51, 55–58, 57n26, 66, 69, 74, 152
  of Ruggieri, 54, 55n19
  type of, 51–52, 141
  of Valignano, 53, 53n17
  of Xavier, 52
Catechismus Christianae Fidei. See Catechism: of Valignano
Categorized Records of the Institutions of the Successive Dynasties (Lịch Triều Hiến Chương Loại Chí), 81
Catholicism. *See* Christianity
Cevallos, Ordonnez de, 24n12, 28n25
Champa, 5
Chang Cheng (Xương Thành), 311–12
Cheng Hao (Trình Hạo), 169n33
Cheng Yi (Trình Di), 65, 169n33
China
  dominance of, 1–2, 5
  Jesuit mission of, 37–38, 54
  literature of, 5n17, 64–65
  origin of Vietnamese cults, 82, 86–87, 92, 95, 103–5, 122
  Rites Controversy, 36–42, 47, 129

Christianity
  and Buddhism, 64, 74, 147, 149–50
  and Confucianism, 147–49
  and Daoism, 64, 74, 147, 149, 151
  and other religions, 145–47
  Rites Controversy in Vietnam, 42–46
Chử Đồng Tử, 11–12, 94, 102n77
chữ nôm (demotic Vietnamese script), xiii, 68, 143–44
chữ quốc ngữ (romanized Vietnamese script), xiv, 26, 58, 62, 68, 328
Chư Vị (the Honored Ones), cult of, 12
Chu Wangying (Sở Vương Anh), 277
Classic of Changes (Yijing, Dịch Kinh), 65n48, 168–69, 173, 173n45, 258
Classic of Documents (Shujing, Thư Kinh), 65n48, 173n45, 180n68, 181–84, 186–87
Classic of Odes (Shijing, Thi Kinh), 65n48, 173n45, 225
Clement XI, 40–41
Clement XII, 42
Cochinchina, 22–23
  Catholic mission, 25–28, 32, 34n49, 44, 130
  trade with the West, 24
Collated Annals of the Mirror of Law (Gangjian Hebian, Cương Giám Hợp Biên), 65
community hall (*đình*), 78–79, 96
Compendium of Nature and Principle (Xingli Daquan, Tính Lý Đại Toàn), 5n17, 65, 166–67, 166n26, 174, 186
Complete Chronicle of the Great Viet (Đại Việt Sử Ký Toàn Thư), 35, 64
Comprehensive Mirror for Aid in Government (Zizhi Tongjian, Tự Trị Thông Giám), 65, 181n75
Conference of the Four Religions (Hội Đồng Tứ Giáo), xi, xiii–xiv, 140, 143–45
Confucianism, 1, 69, 298
  with Buddhism and Daoism, 9–11, 75, 134, 152

with Catholicism, 30–32, 35–36, 46, 54, 56, 69, 128–29, 135, 143, 147–49 (*see also* China: Rites Controversy)
literature, 64–65, 153
Neo-Confucianism, 57, 64, 66, 74, 136–37
ritual of, 74, 79, 106–7, 111, 115
scholar of, xi, xv, 66, 69, 74, 80, 144, 156, 164
in Vietnam, 3–7, 8, 15–16, 161, 213
Confucius, 4, 6, 15, 88, 92, 97, 106, 136–37, 142, 187, 192, 211–12, 215, 236, 298
Buddhist veneration of, 299
cult of, 37, 38n65, 39–40, 42–44, 67, 72, 86–88, 92, 155, 165, 211–15, 299, 323, 325, 329
teaching of, 41, 65n48, 111, 148, 166, 168, 177, 182–84, 186, 226, 258
temple of, 79, 86–88, 92, 214
title of, 86–87n27, 212
Correct Practices of Family Rituals (Gia Lễ Chính Hành), 115, 187, 205

Đại La, 95, 279
Đại Việt, 2, 4–5, 8, 21–22, 43, 87
Dampier, William, xii
Đàng Ngoài, 23. *See also* Tonkin
Đàng Trong, 23. *See also* Cochinchina
dao, 154, 173
Daodejing (Đạo Đức Kinh), 11, 65, 149, 237n8
Daoism, 6
concept of afterlife, 112–13
Confucian view, 36, 133–34
in China, 239–41
origin, 236–38
as philosophy, 11
as religion, 11–12
as sorcery, 243–45
teaching of, 134, 170, 233, 237–38
in Vietnam, 10–13, 241–42
Đế Thích, 255
demon, 77, 255–56, 250, 319, 321–22
Departed Spirits of Viet Realm (Việt Điện U Linh Tập), 4n10, 11, 64, 95n61, 96

Deydier, François, 27n22, 29
Dharma Cloud (Pháp Vân), 101
Dharma Lightning (Pháp Điện), 101
Dharma Rain (Pháp Vũ), 101
Dharma Thunder (Pháp Lôi), 101
Dharmakara, 125
Dictionarium Annamitico Latinum, 63
Dictionarium Annamiticum, Lusitanum, et Latinum, 62
Đinh dynasty, 4, 8, 278
Đinh Tiên Hoàng, 257n72
Dīpankara Buddha, 316, 316n153, n157
Discourses of the Confucian School (Kongji Jiayu, Khổng Tử Gia Ngữ), 2, 29
divination, 258–60, 267–68
Divine Farmer. *See* Shennong
Đỗ Hưng Viễn, 24n12
Đoàn Thị Điểm, 102
Doctrine of the Mean (Zhongyong, Trung Dung), 65n48, 87n28, 170, 173n45, 213
Domenico di San Martino, 71
Dominicans, xi, 24, 28–30, 32, 38–39, 44, 46, 70, 130, 323
Đông Kinh (Eastern Capital), 22, 22n4
Đổng Thiên Vương, 94, 196, 201. *See also* King Gióng or Dóng
Dong Zhongshu (Đổng Trọng Thư), 4, 65, 177
Duke Gao (Cao Công), 310
Duke of River (Hà Bá), 142, 253–54
Duke of Zhou (Chu Công), 86–87, 213, 258
Dutch, the, 15, 24

Early Lê, dynasty, 4, 8
eight trigrams (*bagua, bát quái*), 167n28, 258, 287, 298
Eminent Monks of Thien Community (Thiền Uyển Tập Anh), 8n26, 9n29
emptiness (*kong, không*), 138, 170, 290, 294n93, 294–95, 297
Esoteric Branches (Bí Chỉ), 65, 123, 286n50, 290n88, 295n96
Ex Quo Singulari, 42, 45, 72

Faifo, 24
Family Rituals (Gia Lễ), 65, 114–15, 118, 187–88, 205, 220–22, 224, 226–27, 308, 310
Fan Shiyong (Phan Thị Vinh), 275, 277n26, 284
Fate of Fortune (Lộc Mệnh), 263
Feng Yingqing (Phùng Anh Thanh), 55
filial piety
 as duty, 32, 43, 45, 114, 117–18
 Christian view, 126–32, 225, 228–29 (*see also* China: Rites Controversy)
 as virtue, 4, 78, 108, 111
Five Classics, 5n17, 65, 65n48, 87, 173, 173n45
five elements (*wuxing, ngũ hành*), 11, 121, 189, 259, 293, 296n102
five emperors (*wudi, ngũ đế*), 189n93, 298n106
five norms (*wuchang, ngũ thường*), 31n36, 133
five relations (*wulun, ngũ luân*), 31n36, 69, 164
five virtues (*wude, ngũ đức*), 31n36, 69, 148, 164, 178–79
Foreign Mission Society of Paris, xiii, 27. *See also* MEP
Four Associates, 87n28, 88, 92, 213–14
Four Books, 5n17, 56n24, 65, 65n48, 87, 173, 173n45
four forms (*sixiang, tứ tượng*), 136, 166n21, 167–68, 171, 287n60
Four Letters to Discern One's Fate (Tứ Tự Kinh Tiên Định Số), 261
Francis Đức, 25n16
Francis Xavier, 52, 59
Franciscans, 24, 38
French, the, 24n9
French missionaries, 26–30, 34, 130, 152. *See also* MEP
Fu Yi (Phó Dịch), 64, 278, 278n28, 281–82
Fujian, 38–39
Fuxi (Phục Hy), 189n98. *See also* Taihao

Gao Pian (Cao Biền), 95, 202, 202n137, 231

Geomancy (*fengshui*), 121n29–31, 142, 230–32
Gia Long, 131n50
Giác Hải, 196n122
Gianh River, 23
Gil de Federich, Francisco, 323n1, 323–24
God. *See* Lord of Heaven
Goddess worship (đạo Mẫu), 9, 12, 79, 101–3
Goulong (Câu Long), 188, 190, 190n103, 191
Goumang (Câu Mang), 189, 189n99, 191
Great Duke (Thái Công), 213, 216–17, 219
Great Learning (Daxue, Đại Học), 65n48, 162, 162n12, 173n45, 175, 177, 213, 226, 283
Gregory XIII, 27n21
Guan Yu (Quan Vũ), 89n58
Guan Zhong (Quản Trọng), 218
Guang Yan (Quang Nghiêm), 105, 239–40
Guanyin, 103. *See also* Avalokiteśvara
Guild Founder (Tổ Sư or Tiên Sư), 100–101, 209–10
Gun (Cổn), 180, 180n71
Guo Ziyi (Quách Tử Nghi), 218

Han (Hán) dynasty, 3, 134, 239, 264, 281
Han Gaozu (Hán Cao Tổ), 212
Han Guangwu (Hán Quang Vũ), 203
Han Huidi (Hán Huệ Đế), 212, 218
Han Lingdi (Hán Linh Đế), 240, 242, 277
Han Mingdi (Hán Minh Đế), 67, 134, 275–77, 281–82, 298
Han Wudi (Hán Vũ Đế), 238, 244, 276
Han Xin (Hàn Tín), 218
Han Yu (Hàn Dũ), 64, 282–83, 282n40
Hành Mãn, 320
heaven (*qian, càn*), 173n47, 173–74
Heng E (Hằng Nga), 311–12
Hernandez, Santiago, 29
Hilario Costa (Hilario di Gesù), xiv, 29, 71n68, 71–72, 323–24, 327, 329
Histoire du royaume de Tunquin, 43, 60
History of the Han Dynasty (Hanshu, Hán Thư), 64, 276–77, 300
Hồ Hán Thương, 231n229

Hồ Quý Ly, 9, 90, 231, 231n229, 284
Hồ Sĩ Tân, 114
Hồ Sỹ Dương, 114n11
Hoà Chính, 121n31
Hoảng Đỗ Vĩnh, 65
Holy See, 26, 28, 42n75, 45
Hou Yi (Hậu Nghệ), 312n143
Household Guardian (Thổ Công), 100, 208–9
Hu Guang (Hồ Quang), 65, 166n26
Hu Wufeng (Hồ Ngũ Phong), 178, 178n64
Hu Zhitang (Hồ Trí Đường), 171n43, 269
Huainanzi, book of, 11
Huang Fu (Hoàng Phủ), 231–32
Huangdi (Hoàng Đế), 185n4, 189–91, 238n12
human nature (*xing, tính*), 11, 66, 177
Huyền Vân, 10n37, 241

Ignatius Nhuận, 25n16
imperial ancestral shrine, 86
Imperially Ordered Mirror and Commentary on History of the Viet (Khâm Định Việt Sử Thông Giám Cương Mục), 24
Index historicus, 71, 323
Indra (Đế Thích), 10n35
I-nhi-khu, 24
Inner Way, 123
Instructions on Emptiness (Khoá Hư Lục), 9n29
Introduction to the Holy Teachings of the Lord of Heaven (Thiên Chúa Thánh Giáo Khải Mông). See Catechism: of Majorica
Italians, the, xiv, 29–30, 70–71, 73, 324. See also Augustinians

Jade Emperor (Ngọc Hoàng), 12, 99, 105–6, 142, 239n17, 239–41, 243, 255, 289, 311–12, 326
Japan, xii, 1n2, 22, 24, 25n14, 46, 52–53, 193n110, 318n160
Jesuits, 25–28, 30, 31n35, 32, 34, 70
  in Rites Controversy, 37–40, 43–44

Jia Geliang (Gia Cát Lượng), 218
Jiang Chong (Giang Sung), 244
Jiaozhi (Giao Chỉ), 1n3, 3, 203
Jiaozhou (Giao Châu). See Jiaozhi (Giao Chỉ)
John Paul II, 11n1
Juan de la Paz, 44
Juan de Santa Cruz, 28–29

Kan Heng (Kham Hành), 230, 230n222
Kan Yu, (Kham Dư), 231
Kang Senghui (Khương Tăng Hội), 7n23
Kangxi (Khang Hy), 40–41, 55n23, 129
karma, 10, 30, 113, 123–24, 301, 305, 313–15
Kẻ Chợ, 23, 161, 195–96, 199, 203, 269. See also Thăng Long
Kẻ Sặt, 71
Kẻ Vân, 71
Khmer, 5. See also Cambodia
Không Lộ, 100n71, 196n121
King Bạch Hạc, 257n73
King Bạch Mã, 203, 329
King Gióng or Dóng, 12. See also Đổng Thiên Vương
King Mê Hê, 257n74
King Trèm. See Lý Ông Trọng
Kinh Dương Vương, 196n117
Kitchen God (Táo Quân), 79, 99–100, 137, 142, 205–8
Korea, 1n2, 6, 193n110, 318n160
Ksitigarbha, 124, 314n150

Lạc Long Quân, 196n117
Lady Quế, 257n75
Lady Trì, 257n76
Lambert de la Motte, Pierre, 27–28
Lamp of the Mind (Tâm Đăng), 65, 65n51, 124, 125n40, 141, 272–74, 290n85, 299, 316–17, 319
Land Guardian (Thổ Chủ), 100, 208–9
Lao Tan (Lão Đam), 236. See also Laozi
Laos, 27
Laozi (Lão Tử), 11, 16, 34, 67, 106, 133–34, 137, 142, 149–51, 161, 170, 233, 235–37, 239, 242–43, 270, 289n79, 298, 326
Lê, *Code of Law*, 32, 43, 117n22

Lê, dynasty, 5, 9, 65, 11–12, 22, 88, 96
Lê, kingship, 22–23
Lê Anh Tông, 24n12
Lê Gia Tông, 246, 251
Lê Ích Mục, 297
Lê Ngọa Triều, 279
Lê Quát, 9n30
Lê Quý Đôn, 6
Lê Thái Tổ (Lê Đại Hành), 279
Lê Thái Tổ (Lê Lợi), 231–32
Lê Thái Tông, 88, 90
Lê Thánh Tông, 22, 82, 84, 133
Lê Thế Tông, 24n12
Lê Trung Tông, 279
Lê Tương Dực, 184
Lê-Trịnh era, 23, 80–81, 85–86, 89–90, 105. *See also* Lê dynasty
Leo X, 27n21
Lezzoli, Raimondo, 29
Li Chunfeng (Lý Thuần Phong), 262, 262n88
Li Jing (Lý Tĩnh), 218
Li Rendun (Lý Nhân Đôn), 208
Li Renyu (Lý Nhân Dục), 208
Li Sheng (Lý Thịnh), 218
Li Zhicao (Lý Chi Tảo), 55n21, 56
Liang Taizu (Lương Thái Tổ), 231
Liang Wudi (Lương Vũ Đế), 277, 282, 315
Liao Sheng (Liễu Thăng), 231–32
Liao Yu (Liễu Dư), 121n30, 230–31
Liao Zi (Liễu Tử), 218
Liễu Hạnh, 12, 94, 102–3, 255–56, 260
Liu Ji (Lưu Cơ), 218
Liu Yan (Lưu Ẩn), 231
Local God (Thổ Địa), 79
Lord of Heaven (*Tianzhu, Thiên Chủ/Chúa*)
  Christian doctrine of, 56, 66–67, 172, 302, 315
  as first cause, 67, 168–69
  name of God, 55n20, 141, 155, 162n10, 176
  as object of true worship, 67, 97, 138, 186–87, 192–93, 195, 285
  religion/way of, 33n39, 68–69, 73, 135–36, 138, 147–48, 162, 164, 178–79, 188, 302, 315 (*see also* Christianity)
  as source of blessing, 88, 137, 140, 197, 215, 231, 251
  sovereignty of, 85, 107, 136–37, 142, 185–86, 210
Lotus Sutra, 104
Lü Buwei (Lã Bất Vi), 189
Lü Cai (Lữ Tài), 263–64, 263n89
Lü Wang (Lã Vọng), 89, 92, 216. *See also* Great Duke
Lương Thế Vinh, 133–34
Lý, dynasty, 4, 8, 84, 87, 278
Lý Anh Tông, 8n26, 82
Lý Cao Tông, 5, 8n26, 95
Lý Chiêu Hoàng, 279
Lý Công Uẩn, 279
Lý Độ Văn, 279
Lý Hổ, 273
Lý Huệ Tông, 279
Lý Nhân Tông, 161, 279, 196n121
Lý Ông Trọng, 94, 196n120, 201–2
Lý Thái Tổ, 10n34, 95, 201, 278
Lý Thái Tông, 89, 194n111
Lý Thần Tông, 196n121
Lý Thánh Tông, 8n26
Lý Thường Kiệt, 94

Ma Tian (Mã Điếm), 202
Ma Yuan (Mã Viện), 203, 203n139, 329
Mạc, dynasty, 9, 22–23, 82, 90
Mạc Đăng Dung, 22
Macau, xii, 21, 23, 25–28, 54, 58
Magical Keys to Great Peace (Thái Bình Yêu Thuật), 241
Maigrot, Charles, 37n59, 39–41
Majorica, Girolamo, 52n10, 59
Malacca, 24, 28
Manila, 24, 28, 38, 44
Marini, Giovanni Filippo de, xii, 68n58
Marques, Pedro, 25
martyr, xii, 34n47
Māyādevī, 272, 290
Mencius, 87, 213
Mencius, book of (Mengzi, Mạnh Tử), 63, 65n48, 173n45
MEP (Missions Étrangères de Paris), xiii, 27–30, 32, 44, 46, 130

Mezzabarba, Carlo Ambrogio, 41, 44
Miaoshan (Diệu Thiện, Mẫu Thiện), 104, 318
Miaozhuang (Diệu Trang), 104, 318–19
Miguel dos Santos, 28n25
Ming (Minh) dynasty, 2, 5, 9, 14, 37, 80, 86, 91, 231, 254, 278, 310, 312
Ming Taizu (Minh Thái Tổ), 284
Minh Mạng, 130n50
Mo Di (Mặc Địch), 236n6
Mongols, the, 8, 12, 202n138
monotheism, 30–31, 47, 77, 137, 145, 147, 149
Morales, Juan Baptista, 38
Mount Đồng Cổ, spirit of, 89
Mount Tản Viên, spirit of, 94, 102n77, 196, 329
Mount Yên Tử, 8n26, 10n33
Moussay, Gérard, xvii, 63
Mục Mũi, 141n22, 286n53, 292

Nam Tào, 12
Nan yue (Nam Việt), 3
Nanzhao (Nam Chiêu), 202n138
National Academy (Quốc Tử Giám), 4, 87n30, 88, 213
Néez, Louis, 45, 63n45, 72, 324
Ngô Sĩ Bình, 115n14
Ngô Sĩ Liên, 64
Ngô Thì Sĩ, 14
Nguyễn Bá Tiên (Bá Quang), 254
Nguyễn Bỉnh Khiêm, 6, 13n45
Nguyễn Đức Huyên, 121n31
Nguyễn Hoàng, 24n12
Nguyễn Kim, 22
Nguyễn Phúc Nguyên, 23
Nguyễn Phúc-Ánh (Gia Long), 128, 130n50
Nguyễn Thị Tri, 254
Noah, 67, 181–83
non-being (*wu, vô*), 67, 170
non-contrivance (*wuwei, vô vi*), 11

Opusculum de sectis apud Sinenses et Tunkinenses, xiii–xiv, 70–71, 89, 153, 323–30

Outline of the Comprehensive Mirror (Tongjian Gangmu, Thông Giám Cương Mục), 65, 180n72

Pallu, François, 2n5, 27–28
Pan Gu (Bàn Cổ), 142, 171–72, 188, 191, 198
Pang Juan (Bàng Quyên), 262n87, 262–63
Paul III, 27n21
Paul V, 27n21
Phạm Lang, 99, 206–7
Phạm Nhan, 142, 254–55
Phan Huy Chú, 81
Phan Huy Ích, 14
Phố Hiến, 23–24, 33
Pigneau de Béhaine, 72n73, 129, 130n50
Portuguese Religion, xi, 34n48. *See also* Catholicism; Christianity
Princess Mai Hoa, 24n12
principle (*li, lý*), 11, 136, 166–68, 179
Propaganda Fide, Congregation of, 27, 38n63, 39, 45, 58

Qi Minwang (Tề Mân Vương), 219
Qin Ershi (Tần Nhị Đế), 217
Qin Shihuang (Tần Thuỷ Hoàng), 189n96, 189, 202, 219, 238
Qing (Thanh) dynasty, 278
Quan Âm, 9, 103–5, 318–19. *See also* Avalokiteśvara

Rafael da Madre de Deus, 28n25
Record of Rites (Liji, Lễ Ký), 65, 65n48, 80, 99, 111, 173n45, 186–89, 192, 208, 227
Records of the Grand Historian (Shiji, Sử Ký), 64
Red River, 13
Rhodes, Alexandre de, xii, 21, 21n1, 25–27, 43–44, 51, 58, 74, 108, 127, 131
Ricci, Matteo, 37–39, 41, 54, 131
Ritual
  Chief's Banner Veneration (Tế Kỳ Đạo), 86, 89, 91, 195–97
  Christian evaluation of, 106–7
  funeral and memorial, 220–24
  imperial, 80–93

Ritual (*cont.*)
  Oath-Taking Ceremony (Hội Minh), 89–90, 174, 194–95
  Ranking the Spirits (*tạo khoa bạt thần*), 199
  Rite of Breaking the Prison (*phá ngục*), 125, 313–15, 323, 329
  Rite to Confucius, 86–88, 213–14
  Sacrifice to Heaven (*tế giao*), 82–84, 184, 186–87
  Sacrifice to Shennong, 84–85, 193
  Sacrifice to the Sovereign on High, 184–87
  Sacrifice to the Spirit of Earth, 187–88
Rome, xii, 98, 107
Ruggieri, Michele, 54–55, 59
Ru-ism. *See* Confucianism
Ruiz, Bartolome, 28n25
Rushou (Nhục Thu), 190, 192

Śākyamuni (Thích Ca), 106, 161, 170, 270, 272–75, 290–94, 297–98, 301, 309, 315–16. *See also* Buddha
Santa Cruz, Juan a, 28–29
Secret Book Inside the Pillow (Chẩm Trung Bí Thư), 264
Shang (Thương) dynasty, 190, 192
Shaohao (Thiếu Hạo), 189–90, 192, 260n82
Shennong (Thần Nông), 84–85, 97, 137, 193, 196
Shi Xie (Sĩ Nhiếp or Sĩ Tiếp), 3
Shu (Thục) region, 219
Shu Di (Thục Đế), 310–12
Shu Lianghe (Thúc Lương Hạp), 211
Shun (Thuấn), 180–82, 184, 186–87, 192
Siam, 27, 34
Siddhārtha Gautama, 161n4, 316n126. *See also* Buddha
Sima Guang (Tư Mã Quang), 64, 188n89
Sima Qian (Tư Mã Thiên), 64
Song (Tống) dynasty, 2, 11, 86–87, 91, 134, 188, 246, 278
Song Huizong (Tống Huy Tông), 105, 237–39

Song Renzong (Tống Nhân Tông), 289n79
Song Taizu (Tống Thái Tổ), 212
Song Xiaozong (Tống Hiếu Tông), 188, 283
Song Zhenzong (Tống Chân Tông), 212, 237–38
Sovereign-on-High (*Shangdi, Thượng Đế*), 66, 137, 149, 155, 173–76, 179, 184–85. *See also* Lord of Heaven
Spanish, the, 28–30, 130. *See also* Dominicans
Strange Tales from South of the Passes (Lĩnh Nam Chích Quái), 11, 64, 96
Śuddhodana, 272–73, 89
Sun Bin (Tôn Tẫn), 281n86, 261–62
Sun Wuzi (Tôn Vũ Tử), 218
Superstitious Teachings (Dị Đoan Chi Giáo), 71–72
supreme ultimate (*taiqi, thái cực*), 154
Sutra of Forty-Two Sections (Tứ Thập Nhị Chương Kinh), 65, 149, 274–75, 297–98, 300, 315

Taihao (Thái Hạo), 189, 189n98, 191
Tam Giáo. *See* Three Religions
Tang Codes, 86
Tang (Đàng) dynasty, 1n3, 2, 86–88, 92, 120, 134, 278
Tang Gaozu (Đàng Cao Tổ), 278n28, 281
Tang Dezong (Đàng Đức Tông), 217
Tang Taizong (Đàng Thái Tông), 263
Tang Xianzong (Đàng Hiến Tông), 238, 282
Tang Xizong (Đàng Hy Tông), 231
Tang Xuanzong (Đàng Huyền Tông), 188, 212–13, 216, 219
Tang Yizong (Đàng Ý Tông), 231
Tang Zuzong (Đàng Túc Tông), 92
Tavernier, Jean-Baptiste, xii
Tây Đô (Western Capital), 22n4
Tây Sơn era, 93, 128
Temple of Literature (Văn Miếu), 6, 86, 88, 92. *See also* Confucius: temple of
Temple of the Military (Võ Miếu), 70, 89, 92–93

Ten Commandments, 30, 51, 52n11, 53, 55n19, 59, 61
Ten Philosophers, 88, 92, 213–14
Thăng Long, 22n4, 23–24, 33, 82, 95, 101
Thành Hoàng, 95–108, 137
Thị Nhi, 99, 205–7
three bonds (*sangang, tam cương*), 31n36, 133
three powers (*sancai, tam tài*), 287n59
Three Religions (*tam giáo*), 1–2, 13–17, 133–34, 161–63. See also Buddhism; Confucianism; Daoism
Three Venerables (Tam Tồn), 10
Tian Xiangru (Điền Tương Như), 218
Tissanier, Joseph, xii, 26n17, 98
Tô Lịch River, spirit of, 94–95
Tonkin, xi–xii
  Catholic missions, 25–30, 70–71, 157
  Eastern vicariate, xiv, 29–30, 45, 70–72, 130, 323
  politics, 21–23, 90–91, 194n113
  reception of Christianity, 30–36
  religious life of, 15–17, 43–46, 76–77, 83, 85, 88, 100, 108, 127, 131, 323–24. See also Buddhism; Confucianism; Daoism; Three Religions
  trading with the West, 23–34
  Western vicariate, 45, 63, 72, 130, 324
Tourane, 24
Tournon, Charles Thomas Maillard de, 41. See also China: Rites Controversy
Trần, dynasty, 5, 8–9, 279, 284, 310
Trần Anh Tông, 241, 254–55, 279
Trần Dụ Tông, 10n37, 241
Trần Hiến Tông, 241
Trần Hưng Đạo (Trần Quốc Tuấn), 218, 254
Trần Minh Tông, 241
Trần Nghệ Tông, 9
Trần Nhân Tông, 8n26
Trần Thái Tông, 9n29, 161, 213
Trần Thế Pháp, 64
Trần Thủ Độ, 279, 284
Transmigration of soul, 16, 57, 66–67, 73, 113, 123–24, 295n100, 300–302
Treatise of the True Religion (Phép Giảng Đạo Thật), 140–42

Trịnh Căn, 35
Trịnh Cương, 35
Trịnh Đạo Kiêm, 251
Trịnh Kiểm, 22
Trịnh Sâm, xi
Trịnh Tạc, 1, 22, 25
Trịnh Thiên Xuân, 146, 251
Trịnh Tráng, 21, 25
Trịnh Trí Không, 10n34
Trịnh Tùng, 22, 23n7
Trọng Cao, 99, 205–7
True Meaning of the Lord of Heaven (*Tianzhu Shiyi*). See Catechism: of Ricci
True Record of the Lord of Heaven (*Tianzhu Shilu*). See Catechism: of Ruggieri
Trưng Sisters, 94, 203
Trương Hán Siêu, 9n30
two modes (*liangyi, lưỡng nghi*), 136, 166–68, 175, 186

Updated Family Rituals (Gia Lễ Tiếp Kinh), 115

Valignano, Alessandro, 53–54, 59
Vicente Liêm de la Paz, xi
vital energy (*qi, khí*), 11, 112, 166n23
voidness (*xu, hư*), 134, 170
Vũ Quỳnh, 284

wandering souls, 77, 122, 310, 320
Wang Bi (Vương Bí), 219
Wang Di Tu Wu (Vọng Đế Đỗ Vũ), 312
Wang Xu (Vương Hủ), 261
Wang Yu (Vương Dư), 122, 310n139
Wei Lie (Uy Liệt), 253
Wei Wendi (Nguỵ Văn Đế), 277
Wenwang (Văn Vương), 216–17, 258
Wu Gang (Ngô Cang), 311–12
Wu Ji (Ngô Khởi), 218
Wuwang (Vũ Vương), 217, 252

Xia (Hạ) dynasty, 190, 192
Ximenez, Alonso, 28n25
Xu Zongdao (Hứa Tông Đạo), 10n37, 241
Xuanming (Huyền Minh), 190, 192

Yan Hui (Nhan Hồi), 87, 87n28, 212, 213
Yan Zhaowang (Yên Chiêu Vương), 219
Yandi (Viêm Đế), 189n100, 189–90, 258. *See also* Shennong
Yang Juncong (Dương Quân Tòng), 230n223, 230–31
Yang Zhu (Dương Chu), 236, 236n5
Yao (Nghiêu), 180–83, 187, 192, 298n106, 312
Yaśodharā, 273
Yellow Emperor. *See* Huangdi
Yellow Turban Movement, 10–11, 11n38, 240n25, 242n32
Yên Kỳ Sinh, 10n33
yin-yang theory, 11, 110, 121, 134, 178. *See also* two modes
Yu (Vũ), 180n70, 180–82, 192
Yuan (Nguyên) dynasty, 278
Yuan Liaofan (Nguyên Liễu Phàm), 65
Yuan Wuzong (Nguyên Vũ Tông), 212
Yuanshi (Nguyên Thỉ) celestial god, 105, 239, 289
Yue Fei (Nhạc Phi), 218
Yue Yi (Nhạc Nghị), 219

Zeng Shen (Tăng Sâm), 87, 213
Zengzi (Tăng Tử). *See* Zeng Shen
Zhang Jian (Trương Kiểm), 240
Zhang Jiao (Trương Giác). *See* Zhang Jue
Zhang Jue (Trương Giác), 240
Zhang Liang (Trương Lương), 105, 216–18, 239, 264
Zhang Lu (Trương Lỗ), 240
Zhang Yi (Trương Nghi), 239
Zhang You (Trương Dậu), 240
Zhao Chang (Triệu Xương), 202
Zhao Tuo (Triệu Đà), 202n135
Zhen Xishan (Chân Tây Sơn), 236
Zheng Zai (Trưng Tại), 211
Zhou Book of Rites (Chu Lễ), 82
Zhou (Chu) dynasty, 82, 190, 192
Zhou Gaozu (Chu Cao Tổ), 161
Zhou Jingwang (Chu Kính Vương), 212, 236
Zhou Lingwang (Chu Linh Vương), 211, 236
Zhou Xianwang (Chu Hiển Vương), 213
Zhou of Yin (Trụ Ân), 216–17
Zhou Zhaowang (Chu Chiêu Vương), 9, 2, 42
Zhu Wengong (Chu Văn Công), 188. *See also* Zhu Xi
Zhu Xi (Chu Hy), 166n25, 168, 226–27, 310
Zhu Xi's Family Rituals (Văn Công Gia Lễ), 114
Zhuangzi, book of, 11, 65
Zhuanxu (Xuyên Húc), 185n84, 190, 192, 205
Zhurong (Chúc Dong), 190–91, 205, 208
Zisi (Tử Tư), 87, 213